FROM PRAGUE TO JERUSALEM

FROM PRAGUE TO JERUSALEM

An Uncommon Journey of a Journalist

Milan J. Kubic

NIU Press / DeKalb, IL

Northern Illinois University Press, DeKalb 60115
© 2017 by Northern Illinois University Press
All rights reserved

26 25 24 23 22 21 20 19 18 17   1 2 3 4 5
978-0-87580-764-5 (paper)
978-1-60909-223-8 (e-book)
Book and cover design by Yuni Dorr

Library of Congress Cataloging-in-Publication Data
Names: Kubic, Milan J.
Title: From Prague to Jerusalem : an uncommon journey of a journalist / Milan J. Kubic.
Description: DeKalb, IL : Northern Illinois University Press, 2017.
Identifiers: LCCN 2017011533 (print) | LCCN 2017027983 (ebook) | ISBN 9781609092238 (ebook) | ISBN 9780875807645 (pbk. : alk. paper)
Subjects: LCSH: Kubic, Milan J. | Journalists—United States—Biography. | Foreign correspondents—United States—Biography.
Classification: LCC PN4874.K76 (ebook) | LCC PN4874.K76 A3 2017 (print) | DDC 070.92 [B]—dc23
LC record available at https://lccn.loc.gov/2017011533

For Leesa,
MY BELOVED PARTNER AND WIFE OF FORTY YEARS

Contents

Prologue ix

Part I

CHAPTER 1
THE END OF AN ERA 3
CHAPTER 2
THE FIRST CATASTROPHE: WORLD WAR II 12
CHAPTER 3
AN UNEASY INTERLUDE 32
CHAPTER 4
THE SECOND CATASTROPHE: COMMUNIST COUP D'ÉTAT 47
CHAPTER 5
ESCAPE TO THE US ZONE IN GERMANY 56
CHAPTER 6
IN THE REFUGEE CAMPS 64
CHAPTER 7
WAITING FOR A US VISA 74
CHAPTER 8
AMERICA! 82

Part II

CHAPTER 9
ON THE STAFF OF NEWSWEEK 97
CHAPTER 10
FRUSTRATED IN THE HEMISPHERE 111
CHAPTER 11
MY QUARREL WITH THE *REFORMADORES* 126
CHAPTER 12
THE SIX DAY WAR AND ITS AFTERMATH 144
CHAPTER 13
ARAFAT AND THE RISE OF THE PLO 163
CHAPTER 14
COVERING THE LOSERS' BEAT 174
CHAPTER 15
WATCHING THE SOVIET SATELLITES 186
CHAPTER 16
MEETING THE NEW GERMANS 199

PART III

CHAPTER 17
MY LAST BEAT: ISRAEL   217

CHAPTER 18
MENACHEM BEGIN AND THE RISE OF ISRAEL'S RIGHT   237

CHAPTER 19
ISRAEL'S SECRET KEEPERS—AND LEAKERS   258

CHAPTER 20
POLLARD, IRANGATE, AND BUS 300   269

CHAPTER 21
MY QUARREL WITH ISRAEL   282

CHAPTER 22
THE WEST BANKERS   297

EPILOGUE   311

Prologue

Perhaps, if it were not for my obsession about becoming a journalist, I would have never come to America. I might have spent my life in the beautiful and soulful Czech town of Prague, where I was born. But once the bug bit me—I suspect, in response to the flood of Nazi lies and regimentation to which my generation was exposed during WWII—there was no escaping my destiny. And I eagerly tried to follow it as soon as circumstances allowed. My first attempt was in the fall of 1945, about four months after Nazi Germany surrendered to the Allies and the Soviet troops arrived in Prague.

The empty store windows still echoed the wartime shortages and the roadsides were littered with the debris of war, but the six years of brutal German occupation were over. For my eighteen-year-old classmates and me, it meant the end of ten months of forced labor in factories producing arms for the Wehrmacht, and for my brother Mirek, me, and thousands of fellow Czechs, the end of four days of street fighting against the remaining German troops.

The mere fact that we lived to see the Nazi defeat was a triumph. As the jaunty lyrics of Prague's first postwar hit song proclaimed, "It's All Already Behind Us!" and next, in our naive expectations, were the thrills of democracy. And to get that heady era under way, a few of my schoolmates and I launched a weekly newspaper. Rather pretentiously, we called it *Žihadlo* (The Sting).

Žihadlo was an instant success. The first issue, which consisted of four barely legible mimeographed pages, extolled the quality of American films and American wheat, both of which had just started reaching our long-deprived public. Officially, the Cold War had not yet begun—Churchill's ringing indictment of the descending Iron Curtain was still six months in the future, and the public discourse in Czechoslovakia was full of high-blown rhetoric about "eternal friendship with the Soviet Union," "progress," and "national" unity. But in the streets, schools, and cafés of Prague, a fast-growing lexicon of buzzwords and symbols reflected a rapid polarization. The Czechs were dividing into pro-Western and pro-Soviet camps, and there was no doubt where *Žihadlo* stood.

By praising in the first issue's editorial the products of Hollywood and Kansas, I implicitly detracted from the official laurels ritually heaped on the "wise leadership of Joseph Stalin," "historic inevitability of socialism," and "incomparable achievements of the new Soviet man." (The "Soviet man" was particularly grating. He was always a man, always "new," and in every way superior to any other type of homo sapiens. There was even a Soviet movie showing how the new Soviet man's fun and sense of humor were incomparably superior to anything of that sort in the West.)

Plaudits for the United States, on top of *Žihadlo*'s conspicuous omission of any genuflections toward the East, won instant applause from my similarly minded schoolmates. Possibly even more important was that the price of *Žihadlo* was about two cents, and the four volunteer vendors who hawked the paper during class breaks were among the best-looking girls in the school. The first issue of perhaps two hundred copies sold like hot cakes.

Upon this publication triumph, *Žihadlo* was promptly snuffed out by the Ministry of the Interior, the guardian of state security and one of the key portfolios that had been handed to the Communist Party when the first postwar Czechoslovak government was organized in Moscow. The hasty undoing of *Žihadlo* was really my fault. For its second issue, I asked my cousin Pepík to write an article about jet planes, a new technology that was then of considerable interest. Pepík, who was about eight years older than I was and a graduate student of aeronautical engineering, knew his material but was far from an ideal contributor.

Unpretentious as it was, *Žihadlo* aspired to the democratic spirit of Tomáš Masaryk, a philosopher and university professor who in 1918 had founded the Czechoslovak republic. Pepík, by contrast, unaccountably emerged from World War II as a rabid Stalinist and a Communist Party member. While my *Žihadlo* editorial enthused about Czechoslovakia as a liberal Western democracy, Pepík argued that the Czechs and the Slovaks should give up their "obsolete independence" and "bourgeois nationalism" and become yet another socialist republic in "the workers' paradise," the Soviet Union.

I decided to ask Pepík to write the article anyway. He was very bright, and I knew he would produce a fine article on a mere week's notice. Moreover, while our ideological differences were only recent, Pepík, my brother Mirek, and I had been for years the closest of friends. For me and Mirek, who was two years my senior, Pepík, despite his views, still had the authority and prestige of "Sheriff," the nickname we gave him when playing cowboys and Indians.

Without a second thought, I ran Pepík's article right behind my editorial in which I took an issue with some long-forgotten speech by Zdeněk Nejedlý, the Communist minister of education. The minister was such slavish lackey of the Kremlin that, as the postwar joke had it, he walked under an umbrella in Prague when it rained in Moscow. Proud of my second opinion piece and anticipating another best-selling issue, my classmates and I doubled the *Žihadlo* printing run to four hundred copies.

A couple of days later, the phone at home rang. The call was from Pepík, who had just seen *Žihadlo* for the first time, and he was furious. "I read your shitty poopsheet and I feel like throwing up," he yelled. He was scandalized, he said, to find his name and his article in a "reactionary" publication that stank of "petit-bourgeois values." I was shocked because Pepík had never talked to me in such insulting way before, but I couldn't help feeling amused by his rant about my "petit-bourgeois values." His parents were just as "petit-bourgeois" as mine.

Pepík added something menacing about the sorry fate of the "dupes" who try to stand in the way of "progress" and, suddenly sounding calm and formal, put me on notice that *Žihadlo* was for "the party" a "serious" matter that will be "dealt with." The next thing I knew, the mailman brought me a summons to report to the press directorate of Statní bespečnost or StB—the State Security—and bring along all unsold copies of *Žihadlo*.

At the appointed hour, I found myself sitting in the office of an older, unexpectedly kindly looking police officer who did not strike me as one of the new appointees of the Communists. In fact, he seemed to be almost as ill at ease as I was. He told me that it was prohibited to publish a school newspaper without a license and added, without sounding convincing, that it was reprehensible that I, a student, criticized the education minister. Since this was my first infraction, the officer went on, I would be let go with a verbal reprimand and a warning. *Žihadlo*, however, was finished.

Having said his piece, the man suddenly got up and walked out of the office, leaving—intentionally, I assumed—my dossier on his desk. I leaned over and hurriedly flipped through the reports and depositions. A couple of them consisted of vague statements about my political leanings and character the StB had extracted from my teachers. One agent's report quoted our corner grocer about the reputation of my parents. And at the bottom of the folder I saw there was a letter signed by my cousin and childhood chum, the latter-day Communist Party zealot Pepík. As I had suspected, it was he who had turned me in. Never one to face hostility easily, I left the directorate unbowed but feeling pretty shaky.

My second stint as journalist lasted longer—and ended worse—than the first one. Late in the fall of 1946, I was hired fresh out of high school by *Svobodné Slovo*, the highest-circulation Czech daily, which was published in Prague by the middle-road National Socialist Party, the strongest political movement opposing the Communists. The paper had several regional bureaus where the editors tested such newly hired talent as me. The job that I landed was of the correspondent in Klatovy, a picturesque provincial town in southwestern Bohemia. My tour in Klatovy lasted just sixteen months, and it was once again terminated by the almighty StB.

This time, the cause of my undoing was a scoop about the unsavory past of the top regional cop, an StB colonel whose last name was Havlíček and who, not accidentally, was also a prominent member of the Klatovy branch of the Communist Party. I was tipped off about Havlíček's wrongdoings by the state's attorney who was looking for witnesses of the colonel's conduct while he was a kapo—a prisoner trustee—in a German concentration camp during the war. According to the official, Havlíček had served time, not as a political prisoner but as a black-marketeer, and while in the camp was known for his brutality toward the prisoners. The attorney showed me the testimonies of several former political prisoners who knew Havlíček. They charged that he was a sadist who terrorized the inmates to curry favor with the German guards.

In postwar Czechoslovakia, a country that had suffered bitterly during the occupation, wartime inhumanity or collaboration with the Nazis was an extremely serious crime. The more prominent Czech quislings were quickly rounded up and tried by special tribunals, but many of the smaller-time culprits managed to get lost in the postwar chaos and start a new existence in another part of the country. If they joined the Communist Party—and many did just that—they could even get on the government payroll and make a career under the protection of the party's apparatchiks. The Klatovy prosecutor—a former concentration camp inmate and a tough-minded woman—believed that Havlíček was one of the criminals who got away.

I knew nothing about the StB boss that suggested she might be wrong. Havlíček was a hulking, strikingly handsome man with light blue eyes and an arrogant face whom I had met only once while talking with one of his subordinates. In his Klatovy headquarters, the colonel was loathed as a bully and a political hack who was packing the police force with minions picked by the local branch of the Communist Party.

For the state's attorney, taking on Havlíček was an act of considerable courage. The Communists had enormous power to sway public opinion. They ran the country's only radio station (there was yet no television) and most of the print media, and they were quick to unleash vicious attacks on their opponents. But my source was attuned to different pressures—acquired, I assumed, as a political prisoner. "All I need is an airtight case," she told me. A grim-faced, mousy-looking person, she was after the colonel like a bloodhound. I told her I'd be glad to try to help.

Some of the former inmates whom I managed to trace refused to speak to me; possibly, their own conduct in the camp was not the stuff of legends. There were many shades of gray between wartime heroes and villains, and in the incensed postwar atmosphere, even those midway on the spectrum were not eager for public scrutiny. But three women ex-prisoners eventually came to my small cubbyhole, which was behind a frosted-glass store window of the *Svobodné Slovo*'s Klatovy distribution office.

Most of the interviews took place late in the evening, and the shadows cast by my visitors against the store window prompted sly questions from my friends whether I was "entertaining" girlfriends. One evening, a former victim of Havlíček started taking off her blouse to show me the scars on her breasts caused, she said, by the kapo who put out his cigarette by pressing it against her breasts. Remembering the silhouette she cast on the store window I hurriedly assured her that I did not doubt her story.

When I had enough material for a series of three articles, I sent them to Vladimír Doležal, my boss in Prague, and the newspaper published them in its regional edition. To my surprise, neither Havlíček nor the local Communist Party publicly reacted to the allegations. The only counterblast, which appeared in a regional Communist newspaper in Pilsen, derided my "callow youth" and lack of journalistic experience, not the substance of the articles. On the whole, the explosive series were well received. When I walked in the StB headquarters more people gave me a friendly nod than ever before.

Alas, it was a short interlude. In February 1948, a few weeks after *Svobodné Slovo* ran my articles, Moscow and the Czechoslovak Communist Party brought on the coup d'état for which they had been preparing since the end of the war. Taking advantage of a cabinet crisis, the Communists sent their police and armed militia into the streets of Prague and seized control of all noncommunist organizations and their media.

The next morning I heard, with a mixture of consternation and pride, my name on the radio. A Communist "Action Committee" had taken over *Svobodné Slovo* and announced the first batch of "reactionary" journalists who were being fired. I was right up there, a mere cub reporter in the boondocks, alongside my editor-in-chief Ivan Herben and seventeen prominent editors, senior correspondents, and columnists. It was a wholly undeserved honor that I felt sure I owed to Colonel Havlíček.

Each of my false starts in journalism had a footnote. The first one was the strange fate of Havlíček. About a year after the coup, while I was marking time in a refugee camp in West Germany, I ran into a former police officer from Klatovy who had been active in the underground that briefly sprang up after the Communist overthrow. To my astonishment, he told me that Havlíček had also fled to the West. According to my informant, the colonel had made a complete political about-face shortly after the Communists took power and actually aided the underground in smuggling refugees across the border. My informant believed that Havlíček's wartime record was so bad that, after the coup, even the Communist Party wanted to get rid of him. In the ex-policeman's theory, Havlíček once again reversed gears and fled to Germany to start yet another career.

The second footnote to my start in journalism took place more than twenty years later when I was the *Newsweek* bureau chief in Beirut. One day in March 1971, I got a letter from Cairo, which consisted of a single typed sentence and a signature. The garbled note read: "Milan J. Kubic, please, when you are coming in Cairo let your address or call me on No. 18, Maamal El Sokkar, Garden City. SHERIFF."

There were only two people I could think of who might have written the mysterious note. One of them was an Egyptian army colonel I knew whose name was Mohammed Sharif, but I felt sure that his English was better than the letter writer's. The other person was the "Sheriff" of our childhood games, my cousin Pepík.

A few days later, I pressed the bell of a third-floor apartment in Garden City, a middle-class residential section of Cairo that in those days of the Soviet-Egyptian alliance was full of Warsaw Pact military advisers and their families. When the door opened, a shaft of bright afternoon sun framed a diminutive, unwell-looking woman whom I recognized as Lída, Pepík's steady girlfriend during the last years of the war. She recognized me also and vigorously nodded, casting a worried look at the door of her Warsaw Pact neighbors. Her tension was so palpable that I just stood there and said nothing, waiting for her next move. Pepík was not at home, Lída finally said, almost in whisper, but perhaps we could meet in the evening? I told her I'd expect her and Pepík at six o'clock in the evening in the lobby of the Cairo Hilton, and I left.

The meeting in the hotel was as tense and uncomfortable as I expected—and yet, somehow, different. Pepík and Lída showed up on time, thin-lipped and nervous-looking behind their forced smiles. Riding an elevator to the top-floor bar, my cousin was curtly greeted by a chunky Russian who gave me a look full of curiosity. Pepík, who obviously did not want to be seen in my company in the town's poshest watering spot, broke into sweat and his jaws began working as if he were chewing gum. By the time we finally sat down and ordered drinks, Pepík and Lída were so nervous I almost expected them to jump up and leave.

But Pepík knew that his dice were cast, and after some desultory chitchat about me and my family he said his piece. He'd been in Cairo for over two years as part of a Warsaw Pact military advisory group, lecturing on aeronautics at the Egyptian airforce academy, he told me. His tour was almost over, and he and Lída were due to return to Prague in the summer. Pepík then paused, his mouth twitching, his frozen smile gone, and he tackled the part he disliked most.

"We don't want to go back," he finally said with a shrug of his narrow shoulders. He paused again. "You should understand that," he added in a challenging, almost accusatory voice, and lapsed into silence.

I was half-annoyed, half-marveling at Pepík's refusal to eat crow. This was my chance to bear in and dust off old wrongs. But I, too, said nothing. Instead, I found myself nodding to Pepík to go on.

Suddenly looking relieved, Pepík raised his eyes and asked, almost matter-of-factly, if I could help him and Lída get to England. All they needed, he hurriedly added, was somebody to pull strings in Italy. As a Czech official, he and Lída had to fly to Prague on a Czech airliner whose only stop outside the Iron Curtain was the Leonardo da Vinci airport in Rome. They needed to be spirited out of the transit lounge and put on a flight to London, where they hoped to get visas as political refugees. He looked at me again and asked:

"Can you ask somebody at the American embassy to help us?"

Žihadlo had been dead for twenty-five years, and at the moment it did not even cross my mind. But I was still bitter, for reasons much more painful than anything that had happened to me. I thought about my parents, who after I left the country had been imprisoned and destroyed, physically and mentally, by StB. I thought about the wretched life of my brother Mirek who had been sent to work as a construction laborer, and whose books and plays had been banned. I thought of my Prague classmates whose talents, ambitions, and best years of life had been irretrievably wasted and defiled by tyrants, mediocrities, and apparatchiks who had sold out their own nation.

A generation full of energy and promise had been ground down to a mass of phlegmatic, gray nonentities in an experiment so cruel, so arrogant, and so absurd it made Orwell's "1984" read like nonfiction. In my eyes, the human tragedy inflicted by the likes of Pepík on Soviet-dominated Europe was second only to the crimes of Hitler's Third Reich. Twirling my drink, I felt the swelling of anger that had been part of me ever since, as a small kid, I saw the first Wehrmacht half-tracks rumbling through the streets of Prague.

For a moment I felt like snarling, "Pepík, you miserable son of a bitch, eat the shit you've made," and walking out.

Then I looked at him again in the dim light of the bar and I reflected on how much he had aged and how thin he was. His hair was almost gone, his face was deeply wrinkled, and his mouth was desperately twitching. I glanced at Lída, who seemed to be shrinking in her seat. For some crazy, sentimental reason I suddenly saw in my mind's eye Pepík the teenager, stripped to the waist and throwing a javelin in one of the impromptu sports contests with my brother and me. And then, as the gloomy silence between us thickened, I said what I knew I would say before I even rang the bell of Pepík's apartment.

"OK, I'll try to help you," I promised.

Which I accomplished easily enough, by giving Pepík's address to the Cairo CIA station chief, one of the embassy officials with whom, in those days of bitter Cold War, I and most of us working abroad routinely traded views and news. He took care of the rest; and whatever information he extracted from Pepík was, in my book, a tiny down payment on the debt my cousin owed to the cause of decency in general, and to his fellow Czechs in particular.

PART I

CHAPTER 1

THE END OF AN ERA

Whenever I think of my childhood, my mind always comes up with the walks with my father.

There were a good many things wrong with Dad. He had an explosive streak and sometimes furiously shouted at Mother. I gathered from their nasty quarrels that, especially during the war, he was not a good provider. Dad also had a penchant for borrowing money with the greatest abandon and without equal propensity for paying back. He claimed that being pursued by creditors was fun: "As long as they expect to get their money back," he once told me, "they wave to me and shout 'Hi!' all the way across the street." As soon as he settled the debt, he added, "they look the other way."

There is no question that his failings left a deep mark. For my brother Mirek and me, the fierce exchanges between Mother's tears and Dad's angry voice were a nightmare, and the hounding creditors were a source of profound embarrassment. To this day, I recoil from emotional arguments, and I buy everything in cash.

But Dad also tried to be a good father in the old-fashioned sense, as a moral guide to his two children. I don't mean an arm's-length elder adviser, the way I was to my own sons, Jan and Ben, in my studious effort to avoid any suggestion of value imposition. My Dad's attitude was the exact opposite. He was eager to tell Mirek and me what we should believe and think, and the way he went about it was anything but subtle.

When I was about six or seven years old, he would take me for walks. Not in Vršovice, the humdrum, middle-class periphery of Prague where we lived and where there wasn't any cluster of trees worthy to be called a park, any impressive bit of architecture, or a store window with anything exciting to look at. Dad, whose aspirations always exceeded his reach, would put on one of his natty suits and a homburg hat that made him look like an affluent lawyer, and he would take me to the center of Prague where the broad sidewalks were lined with leafy linden trees, and brightly lit stores displayed luxuries like grapefruits and canned pineapples.

We'd take one of the rattling, ubiquitous streetcars that roamed the Prague streets like an army of ants and we'd ride all the way to the Wenceslas Square, the very heart of the city. The so-called square is actually Prague's version of the Champs Elysées, a boulevard dominated by a huge equestrian statue of St. Wenceslas, a not particularly distinguished tenth-century Czech king. The boulevard slopes down toward the enchanting Old Town and intersects a couple of broad avenues that in those pre–World War II years were full of theaters and bustling cafés.

Dad and I would get off the tram at the top of the square and slowly head for the Old Town. For me, our incursion into the world of affluence was full of thrills. On both sides of the wide boulevard, well-dressed crowds streamed in and out of big stores and movie houses. Posh cars glided past traffic policemen waving their arms. From the square's numerous sidewalk kiosks wafted the mouth-watering aroma of boiled "párky," the elite of world's hot dogs. (Párky, whose subtlety is unmatched anywhere outside the Czech provinces and Austria, are a cultural and historical phenomena. Bohemia and Moravia, once an independent kingdom, lost a crucial battle in 1618 and for the next

This is me, aged seven, walking in 1932 or 1933 in Prague with my father and my older brother, Mirek.

three hundred years became a part of the Austrian realm. The shared mastery of making párky was one of the rare happy results of that shotgun union.)

Dad would hold me by the hand, we'd walk, and he'd talk. He'd talk a lot about Prague, which he loved with a passion known only to natives of very old and very proud European cities. It was a place he knew intimately—every alley, every hidden courtyard behind an unlocked door, every chubby angel perched above a stone water fountain, and many of its roofs and chimneys. Those heights of the town he got to know the hard way, while eking a living as a chimney sweep, a part of his life he hated and tried to hide. But even that humble work added to his bond with Prague. The city was so important to his self-esteem and identity he never spoke about it with his customary irreverence.

By the time we reached the Old Town, Dad would break away from his cherished topic and address the subject of values. As one would expect from a practiced storyteller, his lectures were delivered with flair and dressed up in overstatement, but they always had a valid point.

Unlike many people of his background, Dad had a great respect for higher education, and he would have been elated if Mirek or I had ever earned a doctorate. Upward mobility was one of his hallmarks. An only child, he was taken out of school at an early age after the death of his father, who was a tailor of all-leather work clothes. To provide for himself and his mother, Dad was apprenticed to a chimney sweep, but he never accepted the job's lowly social standing.

After 1918, when the Habsburg empire disintegrated and the Czechs and Slovaks won independence, Dad quickly recognized the status value of a well-pressed military uniform. He joined the new Czechoslovak army and, being bright, witty, and personable, he rose from a private to battery commander in a horse-drawn artillery regiment.

Although he could never afford to satisfy his taste for fine clothes and better things in life, Dad was not envious of people who were more fortunate. But there were three types of individuals my father despised, and whose iniquities he described on our walks with passion. Collectively, he called them "people with no class."

One prominent group in Dad's low-life trifecta were people pretending to excellence by affecting intellectual polish. "Poseurs"—posturing phonies—who put on airs were the worst liars, Dad charged, because they didn't just brag about a thing or two (as he would do), but their whole life was a lie. "With a poseur you never know who he is, Milan," Dad would say, "because he himself doesn't know it, either." The most satisfying punishment that Dad could wish for a poseur was to be found out and held up to public opprobrium, and the more ego-crunching the discovery, the better.

Dad's second category of people unworthy of our planet was *sviňe* (swine). The term covered a mixed bag of unsavory characters, ranging from loan sharks who preyed on orphans and widows to monstrous tyrants like Adolf Hitler. Hitler, by the mid-1930s, was not an abstract term for a Czech schoolboy. I was not quite six years old when der Fűhrer took power in the neighboring Germany, and he very quickly entered my horizon as a dreadful symbol of utmost malevolence and evil. The Czechs had a long history of resisting cultural subjugation by the Austrian monarchy, and the rise of expansionist Nazism across the long Czech-German border was the subject of frequent and worried comments both at home and in school.

The third and numerically largest group in Dad's unworthy menagerie was *pόvl* (rabble), a label he applied to people who were not only ignorant and crude but also indolent and hostile to anyone who achieved more in life. Absence of worldly goods was not what Dad had in mind when he heaped disdain on pόvl—it was a meanness of spirit. Avoiding the rabble was the highest injunction that Dad wanted to impress on his sons. One had to be alert to the menace of the poseurs and the swine, but above all, one had to put inexorable distance between oneself and the slothful, mean-minded, pestilential pόvl.

I still see him, stopping in the middle of the sidewalk, raising his arm above his head like a priest invoking God's righteous wrath, and exclaiming loudly enough to startle the passersby:

"Beware of the poseurs, the swine, and the rabble, Milan!"

The performance was addressed to me as well as to anyone who happened to be within earshot, and Dad's face would light up with delight if he caught the attention of some pedestrian.

In later years, I sometimes wondered how this restless man, full of loud cheer and bonhomie, who bridled against routine and the ordinary, felt about the placid world he had entered in the early 1920s when he married my mother. My mother, the youngest of eleven children in a patrician family, was humorless and withdrawn. We lived in a stolid, turn-of-the-century walkup apartment building that housed most members of my mother's clan. My father fit in like a fox in a chicken coop.

The family that he joined had an undisputed matriarch in my maternal grandmother, Marie Simandlová. Slender and erect, she was the widow of a well-remembered local baker and, in the eyes of our family and neighbors, the first lady of the neighborhood. To go shopping with Grandmother was to bask in her reflected glory. As she strode down the main street, which was just a few steps from our house, merchants outside their stores and strolling burghers would shower her with ornate courtesies. Their greetings, a remnant of the era of Habsburgs, ranged from a courtly "My humble bow!" to an elaborate "I kiss your hand, my gracious lady!" Striding proudly by Grandma's side, I'd get approving pats on the head and, frequently, a piece of candy.

Much of the rest of the house exuded the same ancien régime atmosphere. The ground floor of our apartment house was occupied by my mother's eldest sister, a kindly, always smiling woman who was just as slim as Grandmother. Her husband, Uncle Ludvík, was shaped like a Tweedledum and used to be a well-known Kapellmeister (a band conductor) in the Imperial and Royal Austro-Hungarian Army. His career ended in 1918 when the empire fell apart and royalty went out of fashion. Uncle Ludvík's lustrous past was captured in his near-life-size, hand-colored photograph in a gilded ornamental frame that dominated the Ludvíks' living room. It showed him with a waxed, upward-sweeping handlebar mustache, a shiny pince-nez, and a splendid gold-braided blue dress uniform topped by a broad sash and an array of medals. It was his gala attire he wore when playing at the annual Opera Ball in Vienna, attended by leading members of the Imperial and Royal family and court.

If Uncle Ludvík's world fell apart with the demise of the Austro-Hungarian Empire, he never complained about it. Instead, he conducted Czech orchestras at considerably less prestigious events than used to be his realm and took up carpet weaving to boost his meager income. I remember him best, toiling at the loom while softly humming military marches and melodies from Léhar and Strauss.

On the floor above the Ludvíks lived the family of my mother's eldest brother. Uncle Simandl was the director of Vršovice's major bank, and he looked the part: he was a tall, husky man with heavy eyebrows and a commanding voice and manner. He died when I was very small. His widow was a neat, calm, always pleasant and well-dressed woman. My brother and I called her "Teta Lepší" (Aunt Better) because everything she baked or cooked tasted better than what we had at home. Aunt Better's life was dedicated to the welfare of her son, Milda, and her two daughters.

One of them, Cousin Božena, conceived of the unheard-of notion of following in her father's footsteps and making a bank career instead of getting married and raising children. Under intense pressure from the whole clan, Božena eventually gave in and announced that she'd get married. The whole family celebrated except for my father, who had argued all along that Božena should be left alone. When it turned out that my cousin's fiancé was a printer, a "mere" blue-collar worker, the building almost audibly gasped in horror.

The family citadel had another tenant who did not meet with universal approbation. Uncle Bořik was an avid soccer fan, promoter of a lowbrow amateur theater group, and a supporter of oddball politicians. Worst of all, he had divorced his first wife whom everybody liked, and married an actress who dyed her hair and spent a lot of time at the hairdresser. Mirek and I were very fond of Uncle Bořik. He was generous to a fault and loved children though he had none of his own.

But however likable, on the family prestige ladder Uncle Bořik stood as low as my father, the irreverent outsider. Dad and Uncle Bořik should have been natural allies, but they profoundly disagreed on Czech politics. Dad was a great admirer of Czechoslovak president Edward Beneš, one of the founders of the republic and a highly respected leader of the League of Nations, but Uncle Bořik considered Beneš a wimp.

Except for Grandma Simandlová whom he liked, Dad found the family stifling, and he liked to complain that "there should be a law" against more than two relatives living in the same apartment building. That was Dad's point of view; Mirek's and mine was just the opposite. For us, the close family ties meant security and the warmth of home. Mirek was everybody's favorite. He was tall for his age, strikingly handsome, and had the gentle disposition of Uncle Bořik. I was more in my father's mold, but because I was Grandma Simandlová's youngest grandchild, I was much forgiven. Mirek and I had the run of the house, and we loved the serene years of our childhood.

One of the basic verities to which the Czechs subscribed during my childhood (and which rhymes in the Czech) asserted that "hard work—and striving—is our salvation." As little kids we were taught to take pride in the Czechoslovak democracy, which the republic's founder, President Thomáš Masaryk, consciously shaped on the model of the United States. Czechoslovakia was portrayed to us, not unrealistically, as a small but upright and worthy member of the community of nations.

～

This antebellum bliss lasted until I was almost ten years old and Hitler felt strong enough to start conquering the world. The possibility of a German aggression had been hanging in the air for years, but my first distinct sense of impending war came from a conversation between my father and two of his fellow army officers that I overheard in the fall of 1937.

They talked about Hitler's growing territorial demands on Czechoslovakia and about the scant chances of the Czech army against the mighty Wehrmacht. In the estimate of Dad's friends, the bombers of the German Luftwaffe were poised to devastate Prague and other major Czech cities from at least three directions. I still remember the grim tone of the conversation, which was unrelieved by the usual jokes and bragging.

Newspaper pictures began showing the rallies of Sudeten Germans supporting Hitler's crude verbal onslaughts on the Prague government and President Beneš—"Herr Benesh," as Hitler contemptuously referred to him. An important adjunct to the Nazi psych warfare, thousands of Germans who lived along the Czech border strutted around in the high boots and brown shirts of Hitler's Sturmabteilungen (SA, storm troops), shrieked "Heim ins Reich!" (Home to the Reich!) and battled Czech cops. The Sudeten Germans were Czechoslovak citizens with full civil rights; their elected representatives sat in the Czech parliament, and German, alongside the Czech and Slovak, was an official language. But in those years of worldwide depression, they had many economic grievances, and more than two-thirds of them voted for a Nazi Party that demanded the annexation of Sudetenland by Hitler's Germany.

By the summer of 1938, Hitler's abuse and the Sudeten German antics convinced most Czechs that war was unavoidable. Dad's unit was mobilized, took up positions close to the German border, and he was hardly ever home. With most of the men away in uniform, women and older people were scrambling to prepare for raids by the dreaded Luftwaffe. Every apartment building, including ours, had to convert part of its basement into a bomb shelter. Uncle Ludvík became an air warden. We children carried gas masks to school, and the whole Prague conducted air raid drills with tear gas.

Even among us small kids, anti-German feelings ran so high I remember a whole flock of us jeering a couple of older women who conversed in the street in German. (Ironically, they were most likely members of the large German-speaking Jewish community in Prague.) The one comforting thought that we all shared and that made the strain bearable was that, if Hitler's Wehrmacht got on the move, France and the Soviet Union would fulfill their treaty obligations and come to Czechoslovakia's aid, and Britain would inevitably follow suit.

That naive hope collapsed on September 30, 1938, when a choked-up announcer interrupted the regular program of Radio Prague to read the text of the Munich Agreement. Neville Chamberlain and Edouard Daladier, without as much as consulting Beneš, had handed to Hitler the heavily defended Czech Sudetenland. It was the most shameful political betrayal of the prewar era.

With the stroke of a pen, Chamberlain and Daladier stripped Czechoslovakia of its fortifications facing Germany. France waived its commitment to come to the aid of Czechoslovakia, whereupon Soviet Russia proclaimed void the mutual defense treaty of France, the Soviet Union, and Czechoslovakia. What perhaps hurt most was the message from Munich that in the eyes of the two big Western democracies, the fate of Czechoslovakia did not matter.

It was a country, as Chamberlain famously proclaimed upon returning from Munich, "of which we know little."

I'll never forget the despair of my father who happened to be at home and was about to return to his unit. As the disastrous news sank in, he placed his head in his hands and cried. He did not say anything, he did not even sit down; he just stood there and cried. It was the only time I saw him so desolate.

A little later I went out with my mother to buy some groceries. It was as if the hurt of the Western betrayal had spilled into the streets and bonded the numbed people of Prague into one shocked family. Total strangers would stop in the middle of the sidewalk to denounce the sellout. Women, including my mother, cried openly while shopping.

The fall and winter that followed were so bleak that in retrospect they seem like a long, sad march into the night. Beneš resigned and went into exile in London. Big chunks of Czechoslovakia were ripped off not only by Hitler but also by the fascist regimes in Hungary and Poland. Dad's army was dismantled, a new pro-Nazi government took over, and the state-run radio became an outlet for German propaganda. At the end of November Emil Hácha, a sixty-seven-year-old Czech jurist, was made president of what had become a de facto German fiefdom called Czecho-Slovakia. But everybody knew the process that started with Munich was not finished.

The other shoe finally dropped on March 15, 1939, a miserably cold day. Acting on a consent that Hitler personally extracted from the ailing Hácha, the Wehrmacht troops rode into Prague in a snowstorm and stayed for six endless years and one month. The day they pulled in, Dad came to school to walk Mirek and me home because, as he earnestly explained, Mother wanted to "make sure you don't get into trouble." As we passed a parked convoy of dark-green Wehrmacht trucks full of surly-looking helmeted troops, Dad ostentatiously spat on the sidewalk in front of a German officer. On that first day of the occupation, the German only scowled.

Two nights later, roaring voices in the street outside our apartment made Mirek and me jump from our beds and run to the window. On the main Vršovice thoroughfare, a few yards from our house, a large crowd of young university students marched under the now-banned Czechoslovak flags shouting in cadence "Němci ven! Němci ven!" (Germans, out! Germans, out!). They were headed toward a former Czech army barracks, which by then had been taken over by the Wehrmacht. The streetlights at our corner had been put out, but we could see in the dark about forty or fifty Czech policemen, waiting. When part of the marchers passed by, the cops charged the demonstration with truncheons, cut it in half, and dispersed it.

As protests go, it was smaller and less violent than I was to see later in the Middle East. The cops sympathized with the students, and the students were not eager to face the German guns down the street. By midnight the neighborhood was quiet, but I could not sleep. My heart was pounding in my throat, my lips were parched, and the shouts of the crowd were ringing in my ears. I was only eleven years old and safely behind the closed windows of the apartment, but I was consumed by a sensation that I had been a part of that street protest against a burning injustice.

The fury, fears, and impotence of the students were mine as fully as if I had been one of them, waving the prohibited flag and braving the guns of the invaders. It was a feeling I never forgot. It would come back to me decades later and under much different circumstances when I covered, under the brilliant Middle East sun, Palestinian demonstrations in the Israeli-occupied West Bank and Gaza. But on that night in March 1939, all I vaguely understood was that the world as I knew it was finished.

CHAPTER 2

THE FIRST CATASTROPHE
World War II

Picasso's great mural *Guernica* captured the orgy of war in a single moment of maimed bodies and shattered souls. The war that Nazi-occupied Europe lived through was more like a long trek through a hostile, barren wasteland. It was exhausting, sad and seemingly endless, a relentless, painful education about the limits of human endurance and response to pressure. Moments of joy were rare, and there was only one exhilarating period, which was the utter collapse of the Nazi horror machine in May 1945.

By the time the Third Reich bled to death, most of us who had been ensnared by it had seen enough images of war to fully appreciate Picasso's indictment of inhumanity. But if I were an artist trying to capture my own pain in World War II, I would paint my mother in an ice-cold apartment, bundled in layers of old clothes, and crying despairingly over an empty stove. Or my shocked-looking brother Mirek comforting Helena, a little Jewish girl we knew, after she told us, sobbing, that she and her parents would "soon" be taken to "a camp."

Or me, waking up in cold sweat at three o'clock in the morning at the sound of a turned-off car engine outside our apartment house, terrified it was the Gestapo, holding my breath and expecting brutal men in shining brown leather coats to come upstairs, pound on the door, and drag away Dad. Picasso's war was humanity's heart-rending scream; mine was a succession of private misery, dread, and emotional wounds.

If the war as I knew it lacked epic breadth, the reason was not just my preoccupation with the hardships bearing down on our family. What limited the understanding for all of us in that malignant time and place was a special curse of the occupation that is not well understood by those who have not experienced it. The plague besetting us in addition to constant fear, revulsion, and physical hardship was ignorance. Under the cloak of Nazism, there was no light. In occupied Europe, truth was even more scarce than food, peace of mind, or laughter. For those of us mired in the Nazi cesspool, there was no way to grasp the big picture, to see the full panoply of Hitler's evil.

We glimpsed bits of it on those rare occasions when the Nazis advertised some of their barbarities such as the genocide and eradication of the village of Lidice—to terrorize the Czech underground and populace. We saw Jews—fewer and fewer of them as the war drew on—wearing the yellow Star of David, and we heard rumors about the existence of concentration camps.

We were vaguely aware of Hitler's design for a "new European order" after the "final victory" in which Slavs like us and other *minderwertig* (inferior) people would be "relocated to the East" to make room for the superior, purely Aryan *Herrenrasse* (master race). And throughout the war, we learned about some of the relatives or friends who'd fallen into the claws of Gestapo. But the Nazi grip on the truth was remarkably successful. For years, we did not know the worst.

It was not until the winter of 1944 that "whispered propaganda"—as we called the wartime rumor mill—reported the transit through Bohemia of sealed freight trains carrying, we assumed, political prisoners that were being carted away by the retreating Germans. Only in the spring of 1945, the dying weeks of the war, did we hear from Czech workers who had fled from Germany harrowing reports about hunger-crazed Russian POWs risking a bullet from their guards to pick earthworms and eat them. And it was only a few days after the Nazi collapse that I came face-to-face with a living indictment of the Thousand-Year Reich, a survivor of the Holocaust.

Incongruously, the man was sitting in a Prague streetcar, still wearing his striped camp uniform with a yellow star. He was holding a pair of crutches and his arms, head, and one leg were swathed in fresh bandages that made him look like a mummy. What imperative had compelled him to leave a hospital bed and hazard a trip aboard the rattling tram was one of the myriad mysteries spawned by the horrors of Nazism. I still remember the ex-prisoner's pale, tired face and his fixed, almost apologetic smile, as if in embarrassment over his violated body. I felt humbled by the enormity of his suffering—and abashed at my own good fortune. But the vastness of the Holocaust dawned on us only weeks later, when we saw Allied newsreels from the liberated camps.

What we did know, and intimately, was a tyrannical system that combined physical privation with thought control in an attempt to keep millions of unwilling people in line and contributing to Hitler's war machine. The system was a splendid example of German thoroughness and Nazi venality. It began, even as the Wehrmacht jeeps were arriving in Prague, with the establishment of so-called Protectorate of Bohemia and Moravia, consisting of the post-Munich remnant of Czechoslovakia minus the Slovaks, who became "independent" under the Nazi tutelage. Hácha was allowed to stay in the Prague presidential palace, but the real boss, a Nazi Reichsprotektor, was appointed by Hitler.

Afterwards, the Germans systematically dismantled the Czech army and institutions; looted the Czech economy; enslaved the labor force and established stringent rationing of every commodity needed for survival, from bread and potatoes to clothes, shoes, cooking gas, and coal. Biblical pestilence could not have had more dramatic consequences. Millions of people—rich, poor, and in-between—were suddenly reduced to the same level of privation and forced to scurry around for an extra mouthful. Within a few months, as the last frantically hoarded food ran out, all pursuits took a backseat to mankind's most ancient worry, how to fill one's stomach. The Czechs have a saying to the effect that hardship can teach anyone to play the violin. The wartime quest for survival was a particularly good teacher.

Uncle Ludvík, the musical star of the Habsburgs, filled a niche in the rapidly sprouting black market by making soap, which came to be in much greater demand than his carpets. Every time I saw him he was leaning over the stove, stirring a cauldron bubbling with pungent chemicals and scraps of fat. Like everybody else he was losing weight and, it seemed to me, patience with his small nephews. Aunt Better, who had no special skills, adopted a survival technique followed by thousands of other formerly well-off Czechs. She traded piecemeal her jewelry, wardrobe, and other prized possessions for food. Uncle Bořik earned extra income maintaining a soccer field and stage props. And in our own family, there took place a striking reversal of roles.

Dad, who used to fill the house with bustle and irreverence, went into a withdrawal. Deprived of his uniform and the army, he nominally resumed working full-time as a chimney sweep to qualify for a work ID, without which there was no residence permit or food rations. In practice, he seemed to be doing nothing. Day in and day out, I would return from school in the early afternoon to find him at home, reading newspapers or sleeping with his arms folded on the kitchen table. He was lethargic, like a man staggered by an unacceptable shock. His main contribution to the family's welfare was to make schnapps from fermented potatoes and fruit in a small distillery he rigged up in the bathroom. He sold some of it on the black market and gave away or drank the rest until kidney stones, his mother's bane, forced him into abstinence.

By contrast our normally passive Mother responded to the crisis with an unexpected outburst of energy and enterprise. Since the black market in Prague was for us prohibitively expensive, she set up a food-growing operation of her own in our vacation bungalow in Horní Borek, a village about one hour's train ride south of Prague. In the spring and summer, she raised sheep and chicken. In the fall and winter, she force-fed geese, a difficult and unpleasant chore to which she had to attend every three to four hours, day and night. Part of Mother's production was consumed by us; the rest she traded with local farmers for bread, potatoes, and whatever other food they managed to hide from the authorities.

Every two weeks or so, Mother would pack her provisions and board an evening train for Prague. She traveled at night because the darkness improved the chances of avoiding the policemen at the train station who were on the lookout for passengers with big suitcases. "Hoarding" of food or any other necessity was deemed by the Germans to be sabotage of the war effort and as such was a serious offense. It was Mirek's and my job to meet Mother at the train and help her smuggle the packages past the guards.

The cops never stopped us, but not everything we brought home survived the increasingly time-consuming transit. Throughout the war, Czech passenger trains were routinely sidetracked to make way for Wehrmacht transports. Later on, as the Allies pushed into Germany, trains in Central Europe were also almost daily strafed by American fighter planes we called "steam fitters" because they blasted holes in the locomotives. By the time the war ended, the one-hour trip from the bungalow to Prague could take up to twelve times as long, with sometimes dismal consequences. On one occasion in the summer, Mother arrived home with a ham full of maggots.

On the whole, her brave crusade against starvation was successful—more often than not, Mirek and I went to bed without being hungry. But Mom's addition to the daily menu did not change the fact that our mainstay was potatoes and porridge. *Ersatz* (substitute) was the spirit and substance of our wartime diet. We spread ersatz marmalade made with carrots on ersatz bread baked with potato flour, drank ersatz coffee made from chicory, and supped on rubbery ersatz cheese or ersatz sausages made with flour and boiled blood of beef.

Food became an obsession. Some people, including me, had dreams about eating a full prewar dinner. One of the jokes that made the rounds during the war was about two old friends who had not seen each other for years, were both newly married, specialized in fourteenth-century liturgy, and met at an exhibit of rare lithographs. Question: What was the first thing they talked about? Answer: Where to get black market potatoes.

During the long frigid winters, the discomfort of a half-empty stomach was aggravated by the discomfort of cold because of coal shortage, the only fuel city folks then used for heating. The year's coal ration usually lasted until about mid-January, just as the temperatures dropped lowest. Some people searched the railroad tracks for coal that had fallen off freight trains and tenders, but there was never enough of it to keep the stove going. As the last option, most of us tried to keep warm with table-top gas burners. This prompted the Germans to shut off the gas all but four hours a day and issue a stern warning that igniting the burners at other times could trigger an explosion. Most people were so miserably cold that as long as the burners emitted any flame at all, they were kept going.

On top of this physical misery the Nazi control system inflicted upon us another plague, which was even more insidious because it corroded the mind. It consisted of a blackout of truth and a surfeit of insulting propaganda. To eliminate any interference with the outpouring of official lies the occupation regime shut down all Czech universities, gagged the press, radio, movies, and theater, and outlawed all prewar Czech books about democracy or the historic Czech struggle against the Germans.

Nothing, however, showed more clearly the Nazis' fear that their propaganda machine might fail than their crusade to silence foreign broadcasts. Not only did they jam, all Allied news programs, round the clock; they ordered every Czech-owned radio to be gutted of its short-wave receiver and display a sign under the wave length dial that sternly warned, "Remember, remember . . . that listening to foreign broadcasts is subject to severe penalties!" It was one of the rare official pronouncements of the occupiers that was only in Czech, without the routinely preceding version in German.

At the same time, the regimented media drenched the occupied population with brazen, stupefying, and bottomless propaganda. The Nazi-run newspapers and radio were trying to convince us that American and British "plutocrats" were forever on the brink of either total economic collapse, military defeat, or open warfare against Soviet "bolsheviks," their wartime ally. The media sewage was thick with fantasies about plots hatched by American Jews and Freemasons to dominate the world, old pictures of Great Depression soup lines in the United States, and diatribes against the decadence and depravity of a country whose favorite musician was a minderwertig black named Armstrong. In the absence of facts to distort or stretch, total fabrications filled the void.

In the Nazi propaganda, the disgusting and decrepit attributes of the Brits and Americans were contrasted with the triumphant virtues of the Germans. Especially early in the war, the spinmeisters of the Third Reich proclaimed at least once a month that the Luftwaffe was in control of the air over the British isles; the German submarines were sinking all Allied shipping; and Mussolini's fascist troops—famous as the most fainthearted soldiers of the Axis—were inflicting enormous punishment on the minderwertig Yugoslav and Greek partisans. After Pearl Harbor, the American army was shrugged off by the Nazi-controlled media as fatally inferior because of its racially impure black troops, and the US Navy was proclaimed to be as good as wiped out by the Japanese.

The propaganda machine was powerful and persistent, but not smart. One wartime magazine feature compared the quality of Wehrmacht's and US Army's personal combat gear and came to the inevitable conclusion that the Nazi soldiers were swathed in much more wool, leather, and other fine materials and therefore enjoyed superior protection against the elements. As it happened, the story came out in the winter of 1943, at a time when the Germans ordered us, Czech school kids, to knock on the doors of our neighbors and solicit sweaters and other warm clothing for the freezing Herrenrasse on the Russian front.

Occasionally, the Nazi liars acknowledged that, incomprehensible as it seemed, there were actually some Czechs who doubted the inevitability of Germany's final victory. These individuals were denounced as saboteurs of the war effort, Jew-lovers, bankrupt leftovers of Beneš's "corrupt regime," and enemies of the Czech people whose best interests were generously looked after by Adolf Hitler. The most prominent Czech collaborator of the Nazis, a publicist named Moravec, reminded us teenagers repeatedly that Hitler spared us conscription and bloodshed at the front. And to dispel the rumors about postwar expulsion of all Czechs to Siberia, he assured us that we only needed to fully contribute to the war effort in order to "assure ourselves and our children of a window seat in the Führer's train to New Europe," an event that was to follow the inevitable triumph of the Wehrmacht.

This sort of stuff poured out from every official communication channel, including schoolbooks and magazines for children. It was a vicious crusade to brainwash millions of people that, as luck would have it, I was to experience twice: first at the hands of the Nazis, and later under the postwar Moscow-trained Communists.

The repeated onslaught on human intelligence and sense of decency left me permanently disdainful of propaganda hucksters of all stripes. And it gave me a great satisfaction that, at least in its Nazi version, the culture of official deceit failed. With relatively few exceptions, the Czechs never bought Goebbels's famous dogma that "a lie repeated a thousand times becomes the truth." Not only that: the Czechs, in common with most of the occupied nations, fought against the Nazi propaganda as vigorously as against the ersatz diet.

For example Dad, who was a whiz at electronics, rigged up our emasculated radio with a working shortwave receiver. Despite the threat of harsh punishment, he and tens of thousands of Czechs searched daily for a way to break out of Goebbels's soundproof chamber by twirling the radio knobs until they snatched a few audible sentences of BBC news from London. The nightly ritual rarely yielded more than a dozen words from the announcer before the Nazi jamming drowned out the rest, and listening to these broadcasts was filled with such high tensions that to this day if I hear the BBC's wartime theme tune, "Trumpeter Extraordinary," I feel shivers running down my spine. And yet, no amount of danger could stop the daily routine that became part of our wartime existence. At school, we traded tidbits from the forbidden broadcasts as avidly as gossip about who dated whom.

Nothing proved better the impotence of the Nazi propaganda machine than its hysterical crusade against Jews. The persistence with which the Nazi machine poured out antisemitic filth knew no bounds. Day in and day out, occupied Europe was subjected to a mudslide of falsehoods that made even the "Protocols of the Elders of Zion" look like respectable literature.

We schoolkids had to troop through "cultural" exhibits that consisted of enlarged cartoons of deformed Jews from *Der Stürmer*, the unspeakably racist official organ of Hitler's SA, the Nazi militia of thugs. At one time, the occupying authorities ordered every shopwindow in Prague to display big posters showing dirty, warped faces of bearded Orthodox Jews captured by the heroic Wehrmacht in Poland and Ukraine. Next to the warnings on our radios, this was the most ubiquitous message from our "protectors" that was not bilingual. The Czech-only caption of the posters read: "Are These Your Brothers?"

As far as I could tell, the deluge backfired. In our own non-church-going, nominally Protestant (except for Dad, who was firmly secular) family, religion was unimportant, and such prewar contacts we had with individuals who were Jews were very friendly. One of them was Helena, a gentle little daughter of a Prague family who used to vacation in an inn about a mile from our bungalow in Horní Borek. We used to swim together in a nearby pond, and when, in 1940 or 1941, the tiny girl poured out to us her fears about the "camp," both Mirek and I were in tears. None of the three of us had a clear notion what the term meant, but whatever the Nazis did was terrifying. After that summer, we never saw Helena or her parents again.

The only other Jew I met as a child was a banker named Sommer who on the eve of the Nazi occupation shared a hospital room with my father when they were both treated for kidney stones. Sommer and his wife were farsighted enough to send their only son to relatives in London, but they themselves stayed behind until it was too late. Shortly before they were hauled away to a concentration camp, Sommer asked Dad to safeguard—for "whoever of us returns," as he put it—a few pieces of handsome furniture and a fat manila envelope.

We put the sofa and two chairs in our living room, and Dad hid the packet in our stand-up piano (probably the first place the Gestapo would have searched), thereby committing the "crime" of preserving Jewish property. Later on during the war, after my brother and I became aware that Dad was active in the underground, the stuffed envelope heightened our dread of the Gestapo. To get rid of it, however, would have been unthinkable.

There was an incident that spoke volumes about the disgust of ordinary people with the antisemitism of the Nazis. It happened fairly early in the occupation while I was riding to school on an overcrowded streetcar that included a few Jewish passengers wearing the prescribed yellow Star of David. The presence of Jews in a crowded streetcar was strictly verboten and, at one downtown stop, a German plainclothesman banged on the tram window and ordered the conductor to get them out. The packed streetcar suddenly turned silent as a block of ice.

The conductor repeated the German's order in a convoluted Czech—he said something like "All Jewish passengers have to disembark themselves"—as if to emphasize that the order was not his idea. People exchanged angry glances and some of the faces around me became flushed with emotion. Then, way too late if it had been their original intention, a couple of the men standing near me suddenly decided to get off. They pushed their way to the exit ahead of the two or three Jews who followed them out to the platform.

The non-Jews' departure was an obvious protest, and I remember wishing that the rest of us in the tram had the guts to do the same. We didn't. Defiance in front of an angry-looking all-powerful Nazi cop was fraught with high risk. But staying aboard was not a sign of indifference. After the conductor rang the bell and we pulled out of the station, the tram remained silent. One woman standing near me wiped off a tear, and others stared straight ahead, avoiding the eyes of fellow passengers. The Nazi brainwash did not work.

The barbaric treatment of the Jews was for me such a formative lesson that I emerged from World War II with a deeply felt commitment. Because my generation of occupied Europeans glimpsed what the Nazis did to the Jews, we had a special obligation to never forget. Simply because we suffered less than they did—and we survived, while millions of them did not—we owed them a special respect, in the first place, and compassion.

Years later, when I worked in the Middle East, this attitude influenced my coverage of the Arab-Israeli conflict.

During my first stint in the area, from the Six Day War in 1967 until mid-1971, I was based in Beirut, which was then a key post for watching the Arab world. My encounters with Palestinians were far from pleasant, but after talking with scores of them, Arab officials, and American and foreign diplomats, I concluded that the refugees had been handed by Israel (and their fellow Arabs) a very raw deal. Israel's bulldozing of more than 360 of Palestinian villages in the late 1940s struck me as shocking. The stories of more land seizures in the occupied territories made the record even more grim. It was as if the moral lessons of World War II had never reached the Middle East.

But I never subscribed to the strongly anti-Israeli position that was then common among most foreign correspondents in Beirut. I regarded it as unprofessional, because most of us did not know firsthand the Israeli side of the story: in those days, anyone known to have visited the "Zionist entity" could not get a visa, let alone do any reporting, in any Arab country.

But above all I could not accept it emotionally: Israel was something that my generation owed to Jews who, against enormous odds, survived the Nazi scourge. The crude demonization of the Jewish state that was disgorged daily by the Arab media reminded me so much of the Nazi wartime propaganda that I could not stand it.

~

For teenagers like Mirek and me, the Nazi occupation cast such a deep shadow that, as Aunt Ludvík said, our generation did not know how to be young. It was an overstatement, of course; in due course, Mirek and I tackled the mysteries of dating and sex—Mirek, who was tall and handsome, with much more success than I. Under the guidance of our Cousin Pepík, we took a few experimental puffs on cigarettes and tasted Dad's booze. But Aunt Ludvík was not far off the mark. Wartime regimentation and austerity all but eradicated our rites of adolescence.

Although dancing classes were allowed, public dancing and nightclubs were verboten: the racially inferior Czechs could not be allowed to have fun while the superior Herrenrasse was dying on the battlefield for the Führer and his Thousand-Year Reich. Jazz was verboten as the music of the minderwertig blacks and an example of American decadence. Sokol and all other traditional Czech organizations were disbanded as soon as the Wehrmacht armor rolled into Prague.

Early in the occupation, my classmates and I once in a while organized a small party in the home of one of us, but as the war ground on and the shortages mounted, even those few occasions ceased. The only other opportunities for youngsters of my age to socialize, a handful of authorized youth groups, belonged to something called "Curatorium of Czech Youth," which was a part of the Nazi control apparatus. Quite apart from the question whether we needed any cure, the Nazi affiliation was enough for everyone I knew to give those organizations a wide berth.

This reduced our social contacts to the school, which was a scene of resentment and gloom. We hated the daily classes in German, where we had to memorize lengthy biographies of Hitler and jewels of the Nazi cultural achievement such as the lyrics of the SA's hymn, the "Horst-Wessel Lied." In history classes, we had to blacken out or glue together pages of text with references to the centuries-old Czech struggle against the neighboring Germans.

The study of non-German literature, music, or art was either banned outright or severely limited to a few authors deemed ideologically acceptable to the Nazis. (Shakespeare, for example, did not make the cut, and neither did any American except for the hysterically antisemitic Ezra Pound.) All learning was by rote. To avoid politically incorrect formulations, teachers read their lectures from the censored books, and there were no class discussions.

About the only fun we had in school was pulling night duty as air raid wardens. Starting after the Allied invasion in Normandy, a different group of ten to twelve boys from the senior classes was drafted each day to spend the night in a special classroom equipped with bunks. The supervising teacher slept on a couch in the principal's office, and both he and we were allowed to skip the classes the next day. We had no training, no fire-fighting equipment, no telephone, and no idea what to do if the school were bombed. What we did know was how to horse around until well past midnight, and the teacher knew well enough to leave us alone. But we never escaped the ever-watchful eye of the Thousand-Year Reich.

On one of my tours of duty, the kid in charge of our detail got carried away by his sense of humor and wrote in the logbook that the room's washbasin was "like an oasis: full of mud." The joke was funny until the next morning when the log book was inspected by a German air warden who proclaimed the entry a "sabotage" and ordered it to be fully investigated. In the end nothing came of the incident, but the school principal who had to interrogate us was visibly unnerved and fearful of what the Germans would do next. None of us ever tried to be funny again.

Terror was the fundamental control method of the occupation authorities, and they unleashed it in full force in the summer of 1942, after two British-trained Czech commandos assassinated Reinhard Heydrich, the notorious SS Obergruppenführer who ran the Protectorate. The rampaging Gestapo and Wehrmacht burned and razed to the ground Lidice, the village where they suspected the commandos had been hiding, and summarily executed its entire population except for babies. In the months that followed, the Nazis sent to the gallows more than thirty thousand other Czech men, women, and adolescents in all parts of the country who had nothing to do with the assassination.

It was a general punishment designed to generate nationwide dread. The nominal roll of the victims of what came to be known as "the Heydrichiade" read like the *Who's Who* of importance in prewar Czechoslovakia. It included prominent intellectuals, former mayors, politicians, and senior civil servants. Their names were preceded by a boilerplate statement that "The following individuals and their families were executed because of their approval of the assassination" of Heydrich. For maximum shock effect, the list ran on the front page of every Czech-language newspaper. It included a big photograph of Heydrich and was surrounded by a big black frame like an obituary.

I could always tell that a new death roll was out as soon as I got on the streetcar to go to school. The tram, which in those days was everyone's conveyance, was shrouded in deep silence while shocked-looking passengers scanned the front page for familiar names.

The Czech mood—on the streetcars and elsewhere—got a bit better as the war dragged on and the Wehrmacht heroics declined from grand offensives to stalemates, "tactical repositioning," and eventually, massive retreats. There were some memorable moments of rare cheer: for example, the BBC news about D-day in Normandy, and one of Goebbels's last public rallies to announce a coming "final victory." Speaking in a German war factory, the Nazi propaganda chief swore that "the Allies will find that it's one thing to capture Tobruk or Belgrade, and quite another to take Cologne or Stuttgart." In the movie theater newsreel, the German workers erupted with great shouts of "Sieg heil!" but the most heartfelt response came from the Prague audience: silence. The Wehrmacht was licked. All around me, faces were beaming.

Unfortunately, the worse the war went for the Germans the harder they made it for us. In 1943 they started conscripting thousands of Czech teenagers who were born in 1924 for work in German factories, to replace the purely Aryan Herrenvolk who had been shipped to the front. The next summer, with the Western allies rolling through France and Italy and the Red Army pushing through Poland, the Nazis closed down all Czech high schools and ordered everybody over the age of sixteen to "join the war effort until the final victory."

Totaleinsatz (total effort), as the Nazis' last gasp was officially called, was a fitting climax for our awful teenage years. I happened to be assigned as a lathe operator–trainee in Avia, a huge aviation plant outside the opposite end of Prague from where I lived. It took me one and a half hours by streetcar and on foot to get to work in the morning, and almost two hours to get home in the heavier traffic at night. We worked seventy-two hours a week—from seven o'clock in the morning to seven at night with a half-hour break for lunch, six days a week.

Running the lathe was simple enough, but the long hours, the pounding noise of the machinery, and the pungent fumes of the chemicals that filled the hall were hard to take. Every night I came home dog tired. With Mother feeding geese in the bungalow, the household was run by Dad. He took his homemaking seriously. He'd get up before I did and have my breakfast and my lunch—usually, two big slices of bread—ready by five o'clock in the morning when I crawled out of bed. In the evening, he would have the supper of boiled potatoes or dumplings ready as soon as I got home and washed up. He would then sit in silence opposite me at the kitchen table while I gulped down the food. We did not speak much in those days, but I remember his eyes on me as I ate: they were the eyes of a father who cared. I felt close to him.

The strain of the occupation was hard on family life. Mirek was assigned to a different metal factory, and we did not see much of each other. When we did, neither of us had much to talk about except complain about the tedious work and lack of food. Mother was gone in the hustings. Dad's wisecracks and geniality had dried out already earlier in the war; now, toward its end, he was grim, tired, increasingly on edge. He kept silent about his underground work that, I later gathered, was eventually reduced to aiding families of his executed or jailed fellow army officers. Somehow, he and his friends scraped up enough money to buy black market bread for the most destitute victims.

In keeping with the iron code of wartime caution, Mirek and I asked Dad no questions; resistance was too frightful a subject to be mentioned even in one's own family. But we could see Dad's stress. In the last year of the war, when Prague was frequently roused by air raid sirens, Mirek and I would sometimes balk against trading precious sleep for the dubious security of the bomb shelter. Dad's responses to our protests grew from intemperate to furious.

Aside from the weariness, my most dismal memories of the Totaleinsatz are of my fellow metalworkers. They made me wonder whether Goebbels's propaganda machinery was not onto something I had missed.

Part of the problem appeared to be historical. Under the Habsburgs, Bohemia and Moravia were the industrial heart of the empire, and Czech metalworkers were courted as the elites of the Austro-Hungarian labor force. After Czechoslovakia won independence in 1918, leftist and nationalist parties flattered the skilled workers even more assiduously: for example, machinists were singled out for the honor of leading the annual May Day parade, a major political event of the year, and socialist newspapers hailed them as a class imbued with innate political wisdom and superior character.

As the occupiers, the Nazis—whose organization, after all, was called "the German National Socialist Workers' Party"—stroked the Czech blue-collar ego for all it was worth. The German war machine devoured enormous amounts of military hardware and needed the metalworkers to produce more of it. To keep up their morale, machinists and other skilled laborers in major armament plants such as Avia were given special rations of booze (we, the kids, never got any) and huge doses of praise. They were the "noblemen of productivity" who were forging the "better tomorrow" for the Czechs aboard Hitler's train to New Europe. In school, we used to laugh at such crap. But when I came to Avia, I discovered to my amazement that some of the workers were taking the propaganda seriously.

My foreman, for instance, would stop at my machine once a week or so to criticize my miserly output, and when I complained about the excessively long hours, he would talk about the imperative of the "final victory" of Wehrmacht. American and British troops were almost on the Rhine, the Russians were in Prussia, and this lackey was still talking about Nazi victory. I wondered what he had been saying early in the war, when the Wehrmacht was really winning.

There were also at least three older lathe hands in our department who went out of their way to display their high working morale. One of them, a skinny guy in his thirties, every late afternoon would break into a loud medley of songs, just to show how unaffected he was by the long hours. Another jerk would run from one machine to another banging on each with a big wrench and announcing out loud how close he was to meeting his production quota. It was hard to believe these creatures lived under the same occupation as I did.

The reaction of the half-dozen of us high school conscripts who wound up in Avia was to keep the production mongers—"output noblemen," as we called them—at a distance, which only made us more unpopular. In the class-conscious eyes of the regular workers, our low working morale was not a matter of patriotic duty but the laziness of a bunch of spoiled brats. Within a few weeks the noblemen and we were on a collision course.

My number was up one day in the late fall of 1944, when the foreman saw me expounding something on the john instead of producing engine parts. His patience with me over, I was summoned the next morning to the production chief's office and told that, as a poor worker, I was being transferred to a shipping and maintenance crew. S&M's catchall functions ranged from road repairs inside the plant compound to packing and shipping finished products, a form of unskilled labor unworthy of the "noblemen" in production.

Instead of punishment, I found the change of scenery quite pleasant. Unlike the machinists, the service workers were mostly undesirable elements like me whose main intent was to sabotage the war effort. We loafed with a vengeance, an endeavor that was greatly assisted by Allied bombers who in those waning days of the war had a command of the skies and were busily decimating the Nazi war industry. Since Avia was a likely target, we the workers were instructed to drop everything as soon as the sirens sounded and run out into the fields surrounding the factory. We followed the instructions with such enthusiasm that time and again we did not make it back to the plant for the rest of the day. When there was no air raid, we would find hiding places and take turns goofing off instead of fixing potholes.

My good fortune, however, did not last long. One evening in November 1944, a fellow high school kid and I were sent with two aging Wehrmacht soldiers and a truckload of boxes of engine parts to the main freight yard in Prague, where we were supposed to load them in a railroad car. We made it to the station without an incident, but unloading the heavy crates was beyond the combined strength of my friend and me. We dropped one of them and it, having been nailed together in our department, broke open like an Easter egg. Suddenly, hundreds of closely machined and heavily oiled pieces of steel tubing, no doubt essential for the Führer's final victory, cascaded all over the railroad tracks.

The two soldiers were so infuriated by the incident that they jumped from the truck and turned against my friend and me, cursing and swinging their rifles. At that, the two of us took off for the exit. The soldiers reported us to the Wehrmacht military police at the terminal, and a week later I was transferred again, this time to Avia's Abteilung X (Department 10) in Bránik, another outlying district of Prague. Unlike my previous punishment, the latest move was not accompanied by any verbal reprimand. As I soon found out, that was not necessary.

Working in Abteilung X, which I did for three months, was punishment enough. The plant manufactured parts for V-1s and V-2s, the long-range rockets on which the Nazis hung their last hopes for reversing the tide of war. To safeguard this top-priority production from Allied bombers, the division was shoehorned into deep bomb-proof caves of an old brewery by replacing the huge fermenting bats with rows of lathes operated by delinquents such as me.

The cellars were carved in a solid rock. They were cold, poorly lit and ventilated, and their walls were constantly covered with beads of water. In this Dante-esque environment, we worked from seven o'clock in the morning to seven o'clock at night, seventy-two hours a week, in alternating day and night shifts. Since it was winter and the days were short, I rarely saw any daylight. There were no breaks for air raids, and the relatively small size of each cavern made it almost impossible to sneak out unnoticed and catch a few winks on the john. Just standing at the machine all day was so tiring I sometimes felt that if I leaned against the wet wall I'd fall asleep. I even tried to doze off while keeping open the eye toward the center aisle, which was patrolled by an old German *Werkschutzmann*, a uniformed factory guard. My experiment repeatedly failed.

On the positive side, my foreman this time was a decent sort who never mentioned Nazi victory, and my fellow workers were all Totaleinsatz truants like me. It did not take us long to work out a system of smuggling the same machined pieces from shift to shift, and to have them each time logged in by the Werkschutzmann as new output. The brewery was much closer to our apartment house, which cut short the commuting, and it felt good to sabotage the war effort. But faking work made the time drag even more slowly. By the end of January, I was so worn out I could hardly get out of bed.

The winter of my discontent was abruptly terminated in mid-February 1945. One evening when I got off the elevator at the end of my shift, I discovered that a nearby railroad terminal and surrounding buildings had been bombed out in an air raid of which we in the bowels of Abteilung X knew nothing. For a while, I watched the fires still raging below the brewery and wearily pondered how to get home without the tram, which had stopped running. Eventually I started walking, and the freezing night air and the chaotic scenes in the streets helped me resolve more than the problem of commuting. Jolted out of my robot-like routine and stupor, I came to the conclusion that for me, the Totaleinsatz was over. By the time I got home I knew what I would do next.

Next morning, instead of heading for the brewery I went to the Vršovice railroad station. War-effort deserters like me ran the risk of being caught by German plainclothesmen who patrolled the train stations, but my luck held out and I got on an overcrowded train. Then, just as I felt relieved to be out of sight of the leather coats, the press of passengers shoved me next to an SS-man in uniform. Riding a train instead of working was risky enough; being pinned against an SS-man, under the circumstances, was frightening.

To make matters worse, the soldier was so starved for company he insisted on talking. He told me he was a Romanian. He told me he had found the war "an adventure that's dangerous to your health." He told me about the primitive conditions he saw on the Eastern front. He told me about Russian POWs. When he finally ran out of things he wanted to tell me, he did what I was afraid that he would do: he started asking about me. Frantic to avoid the subject I drew on my high school German to prod him with inane inquiries about the Ukraine and Poland until I, too, ran out of ideas.

By then, fortunately, we were pulling into Benešov, a sizable town about thirty minutes out of Prague, and the SS-man started moving toward the exit.

Emboldened by our impending separation, I asked him the question that was at that time on everyone's mind, namely, how long would the war go on. The SS-man looked at me incredulously as if I was joking, and shrugged his shoulders: "It's all over!" he said. It was my first (and last) conversation with a Nazi soldier, and I was rather pleased by the note on which it ended. Another half an hour later we were in Horní Borek, and I was safe in our *chata*.

A couple of weeks later while I was staying at our bungalow I found out that for some of Germany's most tragic victims, the war was anything but finished. One evening I happened to be passing along a sidetracked, snow-covered freight train at the Horní Borek railroad station when I thought I heard a muffled cry. The voice, which seemed to be emanating from one of the boxcars, was so full of agony that I stopped dead in my tracks. Something was wrong. As far as I could see against the dark sky, the locomotive was pulling only boxcars—no coaches for passengers.

Someone moaned again, and my heart leapt to my throat. I suddenly realized that I was standing next to one of the trains with prisoners that, according to the grapevine, the retreating Nazis were taking along when they were forced to abandon the concentration camps. I looked again, more closely, and felt another jolt. Except for a caboose at the end, the train's silhouette showed no chimney or any other sign suggesting that the cars were heated. It was freezing cold.

I knew I could do nothing and my instinct was to run away, but somehow I managed to suppress the panic. I took a few hesitant steps to the nearest car. "Hello?" I said tentatively in Czech, not knowing what else to say. I kept my voice low.

"Where are we?" somebody inside the car asked in German.

As I started answering, a Wehrmacht soldier in a heavy overcoat jumped out of the caboose and started shouting and running toward me. My heart pounding so hard I could hear it, I turned around and rapidly walked away from the tracks.

There was a terrible tragedy taking place inside the boxcars just a few feet away from me. I conjured up images of freezing prisoners huddling together in the dark, trying to hold on to life through another interminable night. Scores, perhaps hundreds of the poor wretches were dying from the bitter cold and exhaustion aboard that train, just as the Thousand-Year Reich was about to be put out of its hideous existence.

"What swine, what incredible swine," I muttered to me over and over, thinking about the Germans. I thought about the SS-man telling me the war was over. How on earth could members of the human race do this, I thought. The Nazis were finished, and they were still unspeakably brutal. I almost ran back to our bungalow, feeling dizzy. That night, I dreamt about walking down the Wenceslas Square swinging an umbrella with a sharp steel tip. Every time I met a Wehrmacht soldier walking toward me I rammed the umbrella into his gut.

Over the next few weeks, Mirek—who had also walked out on the Totaleinsatz and joined me in the bungalow—and I made several trips to Prague with provisions. By the beginning of April, however, American "steam fitters" made train travel almost impossible, and we stayed in Prague to await the end of the war. It was a sheer thrill to see each day more signs of a Wagnerian *Götterdämmerung* engulfing the Nazis. Allied overflights became so prodigious that the radio stopped announcing air raid warnings.

Another sign of the Herrenrasse's declining fortunes was the shrinking list of European radio stations that each Sunday aired a special concert from Berlin for German soldiers. By mid-April the concert's announcer, who used to list a dozen participating radio stations, was down to Prague and Vienna, the last two capitals still held by the Wehrmacht.

The strutting figures of Nazi officials in green Tyrolean hats and brown leather coats were vanishing from the streets while railroad sidings throughout the city were filling with trainloads of wounded Wehrmacht soldiers pouring in from both fronts. Even Goebbels stopped making speeches promising a "final victory," and the pompous daily military bulletins from "the Führer's headquarters" shrank to a couple of thin paragraphs.

What I watched with particular glee through that early spring of 1945 was the squirming of quislings in the Czech media. Only a few weeks earlier, on the eve of the Yalta conference, Goebbels's Czech mouthpieces were obediently spreading the last-ditch hopes that the Western Allies and the Soviets would soon start fighting each other instead of the Wehrmacht. It was the only scenario that offered Germany some hope of escaping a total rout. But as Yalta came and went, and as Hitler's New Europe kept shrinking between the pincers of the Allied armies, the Czech collaborators sounded less and less shrill and arrogant.

In one editorial appearing at the very end of April, the writer went as far as admitting that "we the activists may not have been accurate in forecasting a German military victory." With the Red Army fighting in the streets of Berlin and the British and American troops on the Elbe, this was the understatement of the war. But after six years of propaganda deluge that tolerated no facts or doubts, reading the editorial gave me a big thrill. I spent the morning on the phone calling the article to the attention of my friends.

When the end finally came, it was swift. In the morning of May 5, 1945, I was at home when the Radio Prague broadcast was suddenly interrupted by an excited voice announcing that the Czech resistance had seized the radio station, and calling on the populace to rise against the Germans. As I ran out of the building, I saw Uncle Bořik and Aunt Ludvík unfurling out of the window a heavily creased Czechoslovak flag they had kept hidden throughout the war. Dad, wearing his old army uniform for the first time in almost seven years, waved to me from the floor above.

Suddenly the town, so weary and dull during the wartime years, overflowed with excitement. People ran instead of walking, exulting out of sheer joy and agitation. In every building, someone would place a radio on the sill of an open window and blare the resistance broadcasts into the street. Around the corner, on the main street, storekeepers climbed stepladders and taped or painted over the signs in German while passersby applauded and cheered. Some merchants brought out props advertising imported products that had disappeared during the occupation. One that provoked salvos of ribald guffaws showed a stork with his beak tied by a rope. It was the trademark of a well-known French manufacturer of condoms.

Astonishingly, the faithful Prague streetcars continued running, though the conductors no longer cared whether anyone had a ticket. Twenty minutes after I first heard the resistance call, I stood outside the downtown headquarters of Radio Prague where a huge crowd sang "Where Is My Home," the banned Czechoslovak anthem. When the singing was over, we just milled around. There was no sign of German soldiers, but toward noon a Luftwaffe pilot did one more heroic deed for his Führer—who by then was dead in his Berlin bunker—by strafing the broadcasting building and the crowd outside. Although some people were wounded, there was surprisingly little panic. We did not disperse, and the plane did not return. By noon, singing and flag-waving crowds of Czechs packed the whole downtown. The radio played Czech national songs and broadcast sometimes conflicting reports about fighting between the resistance and Wehrmacht in various parts of the city.

In the afternoon word spread that Hungarian troops who had fought on the Eastern front had deserted and left a trainload of weapons at the same main freight yard where my friend and I had spilled parts for Hitler's secret weapons. By the time a bunch of us youngsters came running to the scene, German troops had occupied the nearby high ground and fired at anybody who came close. I beat an unheroic retreat, but Mirek, who was toppling the Nazi regime somewhere else, earned his badge of courage. He came home that night with a captured German rifle and a bullet hole in the tip of his hat. I was exuberant, hungry, and empty-handed.

The next morning, we all woke up at dawn to the clanging of picks and hammers out in the street. On instructions from the liberated radio, thousands of men, women, and children were ripping up the cobblestone pavement and blocking street corners with what we considered anti-tank obstacles. Within hours, the citizenry filled viaducts and main intersections with derailed streetcars, heavy trucks, even chairs and desks from schools and office buildings.

When Russian tank crews eventually reached Prague, they treated our piles of stone as a big joke, but on that morning of May 6, we were throwing up barricades with deadly seriousness. As far as we knew, the nearest American units were in Pilsen, fifty miles southwest of Prague. The Russian soldiers were twice as far away to the north, occupying Berlin. By contrast, a German panzer division, which was believed to be preparing to suppress the uprising, was scattered in barracks in several parts of Prague. We expected a bloodbath by nightfall.

On the barricade that I helped to build, just a few steps from our house, the girding for combat produced another incident I still remember. After we piled up the cobblestones as high as we could throw them, the communal harmony dissolved in an argument between a school principal and a furrier whose store was next door to our house. The divisive question was who will defend the barricade when the panzers come out of their lair. It was a hypothetical subject since we had no weapons, but the argument was heated.

The school principal's answer was, "Everybody." The furrier strongly dissented. "If I get killed," I remember him arguing, "who will take care of my family? I am a small businessman. I have no insurance, no pension." In the furrier's view, the fighting had to be done by state employees such as the school principal. At the ripe age of seventeen I was scandalized by such lack of patriotic élan, but since our family never had enough money for fur coats, my views made on the furrier no impression.

The argument was still raging when Uncle Ludvík reported that the resistance was distributing captured Wehrmacht weapons in a nearby restaurant. I ran there, joined the queue, and eventually was handed an unassembled Panzerfaust—the German version of a shoulder-fired bazooka—and a pamphlet with instructions on how to put it together. A young man with a red-and-white armband of the resistance helped us assemble the weapons and sent us off to find positions with a good field of fire. I was told to cover one of the major intersections between Vršovice and the suburb of Krč, from which the resistance expected an attack by German armor.

For the next two days instead of earning battle scars I was on an ego trip. I had no difficulty finding a house with balconies overlooking a large square that by then was blocked off by barricades. I rang the bell of an apartment on the second floor and was eagerly admitted by a slender, middle-aged woman who enthusiastically agreed to let me "establish a position" on her balcony. In her overblown imagination I must have become an underweight Czech version of a John Wayne, about to inflict devastating punishment on German tanks. I was given a heroic treatment in advance of any heroic deeds.

At my hostess's insistence, I pulled in the balcony her cushiest armchair. Minutes later, she showed up with a plate of what must have been the last of her treasured hoard of sardines, liver pâté, and other delicacies. She would periodically replenish the horn of plenty with the help of other housewives who'd appear in her tow, bearing home-made cookies, pastries, and other offerings. For my drinks, my hostess mixed tap water with her last jar of good marmalade. After years of dry-bread austerity, it was a dizzying experience. I spent the day listening to the radio and munching goodies; at night, when my fan club repaired to the bomb shelter to await my victory over the Nazis, I settled in the armchair and dozed off.

As it happened, my trusty Panzerfaust never saw action. During the first night I spent on the balcony, a German tank rumbled within a short distance of one of the square's barricades, but stopped well outside the hundred-meter range of my weapon. Trembling with excitement I crouched next to the armchair, waiting for the monster to start climbing over the obstacle and wondering if the bazooka would fire. Instead, the tank turned around with a big clanging and screeching of tracks and left. That was the last near-engagement in which I took part. Elsewhere in Prague there were outbursts of bitter fighting, but most of the German troops were no more eager to die than the furrier. The next day and night my square was quiet, and on the third day the whole German panzer division left Prague to surrender to Patton's troops near Pilsen.

I said goodbye to my gracious hostess, dropped off the bazooka in the restaurant where I had got it, and ran downtown to see the long convoy of withdrawing Wehrmacht armor slowly making its way through the dismantled barricades. The Germans left scowling just as hard as when they came, but that was the only similarity between the two occasions. The departing troops were either markedly older or younger than those who had occupied the country in 1938, and instead of arrogance, they were nervously training their guns on us on the sidewalks. We watched them in complete silence. When the Germans had first come, people shook fists and cried, and Dad spat on the sidewalk. Six and a half years later, they were not worth even an angry shout. I couldn't imagine a worse condemnation.

The following morning, on May 9, the Wenceslas Square was full of Red Army tanks that had arrived overnight into the liberated city. The long nightmare was over.

CHAPTER 3

AN UNEASY INTERLUDE

As one would expect of the capital of an oft-ravaged country, Prague is a somber city. On most days, its solemn silhouette reflects the town's ten centuries on Europe's fought-over crossroads, and the hilltop church of St. Vitus, the presidential palace, and the Old Town look down on Vltava—the River Moldau—with an air of perpetual brooding. But in May 1945, the town of Bedřich Smetana and Antonín Dvořák sparkled with the zest and cheer of "The Bartered Bride" and "Slovanic Dances."

The sun shone. The linden trees were greening. White seagulls, the perennial harbingers of spring in Prague, circled over the fourteenth-century Charles Bridge, irreverently dotting the statues of saints with their droppings. The barricades of the uprising had been dismantled in record time, and the indomitable streetcars were back in business, clanging and rattling on their meandering ways around the town. Czechoslovak flags, red, white, and blue, still wrinkled from years in hiding, fluttered everywhere.

Each night brought thrilling proof that the Nazi nightmare was over: after years of blackouts, the city was lit up like a Christmas tree. People laughed. Past terrors lay vanquished. For once in its long history, the baroque city on the Moldau caressed its liberated population like a young maiden.

Except for the first day of the liberation, when I entered the postwar era on the wrong foot, I felt as exuberant as everyone else. On the morning the Russian tanks arrived, I volunteered, together with another baker's dozen of neighborhood teenagers, to help round up presumably hiding Nazi officials who were thought to have failed to leave Prague with the retreating Wehrmacht. The job sounded simple enough: the same resistance member who had distributed the bazookas handed us seized German rifles, ammo, and a list of addresses and told us to bring whomever we find there to a nearby gymnasium that had been converted into a makeshift holding camp for POWs. I quickly learned that I was not cut out to be a minuteman.

To begin with, before we even set out on the manhunt, I took a dislike to our self-appointed commander. An assertive, tough-looking guy about ten years older than most of us, he tried to boost our fighting spirit by exhorting us to act "like a Czech Gestapo." I thought that was the most absurd idea I'd heard, the Gestapo being the very last thing I would ever want to emulate. When we hit the streets, toting weapons we barely knew how to operate, the mission became even more dismal. The Nazi menfolk we were after—the bureaucrats and enforcers who had lorded it over us for six long years—had in their vast majority taken the powder before the Prague uprising and were hiding somewhere in Germany.

As we trooped from one address to another, we either found the apartments empty or occupied only by terrified, aging German housewives. Most of them were sitting on packed suitcases expecting to be dragged away to a Czech version of the Nazi concentration camps.

Our instructions were to march all Germans to the gym, but I was never good at following instructions I did not accept, and I did not like these at all. In my experience, the Nazi regime was totally male-dominated, and its occupation and war machines were run exclusively by men. Only because we couldn't find any of them, I saw no need to haul a bunch of scared old women to the collection center. Moreover, I was uneasy about the treatment they'd get before their evacuation to Germany.

The previous afternoon, as I walked home after watching the Wehrmacht armor leaving Prague, I came upon a group of about twenty presumed Nazis and their Czech collaborators who had been put to work removing one of the ubiquitous barricades. It was a shocking scene. The heads of the women had been shaved and marked in black paint with a big letter "K" for *kolaborant* (quisling).

The Czech cops in charge of the detail kept the assumed traitors running with the heavy cobblestones at a frenzied pace, and the dust they stirred, their sweaty, terrified faces, and the furious curses shouted at them by bystanders were frightening. I felt no sympathy for the alleged quislings and hoped the cops had the real McCoys, but this was not my way to celebrate the defeat of the barbarians.

I reflected on this incident the next morning when two other kids and I rang the doorbell of one of the German apartments and found it occupied by two scared women who were easily in their seventies. I took one look at them and decided I had done enough posse duty. Disregarding our orders, I indignantly informed the women we're not taking them anywhere "because we're no Nazis," and I told my companions that we were leaving the oldsters alone.

My leadership potential is negligible to none even under the best circumstances, but my fellow minutemen obviously shared my feelings. We walked out with no prisoners in tow. In the afternoon I turned in my rifle and told the resistance leader that I would not be coming back.

The following morning I did what everyone else was doing: went out to greet the Russian soldiers. Friendly and unpretentious, these "Ivans," as we affectionately called them, were General Konev's elite troops who had broken through the last Wehrmacht defenses and conquered Berlin. Presumably, they had done their share of the monumental rape and looting that marked the Red Army's advance through Germany. But as the fighting ended and they relaxed in their makeshift bivouacs in the parks of Prague, these burly sons of the vast Russian motherland were as kindhearted and well-mannered as the Salvation Army in December. Until the crews and their tanks pulled out, a few days later, Russian accordions and vodka filled the center of Prague with genuine friendship and cheer.

Much of the fraternizing was done by high school youngsters like my schoolmates and me, and our visits with the soldiers soon took on a fixed pattern. In groups of three or four, we'd march up to a tank, beaming and mixing our Czech with a quickly learned greeting in Russian, "Dah zdrahstvooyet!" (Hello, how are you doing?). The soldiers would grin back and urge us to make ourselves comfortable on the grass. We'd offer them "liberated" German cigarettes that had suddenly appeared in the Prague stores, but most Ivans would politely decline. They preferred to tear off a piece of newspaper, reach in the pocket for a pinch of tobacco, and with one hand roll a *makhorka*, a pungent cigarette shaped like a small ice-cream cone.

After this opening ritual, one of the soldiers would vanish into the bowels of the tank and emerge with a bottle of vodka and a hunk of bacon. After a few ceremonial puffs, mouthfuls, and gulps, the Russians would pull up their sleeves and show off their collection of *tchasy*, the "liberated" watches they'd seized from their German prisoners. The order of "Davai tchasy!" (Hand over your watch!) was as familiar throughout the Russian-occupied Germany as "Hands up!" in the old West. It was not uncommon for an Ivan to sport several watches on each arm.

We'd appreciatively chortle and congratulate the soldiers on their victory over the Wehrmacht. The Ivans would beam and modestly decline to take much credit. "Eto nitchevo, nas mnogo" (It's nothing—there are many of us) was their frequent reply. We'd insist on praising their bravery, which, from all we'd heard, was truly impressive. The Ivans would reciprocate by pronouncing the Czechs *"kharasho partyzany"* (good partisans), as opposed to the Ukrainians and Poles, whom they would curse as *"fashisti."*

Practically every Russian soldier I met in those days told a story about a trinity of captured enemies—a German SS-man, a Ukrainian, and a Pole—that said volumes about the rules of war on the Eastern front. The location and circumstances of the incident varied with each Ivan's imagination and storytelling talent, but the punch line was always the same. After describing the events leading to the capture and the despicable qualities of the prisoners, the soldier would challenge the listener to guess what sort of justice he had meted out to each of them.

"So what did I do?" the Russian would ask, fiercely frowning, and then, slapping his holster for emphasis, he would add: "I pulled out my pistol and shot the German, and the Ukrainian, and the Pole." My high school buddies and I were not exactly comfortable with the speed of these verdicts, but we loved the tank crews, and hated all "fashisti." When our hosts laughed, we laughed.

Several drinks later, the soldiers would politely inquire if any of us had a sister. Most of the Russian soldiers had not seen their wives or girlfriends since the start of the war; as for the Soviet nurses who accompanied the troops in battle, the soldiers complained that "they slept only with officers." By the time the bottle was empty, one of our hosts would pull out an accordion and start playing soulful Russian songs. His comrades would spread their arms, throw back their heads, and dance to the music, crying real tears.

It was all very moving. The Czechs have a thing about their fellow Slavs, and our encounters with the tank crews were full of brotherly feeling. The Russians were generous to a fault, they were brave, and to us at least, they were charming. They had suffered enormous hardships during the war, and their casualties were legendary. They certainly deserved our affection and gratitude. But I had difficulty sorting out the rest of my feelings about our liberators. In some ways the soldiers sounded too childlike and simplistic. The trait was pronounced and common, and some of the Ivans not only admitted it, they had a derogatory term for it: they called themselves *niekulturniy* (uncultured).

After the Russians left—it was still May, and the schools remained closed—I went to see the American soldiers, the other Allied troops that had advanced into the heart of Europe to defeat Hitler. By May 5, General Patton's Third Army had reached a line running through southwestern Bohemia that included Pilsen, the Czech beer capital. Patton could have liberated Prague the same day, sparing us the agony of the uprising: the remnants of Wehrmacht were as eager to surrender to the GIs as they were scared of falling into the hands of the Russians. But Stalin wanted no American influence in a country he wanted within the Soviet orbit, and at

Yalta he won the green light for the Red Army to occupy all but the westernmost slice of Bohemia. To meet the Yankees, most Czechs had to take an overcrowded train to Pilsen. Thousands did, including me.

I spent a whole week touring the US-liberated part of Bohemia, but it took just a day or two to understand why Stalin wanted no Yanks in Prague. Compared with the poverty and shabbiness of our long dreary existence under the Nazis and with the scruffy, unkempt Russians, the GIs were enormously impressive. They were scrubbed and clean-shaven, wore crisp uniforms with rubber-soled, comfortable-looking boots, and smoked cigarettes that wafted aroma instead of odor. To us they looked like aliens from a rich planet, and they even behaved that way. Because the Third Army's theaterwide regulations did not distinguish between the defeated Germany and the liberated Bohemia, the GIs in the Czech towns and villages were not only prohibited to fraternize with the local population but had to run armed patrols as if they were in enemy territory. Political subtleties were never the US Army's strong suit.

But despite—or perhaps, because of—the arm's-length distance, the GIs were good ambassadors for their country. They were relatively unobtrusive and easy on the nerves of the local populace. The Third Army units stuck to their own installations, ate their own food, and watched their own movies. They drank less—at least less in public—and were better disciplined than their Soviet counterparts, who were often drunk and sometimes shot up a whole neighborhood just for the hell of it. I saw some GIs carrying paperback books, at that time a novelty, and couldn't help making mental comparisons with the Russian troops. Many of the Ivans were illiterate, and their closest contact with literature was the torn pages from the "liberated" books that they rolled into their makhorkas.

What I found most appealing about the Yanks was their informality and easy spirit, which came through despite their aloof behavior and the language barrier. The GIs behaved like true civilians in olive drab: they struck me as relaxed, unregimented, non-bellicose, and utterly unlike the Wehrmacht. This was not based on any close personal contact, because I spoke no English, but simply from seeing the informal way they ran their patrols, talked with their officers, or made their few appearances before Czech audiences.

I saw one of these rare events in Domažlice, a town in southwestern Bohemia. It was a close-order-drill demonstration by an infantry unit that was attended by "Blood and Guts" George Patton himself, wearing his riding britches and pearl-handled Colts, and the troops, I felt sure, were putting on their very best performance. The drill sergeant bellowed like a foghorn, the GIs' boots and rifles were spit-and-polished, their moves were snappy as machine-gun fire. Unfortunately, that prompted an approving roar of the Czech audience so loud that it drowned out the sergeant's commands. The result was total confusion: the troops slapped their M-1s when they were not supposed to, flanked-marched instead of to-the-rear-marched, and spread out all over the field instead of merging or marching in place.

In the Wehrmacht, such public mix-up would have been unthinkable. Even in my father's army, havoc on a parade ground would have been a red-faced disgrace. But to my great delight, the American troops—and the officers on the reviewing stand, including Patton himself—just laughed. For an impressionable youngster who had for six years watched the world march in lockstep, the lighthearted response was potent stuff. Aboard the train going home, I tried to put my finger on what—in addition to their affluence—made the Americans so different. The best explanation I could think of was that they were self-confident and unafraid.

I returned to Prague and to more marvels of the liberation. One major event was the return from exile of the last Czechoslovak president, Edward Beneš. Before the war Beneš was regarded as an intellectual, a statesman, and a decent man—a sort of Czech Adlai Stevenson—but not a strong leader. His stature, however, rose dramatically during the hectic months before Munich when Hitler denounced him at his rallies, the Sudetenland Nazis rioted for annexation by Germany, and the intimidated leaders of England and France mumbled that Czechoslovakia was a small country "about which we know nothing." Beneš stood up to the wrenching pressures with impressive dignity.

After Munich, Beneš resigned and went into exile, first in Paris and later in London, and was eventually recognized by the Allies as the legitimate spokesman of his occupied nation. By the time he returned to Prague—following a politically unavoidable if fateful stopover in Moscow—Beneš was a highly respected national figure who for most of us symbolized the restored democracy. The day he arrived to a hero's welcome in the liberated capital, Dad opened a bottle of champagne he had been saving for the occasion since 1938 when Beneš left the country.

The champagne had over the years acquired a sediment, but as everybody happily noted, at least the president and his wife, Hana, looked well. It was also reassuring that the foreign minister of the provisional government was Jan Masaryk, the urbane son of the first president, whose democratic credentials were taken for granted. The reality behind these early impressions was far less bright. In fact, Beneš's health was bad and getting worse; Masaryk turned out to be less than a tower of strength; and about half of the ministers that Beneš had to include in his cabinet during his stopover in Moscow were outright retainers of the Kremlin. Contrary to our overblown hopes, the country was teetering on the brink of a precipice in the path of an avalanche.

In the first few weeks after the liberation, however, worries about the future for youngsters like me took a backseat to the sheer thrill of renewed contact with the Western world. After a six-year ban on "racially impure" music, Radio Prague brought out from hiding old records of Satchmo's "Blueberry Hill" and Gershwin's "Rhapsody in Blue" and played them several times a day. Packed movie houses showed a flick starring Rita Hayworth, the first Hollywood movie to hit the Prague screens since 1939. Mirek and I went to see it at eleven o'clock at night, the only showing for which we could get tickets. The movie was terrible, and we loved it.

Shakespeare and other banned classics reappeared in bookstores. Newspapers once again expressed different views and became fun to read. The reopened universities were flooded with a huge backlog of students who had finished high school during the occupation and spent the rest of the war doing forced labor. Bars and dancing halls resumed business, and even the food was getting better. Although rationing continued for a while, as soon as the first American wheat shipments reached Prague, bread tasted like bread again. The wheat was followed by emergency shipments of US Army K-rations. One day, my mother triumphantly brought home from the grocer a ten-pound can of a hitherto unheard-off American delicacy called peanut butter.

Thousands of families celebrated the return of relatives—prisoners from concentration camps, exiles from Britain, partisans from the mountains, and slave laborers from Germany. Thousands of others learned that their friends and relatives had not survived the Nazi jails and concentration camps. And our own family was electrified by the return of Sommer's young son, who one day showed up at our door wearing the uniform of the Czechoslovak brigade of the British Army.

It was a big event. Dad opened a prewar bottle of Tokayi, his favorite Hungarian wine, and solemnly handed Sommer his father's sealed envelope. Sommer opened it and found it to be full of pre-war Czechoslovak currency that once represented a small fortune but by now had become completely worthless. We drank the wine in a somber mood. Young Sommer confirmed our fears that his parents had died in a concentration camp.

Politically more savvy than his parents, Sommer stayed in Prague only briefly and after his discharge from the army emigrated to Australia.

The postwar elation lasted till the end of the summer. I missed most of it harvesting wheat—not in Horní Borek but in the Czech border region whose former inhabitants, mostly supporters of Konrad Henlein's "Heim-ins-Reich!" Party, had been expelled with the Allies' approval to Germany. The former

Sudetenland became part of Czechoslovakia again, but the area was practically unpopulated.

To save the precious crops standing in the fields, the Prague government sent to the border voluntary labor brigades made up of high school students. For several weeks, we were gloriously out of the reach of our teachers and parents and even managed to get most of the grain under the roof. But when we returned to school, the fun was over. For one thing, our schedule was sped up so that we could make up for the year lost to the Totaleinsatz. The workload was correspondingly heavy. Another serious development that changed the happy postwar atmosphere was the scheduling of the first postwar elections for the next spring. The announcement triggered a major political battle.

The 1946 election campaign—the first and last free Czechoslovak political contest in which I took part—turned out to be a memorable event for the whole country, including my schoolmates and me. It hardly could have been otherwise: we were eighteen-year-olds and had lived our formative years under the occupation—a period of monstrous fraud, grotesque propaganda, and brutal oppression. After that experience, politics for my peers and me took on an almost tangible meaning. Without realizing it, we learned under the Nazi tutelage that the free exchange of ideas is a necessity as vital as air and food. As the election campaign got under way, no amount of schoolwork could stop us from avidly scrutinizing the political landscape—and what we saw was far from reassuring.

On paper, the election campaign looked respectably democratic. Beneš's provisional government consisted of four parties of the so-called National Front that offered the voters a reasonable choice of policies. On the left were the Communist Party and its ally, the Marxist Social Democrats; on the right, the People's Party that was close to the Catholic Church; and in the center the National Socialists, a middle-road party that used to be headed by Beneš before he became president. The only banned prewar parties were far-rightist groups that had participated in the short-lived pro-Nazi regime between Munich and the occupation. Nobody I knew mourned their demise.

That was the facade. Underneath, the race had been seriously skewed the day Beneš bowed to the realities created by the Yalta agreements and the presence of the Red Army in Eastern Europe. Although before the war the Communist Party usually polled a little over 10 percent of the popular vote, the provisional government concocted in Moscow was dominated by highly disciplined, Soviet-trained apparatchiks who took directions not from Beneš but from Stalin. In addition to Klement Gottwald, the Communist Party chairman and a deputy prime minister, they included Václav Nosek, the minister of interior, who controlled the police and the security apparatus; Viliam

Široký, the minister of information, who ran the radio stations, subsidized numerous newspapers, theaters, and cultural and artistic groups, and put out thinly disguised Communist propaganda; and Zdeněk Nejedlý, the minister of education who hired, promoted, and fired all teachers and university professors and controlled what students like me learned in school.

As if that were not enough, the Communists held two other vital portfolios through their moles or *vtytchkas*, as Communists-in-disguise were called by Lenin. One vtytchka was the provisional prime minister and chairman of the Social Democrats, Zdeněk Fierlinger, who even looked like a rat. He served Moscow faithfully, and on the day of the coup d'état announced his party's merger with the Communists. The other mole was the "non-party" minister of defense, General Ludvík Svoboda. He, too, revealed his true colors in February 1948, by throwing the army's support behind the Communists.

Key portfolios, moreover, were only one set of power levers controlled by Gottwald and, through him, by the Soviet ambassador in Prague. Also highly important were government-subsidized, monopolistic, and allegedly "nonpartisan" organizations that sprouted like weeds all over the liberated landscape. Ostensibly these labor, trade, professional, veterans', students', artists', youth, anti-fascist, ex-prisoners', "Soviet Friendship," "Friends of Red Army," and you-name-it "grassroots" organizations and societies promoted the causes advertised by their titles. In fact, almost without exception they were front organizations run by the Communists.

Once founded, each group published its own information ministry–subsidized newspaper or some other periodical, and its "progressive" programs and activities were promoted and praised by the information-ministry-run radio. In no time at all, a motley collection of these groups was established in every sizable Czech and Slovak city and town. There was a great pressure on everybody to join these "mass movements." According to the mythmakers, in a "progressive" society (and nobody dared question precisely what that meant), individualism was a symptom of a reactionary attitude; worthy societal accomplishments, from mountain climbing to poetry writing, came only in closest association with the "masses."

As the anointed vehicles of "progress," these nouveau "representatives of the people" conducted membership drives, rallies, public meetings, memorial festivities, celebrations, marches, petitions, exchanges, congresses, and dozens of other hyped activities, all of which directly or indirectly trumpeted the "forward-looking" program of the Communist Party. And as the elections drew closer, these puppets of Gottwald held huge rallies in Prague that filled the Wenceslas Square with red flags and filled the airwaves with slogans extolling Stalin, the Red Army, and the future of "progressive" Czechoslovakia.

The fraud and hullabaloo that accompanied these congresses matched almost anything invented by Goebbels's Agitprop. Before each such "manifestation of irresistible popular will," squadrons of government-paid carpenters covered public squares with platforms, arches, pillars, and posters displaying red flags, slogans extolling "Czechoslovakia's March toward a Socialist Tomorrow," and flattering portraits of political leaders who all happened to be Communists. Afterwards, when the "progressive masses" arrived for the freebie shindig by special buses and trains decorated with still more flags, slogans, and posters, the comrades put on displays of street power reminiscent of the intimidation rallies of Hitler's SA in the 1930s.

There were endless marches under a sea of red flags. There were mass assemblies that roared instant approval for "progressive" programs and demands read from the platform. There were special editions of the Communist Party organ *Rudé Právo* that hailed the extravaganza as another "hard blow at the forces of reaction" and a "historic step toward a better tomorrow in the socialist camp headed by the great leader of the world's anti-fascist forces, Josef Stalin."

There were ceremonies awarding prizes to the most deserving comrades. There were Red Army songs lustily sung by big male choirs. There was organized "spontaneous" dancing in the streets. There were evening fireworks. In short, there was a contrived theater and frenzy to create the impression of an unstoppable force surging toward the Communist Party's goal of winning 51 percent of the votes.

In the electoral propaganda that blanketed the country, the Communists claimed the sole credit for heroism in wartime underground, for the defeat of Nazi Germany, for the ideals of social and economic equality—and of course, for the economic, social, and cultural paradise that would follow their victory at the polls. The blessings of socialism that awaited the Czechs and Slovaks "in brotherly cooperation with the Soviet Union and its great leader, J.V. Stalin" beat by far even the window seat in Hitler's train to New Europe promised by the Czech quislings. In one memorable example of illusory braggadocio, the Communist-run Writers' Union pledged to make Czech "a world language."

By contrast, whoever did not buy the Communist line was a willful or witless supporter of fascism, racism, colonialism, capitalism, and other forces of reaction that kept humanity in the chains of disease, ignorance, and poverty. This earnestly propagated smear was spread particularly thick on the National Socialists and the People's Party—in Bohemia and Moravia, the only two non-Marxist contenders for the votes—who were depicted as rotten leftovers of prewar Czechoslovakia, a country that according to the Communists had been a backward monstrosity just this side of feudalism.

What irked me most, because I understood it least, was the cheering and endorsements lavished on this orchestrated make-believe by some of the most prominent names in the Czech arts and sciences. Among the most disheartening phenomena of the postwar Czechoslovak scene was that the Communists had fervent allies among scores of bright, sometimes outstanding individuals of talent and merit who enjoyed great prominence and prestige in public life, arts, and academia. It was a baffling phenomenon: here were scores of intelligent people who had gone through the same Nazi crucible as the rest of us only to clamor for more regimentation, servitude, and corruption dressed up in different colors. Whether out of greed for the fancy jobs handed out by the Communists, or out of abysmal romanticism and naiveté, they parroted the party line with a slavishness that made one wonder about the state of their faculties. The bottom line was that they lent the Communist Party and its mediocre, obscure leaders, badly needed glitter and resonance.

Lenin, who also made use of this breed of high IQ political simpletons, disdainfully called them "useful idiots." In postwar Czechoslovakia many artists, writers, scientists, and university professors fully earned the sobriquet. They sang, recited poetry, penned essays, produced plays, authored novels, marched in rallies, orated, and eagerly attached their names to petitions that fueled the Communist steamroller.

Some of the younger members of the "progressive avant-garde" came to see the light two decades later, and became the revisionist stars of the short-lived "Prague Spring." One of these original True Believers—the wife of a member of the Central Committee of the Communist Party—changed her colors so thoroughly that the post-Communist Czech government sent her to Washington as ambassador. In my book, their conversion—like my Cousin Pepík's—came far too late. In 1946, when they could have been a force for democracy, they added to an atmosphere in which by far the easiest thing to do was to vote for ticket Number One, the electoral list of the Communists. To not vote for Number One required serious thought and resistance to public pressure.

My own doubts about Communism set in well before the election campaign, at a time when the sum total of my political views was abhorrence of the Nazis. The first incident that raised my eyebrows happened a few weeks after the war, when I testified before a special retribution council about the wartime conduct of my former foreman at Avia. As I was leaving the room, I saw him standing outside, presumably waiting to defend his enthusiasm for a German victory. The thing that struck me was the pin in his lapel: it was the hammer-and-sickle emblem of the Communist Party. How gross, I thought. Only a few months before, he was pushing production for the Wehrmacht, and now he was part of the "progressive masses."

A more important straw in the wind—that directly led to my founding of *Žihadlo*—were articles in *Rudé Právo* disparaging the historic role of Thomas Garrigue Masaryk. "*Tatíček*" (Daddy) Masaryk was not a man whose name I took lightly. He was the George Washington of the Czechs and Slovaks, a national icon about whom my father and everybody else I knew talked with admiration bordering on worship.

Masaryk—"T.G.M.," as he was also called—was a man of towering decency, intellect, and integrity. The son of a coachman, Masaryk started in life as an apprenticed locksmith. He married an American studying in Vienna and went on to become a philosopher of democracy and humanism. After a lifetime in the academe, he entered politics at age sixty-four and quickly emerged as the chief spokesman of the Czech and Slovak demands for independence from the Habsburgs. In 1918 he proclaimed—symbolically, in Philadelphia's historic Independence Hall—the birth of the Czechoslovak republic, was elected as its first president, and made the country a model democracy.

For the man on the street, "Daddy" Masaryk was far more than a statesman. Tall, slender, austere in his looks, language, and habits, Masaryk was a beloved father figure, a genuine folk hero, and a paragon of homespun wisdom whose pithy injunctions and adages were quoted like the Bible. It was Thomas Masaryk who gave the Czechoslovak republic its sanguine official motto "Truth Prevails!" My father hung it in the living room next to another of Masaryk's favorite injunctions, "Be Honest and Don't Be Afraid!"

My own cherished insight of Masaryk was "Thinking Hurts." I could vouch for its accuracy. An author of erudite books, Masaryk preached social justice and personal and political decency with vigor and conviction that shaped the values of several generations of Czechs. When he died, not long before Munich, there was not a dry eye in Prague. Dad, who was not a sentimental man, took my brother and me to see the ex-president's funeral. To write off T.G.M.—as the *Rudé Právo* did—as a figurehead of "the bourgeoisie, capitalists, and rich landowners" was simply revolting.

The undoing of *Žihadlo* sealed my attitude toward the Czech stand-ins for Moscow, whose arrogance, radicalism, and stupefying propaganda were rapidly dividing the country. By late fall of 1945, not only adults but even most of us at school were divided between those who did and who did not place make-believe, Marxist-style "progress" above democracy. The feelings ran so high that no boy or girl would be invited to a party if he, she, or their dates belonged to the opposite political camp. Romances were made and unmade in the course of increasingly fervent political arguments.

Except for two or three exceptions, my classmates and I were solidly in the anti-Marxist camp. We loudly applauded when our physics teacher baked samples of flour from donated American and Soviet wheat, and the American bubble was bigger, which we took for evidence of superior quality. We booed when another teacher accused the United States of having "plundered Europe of its most energetic and enterprising individuals" by letting them in as immigrants. However unlikely it may sound, in the bull sessions of my friends and me, politics were as likely to be a topic of discussion as the attractions of our girl classmates.

In this charged atmosphere, it was only natural for me to tackle Marxist-Leninist writings to find out what made them suddenly a holy writ. The research was cheap, because the Communists brought back from Moscow a huge supply of hardbound works of the anointed Marxist ideologues and sold them, literally, for pennies. A two- or three-hundred-page volume would cost the equivalent of ten cents. At first sight, the super-cheap tracts looked like another feather in the cap for the Agitprop, but once I started reading the stuff, I thought the Communists were out of their minds.

Even to my unsophisticated eye, Karl Marx's economic determinism—the guts of his doctrine—looked like so much bunk. If man truly responded only to his material needs, why didn't the whole Czech population collaborate with the Nazis? Everyone knew that quislings got far better rations than the rest of us. Why did Stalin proclaim World War II "the Great Patriotic War" instead of, say, "The War to End All Queues and Shortages?" And what about the intense nationalism of the Czechs and other Austro-Hungarian minorities that led to the downfall of the Habsburg empire?

As for the Marxist vision of the future, it had nothing to do with reality as I knew it. First of all, I couldn't accept the arrogant assertion that Marxists knew what history will bring because Marxism was a "science" and, as such, predictive. If that were the case, why was the Red Army caught flat-footed by the Wehrmacht's invasion of Poland? Another part of the dogma that riled me was that under "scientific socialism," man would shed his egocentric nature and become an altruistic contributor to the collective.

Come the Communist nirvana, the Marxist-Leninists claimed, the "New Socialist Man" would spontaneously work "according to his ability" while consuming "according to his needs." Stalin, another heavyweight Marxist thinker, even discovered that socialism "changes labor from a shameful and heavy burden into a matter of honor, a matter of fame, a matter of valor and heroism." On top of these flights of fantasy, Karl Marx scientifically predicted that the state was going to "wither away," and ordinary workers would take turns running the "irreducible minimum" of bureaucracy.

From what I knew about people, this was all science fiction.

But as I kept reading Marxist-Leninists, what bothered me most was the hatred they peddled as a "liberating" doctrine. Lenin, for instance, called for "the fiercest, sharpest and most merciless war against the bourgeoisie"—that is, folks like our family and everyone I knew—in order to establish conditions he described as "the domination of the proletariat over the bourgeoisie, untrammeled by law and based on violence." For Stalin, the Communist Party was "the military staff of the proletariat" or "the weapon in the hands of the proletariat for the conquest of the dictatorship." The prime duties of such dictatorship, Stalin wrote, included "maintaining iron discipline."

If I had learned anything under the Nazis, it was to profoundly appreciate the importance of decency in public and personal life, and to abhor the sort of toxic and rigid dogma openly preached by the Communists. Statecraft was about a maximum of harmony and a minimum of friction, not about a war on "bourgeoisie" followed by the "dictatorship of the proletariat." The state was supposed to serve its citizens, not the other way around. The Nazi shirts were brown and Enemy Number One was the Jews; the Communist flags were red and the Enemy Number One was the middle class. Otherwise the mentality and the means were just about the same.

These were all fairly obvious thoughts, considering the time and place where I grew up; what was less clear was how long such views would be tolerated. Throughout Central and Eastern Europe, a deafening chorus of Communist and Communist-front media proclaimed the invincibility of Marxism, and the native hacks of Kremlin were embracing police regimes and command economies serving the Soviet Empire. The West and its ideals of freedom were denounced as decadent, corrupt, devoid of vision, deprived of energy, rejected by the unerring masses, and about to be discarded into the garbage dump of history. Goebbels didn't do as good a job as his Communist counterparts.

As Churchill put it, an Iron Curtain was descending from the Baltic to the Adriatic. The process was plain to see even from Prague, but many of us entertained a hope that the lowering cage would leave a small opening, because, it was commonly thought, even Stalin needed a democratic showpiece and a window on the West. Czechoslovakia would be it—provided we withstood the electoral onslaught of the Communists.

It was in this atmosphere that I decided to become a journalist. I liked writing, and the two issues of *Žihadlo* had whetted my appetite for the semi-public status attached to people in the trade. I enjoyed the little stir that my humble publication had caused before its demise. Like most kids of my age, I reveled in excitement and challenge, but I also wanted to do something that mattered. During that period I had a recurring dream in which I could see myself pushing at the wheel of a creaking cart that, to me, symbolized progress toward a world of decency. The allegory, of course, was pretentious. But at the end of 1945, when terrifying memories of Hitler mingled with mounting forebodings about Stalin, the personal goals of many of my generation were shaped by what we perceived as society's foremost need.

The cart, I thought, needed a lot of pushing.

CHAPTER 4

THE SECOND CATASTROPHE
Communist Coup d'État

The first postwar elections in Czechoslovakia confirmed that I was right. The voracious Communist propaganda aside, the elections were reasonably fair. Although criticism of the Soviet Union was an unwritten taboo, the domestic issues were spelled out; the turnout was high; and the vote count was honest. And the results gave the Kremlin's proconsuls a landslide victory.

Ostensibly, the Communists fell short of their electoral goal of 51 percent of the vote, because only 38.7 percent of the voters cast the Number One ballot. But "KSČ"—the Communist Party of Czechoslovakia—emerged as by far the strongest power, and in Bohemia and Moravia its triumph was clinched by the fellow-traveling Social Democrats, who added 13 percent to the Marxist tally. By contrast, the National Socialists—the choice of most members of the Simandl clan, including Mirek and me—came in an out-of-sight second with 18 percent, and the People's Party finished third with 16 percent of the vote. What saved the bottom from completely falling out was a strong anti-Communist showing in Slovakia, but this only added to the elections' poor aftertaste: many of the right-wing Slovaks who dominated the province's politics were former followers of the pro-Nazi Father Tiso.

For once, *Rudé Právo* did not need to lie. The elections in May 1946 were almost as "red" as the Communists had predicted. Although (thanks to the appointment of one Slovak minister without portfolio) the noncommunists had a thirteen-to-twelve edge in the cabinet, Klement Gottwald became the prime minister and formed a cabinet where Communists and Social Democrats held all but two important portfolios. One of the exceptions was the ministry of justice, which went to Prokop Drtina, an able National Socialist; the other was the reappointment—at Beneš's insistence—of Jan Masaryk, who had no party affiliation, as the minister of foreign affairs.

Given the size of the stakes and the pressure from Moscow, the razor-thin noncommunist majority could not last long, and it didn't. But in the spring of 1946, when I was about to graduate from the commercial academy, the world had yet a lot to learn about the tactics of Stalinism. As I said good-bye to school, I was hoping to lending a hand to the cause of democracy.

Alas, my early ventures outside the school room were inauspicious. At first I got a job as a clerk in the export department of Koh-i-noor, a firm producing (of all things) buttons. I quickly realized this was no substitute for my real ambition—to be a journalist. When, in the summer of 1946, the government ordered a "mobilization" of all members of my age group to "fight the battle of the harvest," I cringed at the militant Communist-speak but I was happy to comply. I quit the job at Koh-i-noor and went to Horní Borek, where I spent the requisite six months working for a local farmer.

It was during this rustic interlude while I was harvesting spuds and spreading manure that I got the first big break that shaped my career. I wrote a longish article about a nearby training camp for women in the Czech national guard and sent it to *Svobodné Slovo*, the official organ of the National Socialist Party and the highest circulation noncommunist daily in the country. The article appeared shortly afterwards on the regional page of the newspaper, which encouraged me to write the editor that I'd like to become a reporter. At the end of the year, when my farm "battle" was over and I returned to Prague, the editor of the regional editions invited me to come to his office.

I was excited, to say the least. This was my chance to break into real journalism, and politicized as I was to the eyeballs, I expected to be grilled about the great issues of the postwar era. Riding the tram to the newspaper headquarters on the Wenceslas Square, I tried to formulate impressive positions that would land me the job.

A few minutes later I was sitting in the cluttered office of Vladimír Doležal, a thirty-something editor of the regional pages, ready to impress him with my insights and wit. I was clutching a folder with my graduation certificate, my birth certificate, and a certificate from the "security referent" of the Vršovice town hall confirming that during the occupation I behaved in a patriotic manner, meaning that I did not collaborate with the Nazis. After the war, every Czechoslovak citizen was examined for his wartime activities and received an official statement on whether or not he or she passed muster.

I also brought along a military citation I had received for sitting on the balcony with a Panzerfaust (and eating the last wartime goodies of my hostess). In short, I was primed for action. Unfortunately Doležal—curly-haired, tall, and skinny—was not asking me anything. When I walked in, he merely waved me into a well-worn chair and went on marking up a piece of copy. I kept opening and closing the folder while my tensions mounted.

At long last, the editor looked up from his work. He tugged on his long prominent nose and gave me a mirthless look through his round steel-frame glasses. For a moment his eyes became unfocused as if dismissing my presence and thinking about something else. Oh no, I thought. He's hired somebody else and doesn't need me. Finally, Doležal looked at me again and spoke up.

"When are you ready to go to work?" he asked.

I was so surprised I almost jumped up. In later years I learned to appreciate no-nonsense, straight-shooting editors of Doležal's type, but right now, I was startled. The man did not seem unfriendly but he did not believe in smiling in vain, either. When he spoke, his face didn't move except for his lips. This guy is all business, I thought. But flustered as I was, I took no time answering his question. If there was something I could never turn down, it was challenge.

"Tomorrow," I said.

"All right," Doležal nodded. "Go to Klatovy and take over our office there."

That was another jolt. I had assumed that if I landed a job, I'd be sent to one of *Svobodné Slovo*'s regional branches, but I took it for granted that first I would spend some time in the Prague headquarters to learn the ropes. Doležal's full-speed-ahead decision-making was most unsettling. My total journalistic experience was two articles in *Žihadlo* and the feature in *Slovo*. I'd never been to Klatovy, and I knew virtually nothing about the techniques of news reporting. I could see from Doležal's body language that I was about to be dismissed, but there were so many questions crowding my mind I had to ask at least some of them.

"How am I going to know what to do when I get to Klatovy?" I finally blurted out. Immediately I felt stupid, but it was too late. Still poker-faced, Doležal gave me another piercing look.

"Same way Indian kids learn how to swim." He did not elucidate, but the message was clear enough. Doležal's time was not to be wasted by questions from his underlings.

He added something about my minuscule starting salary and the length of the tryout period. Then he returned to the copy in front of him, terminating the interview. As I learned the next day, Doležal did not drop me into the water hole entirely unassisted. When I arrived in Klatovy, a pleasant small town about eighty miles southwest of Prague, I was awaited by Vlasta Lorenz, the outgoing bureau chief who was about five years older than I was.

Lorenz, who was being transferred to a bigger branch office, was square-jawed and athletic, smoked a pipe, and most impressive of all, exchanged letters with Doležal. A young man clearly on his way up, Vlasta turned out to be only slightly disdainful of "snowmen," as old pros called the cub reporters. He stayed with me for a whole week and taught me the ABCs of my job.

After Lorenz departed, however, I was left totally to my own devices, and the first few months were hard. Doležal was not a man I dared to call up to ask questions, and anyway, in those days of postwar austerity, the newspaper discouraged long-distance phone calls. There were times when I felt lonely and deeply uncertain about what I was doing. There were days when I was frantic to meet my deadlines, and there were stories I bungled. But somehow I muddled through. On the whole Doležal's swim-or-sink system worked.

In retrospect the fifteen months I spent in Klatovy were probably as good an all-round on-the-job training as a budding journalist could get. The area I covered consisted of several farming districts, a good stretch of the mountainous Czech–West German border, and three small historic towns, Klatovy, Domažlice, and Sušice. Except for one large matches-manufacturing plant, my beat had no commerce or industry to speak of, no fancy resort town to attract celebrities, and no big-name politicians.

The paltry turf notwithstanding, I was responsible for reporting, writing, and getting to Doležal by the end of each day enough copy for one full ads-free newspaper page. This output, which appeared as the regional page of the national edition, consisted of a fixed number of news items, a brief editorial, one sizable feature, and assorted artwork and photographs. All copy had to be written to space, including the headlines and subheads, and marked up for the typesetter. The drill was repeated six days a week including Saturday, when the news stories I sent to Prague were supposed to be particularly gee-whiz and the feature prose purple because of the paper's bigger circulation on Sunday. I could take a break on the biblical day of rest only because the Monday page was filled with the regional sports news covered by a stringer.

It was a job for a tenacious jack of all trades with a good pair of legs and nothing else to do but work. Since phones in Klatovy were scarce, I spent every morning making the rounds of the city hall, the main police station, the courthouse, and assorted offices of civic and business organizations, scribbling notes on humdrum events and unexciting views. Added to whatever contributions arrived by mail from volunteer stringers—mostly teachers—in the boondocks, my morning gleanings provided the bulk of the hard news.

After a bite for lunch I would search, sometimes desperately, for material for the daily feature. In the placid Klatovy (population about fifteen thousand), coming up with a gripping read usually was the toughest task of the day. More often than I liked, I wound up interviewing yet another local hero of the wartime resistance or, even worse, visiting a twenty-five-employee shirtmaking factory whose sole claim to fame was a small export order from England.

Each day I had to have all the copy written by 5 p.m. in order to catch the last train to Prague. The filing system we used was an updated version of the runner and cleft stick. Racing against the clock, at 4:45 p.m.

sharp I'd stuff the copy and photos in a big manila envelope, jump on the office motorcycle, and head for the train station. I'd park the bike, run to the steam-belching locomotive, and hand the envelope to the engineer. He would take it to the Prague terminal and pass it on to a waiting messenger from *Svobodné Slovo*, who would leap on another motorcycle and rush the copy to Doležal's cluttered desk.

There was practically no backup arrangement if I missed the train. Telex in those years and in that part of postwar Europe was almost unheard of, and there was nobody in the home office who could take my dictation by phone. If I got to the station late, the only recourse was to try to catch up with the train at the next stop, some five or six miles away. The road was full of potholes and slow-moving horse- and cow-drawn farm wagons. I learned not to miss the five o'clock evening trains, especially after a snowfall.

I worked long hours, lived in a tiny sublet room and earned peanuts, but I absolutely loved my job. Once I managed to establish good working relations with most of the Klatovy movers and shakers, including the mayor, the bureaucrats, and the senior detectives in the StB headquarters (not one of whom, in this backwater town, was Communist), putting together the daily page became almost fun.

The detectives would squeeze me in their squad car when they went out of town to investigate an interesting case. The mayor, an ambitious National Socialist, was generous with background dope about local politics and helped me with some contacts. City hall officials gave me carbon copies of their reports, and the chamber of commerce fed me statistics. The court house, another domain of noncommunists, was full of good sources. I learned that there is an advantage to being eighteen years old, assiduous, and obviously eager to do well. People gave me a hand. And of course it did not hurt that I was the only full-time reporter in town, because no other newspaper bothered to open a bureau in a place as small as Klatovy.

Aside from Havlíček, there was only one VIP in town with whom I did not get along. He was the Klatovy high school principal and amateur dramaturgist who, as the local chairman of the National Socialists, kept demanding that I publish more news about the party activities. There was no avoiding the fact that the local party branch was entitled to some space in the party's newspaper, but I regarded the blurbs about their "successful" meetings as the most boring waste of space. I would dutifully attend the regular party meetings, take notes, and then throw them away. Two days later, "brother" chairman ("brother" was the National Socialist counterpart of the Communist "comrade") would drop in on me and give me a stiff reprimand for failing to chronicle yet another historic political palaver.

His patience with me finally ran out when I panned an amateur group's presentation of Ibsen's *Peer Gynt*, which he directed. Doležal, who must have smelled trouble, softened the headline of my piece—it was one of the few times he changed anything in my copy—but that did not lower "brother" chairman's blood pressure. The morning the review came out, he was waiting for me on the sidewalk outside my office.

"Ridiculous! Ridiculous!" he yelled, all red in face, waving a copy of my article. I was astonished how seriously he took that little story that did not run more than four to five column inches. Not satisfied with the oral chewing out, the party chief wrote a blistering attack on the "greenhorn pencil-pusher from Prague" and posted it on the bulletin board of his theater group. Later I learned he also had written my editors on party stationery to formally complain about my "unhelpful" attitude. To Doležal's credit, he ignored the whole episode.

Doležal, in fact, generally stuck to his hands-off method from the day I was hired until the Communists fired both of us. During my first months in Klatovy, he would occasionally send me a marked-up tear sheet of my page. His laconic comments ranged from "This is stupid!" to "Old hat" to "Not bad" to an occasional "Good."

But in subtle ways, Doležal kept building up my self-confidence. He never spiked my stories and only rarely changed a word in the text or the headline. On a couple of occasions, he asked for more data supporting my reporting, but he did that only after the article was published and if an injured party threatened with a libel suit. Sometimes I wished Doležal would have less confidence in me and take some of the responsibility off my untried shoulders. Particularly when I worked on the high-octane Havlíček expose I would have loved some support, but that was not Doležal's style. His Indian kids either swam or drowned.

My sojourn in Klatovy would have been even more fun had it taken place against a less dismal political background. While I was making moderate progress cutting my teeth as a cub reporter, the Communists were sinking their fangs into the country's shaky democracy. Their savage forays began soon after I got to my new post. In July 1947 the Prague cabinet voted for participation in the Marshall Plan only to be brusquely slapped down by Stalin, who summoned Jan Masaryk on the carpet and ordered him to reverse the decision. The cabinet hastily complied even before the reprimanded Masaryk returned from Moscow.

In September, three leading National Socialists—including justice minister Drtina, the gutsiest democrat in the cabinet—received booby-trapped packages. Through sheer luck the first bomb failed to go off, and the resulting alarm forestalled the opening of the two other parcels whose origin was later traced to a group of Communists led by Gottwald's son-in-law. By the end of October, the Communist-run ministry of interior practically put the Slovak National Democratic Party out of business on unsupported and unspecified charges of "treasonable activities," thereby making the thirteen-to-twelve cabinet majority still more shaky.

The next month, the Communists created yet another major crisis by accusing the National Socialists of running an "anticommunist espionage ring," whatever that was supposed to mean. The Communist press that trumpeted these charges was very long on sweeping accusations but very short on evidence.

While I followed these developments with considerable foreboding as a citizen, my main regret as a journalist was that none of this history played out in my unexciting bailiwick. I kept my ear to the ground for local echoes of the epic struggle in Prague, but except for the series on Havlíček I found no real ammunition for the hard-pressed democrats. In fact, the only other memorable experience before my journalistic apprenticeship came to an end had nothing to do with postwar politics. It was the execution of a former Gestapo Gauleiter who was captured after the war and tried in Klatovy as a war criminal. The Nazi was so exceptionally tall that his feet touched the floor of the makeshift stand where he was hanged, and he kept gasping for breath until the executioner—who was wearing a cutaway coat and a top hat—broke his neck. Despite my usual need for exciting copy, that aspect of the event went unrecorded in the next day's *Slovo*.

I did better with the more conventional coverage. After less than a year on the job, I put together a special page for the 1947 Christmas Day edition that won a prize in an internal competition of all the regional bureaus. My award was a couple of books published by Melantrich. Soon afterwards, Doležal ran my series on Havlíček that brought me kudos from some of my sources and readers. I got better at handling the pressure of deadlines and even found time for a couple of dates a week. With the Havlíček hurdle successfully behind me I began wondering how soon I could ask Doležal for a transfer to a bigger bureau, or perhaps even to Prague. And then, in the space of a few days, the whole world turned upside down.

On February 13, 1948, the gutsy Drtina accused the Communist interior minister Václav Nosek of systematically packing the top police echelons with Communist Party members. With 85 percent of the senior jobs in the State Security already in his party's hands, Nosek had carried out another series of Communist promotions, and Drtina demanded that they be canceled. His proposal was carried by a narrow majority of the cabinet, but Nosek refused to comply.

As tensions mounted, Stalin's deputy foreign minister Valerian Zorin suddenly arrived in Prague to personally supervise what rapidly escalated to a decisive duel between the democratic camp and the Left. The day after Zorin arrived, all ministers of the non-Marxist parties walked out of Gottwald's cabinet in protest against Nosek's defiance of their decision. Their assumption, which turned out to be disastrously wrong, was that President Beneš would reject their resignation and reprimand Nosek for ignoring the cabinet vote.

The Communists, of course, had no use for such bourgeois maneuvers. With the pressure ominously mounting like the drums and trumpets in Tchaikovsky's *Overture of 1812*, Gottwald pressed all his considerable power buttons, and unleashed a swift coup d'état. Hidden party moles came out of the cold, fellow travelers rallied to the cause, and the party minions dutifully staged what the party subsequently called a "proletarian revolution."

Before Beneš had a chance to act, his office was besieged by demonstrators and "people's" delegations demanding his acceptance of the resignations and appointment of a "progressive" cabinet. Defense minister General Ludvík Svoboda—ironically, the last name means "freedom"—confined the army to the barracks and declared that the democrats who resigned were "a menace and must be removed." Zdeněk Fierlinger, though no longer the chairman of the Social Democrats, lined up all of his party's ministers behind the Communist demands.

The usual gaggle of university professors, artists, writers, actors, and other celebrities signed a petition calling for the victory of the "progressive forces." The Communist Party's general casting organized three huge rallies in the Wenceslas Square in the space of four days. And in a faint echo of the bolshevik storming of the Winter's Palace in St. Petersburg, the Communist-led trade unions staged a general strike and sent fifteen thousand rifle-toting militiamen marching through the streets of Prague.

After ten days of this barrage, the Communists judged the time was ripe for the last blow. During the night of February 24, Nosek ordered the State Security to occupy the offices of the democratic ministers, the headquarters of the National Socialists and the People's Party, and take over all noncommunist newspapers. Communist "Action Committees" moved into the ministries and the editorial offices together with the cops. The various and sundry professional, artistic, trade, and other organizations not yet fully in Communist hands were also taken over by "Action Committees," which promptly began to issue the names of purged "reactionaries," including mine.

Confronted with brute force, most of the democratic ministers scattered. Drtina attempted a suicide. And the ailing Beneš crumbled. When, at eleven o'clock in the morning on February 25, Gottwald presented him with a list of the members of a new, "progressive" cabinet, Beneš signed it.

CHAPTER 5

ESCAPE TO THE US ZONE IN GERMANY

At about the time Beneš legitimized the coup, I was boarding a local train at a small station outside Klatovy, on my way to Prague. Earlier in the morning, after I heard the news of the coup and my name on the radio, I was so rattled that all I could think about was to go to the office and try to call Doležal. Under the circumstances it was probably the most stupid thing to do, but luck was on my side. Walking toward the main square, I first ran into a couple of plainclothesmen I knew who were carrying stacks of *Svobodné Slovo* and other noncommunist newspapers they had confiscated from news vendors. One of the detectives mustered a friendly smile and tried to make a joke. "All the hard work you've done," he mumbled, "and it's all for nothing."

I was in such turmoil I barely heard him. A block later I spotted a uniformed police sergeant whose face I also vaguely recognized. He, too, was confiscating newspapers that had been shipped before the "Action Committees" took over the printing plants. The policeman glanced at me and his eyes froze; it was obvious he knew who I was. As I passed by the kiosk, he looked away from me and said in a low but distinct voice, "Get out of town, but don't go to the train station."

What he said reinforced a thought that was forming in the back of my mind since I heard my name included among the *Slovo* journalists who had been purged: this was Havlíček's day to get even, and I had to get away from Klatovy. I hoped that I had at least a few hours before it was too late: considering how many much more important "enemies of the people" his StB had to round up, it probably would not go right away after a small fry like me. The Klatovy train station, however, was a logical place for Havlíček to have staked out; it was not a place to show my face.

I kept on walking, trying to think what to do next. I realized that I was taking chances by going to the office, but I still could not fully believe what was happening. I had to try to call Doležal.

I passed by the front window of the *Svobodné Slovo* and saw no sign of anybody in my cubicle. The town square, usually busy at this time in the morning, was also quiet and almost empty. I took a deep breath, unlocked the door, and stepped in my office. The desk was as messy as I had left it the night before. I picked up the phone and placed a call to my headquarters. The call went through almost instantly, but it was not answered by one of the women at the *Svobodné Slovo* switchboard. The deep-throated voice I heard conjured up the face of a chain-smoking cop. My heart sank, but I asked to be switched to Doležal. "The lines are all down," the voice said.

I hung up, took another deep breath, and made for the door. Back in the square, I rolled up the collar of my heavy winter jacket and walked into a nearby doorway to let the panic pass and collect my thoughts. I saw only one chance to evade Havlíček's clutches, and I took it. Leaving all of my meager possessions behind, I started walking to a small train station north of Klatovy that was serviced by commuter trains. As I remember, it was more than an hour's walk along a snow-covered road, but I was feeling numb and oblivious to the cold. My only vaguely felt concern was whether I had enough cash for a ticket to Prague.

As I had hoped, there was no sign of the StB at the small railroad stop. I boarded the first train for Pilsen, changed to an express train, and arrived in Prague still shrouded by the mental fog that had set in the morning. When I came home I hardly said hello to my parents and went to bed. My mother cried and Dad looked upset. Mirek had been drafted in the army some time earlier and was at his post. I felt feverish, unable to think about anything in particular, least of all the coup. Time rolled by like a slow-motion movie showing a blank wall.

The next morning, I went to Doležal's home. He was in bed, exhausted from the days-long crisis. His steel-rimmed specs shined against dark circles under his eyes, and he looked thinner than I remembered him, but otherwise he was still the no-nonsense man in charge. He approved my escape from Klatovy but warned me that unless I found a new job soon and established a legal residence in Prague I would get picked by StB as a "social parasite" and possibly be handed to Havlíček.

Since we were both unemployed, Doležal said, we should launch a pro-forma job hunt, both to keep the StB off our backs and to have a cover for a daily contact. But our main job would be to help other people stay out of jail and, if need be, help them escape abroad. Doležal, who had obviously done a lot of thinking since the coup started, also hinted that I might have to risk a quick visit to the border area west of Klatovy to link up with a group of professional smugglers about whom I had written one of my features. As I was leaving, Doležal gave me one of his piercing looks.

"Not one word about this to anybody," he said. I nodded without enthusiasm. The Nazi occupation had ended less than three years ago, and here we were, talking about going underground against another dictatorship—this time run by people who spoke Czech. I found the thought so depressing that for a few days I could hardly function. Sometimes, for no obvious reason, a great wave of sadness would wash over me and I'd hide somewhere and bawl like a child. Eventually I would calm down but inside I felt frozen, as if drugged.

Doležal and I would get together every couple of days or so and test some of his ideas. Not all of them worked out. In the middle of March I took, as he suggested, the trip to the border, but the smuggler I knew was gone, and another of my contacts did not pan out. Our job hunt was also getting nowhere. Doležal and I kept dutifully applying for work in various state enterprises, but wherever we went the comrades in the "Action Committees" just laughed at us.

"We're in the process of weeding out reactionary elements just like you," one newly appointed personnel chief told us, "and you're asking me for a job. You must be kidding." I appreciated his logic, but that was no consolation for the fact that it put Doležal and me in a predicament that would now be called "Catch 22." As certified societal outcasts, we could not get a legitimate job; and since we didn't have a legitimate job, we were societal outcasts. The way the people's republic dealt with social parasites was to charge them with "shirking work" and assign them as laborers to mines or construction projects away from Prague.

In contrast to our make-believe job hunt, Doležal's clandestine work was making progress. He kept mum about most of his activity, but I gathered he was running something of an underground railroad that spirited prominent anticommunists across the border into the US Zone in Germany. An essential component of the operation was an accomplice—Doležal never even hinted who it was—inside the Prague headquarters of the State Security who provided him with a carbon copy of the list of "reactionaries" who were due to be arrested.

Since the cops were overworked and the jails were overfilled, there was a lag of up to a couple of weeks between the time the names appeared on the list and the time the StB rang the bell. This gave us a chance to warn the targeted individuals and, if they wanted to flee, arrange for a guide to take them across the Czech border to Western Germany. After I failed to reach the smuggler I knew, Doležal established a link with another group whose competence I eventually came to appreciate.

My own small role in Doležal's illegal enterprise was to locate a few of the people on the StB list and shove under their door or in the mail slot a typed warning of their impending arrest. It was a nocturnal task that Doležal assigned to me only occasionally and that, I assumed, I shared with other members of his cell. Each mission sent my heart in my throat—what if the apartment was watched by StB?—but we could not devise a less risky system. We could not use the bugged telephones, and short of that nothing was as quick as the surreptitious visits.

Another adventure that made my nerves tingle was casting somebody else's vote in the May 1948 "elections" called by the Communists, who wanted to put a veneer of legality on their takeover. For some reason, Doležal wanted the StB to think that one family whose escape he had arranged was still in the country, and it was therefore important to have their names checked off at the polling place as having voted. I was chosen as a stand-in for the family's son, a youngster of about my age. Doležal gave me the escapee's ID card, the address of his polling place, and—he added with a crooked smile—permission to vote for whomever I wanted.

It was black humor on more than one level. Together with the Communists and the subsequently absorbed Social Democrats, the two stage props participating in the elections were the reconstructed National Socialists and the People's Party, both of which had been taken over by "progressive elements." As a result, the only way to show dissent was to use the voting booth to pull the four ballots out of the envelope and then drop it, empty, into the box. But even that option was iffy. In the final two weeks before the elections, Communists and Social Democrats all over the country publicly pledged to vote "proudly," that is, by showing the ballot they chose before dropping it in the box. Chances were high that, at least in some polling place, all voting would be done in the open.

On election day I went to the fugitive's polling place in mid-morning and walked around the neighborhood until close to noon, when the lines of voters stretched well outside the school building. I then joined the queue, hoping that by the time I got to the poll watchers' table they would be too rushed and hungry to compare my looks with the photo in the ID.

The line moved slowly, the sun was hot, and the two policemen who watched the queue made the progress seem even slower and the air hotter. By the time I reached the voting room I was all nerves, but Lady Luck was on my side. As I hoped, the two women who checked the names of the voters only looked at the ID card in front of them and barely gave me a glance. To add to my relief, practically everybody in the line in front of me used the voting booth. I felt safe enough to follow suit, stuff the ballots in my pocket, and cast an empty envelope.

That chore finished, I took a deep breath and went straight to my own election place, where most people also declined the "proud" option. It felt good voting twice against the regime although, of course, it was an empty gesture. The announced results were a 98 percent support for the new Communist government, a figure that is the standard lie for all so-called elections in the Soviet orbit. The Kremlin and its Czech stand-ins were firmly in charge, and there was no force on the horizon that could remove them from power. Not for forty-one years, anyway.

~

A few days later, Doležal told me that my name showed up on the upcoming arrests list just as he was concluding arrangements for another escape. The smugglers with whom he dealt were pros who after the war made good money backpacking goods—mostly American cigarettes—from the US Zone in Germany to Czechoslovakia. Following the Communist coup, they added a new and even more profitable line to their business, that of guiding political refugees from Czechoslovakia to the US Zone.

Their price was steep, but the man whose escape Doležal was preparing, a wealthy landowner from Southern Bohemia, was willing to pay the smugglers' fee for four refugees. The group that Doležal had put together before my name appeared on the list was made up of Václav Mašek, the estate owner; his daughter Romana; and Ilka, the fiancée of my former colleague Vlasta Lorenz who had fled to Germany a few weeks earlier. Now, just a few days before the planned crossing, Doležal added me as the fourth member of the group.

The short notice was a blessing. I had no need for long preparations—the smugglers' instructions were that each of us could carry only one small, dark-colored valise with a few toilet articles and some clothing, none of which was to make any noise when carried. And the early departure date mercifully reduced the pain of leave-taking, which I tried to make as brief and undramatic as possible.

During my last few days at home I felt tired and empty. I said nothing about my plans to anybody but my parents and Mirek, but the word somehow spread, and some members of the Simandl clan quietly brought me little presents to take along on the trip. I was particularly touched by my Cousin Míla who was still running the closely controlled foreign currency department of the Czechoslovak National Bank. He falsified the bank records to show that he had issued one hundred German marks to a nonexistent official, paid for them out of his own pocket, and left the money with my aunt. Another selfless gesture was my brother's insistence on packing in my valise his best suit. Mirek was twenty-two years old and dating a lot; handsome as he was, he needed the suit badly.

The poignant gestures made the emotional strain of my parting even harder. The morning I left my home for the last time, Mirek was on military duty. Dad gave me a hug and stood outside the door of the apartment until I walked out of sight. As for my mother, she insisted on taking my bundle to the main railroad station by a separate streetcar and handing it to me just before our group boarded the train. It was more a symbol of her support for my decision than an attempt to foil the StB. She stood near the main entrance to the station with tears rolling down her ruddy cheeks. We quickly embraced, I grabbed the suitcase and headed for the door of the terminal. My eyes, too, were full of tears.

Mašek, the two girls, and I took a train to Cheb, a town in western Bohemia close to the German border. After the overthrow, the Communist regime had created a forty-kilometer-deep zone along the western border that was closed to outsiders, but for reasons I no longer remember the ban was suspended for a few days in June so that Cheb was accessible for people who didn't live there. Once on the train, the four of us divided into two pairs and took seats in different compartments, which gave each of us a much-needed company as well as a hoped-for alibi if we should be questioned by StB plainclothesmen who we assumed would patrol the train.

Ilka and I had agreed to pretend we were engaged and on the way to visit her old aunt; Mašek and his daughter invented a relative in a Cheb hospital who was expecting their visit. Neither story would have withstood even a superficial check, but once again we were lucky. No plainclothesman showed up during the trip, and when we arrived in Cheb, the policeman at the station did not seem to care who got off the train.

Encouraged, we all checked into a small inn whose name was given to Doležal by the smugglers. I shared a room with Mašek. All I remember about the rest of the day is that I was calm. After dinner, I played—badly—the piano that stood in the room of the two girls. Afterward, to my surprise, I slept as soundly as if I had been on a school outing.

The next day we killed time in our rooms until late afternoon, when we took our bundles to the tavern downstairs and, as was prearranged, waited for our guides. By then the strange ease of the previous day had dissipated, and the afternoon vigil was hard. It did not add to my peace of mind that the smugglers failed to show up at the appointed time. As time dragged on and we were still sitting alone in a mostly empty tavern, I felt we were increasingly

CHAPTER 5

conspicuous and easy targets to be arrested. We had no idea whom to contact in Cheb—all we were told was to wait in the tavern. As the sun went down, I was more and more worried.

Finally the door swung open and an older man with a weather-beaten face walked in, followed by a young companion. The two nodded to us cheerfully as if we were old friends and, to my surprise, sat down at a separate table and ordered a beer and schnapps. Their Czech was so poor I realized with a shock that they were Sudeten Germans—hopefully, I thought, non-fascists who had been spared the postwar expulsion from the border area. Despite this smidgen of comfort, the sudden discovery that our escape would be handled by a couple of Germans only added to my jitters. For once, I felt, Doležal should have been less tight-lipped about his contacts.

While the four of us kept up a desultory conversation, the smugglers sipped their drinks as if they had all the time in the world. Finally, when it began to turn dark, they got up and nodded to us to follow them. Outside, they wordlessly helped us climb into the back of a small canvas-covered pickup truck with a Cheb license plate. The older man got behind the wheel, the young man sat next to him, and we were off.

As best as I can reconstruct the itinerary, we took a secondary highway through a wooded countryside for about three-quarters of an hour until the road came close to the border. At that point the smugglers pulled over to the shoulder, turned off the lights, and jumped out. Working with great speed, they jacked up the front end of the vehicle and removed one wheel, pretending that they had a flat in case a police car went by. Next thing we knew, the younger man pulled apart the canvas cover and hissed to us to jump out. No longer looking relaxed, he immediately ran into the nearby woods and waved to us to follow.

For the next hour or so, we silently walked in single file through the woods behind our guide. I was followed by Ilka and Romana, and Mašek, who had a revolver, brought up the rear. Except when crossing a couple of logging roads we kept deep inside the forest. The farther we walked the more frequently our guide would stop for a while to listen. At one point, he dropped down to the ground and hissed to us to follow suit.

For about ten or fifteen very long minutes we hugged the ground waiting, I assumed, for a Czech border guard to pass by so that we could move on. Whispered words sounded like a loudspeaker; body movements broke twigs and produced noise that seemed to give us away all the way to Cheb. There was nothing to do but wait and worry, but I remember that Ilka and I, laying side by side, exchanged grins and quiet chuckles. It felt good to be on the move—much better than sitting in the tavern. Eventually our guide stood up and walked away, but in a few moments he was back, waving us back on our feet.

We formed again a single file and set off at a fast pace. Another twenty minutes or so later, we came to an open field from which we could see distant lights. The smuggler stopped and, still speaking in a hushed voice, told us to cross the field and follow a road toward the lights. We were in Germany, he said, and we should report to the police station in the village. Mašek handed his gun to the smuggler, saying he would no longer need it. The smuggler took the weapon, turned around, and disappeared in the woods.

Without exchanging a word, the four of us broke into a run across the field. Even after we reached the dirt road, we moved fast and exchanged only a few words in whispers. We were still uncertain whether we had indeed crossed the border. In the darkness, the road looked like any empty country road anywhere. The longer it stretched, the more anxiously we searched for a sign confirming that we were in Germany.

Finally, we reached a clearing with a tavern whose door was wide open. It was too dark to see any sign above the door, but behind it we could see a table lit by two stubs of candles in a puddle of congealing wax. On top of the table, casting a flickering black shadow against the wall, was a small beer keg. It was propped up by bricks at a steep angle to drain the last dregs.

It was a scene fit for a Rembrandt, but all I could feel was a surge of relief running through my whole body. Whatever else was in short supply in Czechoslovakia, the pubs had plenty of beer. For the moment, our worst fears were over. We were in Germany.

CHAPTER 6

IN THE REFUGEE CAMPS

By making it through, under, or around the Iron Curtain after the February coup, a Czech escapee became a nonperson: under a law issued by the new regime in Prague, upon crossing the border, all political refugees automatically lost their Czechoslovak citizenship and property. For our foursome, lost belongings were no burning worry. Mašek's considerable wealth had been confiscated as soon as the Communists took over, and all I had left behind was a half-share in our humble family bungalow in Horní Borek. But as Mašek, the girls, and I walked into Selb, a small German town hard by the Czech border, we did want an official acknowledgment of our presence in Germany. It turned out to be a remarkably fast and simple process.

It was close to midnight when we walked into the local police station and reported our arrival to a bored-looking sergeant. Showing no surprise at our sudden appearance, he made a short phone call and wrote our names in the blotter. Less than fifteen minutes later, a couple of US Army military policemen pulled up in a small truck and took us to a German border post where we were registered as stateless and visa-less refugees. This time, each of us got a piece of paper with a stamp confirming our status and identity. Shortly after one o'clock in the morning we were back at the Selb police station, asking about a place to sleep.

The desk sergeant, who had seen the likes of us before, knew the answer. He nodded to a sleepy-looking duty cop who yawned, put on his regulation cap, and walked with us to a local barbershop. The owner, already alerted by the sergeant, was waiting at the door. He showed us how to lower the back of the four seats in his establishment, accepted a couple of packs of cigarettes as payment, and left. I leaned back in the barber's chair and fell asleep almost immediately. I had a vivid dream in which I retraced every step we took after we jumped off the smugglers' truck.

In the morning another cop put us on a train to Hof, a Bavarian town not far from a refugee camp just outside a village called Moschendorf. Hof, which was about the same size as the Czech Cheb, was our introduction to postwar Germany, and it was a shock. Cheb was nothing to brag about, but it was a functioning place where food and other basic necessities were readily available. Hof, three years after the war, was a showcase of the drastic price Germany had paid for its love affair with Hitler. The town was a skeleton: destitute, hungry, and eerily lifeless.

The few people in the streets were dressed even more shabbily than was the norm in Czechoslovakia, where clothing was still scarce. Most of the buildings were bullet-marked, and the holes in the walls were at best patched up with raw cement. Store windows were broken and covered with wooden planks, and the pavement and sidewalks were crumbling. Except for a few drab olive jeeps with American GIs there was no traffic.

What I found particularly ominous was that food in Hof appeared to be as scarce as it had been in Prague during the war. I noted with a depressing sense of déjà vu that the store window of the main street's biggest grocer held nothing but three rusting cans labeled *Ochsenschwantzenartsuppe* (Oxtail-style soup), the same ersatz concoction we used to eat during the war. I realized that, if this was the German menu, we were about to go hungry. But even more foreboding was the only store window, farther down the street, that showed a variety of products. The store was a pharmacy, and its display consisted entirely of artificial arms and legs, items that must have been in great demand by the former soldiers of the Wehrmacht.

The town was a good introduction to the nearby Moschendorf refugee camp where we arrived on Sunday morning, June 19, 1948. Run by the Bavarian Red Cross, the establishment consisted of several rows of primitive wooden barracks that had held prisoners of war. After the war, the barracks were used to provide temporary shelter to the human flotsam—refugees like the four of us—who were straggling in from the tormented Central Europe. Three years after the war ended, the camp was still surrounded by a barbed wire fence, but the gate was kept open.

In the reception barracks, an old man wearing a cap with the Red Cross insignia told us that if we wanted lunch, we had to bring our own mess kits. Seeing our blank stares, he advised us to go a GI garbage dump just outside the fence and pick out some empty cans. We trooped to the smelly pile and did as the man said, feeling—at least in my case—a touch of panic. But the worst part of our new existence was yet to come.

That Sunday's lunch, the main meal of the day, for each of us consisted of two dark unpeeled boiled potatoes and one ladleful of boiled red beets. For dinner, the two old women who comprised the mess hall staff gave every refugee a ladleful of boiled raisins. The next morning's breakfast was about a pound of bread—the whole day's ration—and two pats of pale margarine. During the three weeks we spent at the camp, the menu hardly changed.

Within a week, I was hungry—not in the old wartime sense of half-empty stomach at bedtime, but so famished that sometimes I couldn't stop thinking of food. To make matters worse, the black market German marks I had brought from Prague turned out to be a bitter joke. As fate would have it, a few days after we crossed into Germany, the United States, British, and French authorities declared the Hitler-era currency invalid in their zones of occupation. The ersatz oxtail soup and other unrationed nutrients we thought we could buy were suddenly out of reach, casualties of Germany's desperate need for new, hard currency.

The historic *Währungsumtausch* (currency exchange) was the curtain raiser on the separation of the Western and Soviet zones of Germany, and in an amazingly short time triggered the famous West German "economic miracle." For refugees like us, however, it was not an immediate blessing. Each of us received the same sixty spanking new marks—worth twenty dollars—that were issued to all Germans in the western part of the country. But food rationing continued. Moreover, with no job opportunity in sight, the Deutschmark became each refugee's last-ditch reserve that most of us were loath to spend.

The stomach pangs added to a dismal environment. Mašek, the girls, and I were assigned to room no. 3 in barracks no. 37. The room held twenty-six bunk beds covered with mangy straw sacks impersonating mattresses, two tables without drawers, and six chairs. We were informed that when it rained, the roof leaked.

Our arrival brought the total occupancy of our room to four women and twenty men, all of them fellow Czechs. Despite the common language and origin, our roommates were a tight-lipped lot. One of the assumptions that had wide currency in the camp was that it was infiltrated by StB informers, and as a result nobody revealed anything about himself or herself, including the last name.

The secretive nature of our roommates did not stop us a few days later from electing a Moravian judge as a spokesman. He was a skinny, towering character—he must have been about six feet five inches—who delighted in referring to himself as "a small country person."

Hunger and worries being my steady companions, I adopted a lifestyle that was typical of many refugees in the postwar camps: I spent long hours each day lying on my bunk, thereby husbanding my meager energy, and applied my anxious mind to memorizing a Czech-English dictionary, the only book I had brought from Prague. It was something to do for my future as well as, thanks to the beautiful simplicity of the Shakespearian language, a sorely needed morale-boosting experience. As soon as I mastered a few hundred words in English, I found I could decipher articles in the *Stars and Stripes* magazine the GIs tossed in the garbage dump. By the end of the year, I managed to read my first book in English, a GI paperback edition of Ernie Pyle's World War II essays titled *Here Is Your War!*

Linguistic progress was the only bright memory I have of camp Moschendorf, which ranks in my experience only slightly higher than the wartime Abteilung X. The dingy barracks were so depressing that, despite the need to preserve energy, practically all of us in room no. 3 took daily walks to the surrounding countryside. The excursions killed time, but as a change of scenery they were not particularly rewarding. Usually we ended up in a small forest not far from the camp that, to me, was another symbol of the ruin to which Hitler had brought Germany. A witness to the wartime shortage of coal, the trees were stripped of all bark and branches as high as a man could reach; the underbrush was cut down; and the ground—and this I found truly astounding—was swept clean of all needles and twigs. Each time I saw the naked trees and the barren ground an inner voice told me that I had to get out of Moschendorf before the winter.

Adding to the gloom of the Red Cross camp was the grim discovery that as the Johnnies-come-lately among more than two million stateless refugees, we were at the end of every queue leading to a more tolerable existence. Hundreds of thousands of Ukrainians, Lithuanians, Hungarians, and Poles—some fleeing their pro-Nazi past and some their Communist future—were way ahead of us in applying for emigration, for jobs with the American military or the United Nations' International Refugee Organization, and for better preserved barracks. Coming to Germany at the time we did was like entering a race three years after it took off.

Perhaps the worst news we heard in Moschendorf was that our best hope for emigrating to the United States—the Displaced Persons Act 774—authorized admission of refugees who had fled to the West within three years after the end of the war in Europe. The law's deadline allowed ample time for escapees from countries where the Communists took over immediately upon the arrival of the Red Army, but for the Czechs and Slovaks, the door to the United States seemed to close four months after the February coup d'état. It was only later we learned that the DP Act was signed into law on June 25, 1948, which meant that the four of us qualified for the immigration quota with six days to spare.

On top of everything else, I was increasingly distressed by the company we kept. The Red Cross employees wasted no sympathy on the down-and-out

Czechs who only a while back had celebrated the defeat of Nazi Germany. Even less congenial were some of the new arrivals from the Soviet-occupied zone of Germany. One morning, for instance, I noticed that the guy taking a shower next to me had under his armpit a fresh patch of implanted skin. It was a dead giveaway of a former SS man trying to hide his tattooed service number.

Of the four of us, only Ilka managed to get out of Moschendorf early. One evening a few days after our arrival, she was spirited away by Vlasta Lorenz, her fiancé, who had fled ahead of us and managed to get a job in the Czech section of Radio Free Europe in Munich. I never asked Vlasta how he achieved this formidable feat, or how he knew that Ilka was in the camp. The unwritten rule in the camps was to say nothing that could reach the ears of the StB moles we suspected to be in our barracks.

For Mašek, his daughter, and me the hoped-for parting with Moschendorf came, unexpectedly, one morning in July. The night before, the camp had received a large group of former Hungarian soldiers who had fought on the eastern front alongside the Wehrmacht. The same night, they got in a fistfight with a bunch of young Czechs from another barracks. The fracas prompted our departure. The next morning, a convoy of US Army trucks picked up all Czechs and Slovaks and took us to a railroad station where we were put on a train to Schwabach, a small town about ten miles south of Nuremberg.

Our new camp was overcrowded and not much better than Moschendorf, but since its residents were only Czechs and Slovaks, the atmosphere was free of ethnic tensions. Another morale booster was a bulletin board listing several immigration programs opened to refugees, which eased the nagging worry that we might get stuck in Germany. On top of this good news, we learned that the United Nations' International Refugee Organization (IRO) granted all Czech and Slovak political refugees the status of Displaced Persons, and that we would be transferred to more permanent—and presumably better—quarters in IRO's care.

This expectation came true early in the fall of 1948, when all three thousand or so of us in Schwabach were brought by train to Ludwigsburg, a largely undamaged town near Stuttgart. It was the most pleasant location by far we had encountered since arriving in Germany. The town's old buildings were well preserved and included three eighteenth-century castles of the king of Württemberg, one of which—a beautiful, 450-room example of Baroque extravagance—was surrounded by a huge, lush public park. Some of the downtown stores were prosperous-looking and beginning to show the beneficial effects of the Marshall Plan for Europe's economic recovery.

And by moving to the southern tip of Germany, we could look forward to a mild winter.

Best of all, IRO put all of us into three well-preserved complexes of the Wehrmacht's military barracks and let us elect our own government. Our threesome was assigned to Jägerhof Kasserne, a group of nondescript five-story brick buildings surrounding a big exercise yard. Compared to the wooden barracks at Schwabach and Moschendorf, the rooms, which were big enough for a dozen refugees each, were a major step up, at least for us men. The most critical shortcoming was the absence of separate toilets for women. It was not unusual (though to me, invariably shocking) for female refugees to charge into a men's room full of peeing males and, with their eyes averted, head for the stalls.

A continued woe was our starvation diet. Eating was a serious business—not only because it calmed the hunger pangs but because it was a protection against tuberculosis, of which there were several cases in every camp. TB was greatly feared. Emigration—and emigration to America in particular—was uppermost on everybody's mind, and the United States, or so we were told, did not admit tubercular refugees.

For me—and I believe that for most of us—to be refused a US visa would have been a crushing blow. The attraction of the New World was not only its high standard of living. America was the world's strongest and most successful democracy; it was the only real bulwark against the unbridled Soviet expansionism; and it was a country where an immigrant could become a citizen in just five years. It took much longer to get an immigration visa for the United States than for any other country that admitted refugees, but America was worth waiting for—provided one did not get TB in the process. Food therefore was of the essence.

I had an especially good opportunity to keep informed about the camp nutrients. As it happened, shortly after the Communist overthrow, Jana Poučková, my very good high school friend and co-publisher of *Žihadlo*, married her fiancé and on the night of their wedding they fled to Germany. After the usual sojourn through several Red Cross camps they wound up in Jägerhof where her husband, Eugene Pohořelský, became the chief mess officer.

Gene did a great job trying to ward off TB, but he couldn't change some basic facts of camp life in postwar Europe. Theoretically, each refugee was entitled to two thousand calories a day. In practice, the camp rarely received from IRO's German suppliers more than two-thirds of its rations; the rest, Gene assumed, had been siphoned off along the way and diverted to the still shortages-prone German market.

Like his colleagues in the other refugee camps, Gene tried to stretch the meals by boiling the meager vittles into soups, which usually came out tasting the same. But Gene was always on the lookout for improving our calorie count and won great acclaim by replacing knives with peelers for cleaning our main ingredient, the potatoes. The stratagem saved considerable quantities of spuds—but of course, most of us were still hungry.

Another scarcity that caused much griping was clothing. IRO supplied the camps with truckloads of brand new trousers and shirts that were made from the same material as the uniforms of US Marines, but even skinny characters like me could not find an item that would fit. The biggest pair of pants I saw would have been scarcely comfortable for a twelve-year-old. The shirts were in the same category. Our assumption was that the German manufacturer had used the scarce American material to sew up the required number of clothing items but made sure to have cloth left over for other customers.

Women had a similar problem. One day, I saw a group of excited female refugees standing outside the camp administration office with a basketful of bras from a just-delivered IRO shipment. The undergarments, the delegation complained, were barely big enough for children. Ripping off the DPs was obviously a thriving industry.

For all its shortcomings, however, Jägerhof was not a bad haven. Once a year, each Ludwigsburg IRO compound elected a council that appointed a camp leader who operated pretty much like a town mayor and received a modest IRO salary. The refugees were in charge of the administration and all camp services, from cooking to police, sanitation, and the health clinic.

The camp population was relatively homogeneous. The largest group by far was single men in their twenties and early thirties. Another sizable category was married men in their forties, some of whom, I suspected, were as much on the lam from their unhappy marriages as from the Communist rule. By contrast, only about 10 percent of the refugees were women, most of whom were accompanying their husbands. Single women and children were a rarity. One surprise was that in my estimate 60–70 percent of the men among the thousand-odd residents of Jägerhof appeared to have been former factory workers or small farmers. Obviously, the "workers' and peasants' paradise" promised by the Communists had its skeptics.

One strikingly underrepresented group in Ludwigsburg was professional politicians. Prominent refugees as a rule did not stay in the camps. Cabinet members, most members of the parliament, and such public figures as was my former editor-in-chief Ivan Herben were put up by the CIA in special quarters, debriefed, and in most cases quickly granted political asylum in the United States.

Each camp also housed a few smugglers and other adventurers who seemed to be unfazed by the Czech border guards and severe penalties for illegal border crossing. Some of them were ordinary refugees with an extraordinary nerve: one youngster I knew, about two years my junior, went back to his Czech home town three times in as many months. A retiring, soft-spoken kid, he told me he knew a route through the woods that brought him to a bus stop where he could get a ride to Cheb. He even knew the bus schedule. I never learned why he kept going back, but I guessed he was visiting a girlfriend.

The smugglers were important, because for most of us they provided the only link with families and friends left behind. Some of the smugglers were an unsavory lot, but one that I liked was a twenty-year-old, baby-faced, bald-headed guy everybody called "King Kong" because of his broad shoulders and athletic build. He looked like the Jolly Green Giant of old TV commercials except for his missing front teeth, which he said had been knocked out in fights with border guards. Blessed with a sunny disposition and a talent for storytelling, King Kong regaled us with tales from the Czech-German border that were the stuff of a novel. The way he described them, the border guards and the contrabandists—both Czech and German—were like the Montagues and Capulets, laying ambushes for each other and brawling in taverns on both sides of the border. Listening to him, I wished I had known him when I was grinding out my features in Klatovy.

Despite the odd population mix and our footloose existence, the camp life was remarkably orderly. Since jobs were extremely scarce, the day's routine for most of us consisted of queuing up for food, cleaning the room, taking walks, and writing letters or reading. Although many of us were ripped off by the smugglers whom everyone used to maintain some cross-border contacts, theft in the camps was rare, and the meager possessions we kept in our unlocked rooms were safe. Since no one had money to spare, drinking was uncommon, although wine was one of the more readily available articles in German stores. Practically everyone, me included, worked hard at learning English.

Considering the circumstances, the atmosphere at Jägerhof was relatively upbeat. Individual refugees had ample reasons to feel depressed: we were almost constantly semi-hungry; the empty hours were hard to fill; emigration procedures seemed to be excruciatingly slow; and worst of all, practically everyone had left behind a family, a girlfriend, or someone else who was sorely missed. Still, the relief of getting out of the clutches of the Prague regime and the hope for a new life abroad were so potent that I don't recall a single case of mental breakdown in the camp. It was only years later, when we were all well into our new existence, that the accumulated pressures appeared to take their toll.

One of these victims was my former colleague Vlasta Lorenz. When I visited him and Ilka as a GI in Munich in 1952, they had two small daughters and seemed to be a happy couple. But after they emigrated to the States, something went wrong. Vlasta could not get back into journalism and wound up working as a trainer in a New York health club. The marriage fell apart, and he took his own life.

Future stress, however, was not what worried us at Jägerhof. The main concern was emigration: to be admitted into the United States in those years required, in addition to the DP status, an American sponsor—some brave and kindly soul who would assume the responsibility for making sure that the immigrant would not become a public charge. That was a high hurdle, but we were fortunate in appealing to a generation of Americans who were astonishingly generous. After paying the enormous price on the battlefield, American taxpayers donated billions for the Marshall Plan and then reached still deeper in their pockets to ply millions of DPs with CARE packages or to help them immigrate. Although almost none of us had any contacts in the United States, everyone I knew eventually found a sponsor.

Still, for a young guy with only rudimentary English and no job record (in fact, no documents at all), finding a signatory for the affidavit was a daunting task. Like practically everybody else in the camp, I dipped into my sixty new marks for stationery and postage and became a prodigious letter writer. I penned notes—some in Czech, some in broken English—to every hapless American whose address fell into my eager hands. Some addresses came my way through fellow refugees who had already found a sponsor and had a prospect to spare. Others I copied from Czech-language American newspapers for which I wrote, free of charge, features about life in Communist Czechoslovakia and in the DP camps.

Some of the refugees made sponsor soliciting an art form. One friend of mine, a talented artist and feature writer who used to illustrate his own articles in Czech magazines, made up for his lack of persuasive English by adorning his letters with cartoons. His illustrations not only landed him a sponsor—a Chicago widow. They were so effective that soon after his arrival to the United States, the two got married. Another fellow refugee, an accomplished musician, achieved the same result by sprucing up his correspondence with little musical compositions. Years later, my wife and I visited him and his American wife in Cedar Rapids, Iowa. My friend's spouse ran a restaurant, and he played piano for the dinner guests.

My own pitch was run-of-the-mill. I usually described the coup d'état and my reasons for fleeing and threw myself at the addressee's mercy. I stressed that

I did not want money, I could do without food packages, but I badly needed a sponsor for my immigration visa. My campaign produced several friendly responses, including one from a Nebraskan who offered to underwrite my immigration if I would work on his farm.

With considerable misgivings, I wrote him a letter politely turning down the offer. I'd learned enough about farmwork to know that I was not cut out for it, and it would have been unfair to take advantage of a friendly stranger by accepting his sponsorship only to leave him as soon as I'd found another job. Moreover, I had one very important reason for temporarily suspending my visa quest. By the time I got the farmer's letter, in the summer of 1949, my relationship with Romana, Mašek's daughter, had developed beyond a casual friendship. I hoped that we might emigrate together, as a married couple.

CHAPTER 7

WAITING FOR A US VISA

Next to emigration, keeping in touch with the folks at home was the refugees' most nagging and universal worry. For our foursome, the problem emerged immediately after we arrived in Germany and learned that the Czechoslovak post office was refusing to accept sealed letters mailed from Germany—I assumed, because the StB was too busy arresting people to steam the envelopes. This left each of us with no option but to send home an elaborately innocuous-sounding postcard, signed with a phony name, to indicate that we were across the border.

After that desperate attempt at communication (which, I later learned, never reached my parents), I never used the StB-monitored mails. It was only after I was in Jägerhof that I sent a few letters by a carrier that was supposed to bypass the StB: international trains. It was not a good system. These trains—or more precisely, their smuggling cooks and waiters in the dining cars—put an important hole into the Iron Curtain by regularly crossing the Czech-German border. Some of their exploits were worthy of the pen of John le Carré. For example for a fat fee, they helped a young journalist I knew flee the country by lying on his back inside the water reservoir under the roof of the dining car. He made it to Germany chilled to the bone, but safe.

But using this underground mail for correspondence was problematic. In Prague, the letters could be received from or handed to a dining car crewman anywhere outside the train station. Retrieving them, however, entailed a cumbersome procedure. The crewmen, who insisted that the train stops in Germany were watched by StB agents, would hand over or accept the mail only when serving meals between stations.

This made the system expensive; moreover, there were reasons to suspect that the underground post office was also used by the StB. Time and again we heard reports that a smuggled letter about the harsh conditions in the camps appeared verbatim in the *Rudé Právo* or other Communist newspapers, where it was presumably published to discourage would-be refugees. The way I rationalized the couple of letters I sent by train was that I wrote nothing about the camp's conditions.

The caution was probably unnecessary, because security in the camps was a joke. While I was still in Moschendorf somebody—presumably, an StB agent—broke into the Studebaker of a young captain of the US Army Counter-Intelligence Corps (CIC) and stole a box with the refugees' debriefing records he kept on the backseat. The loot consisted of scores of unguarded interviews in which the newly arrived refugees disclosed some of the most sensitive information, such as who helped them flee. The captain, incidentally, was not exceptionally incompetent. His counterpart in Schwabach was so unconcerned about our security that we called him, in a Czech takeoff on the initials CIC, *blbec z cícu*, meaning roughly "the tit's idiot."

One important reason I was reluctant to get in touch with my parents was my fear that, sooner or later, StB would catch up with them. The fact that I had escaped was damning enough; what worried me even more were hints I heard from Dad before leaving that he and his former army buddies were once again involved in some underground enterprise. In February 1949, my fears came true. According to a veiled reference in a letter Mašek received from his former wife in Prague, my mother, Dad, and Mirek had all been arrested and the family apartment was sealed.

Years later, Mirek told me what happened. One late afternoon, when he returned home from a military exercise, he found six agents of the Czech military counter-intelligence systematically searching the apartment. Dad and Mother sat under guard in the kitchen, and one of the gumshoes avidly pored over Mirek's sizable collection of love notes from his girlfriends. Eventually the agents gave up and took away the whole family. My father and brother were carted away to a downtown military prison, and my mother was put in a jail for civilians.

Mirek, who was an army lieutenant on active duty, was locked up for a week in a windowless solitary cell and put on a bread-and-water diet. His room was kept lighted day and night and his only diversion was eavesdropping on security agents whose office was next to his cell. One of the conversations he overheard included the names of several people who apparently were under surveillance in Kladno, the town where Mirek's unit was stationed. After he was released, without any apology or explanation, Mirek returned to his unit, ate, shaved, and rushed out to warn the people whose names he had heard through the wall.

Mother was incarcerated for five months during which she was denied all contact with the outside world. Uncle Bořík managed to find out where she was imprisoned and tried to visit her each weekend. He never succeeded; the

CHAPTER 7

My parents and brother shortly before they were arrested after my escape to the US zone of Germany in June 1948.

guards refused to pass on to her even a change of underwear. Dad was brutally beaten and was kept in solitary for eight months. Like Mother, he was allowed no contact with anyone outside the prison.

Mirek in the meantime grew increasingly worried that the agents would return for another search of the apartment and perhaps find some hidden evidence against the family. One weekend Uncle Bořík helped him crawl into the sealed apartment through a bathroom window, and Mirek combed it for overlooked clues about Dad's underground work. He found nothing, and the agents never returned—not even to remove the official seal and tape from the door.

In October Dad was put on trial with several other officers for various crimes against the state, the most serious of which was an alleged attempt to organize the escape to the West of Hana Benešová, the widow of the former president. The evidence against the whole group was so flimsy that even the Communist judge threw the case out of court. Dad was released from jail, but he and Mother were so broken by the experience, both physically and mentally, that they were on and off in psychiatric care until they died a few years later.

For me, the arrests in Prague couldn't have come at a worse time. By the end of my first year in exile, I was in love with Romana, Mašek's fair daughter, and the feeling was mutual. Both Romana and I were young, unattached, and suspended in the same hiatus. The shared hardships, isolation, and uncertain future almost unavoidably drew us together, and each day in the camp made the tie grow stronger. It did not take long for Mašek to find out what was happening; and since he totally disapproved of me as a prospective son-in-law, he set out to bring our romance to a halt.

The showdown came one late fall afternoon, when Romana's father and I happened to be alone in the room. A short, strong-willed man in his early fifties, Mašek was accustomed to having his way. He fixed me with his pale blue eyes and bluntly announced that I was an unformed adolescent who was unfit to court his daughter.

"Women are weak," he told me, "and that's fine for us men because it makes our lives more interesting. The other side of the coin is that we have to bear responsibility for the results. And," Mašek pressed on without taking his eyes off mine, "you're not ready to accept responsibility for what happens to my daughter." He went on for a while about the difference between Romana's and my social backgrounds, assured me that I could not support his daughter in the style to which she was accustomed, and flatly concluded that "your affair with her must end."

As Mašek spoke, I was acutely aware that his points were well taken. Until the previous February, he was a wealthy member of the Czech landed class, secure in old money and connections at the highest levels of the pre- and postwar Prague governments. Twice divorced, Mašek lived with his only daughter, Romana, in a large historic mansion surrounded by servants. The family estate included a brewery, a cheese factory, two inns, and thousands of acres of forests and fields that produced an annual income I couldn't even dream about.

Before the Communist coup, both Romana and her father moved in the best social circles: Mašek, who as a young man was the agricultural attaché in the Czechoslovak consulate in San Francisco, spoke fluent English, was an avid hunter, and frequently hosted on his estate the American ambassador and influential members of the Prague parliament. To make my relative standing still more wretched, I owed Mašek for escaping the clutches of StB—after all, he had paid my smugglers' fee.

But at the ripe age of twenty-one, none of this weakened my resolve to court Romana, despite the distressing consequences for the atmosphere in the room I shared with her, her father, and three of their relatives. For two of them—Vladislav Brdlík, Romana's maternal grandfather, and his wife, Elizabeth, or as Brdlík called her, "Liška"—I became an anathema. For me, this was a painful blow because the couple, who were well in their seventies, were among the most impressive people I had ever met.

Brdlík was a former professor of economics at the Charles University in Prague and the finance minister in the prewar Czechoslovak government. He was a powerfully built grand old man with bright eyes, a halo of unruly white hair, and great unaffected dignity. He ignored the physical discomforts and limitations of camp life as if they did not exist and was constantly immersed in arcane economic studies and correspondence with several universities in the United States and England.

His wife—a slim, regally erect, onetime beauty—was also a remarkable trooper who seemed to be as oblivious to the hardships of the DP life as was her husband. Liška could have been exempted from all camp duties because of her age, but she insisted on doing her share of washing stairs and standing in long lines for food. She took turns with me typing her husband's letters. Never idle, she also sewed, and one of the garments she made, without a sewing machine, was a handsome nightgown. I particularly admired the way Liška showed her breeding without appearing to be condescending or arrogant. She moved with poise and elegance that defied her age, practically never complained, and occasionally delighted us with amusing stories about her wealthy social set in Prague. She could make even serving the camp porridge a festive occasion. Now, this couple that I so greatly admired, solidly lined up behind Mašek's campaign to stop my courtship of Romana.

Brdlík was the first to confront me, in a way that was relatively low-key. Shortly after Mašek issued his dictum, the old man took me aside and bid me, in a firm but dispassionate way, to leave his granddaughter alone. The time to get seriously involved with a young woman, he said, was when I was settled somewhere outside Germany and had a promising job. Unlike Mašek, Brdlík did not dwell on my potential to live up to Romana's expectations, but he made it quite clear that by courting Romana I was socially out of my depth—at least, as he put it, in the eyes of "other members" of Romana's family.

One of those "other members" was Liška. Upon learning of my advances to her granddaughter, the old lady's egalitarian attitude underwent a total reversal. Unlike her husband, Liška did not deem me worthy an open encounter. Her approach was to dismiss me entirely, except when I dared to say anything in her presence, in which case she would make an exasperated grimace and roll her eyes to the ceiling in a gesture that clearly meant to be insulting. Otherwise, I became for her thin air, a non-person.

As if my affair were not enough to cast a pall over our room, in the fall of 1948 Mašek got news that effectively buried his hopes for a new career in the United States. Before his escape, officials in the US embassy in Prague apparently had raised the possibility that when he reached the States he could get a senior position with the Voice of America (VOA). If that did not work out, Mašek hoped to land a good job as the former head of the Rotary International in Czechoslovakia.

Within six months after we arrived in Germany, both of these hopes suffered reversals that would have crushed a lesser man. First, Mašek's friend Laurence Steinhardt, the former US ambassador in Prague, died in an airplane crash in Canada. With his death, Mašek's VOA prospects effectively vanished. He had no background in journalism, and no other influential supporter in the State Department.

The second blow, this one from the headquarters of Rotary International, came shortly afterwards. The organization's response to Mašek's plea for help was an indignant letter informing him that he was no longer a "fellow Rotarian" because the Czech and Slovak Rotary clubs had been disbanded by the Communist government. After a great deal of correspondence with individual members, the only job Mašek was offered by a would-be sponsor was as a gas station attendant in Dearborn, Michigan. In the end, he felt he had no choice but to accept it.

To my admiration and to his great credit, Mašek took these setbacks with the same steely fortitude with which he had rebuked my advances to Romana. There were many mornings when, after reading his mail, he would turn his back on the rest of us and without a word stare out of the window for what seemed like an eternity. He never complained, but the long silences were the evidence of his hurt.

As if Mašek's disappointments, my parents' imprisonment, and the Brdlík's reaction to my amorous advances were not enough to make the gloom in our room thick enough to cut, a shocking event in the spring of 1949 made the tensions almost insufferable. It involved the Brdlíks' only son, a reedy twenty-something who had also fled to Germany and who worked as an IRO policeman in a camp not far from Jägerhof. One day, while interrogating a refugee suspected of stealing food from the kitchen, the young Brdlík and several other camp cops beat up their prisoner so severely that the US occupational authority put them all on trial for police brutality.

The news of young Brdlík's arrest plunged our room into a sepulchral silence. To outsiders, Romana's patrician grandparents showed nothing but enormous fortitude. The professor spent many hours conferring in whispers with the court-appointed defense lawyers, and Liška continued taking her turn to queue up for our food. Throughout the weeklong trial, both of them unflinchingly watched their son's ordeal from the front row of the courtroom. No one who lived as close to them as I did could miss their suffering.

The American judge sentenced each of the cops to several months in jail after pointing out that police brutality was a hallmark of the regime the refugees had fled. The severity of the sentence, its impact on their son's chances to get a US visa, and the ignominy and strain of the trial had a devastating effect on what was left of our room's social relations. By late spring the mood in our room was so desolate that I sometimes took a deep breath before walking in.

And then, in July, several developments brought a sudden relief. First, the Brdlíks received their US visa and emigrated, leaving their son and his wife to follow suit after he finished his jail sentence. Next, Romana's father was elected the Jägerhof camp leader. And I, thanks to my memorized English, landed a job in an IRO emigration office.

Since married IRO employees were entitled to their own room, and since my modest income bought solid food on the increasingly recovering German market, Romana and I decided to get married. On September 18, 1949, we walked over to the Ludwigsburg city hall. In a brief ceremony, we were married by the town clerk with Eugene and Jana Pohořelská serving as our witnesses: I had been the godfather of their son Viktor, who was born in the camp, and they were my closest friends.

Mašek left the town on our wedding day, but three weeks later he asked Romana to prepare a dinner for the three of us. I accepted his invitation with some misgivings, but Mašek chatted with both of us as if the previous antagonism had never happened. At the end of the unexpectedly pleasant evening he announced that we all ought to emigrate together "as one family." I could hardly believe my ears. As if stage-managed, the reconciliation was shortly followed by more good news: my former editor Herben, who by then lived in

New York, signed the necessary affidavit for Romana and me, which made us eligible for immigration.

Despite these encouraging developments, in one important aspect my last winter in the camp was as depressing as the previous one. The news from Prague continued to be bad. In November, the train smugglers brought a note from Mirek that both Mother and Dad were in bad shape. Adding to my distress and sense of guilt for their misfortune was a report from a former member of Dad's underground group who had fled to Germany and contacted me shortly before Christmas. He said that my father had been severely and repeatedly beaten by his interrogators, and that he was "a broken man."

It turned out to be my last Christmas as a DP. In February 1950 the visa for Mašek, Romana, and me came through, and we were all transferred to an embarkation camp in Hamburg to wait for an empty troop carrier to take us to the States. The Cold War was going full blast and US Army transports were bringing thousands of GIs to Europe to serve in the newly established bases of the North Atlantic Treaty Organization (NATO). On President Truman's orders, the empty ships picked up DPs when returning to the States.

Our crossing aboard the USAT *Gen. A. W. Greely* was so rough that the ship's propeller was one-third of the time out of the water, winds pushed us off course, and the normally weeklong crossing took eighteen days. Since we had no drugs against seasickness, most of us ate little or nothing until we reached terra firma. Otherwise, except for a glancing collision with another army transport in the foggy English Channel, the trip was uneventful. When I was not too seasick, I worked behind the counter of the ship's PX and helped put out the souvenir edition of the ship's journal.

Each refugee on board received six dollars as a gift from the American Red Cross, a sum that at contemporary prices translated into 120 candy bars, Cokes, or packs of chewing gum. In the PX we sold sodas, Hershey bars, Oh, Henry! bars, V8 juice, and wonder of wonders, nylon stockings for women. Every time the crazy sea calmed down enough for the PX to open, the store was mobbed by eager customers. By the time we pulled into New York harbor on a freezing cold morning of March 3, 1950, the PX wares were practically all sold out.

I saved the "Souvenir Edition of the USAT Gen. A. W. Greely Journal" for which I wrote—in capital letters for emphasis—the leading piece. It was my first published effort in English, and describing the DPs on board, I informed the reader that "WITHOUT ANY DOUBT, WE ARE STRANGE PEOPLE." What I meant to say was that we were no ordinary travelers, but the way it came out it was no abuse of the truth.

CHAPTER 8

AMERICA!

It is hard for me to write about my first years in the States without sounding sentimental. This is not an apology but, rather, a salute to the society that took me in and of which I was delighted and grateful to become a part. The America I encountered in 1950 was a country that was strong without arrogance: justifiably proud of its victories in World War II, self-confident about its impressive economic progress, and aware of its responsibility for saving democratic values from being extinguished by Stalin's brutal Soviet Union. To me, America exemplified the human decency that I so sorely missed under the two authoritarian regimes of my earlier years. And it was a society that gave me a home, after the Kremlin's Czech lackeys had made me homeless.

For America, the more than 620,000 postwar DPs were probably the last major wave of old-style European immigrants. We got off the boats empty-handed but overjoyed to be given a new chance, went to work without complaints or demands for entitlements, eagerly assimilated, and in most cases prospered. Becoming an American in those years meant far more than getting a passport of convenience and social benefits: it was a matter of honor and a privilege. It also meant making a special effort to belong, assuming new identity, and being deeply committed to the new country.

Individually and collectively, we experienced the true greatness of the United States. When Romana and I stood on the New York pier on March 3, 1950, waiting for customs to clear our wooden box with old clothing, I did not know a soul in the country except for Herben, my erstwhile boss, who himself was barely eking out a living at a down-at-the-heels newspaper for Czech émigrés. Our total financial resources were forty-two dollars, the sum of gifts from the Red Cross and from Romana's father. My English was at best shaky.

Yet eight years later, I was back in journalism, a dream I thought I would never see come alive again. I had a slightly different name: as part of my naturalization in 1954, I changed my name from Milan Bořivoj Kubík to Milan James Kubic, and everybody called me Mike. I felt I was part of the American mainstream, accepted or rejected on the same grounds as everyone else, which meant, primarily, on merit. I had a new self-confidence, a new future. It was part of my marvelous fortune to personally experience the thrill and optimism that Dvořák poured into his New World symphony.

I came to America enormously relieved to be out of Europe, a continent of bad memories, and it undoubtedly helped that I had no illusions about what to expect. The few books I read in the camps and the vile lies of Nazi propaganda aside, what I knew about life in the United States came mostly from the few American movies the Communist-run ministry of information allowed us to see after the war, and in those years it was recognized (and, in our drab environment, appreciated) that the products of Hollywood were mere fairy tales. Nobody thought that the gorgeously slender, posh secretaries and their boyfriends in tailored suits that never wrinkled had any connection with reality.

Romana and I were therefore ready to start from scratch, and the International Relief and Refugee Committee (IRRC), a Protestant agency that handled our resettlement, had a job for us. Herman J. Finder, a Chicago industrialist, had asked the agency to find for his home a butler and a maid and left the choice up to the IRRC representative in New York. He picked us. Finder even advanced the agency money for the couple's train fare, and soon my wife and I were on the way to Chicago.

My first boss in America, Finder is inscribed in my memory as a classic American millionaire. He was tall, robust, handsome, and totally self-assured. He wore big, dark-framed glasses that gave his massive face the looks of a thoughtful owl, and he had a young, slender second wife and a small son named Michael. A self-made man in his early sixties, Finder seemed to have everything the American dream offered in those postwar years, including a big pseudo-Greek mansion in Woodlawn, a parklike section in Chicago's South Side, a white yacht on Lake Michigan, and a brand new black Cadillac.

The boat—next to Michael—was Finder's great love. During most of the five months we worked in his house, Finder looked forward all week long to a sailing picnic on Sunday. His wife, a birdlike but resolute person, just as wholeheartedly loathed it. Returning home from a Sunday on the yacht, she would roll her eyes to the ceiling, cry out "Punishment!" or a similarly disdainful comment, and head for the privacy of her bedroom. Finder, who trailed her with an empty jug and a picnic basket, would puff on his cigar and look mad as a bear. Afterwards, he would go in the living room and neck with Betty, the slim Southern belle who took care of Michael.

Finder was the only person except for the Communists who ever fired me, but I respected him all the same. The son of Jewish immigrants, he told me that his first job, at the age of sixteen, was loading sand and stones in a quarry. By the time he hired us, he was the chairman of the board of Mohawk, a Midwestern paper company. Finder ate big meals, drank Scotch, was never sick, and when I asked him if I should buy health insurance for my wife and me, he looked at me as if I were nuts. "What do you want to get sick for?" he asked.

As I learned within a couple of days on the job, the butler in movies who serves drinks in the living room represents only the glamorous tip of the job, 90 percent of which consists of scrubbing a myriad of objects until they show no sign of human or environmental impact.

I started each day early by washing the black Cadillac, and ended it late in the evening by mopping the kitchen floor. In between, Romana and I cleaned all the rooms of the house, of which there were a great many. There were bathroom tiles to be washed, rugs to be vacuumed and shampooed, curtains to be taken down, laundered, ironed and rehung, walls to be sponged, windows to be washed, and furniture to be dusted and waxed. I did a lot of work on a stepladder, and even more on my knees.

In the afternoon, Romana suspended the cleaning activities and went downstairs to help Emily, the cook and head of the household staff, to prepare the meal for the family. At seven o'clock in the evening I dressed in a white jacket, black pants, and a black bow tie, all of which were about two sizes too big for me, and served the dinner. The ill-fitting clothing, originally bought for my husky predecessor, added to my unease when the Finders gave one of their frequent parties. I was so stiff and awkward fetching drinks that my boss would joke to his guests that I was struck by "Stage Fright," which was the title of a then-popular movie. He was right.

I was not a good butler. Since I did not know how to drive, I couldn't take the Cadillac out of the dark garage and check the polish in the broad daylight. As a result I missed dull spots that my boss was careful to note in the morning and comment on as reprehensible. I knew nothing about American appliances and gadgets, and I could not adequately communicate with Emily, my immediate supervisor, who had a heart of gold but also a deep Mississippi accent that hopelessly befuddled my untrained ears. Since Emily did not understand my Czech-accented, dictionary-English, we were like ships passing at night. Another problem I had with Emily was that she daily Scotch-taped her disintegrating house slippers. The stuff stuck to the kitchen floor and I had to scrape it off every night with a knife.

Betty, the fourth member of the household staff, kept pretty much to herself, devouring paperback mysteries. Her charge, however, was a different story. The boy was cute and the apple of his father's eye. Finder's secretary had a standing order each day to put a new toy in his pocket before he went home. Michael played with it for about three minutes before turning to something else. The abandoned toy would enter the ever-growing collection of playthings the boy scattered throughout the house, the garage, and the driveway. It was part of my job to help Betty find them and produce the one that Michael wanted to see again, sometimes days later. On his third birthday, the kid celebrated the occasion by emptying a pound of salt on the kitchen floor.

My career as a house servant was going nowhere when, in August 1950, it was terminated due to the lack of my own mailing address. Eager to do something more satisfying than sloshing water, I had written a couple of universities for information about their evening courses, and they responded with big envelopes stuffed with catalogues. When Finder found them in his mailbox, he charged me with disloyalty and gave Romana and me two weeks' notice. He was matter-of-fact, not angry or nasty, and I could not blame him for wanting a better butler. We parted without regrets or sore feelings. By then Finder had deducted from our pay the money we owed him for the railroad fare, but our bed and board had been free, and we had managed to save about two hundred dollars. We had no trouble finding a small apartment on Chicago's blue-collar West Side.

My second job in America was in an old dilapidated factory of the Overland Candy Company whose continued operation I could only attribute to the municipal inspectors' severe eyesight and hearing problems, or bribe-taking. It was another false start. At first, I ran a rattling old mixer where freshly baked malted balls were coated with fine starch powder to keep them from sticking together. The problem was that I wore glasses, and to be able to see anything, I had to keep running to the water faucet to wash off the powder that billowed over the mixer like a tropical rain cloud. This interfered with the speed at which I was able to load and offload the hot balls, thereby displeasing my foreman.

When I asked him for a powder-less job, he put me in the so-called kitchen, where I worked in tandem with a swarthy, thick-set Native American. Our job was to boil gallons of thick sugary syrup in huge copper vats, carry them across a wooden floor that constantly trembled from the running machinery, and dump the scalding-hot stuff into a mixer. It was still August, with outside temperatures in the hundreds. The kitchen had no air-conditioning; the gas burners were hot as hell, and my partner was about two inches shorter than I was, which made the hoisting of the vats and the sweaty walk across the shaking floor even more precarious. On top of everything, both the foreman and my sturdy partner insisted on my working ten to eleven hours a day, including Saturdays. The paychecks were relatively robust, but I was so exhausted that at the end of each day I had to sit on the sidewalk while waiting for the streetcar. After three weeks in the sweet-smelling purgatory, I quit.

After that my wife and I found jobs that put us on the right track. Romana became an assistant buyer for a big department store in the Chicago Loop. And I, ironically, got a new beginning thanks to the Korean War and a skill I had acquired during the Nazi Totaleinsatz. We were still at the Finders' at the end of June when the North Korean army crossed the 38th parallel and President Truman launched the United Nations–sanctioned "police action" to save South Korea. By the time I left the candy factory, two months later, orders from the Pentagon were pouring into the metalworking plants not far from our small apartment. The first shop I walked in to ask about a job, I was hired.

A foreman took me to a lathe and asked me to machine a small ring. It was a joke; the controls hardly differed from the equipment I had used at Avia. Ten minutes later I gave my name and address to a clerk in the office, and Gits Bros., a medium-sized manufacturer of lubricating devices, had a new lathe operator at $1.85 an hour. In those days that was not a bad wage—and I, no longer bent on sabotage, was not a bad lathe hand. With time out for a two-year military service, I worked for the company for almost eight years, full-time whenever I could, and part-time when I studied at the university.

Six months out of Jägerhof, Romana and I had begin to taste a slice of the good life, which on the West Side of Chicago was redolent with memories of my childhood. An enclave of "Bohemians," as the previous generations of Czech immigrants were called in the Windy City, the neighborhood stores abounded with local versions of Prague ham, Moravian sausages, crusty farm bread, and koláčky, a Czech pastry. For those who wanted to support the Communist-run Czech beer industry, there was even an ample supply of imported genuine Pilsner and Budweiser.

Czech language was in evidence everywhere, from the lawyers' shingles to the Sunday hymnals in West Side churches. The Jan Toman branch of the municipal library was full of books in Czech, including some thinly disguised propaganda donated by the Communist Ministry of Information in Prague. At Christmas the department stores resounded with the strains of Czech carols and "Good King Wenceslas." It was an environment created by immigrants who had come to the States in the early 1900s, and in some ways—especially the culinary ones—Romana and I found it congenial.

After a while, however, the enduring ethnicity of the old immigrants became hard to take. The Czech-language Chicago newspapers—for some of which I used to write in the refugee camps—were full of idealized reminiscences of Czech rural life before World War I. The émigré societies were steeped in the romantic patriotism of the Habsburg era, when the Czechs were fighting for independence after three hundred years of Austrian rule. And some old-timers even regarded the Communist regimes in Eastern Europe as an expression of pan-Slavism. Pan-Slavism was a nineteenth-century movement preaching the unity of all Slavic nations, an idea that Marxists denounced as petty bourgeois.

None of these sentiments had anything to do with the immigrants' own lives in America. The "Bohemians," mostly plain, hardworking folk, were stragglers between a Czech past that no longer existed and an American present they were reluctant or unable to enter. They were like the White Russian émigrés in Paris—but without their money, the pictures of Czar Alexander, and the silver-plated samovars.

One evening, Romana and I were invited to one of the Czech clubs for an "entertainment" that consisted of nine aging men marching in a circle and singing Czech songs. Watching them and their misty-eyed audience, I reflected on my own sense of detachment. As best as I could pinpoint it, my emotional ties with my homeland had snapped the day I walked out of my office in Klatovy and in a daze made my way back to Prague.

Emotionally unencumbered, I was eager to get to know America, and I liked most of what I saw. My wife and I began making the customary down payments on a used car, TV, and assorted gadgetry. We discovered pizza, popcorn, apple pie, and the world's best ice cream. Along with what seemed like everybody else in Chicago, we took long Sunday rides to the countryside and picnicked under the magnificent trees in the nearby Morton's Arboretum. We acquired a badly needed new wardrobe.

One of my strong early impressions came from contacts with the authorities, such as getting a driver's license or a social security number. In my childhood, relations between ordinary people and bureaucrats were part of the heritage of the Habsburg era, when Czech subjects facing German-speaking factotums were supposed to quake. Officious snarling was de rigueur, and any ordinary citizen's statement not supported by stamped documents was assumed to be a lie. It was one of my great thrills as a new immigrant to learn that in America, the presumption was just the opposite. Nobody ever wanted to see my birth certificate, immigrant's ID card, or that document that had been inseparable from every contact with the bureaucracy during and after the Nazi occupation, a certificate of clean police record. Civil servants in Chicago were actually civil. Despite my status as an alien, I felt for the first time treated like a citizen.

My contacts with ordinary Americans were also surprisingly easy. I was very much an oddball among the Gits Bros. lathe hands, who were about equally divided between second- or third-generation "Bohemians" from nearby neighborhoods and blacks from the South Side of Chicago. My English was still basic and my total disinterest in baseball and football left me outside most lunchtime conversations. Yet my relationship with the factory hands was unburdened by the palpable tensions that used to separate me from the class-conscious "noblemen" at Avia. Chuck Kiedaish, my setup man, and I became friends and exchanged letters at Christmas for almost two decades after I left the factory.

One thing I particularly appreciated about my fellow workers was their apolitical attitude. They read the sports section of the ultra-conservative *Chicago Tribune*, voted a straight Democratic ticket, and, except at election time, it was impossible to make them discuss politics. On a couple of occasions when the lunchtime weather was good and a bunch of us sat in the sun outside the plant munching sandwiches, I tried to explore their reaction to some of the ideological pap the Communists fed factory workers in postwar Czechoslovakia. The looks I drew were so blank that I hastily dropped the subject. At Gits Bros., the dictatorship of the proletariat did not sell.

Another early impression was of our first American Thanksgiving. A young couple who lived on the floor below Romana and me—Bob Schutt, a railroad worker, and his wife, Ruth, a librarian—invited us for the traditional turkey dinner a couple of days after we met them on the stairs of our apartment building. Nothing momentous transpired: we chatted about Europe, our hosts chatted about America, and I took my first and last bite of a pumpkin pie. What to me made the afternoon special was its uniquely American character—a relaxed and friendly get-together of people who barely knew one another. When I later learned that both Bob and Ruth had advanced college degrees, I was doubly impressed. In Europe, university-educated people did not ride the caboose and did not mingle with blue-collar immigrants.

None of these early American experiences influenced me and my future so profoundly as the Korean War draft and the two years I spent in the US Army. I was not an enthusiastic soldier like my Dad. I did not like to wear the uniform, and I loathed the pecking order and the by-the-numbers rigmarole that was euphemistically called "the army way" of doing things. I griped about the many restrictions on my personal freedom and avidly counted the days till I would return to civilian life. In short, I was just another GI.

But after I left the army I recognized that it had made two major contributions to my development. One was physical fitness and endurance. As a 130-pound urban-bred non-athlete, I took pride in my ability to tolerate the army's exhausting physical training and the grind of hard work; physical exercise and a can-do attitude became my lasting assets. The other, and even greater, gain

I brought home from the army was a new sense of being an American. It was my service in the army, more than anything else, that made me feel equal and at home in the United States.

My army experience followed a routine that is familiar to millions of GIs. Late in the fall of 1951, the mailman brought me the customary "greetings" from my "friends and neighbors" on the draft board, and shortly after Christmas I reported for a preinduction physical at a Navy Pier recruiting center. That chore over, a bunch of us in skivvies took the requisite step forward, thereby pledging to defend the Constitution and the colors. In recent years I've read allegations that the Korean War draft met a resistance similar to Vietnam. As a GI, I never encountered the slightest hint of it. In the group with which I was sworn in, about half a dozen husky youngsters even volunteered for the Marines.

Basic training, which started in mid-January 1952, was, as the commanding general promised us when we arrived, tough. Camp Breckenridge in Kentucky, the home of the 101st division of D-day fame, consisted of bleak rows of aging clapboard barracks flanked by dusty drill areas and, outside the gates, beer joints, whorehouses, and assorted honky-tonks. Between the blocks of barracks, equally dismal-looking PX shops sold ice cream, 2 percent beer, and shoe polish and offered the services of a barbershop with a sign advising patrons that for the fifty-cent standard fee they were entitled to "three minutes in the chair." The camp also included a couple of fenced-in stockades and a few movie houses that showed some of the worst cultural atrocities ever perpetrated by Hollywood.

The background was bleak, but the quality of the training provided by the "Screaming Eagles" cadre was tops. Sergeants are the almighty gods-in-residence of every training outfit, and most of ours were World War II paratroopers determined to live up to their glorified image in the comic strips. My company's top kick, for example, was an enormously fit-looking specimen with a Ukrainian name and an incredibly neat foot locker and bunk. His other distinguishing features were boots shined to a mirror and a disdain for any recruit who would dare approach him with a grin on his face. The sergeant's response to such unseemly sentiment was a curt warning, delivered in threatening voice, "Never smile at me unless you're a woman." When he wore the dress uniform, which was rarely, his chest was full of combat medals.

Our cadre were expert at reducing recruits to utter physical wrecks and then remolding them into what the army called "fighting men." We drilled and drilled and double timed and double timed. When we thought we could not take another step, the noncoms would make us run like the possessed and shriek "Yessir!" when they asked if we were happy and "Nosir!" when they asked if we were tired. Horseplay was encouraged whenever we paused in drilling, and the minimum punishment for anything was twenty push-ups. KP—the dreaded nonstop mess-hall and kitchen detail—started at four o'clock in the morning and ended twenty-one hours later. We griped in the best GI tradition, but we also realized that physical toughness was a key to survival in Korea. There were no AWOLs and very few goof-offs in our unit.

After four months of push-ups, side-straddle hops, and what seemed like no sleep at all, I felt mean enough to sign up for airborne training. The army deemed otherwise—the five members of my platoon who were accepted were far more husky than I was—and thereby changed my life. At the end of summer 1952, practically my entire outfit was shipped to Korea. The mission was to stop the Chinese troops who were pouring into North Korea across the Yalu River after General MacArthur overplayed his hand and pushed too far north. As one of my buddies later wrote me, one-third of our training company became casualties within a couple of weeks at the front.

I was spared by an alert one-stripe PFC who spotted in my documents the results of several foreign language tests I had taken in the induction center. In addition to Czech, Slovak, and German I had groped my way through Polish and French. It was no great linguistic accomplishment, because the three Slavic languages share many similarities, but the total of five languages looked, I guess, impressive.

GIs with Central and Eastern European languages were in demand. The Cold War was in full swing, and army linguists were in far shorter supply than infantrymen or paratroopers. As a result instead of sailing for Korea, I was shipped—aboard the same type of troop transport that had brought me to America only two years earlier—to Livorno in northern Italy. There, in a reception center a chunky army major handed me a piece of paper and pencil and told me to describe what I saw. I wrote out two paragraphs speculating on who scratched the desk at which I sat, and why. The major read my little composition, nodded, and told me I was assigned to a military intelligence unit in Linz, Austria. We left by train the next morning.

My sixteen months with Company B of the 533rd Military Intelligence Service (MIS) battalion were a seminal piece of good fortune. Instead of dodging bullets in Korea, I was given a desk job in a small unit that collected information about Soviet satellite countries. The creature comforts were well above the army norm—for example, we each had our own room, and the abominable KP was pulled by hired employees. The work was challenging and interesting, occasionally very much so. I found myself in the company of bright and well-educated people. I was twice promoted, and I did not even have to wear the uniform. The army put me in civilian clothing.

Moreover, the intelligence work did for my intellectual self-confidence what the Camp Breckenridge noncoms had done for my physical stamina. It gave me the morale boost I needed to try for a return to journalism.

The desire to go back to the news business had always lingered in the back of my mind, but after I escaped to Germany it seemed to be a hopeless illusion. I doubted I could ever hone my English to the precision required for reporting. Even more important, I could not believe I could ever make up for the twenty years of growing up in America that I had missed. Where I came from, newsmen were supposed to be deeply rooted in their native land's traditions and spirit, and I believed that for an immigrant such intimacy was out of reach. The army tour in Austria gave me a new and more hopeful perspective.

My main job was to interrogate selected refugees from behind the Iron Curtain and write detailed reports about what they had told me. Producing thousands of words every week and rereading them after they had been edited by fellow GIs who were college grads was a great boon for my self-taught English. Translating from one vernacular to another with the sort of accuracy that was required of us was a real challenge, but it paid off. The more I did of it, the more I developed a feeling for the beauty and rhythm of the English sentence. Moreover, I had time to take a correspondence course in American history and do reading that dispelled my European assumptions about American journalism. I learned, for example, that Joseph Pulitzer was a Hungarian immigrant, and that some of the most perceptive reporting about America had been done by Alexis de Tocqueville, a Frenchman.

I also drew encouragement from working closely with the sort of people whose performance I knew I would have to match if I was to advance from the lathe department at Gits Bros. Our unit was an excellent proving ground. In addition to the GI editors and a few foreign-born linguists like me, our company consisted of World War II field-rank officers who had been recalled to active duty after the Korean War started and had undergone intensive linguistic training. Working with them on a daily basis, they impressed me as being a great deal more competent than the CIC bunglers we used to laugh at in the DP camps.

Since I thought so well of them, I was greatly encouraged by the results of a three-week intelligence course that was required for all new members of the unit. I finished with the highest score, ahead of about twenty enlisted men and officers, including Major Allen, an affable Georgian who was my section chief. I suspected that I had taken the course more seriously than the rest of the students, who probably did not share my pressure to prove themselves. Still, the message I got was that if I worked hard enough, perhaps I could start thinking the unthinkable.

CHAPTER 8

What gave me the final push was Joe McCarthy, the bête noire of the American politics of the 1950s. I must confess that I never fully understood the hysterical alarums the junior senator from Wisconsin inspired in American living rooms and media. There was no question that McCarthy was an unsavory wart on the otherwise sturdy American body politic. But after seeing real political heavies cracking democratic institutions like walnuts, McCarthy struck me as a flashy but essentially pathetic demagogue—a right-wing Don Quixote who had some nuisance value but not much else. In a country whose love affair with liberty and democracy had survived the Civil War and the Great Depression, a mean and execrable creature like McCarthy was no real menace. I saw him as a temporary phenomenon that would self-destruct long before he could rock a ship as big and solid as the United States.

Still, watching McCarthy's antics brought back some of my worst political memories. His insistence on repeating the same lies over and over echoed Goebbels, and his ominous and undocumented accusations reminded me of the postwar tactics used by Gottwald and Nosek. And as luck would have it, just as I got comfortable in my job with the 533rd, McCarthyism also affected me personally. It happened in the summer of 1953, when the Wisconsin senator dispatched his two junior sidekicks, Roy Cohn and David Schine, to GI bases in Europe with a mission to ferret out hidden Communists.

It was purely a headline-fishing expedition because there were no commies in the three services, but the junket triggered an army probe of its security procedures. The upshot was a discovery that three foreign-born non-citizens in our battalion did classified work for which we could not be cleared, and thus were potential game for McCarthy's spy hunt. In fact, we were a security menace in more ways than one. In the first place, the presence of the 533rd in Austria was not sanctioned in the four-power occupation agreement—that's why we wore civilian clothing—and therefore the likes of the three of us were not supposed to even know about it. (Incidentally, a Red Army intelligence outfit then stationed in Vienna was just as unauthorized as we were.)

Even worse, some of the information my two Czech-speaking colleagues and I collected from political refugees was exceptionally sensitive. This was particularly the case with our unit's foremost intelligence target, the Jáchymov uranium mines in Bohemia, whose entire production was being shipped to the Soviet Union. Since anything bearing on the Russian atomic bomb development was of the highest intelligence interest, debriefing a Jáchymov engineer about the mines' output, or the town's station master about the ore shipments, was for our unit a feather in the cap. Such reports were rapidly edited, stamped "Top Secret," and rushed to our intelligence bosses in Washington.

The Catch 22 was that were Cohn and Shine to find out that the interviewing had been done by three GIs with no security clearance, some heads would have had to roll. Clearly, something had to be done, and just before the gumshoes arrived in Europe, it was. Disregarding as inconsequential the fact that one of us could not drive at all and the other two (including me) had never driven a truck, our battalion commander sent all three of us to an army base near Linz to take a two-week course in truck driving under combat conditions.

I realized that the commander did the prudent thing, and I did not blame him personally for making me drive, utterly terrified, a huge six-wheeler with no lights at night over narrow winding roads in the Alps. I was sure that had the spy-chase taken place during a less nerve-wracking army course (say, on baking doughnuts), the lieutenant colonel would have sent us to learn how to make doughnuts. But seeing the proud US Army that had taken on both Hitler and the Japanese emperor quake before two junior publicity hounds made me cringe. Now I really wanted to return to my old profession and take another crack at covering politics.

By the time the army brought me back to the States and gave me a discharge, in January 1954, I knew pretty well what my next step should be—it was to go back to school and get a degree in journalism. But I was still equivocating: I was already twenty-seven years old, with no resources to fall back on, and four years in college seemed like a long time to wait before getting a real job. When I got out of the army, I decided to return to my lathe at the Gits Bros., and make just one try for the brass ring without a sheepskin.

One spring morning I took a few hours off from work, and clutching samples of my writing and an album with pictures I had taken in Europe, I called on Isaac Gershman, the manager of the Chicago City News Service. CNS was a well-run local wire service that paid peanuts but provided good training to young journalists, most of whom went on to be hired by Chicago and Midwestern newspapers. I remember Gershman as an old man with thick glasses and a face that was both kind and wise. He saw me right away—in those days, it was still possible to see even busy people without an appointment—but he hardly looked at the proferred examples of my excellence.

"That's not the way to do it," he said, squinting at me through his glasses and disapprovingly shaking his head. "Go to a journalism school and get a degree. It's like a union card; you have to have it to get a job anywhere. Then, come back."

I took his advice but still hedged my bets. I first enrolled at the University of Illinois and took two years of business administration, just in case it should turn out that my ambition exceeded my reach. When I finished the two years with straight As, I transferred to the Medill School of Journalism at Northwestern University in the Chicago suburb of Evanston.

I had my hands full: I carried more than a full schedule, worked part-time at Gits Bros., and commuted daily to the campus that was as far from our West Side home as Avia had been from our house in Prague. But hard work aside, things were looking up. Romana was working full-time, my GI Bill of Rights paid most of the tuition, and on top of that, Medill gave me a scholarship. While I went to school we not only bought our first new car—a nineteen-hundred-dollar Plymouth that fell apart in two years—but we even took a three- to-four-week vacation every summer camping in the Rockies.

Scholastically, I certainly could have spent the time better. I had only one memorable teacher, Jacob Scher, who taught several courses in journalism at Medill. He was a committed liberal and a passionate believer in the freedom of the press. Journalism, he forcefully argued, was the free society's most potent rampart against oppression. To do the job well, Scher taught us, called for more than good English and technical skill: it required integrity, judgment, and courage. Scher preached what I sensed as a cub reporter in Klatovy: journalism was not about making a career behind a typewriter but about being one of society's watchdogs.

But if Scher was inspiring, the rest of the journalism classes left me cold. One of Scher's colleagues insisted on teaching us how to use the California job case, an archaic printer's device that belonged in a museum. Another teacher praised as the height of "professionalism" the ability to argue with equal conviction opposing sides of the same issue. I soon came to the conclusion that except for Scher, I would have done better taking a degree in political science or history.

But in the end, Gershman was proven right. About a week before I graduated in the spring of 1958, Malcolm Muir Jr., then the managing editor of *Newsweek* magazine, made a tour of the nation's six leading journalism schools to interview the top graduates interested in a summer job. At Medill, I was the top grad. "Mack" Muir and I had the usual awkward conversation between a potential employer and a would-be employee. Its nadir came when he asked—twice—what was my "strong suit" as a journalist.

Since talking about my work for the *Svobodné Slovo* sounded too complicated and I had no expertise on American politics, all I said was that I was totally unsuited to be a sportswriter. I parted from Muir convinced that I had blown my great chance and resumed working full-time at Gits Bros. Two weeks later I got a letter from Muir asking me to report on a tryout basis to the Chicago bureau of the magazine.

I was hired. I was already thirty years old and my salary was eighty dollars a week, but I knew where I was headed, and the door was open.

PART II

CHAPTER 9

ON THE STAFF OF NEWSWEEK

Journalism sinks many hooks in its practitioners, and in my case, most of them were firmly in place by the time I left Klatovy. I had learned that for a reporter there is no humdrum routine. Whenever anything became boring, it was a signal I should be doing something else. I had also learned that events and newsmen are locked together in a race with no letup or time out. Reporting is hard work, but I thrived on the round-the-clock hustle and the sense of purpose that went with it. I liked the job's greatest prize and its punishment, which is the readers' approval or criticism of a published article. The morning's judgments of the previous night's work are a Damocles's sword over every journalist's head, but also his or her distinction as a public person.

I had learned already in Klatovy that reporting is not a job but a way of life. But it was only in Washington, DC, where I was transferred after five months in *Newsweek*'s bureau in Chicago, that I was introduced to another heady inducement of the trade: the company of elites.

In January 1959, when I first reported to Ken Crawford, my new bureau chief, the American Century was at its zenith. As the popular lore had it, the United States was by far the world's leading economic and military power and the biggest creditor nation on earth. American industrial and technological supremacy were undisputed; its Protestant work ethic was intact; the already high standard of living was rapidly rising; and the moral renaissance of the Civil Rights crusade was in the air. Government was run by some of the nation's best and brightest; politicians were respected; and the presidency, in Dwight D. Eisenhower's words, was "cleaner than a hound's tooth." All this made Washington the world's most important news center and the coveted Mecca of journalism. A transfer to the nation's capital was heady stuff even for a seasoned pro; for a legman less than nine years out of a DP camp, it was a thrill beyond my wildest dreams.

It's not that reporting from Chicago was without excitement. On one of the stories I covered, for example, I met two prominent figures of the world of grand opera. In the fall of 1958, the Soviets responded to a brief thaw in the Cold War by sending to Chicago Kyril Petrovich Kondrashin, the conductor of the Bolshoi Opera in Moscow, for a few guest appearances in *Madame Butterfly*. Such was the state of US-Soviet relations that Kondrashin's direction of music that included the motif of the American national anthem was regarded as an important diplomatic signal and therefore rated news coverage.

I did the story for *Newsweek* and found it doubly fascinating. The three days I spent with Kondrashin during the rehearsals filled me with awe at the extraordinary talent—not to mention the profuse sweat and stamina—that goes into a major opera performance. One spell-bounding experience was standing next to Renata Tebaldi when the great diva and Kondrashin held a piano rehearsal. When the famous soprano switched from sotto voce to full voice, the windows of the small room literally shook as if hit by a hurricane. Even for a musical ignoramus like me, the power and purity of Tebaldi's voice were out of this world.

Music aside, the best part of trailing Kondrashin was getting to know him and Nikita Sanikov, his young official interpreter, who had never been outside the Iron Curtain. Kondrashin was friendly, intelligent, and sensitive and enjoyed the Chicago scene so thoroughly that I was sure he was not an enthusiastic admirer of the Soviet regime. Sanikov, to my big surprise, was not a KGB type, either, although his standing in the eyes of that agency obviously was good enough to let him to travel outside the Soviet Union. He was a bright, pleasant guy about my age who told me he had learned English entirely from books and recordings and got most of his information about Chicago from Upton Sinclair's muckraking book *The Jungle*, which was published in 1906.

Nikita soon began questioning the differences between what he saw and Sinclair's 1906 exposé, and toward the end of his visit he asked me to show him how the Chicago "proletariat" really lived. We agreed that a public housing project was a good place to start, and on Saturday morning we drove to one of the grim high-rise buildings on Chicago's predominantly black South Side. We got on the elevator and Sanikov picked a floor. I rang the bell at couple of apartments and asked whoever answered if they would show their home to a Soviet visitor.

Today, an excursion of this sort would be at least in poor taste and possibly risky, but in late 1950s the Cold War trumped racial tensions, and the folks we dropped in on were cheerful and cooperative. Sanikov asked questions about salaries and the standard of living and received answers reflecting the relatively good income of our hosts. Both apartments contained the full array of electric appliances and gadgets of a typical American household, and one of the families boasted two TV sets. At that time, even the Finders had only one. Another impressive sight was of the building's parking lot, where residents were washing their reasonably recent-vintage products of Detroit.

When we left the project Sanikov, after a few minutes of silence, asked me if I could drive him somewhere outside the city. I took him to the campus of my alma mater, the Northwestern University, and we walked together to the edge of Lake Michigan. Sanikov squatted down and for a long while looked intently at the water. Then he said, slowly and distinctly, "This is the first time since I've left Moscow that I feel I am in touch with reality."

I was impressed by his integrity and courage. In those years, it was a very bold act indeed for a Soviet citizen to be frank with a foreigner. After Kondrashin and Sanikov left the States, they mailed me a letter from the Orly airport in France, their last stop in the West before landing in Moscow. The letter said, in essence, "Don't write to us." Their caution was hardly necessary—I was not corresponding even with my own parents or Mirek for fear of bringing upon them the wrath of the state police.

I stayed in Chicago only six months as a result of a disaster. At 2:40 p.m. on a cold and clear Monday in early December 1958, Our Lady of the Angels, a fifty-year-old parochial elementary school on Chicago's West Side caught fire that, according to first radio reports from the scene, killed at least eighty-seven small children and three nuns. It was an enormous tragedy that on any other weekday would have been covered by the bureau chief—except that for a newsweekly, what happens on Monday is a nonstory. By Saturday, when the magazine goes to press, the event is usually spiked as too old. As the junior member of the bureau, I was told to do the presumably doomed story, just in case.

By the time I reached the scene, the toll of dead children had climbed past a hundred, and by next morning it was, as I remember, over two hundred. I had three-and-a-half days to weave the eyewitness accounts of nuns, firemen, parents, and children into a "tick-tock," a minute-by-minute chronology of the inferno, and the magazine spread it on two pages. I even got a byline, at a time when *Newsweek* bylines were a great rarity. A few days later, the brass in the New York headquarters of the magazine picked me as a new hand to send to the prestigious bureau in Washington.

I left Chicago and entered an impressive environment of real talent and savvy, not to mention big egos and vanity. The *Newsweek* bureau in Washington was at that time only about a dozen strong, and our quarters were a string of modest rooms on the twelfth floor of the then run-down National Press Club building at 14th and F Street—a far cry from the posh suite a block from the White House where the bureau moved years later. But if the surroundings were unimpressive, the bureau staff and atmosphere were first rate. They were an example of what was called—in those years, admiringly—the "Washington Establishment," an elite I quickly learned to respect and admire.

There was, first and foremost, the bureau chief Ken Crawford. All publications put their best foot forward in picking their top man for Washington, and a good deal about the Fourth Estate's values can be gathered from the character and ability of the media bureau chiefs in the nation's capital. Crawford, slender, tall, and craggily handsome, was a thoroughly decent person, a great boss, and a first-class professional totally dedicated to the integrity of his craft.

There were no smooth edges on Ken Crawford. His PR quotient was close to zero, his small talk negligible, his suits rumpled, and his TV manners so painfully uptight that when he was recruited to do commentary for the *Washington Post*-owned TV station, I could not bear to watch him. But among the people who knew him best—his crew of veteran reporters, who could smell a phony all the way to Baltimore—Ken had the stature of an Olympian deity.

His career was legendary. Before coming to *Newsweek*, he had labored first in the underpaid sweatshop of the old United Press, and later the equally stingy *New York Daily News*. During World War II, his datelines included the North African battlefields and the beaches of Normandy, where he landed with one of the first waves of the invasion. It did not hurt Crawford's reputation that he had been one of Ernest Hemingway's drinking buddies in the bars of liberated Paris and that, after the war, he fought and won his own war against alcoholism. By the time I was assigned to his bureau, Crawford was known as one of the handful of journalists who enjoyed the personal respect of both Presidents Truman and Eisenhower.

He had a brass spittoon under his desk and a beaten-up old Underwood on which he pounded out his weekly reports or "files," as we called them. Later, he wrote a weekly column. In the informal atmosphere Ken maintained in the bureau, we all read each other's copy. His was triple-spaced, most every adverb or adjective was changed once or twice, and he hit the keys so hard his *o*s cut a hole in the paper. Crawford wrote the way a smith works a piece of hot iron, hammering and rehammering every sentence until it said precisely what he wanted.

Best of all, he was a paragon of personal integrity. He was unafraid, uncorrupted, and unimpressed by the trappings of power. I learned about that after I interviewed Arthur Summerfield, a Republican biggie and Eisenhower's postmaster general, for a cover story on the US mail system. I did not write an admiring piece and when the story came out, Summerfield called me up and gave me hell. When I mentioned it to Ken, he got Summerfield on the phone and chewed him out like a lance corporal. "You've got a complaint, you call me," Crawford snarled at the Republican heavyweight. "I resent it when people try to intimidate my reporters."

It took a man of Crawford's caliber to win the respect of the "troops," as he sometimes called his staff. Except for me and Ward Just, another newcomer (who went on to become a successful author of several novels), the bureau was made up of old Washington hands who were not shrinking violets. My favorite prima donna was Teddy Weintal, the diplomatic correspondent and a superb linguist who came to Washington in the 1930s as an Oxford-educated Polish diplomat. When Hitler and Stalin swallowed his country, he resigned and later joined *Newsweek*.

Teddy, a courtly bachelor, was a quintessential Washington insider who wore out a tuxedo every couple of years by attending parties and dining with ambassadors and foreign policy makers. A typical Weintal feat was a small dinner in his Georgetown house whose guests included Christian Herter, Eisenhower's secretary of state, the same day he returned from his first official visit to Moscow. Given the paucity of top-level US-Soviet contacts at the time, Herter on that particular evening was undoubtedly the most sought-after dinner guest in the capital. The fact that he accepted the invitation spoke volumes about Teddy's standing.

Another superb professional was Ben Bradlee, who happened to be a close friend of then-senator John F. Kennedy. Ben was a genial comrade-at-arms, a warm human being, and an outstanding wordsmith. He succeeded Ken Crawford as the bureau chief before becoming the editor of the *Washington Post*, a job in which he made journalistic history by his gutsy publishing of the exposé of the Watergate scandal that led to the resignation of President Nixon.

Sam Shaffer, the bureau's chief congressional correspondent, by the end of the 1950s had covered the Hill longer than anybody else in town and was recognized as a walking encyclopedia of American politics. He was also a man of great erudition and an accomplished musician who played flute in a quartet that included a couple of senior senators. A heavyweight fact finder who knew more about Lyndon Johnson's machinations than anyone else in the media, Sam was also one of the Senate's most popular figures. When in 1960 Senator Hubert Humphrey announced in the press gallery his bid for the Democratic nomination for President, he only half-jokingly added that if elected he would let Sam Shaffer use the White House swimming pool.

The bureau's top Russian expert was another media celebrity. Leon Volkov was a former colonel in the Soviet air force who in the late 1940s was sent on a mission to Paris, whereupon he deserted and offered his services to the CIA.

Leon had a photographic memory that made him so prodigiously informative that the agency spent a whole year debriefing him before it spread the word in Washington that Volkov would make a fine reporter. Crawford hired him to write columns about Kremlin's impenetrable politics, and Leon handled the impossible task so well that he remained Washington's most-sought-after Kremlinologist even after he predicted the demise of Georgy Malenkov the very same week he succeeded Stalin.

I was personally closest to Weintal, Shaffer, and Volkov, but this did not diminish my admiration for the rest of Crawford's "troops," who became my role models. Lloyd Norman, the bureau's veteran Pentagon correspondent, produced a clean scoop every week. Bart Rowen was a top economic writer and analyst who later became a *Washington Post* columnist. Hank Simmons, the bureau's scientific reporter, shocked a nationally televised press conference about the first US space shot by disputing some of the officially announced figures—and he turned out to be right.

In short, in Washington I felt I was in a journalistic heaven. When, a few months after my arrival, Ken Crawford took me to the Press Club for breakfast to tell me I had become "one of the pillars" of the bureau, I was torn between triumph and disbelief.

~

My first regular beat in Washington, the Senate hearings, only increased my admiration for the capital. The immodestly self-styled "world's most exclusive deliberative body," the US Senate at the end of the 1950s was full of towering personalities. It's hard to say who was the most impressive because they stood out in different ways.

My favorite character was Everett Dirksen, the witty, craggy-faced Illinois Republican who was the minority leader. A sensible middle-of-the-road politician with perpetually tousled hair that gave him the looks of a violin virtuoso, Dirksen was probably the finest American orator since William Jennings Brian. From time to time he would walk into the Senate press room, climb on a desk, and deliver in his wheezing voice off-the-cuff briefings that were verbal masterpieces. Dirksen's attacks on his political opponents were so funny, pugnacious, and chock-full of delightful bon mots that I could hardly concentrate on his political message. In my experience only Abba Eban, the great orator of Israel, came anywhere close to Dirksen's silver tongue, though Abba Eban was no match for his wit.

Hubert Humphrey, another colorful figure I liked as a person as well as a politician, was so full of ideas that he had something intelligent to say on almost anything. I would call him up for comments on the nuttiest subjects, including women's hats and hula-hoops. Nice guy that he was, he would always call back and come up with a quote I could use.

Lyndon B. Johnson, the majority leader, was hardly my favorite source, but this did not detract from my appreciation of him as a politician. Johnson was enormously effective, and his skill and cunning as the Senate wheeler-dealer was a Washington legend. What added to his aura of power, if not popularity, was that he was also secretive, domineering, vindictive, and ridiculously sensitive to the slightest perceived slight.

In one incident that stands out in my memory, Johnson made Sam Shaffer, who had a heart condition, get down on his knees and in full view of the Senate gallery examine Johnson's wrist. The reason for this humiliation was Sam's article that mentioned Johnson's gold cuff links, a bit of information Johnson did not care to share with his Texas constituency. The morning the story came out, Johnson, sitting as usual in the majority leader's chair on the floor of the Senate, started his regular press briefing by stretching his arm below his knee and bidding Sam to take a look at his cuff links. Of course, this time they were not made of gold.

In a more positive way, I was also greatly impressed by John McClellan, who fought labor racketeers with every grim ounce of his spare body. Watching his performance in the hearings, I always felt that unlike Lyndon Johnson, who was first and foremost a politician, McClellan's political persona was secondary to his primary talent and inclination, which was that of a prosecuting attorney. In a place overflowing with political theatrics and egos, McClellan's unpretentious and edgy presence made me feel that with senators like him, the republic was in good hands.

And coming up behind the senior celebrities there was a whole flock of bright new faces elected in the Democratic sweep in 1958—senators like Frank Church, William Proxmire and Edmund Muskie. After my first few weeks in the periodic press gallery, I concluded that all senators—except for John Pastore, who was very short—were over six feet tall; six out of ten were millionaires; and about one out of six was a potential presidential candidate.

The charisma of John F. Kennedy—"Jack," as he was then called by the press corps—particularly exceeded everything in my previous experience. I was by no means one of his favorite reporters, and in common with other legmen on the Hill I had no use for his prickly sensitivity to media criticism. Once I showed him a page-long story that was easily 80 percent favorable to his handling of the hearings on the Kennedy-Ives Labor bill, which was one of his stepping stones to the nomination for president. Kennedy—who, like Proxmire, was a speed reader—took just a few seconds to spot two paragraphs where I quoted his Republican opponents. Kennedy's face froze, he dropped the magazine on the desk of his secretary and charged out of the office snapping, "I disagree." Humility was definitely not among JFK's virtues.

But like practically all of my Washington colleagues I was far from immune from what Ben Bradlee in his first book about Kennedy called "that special grace." The senator's style was precisely the opposite of Summerfield's. He kept aloof, but his charisma was such that his mere presence filled the room with tension. Kennedy's effect on even sophisticated audiences approached mass hypnosis. He did not smile easily, but when he did—whether at a chichi cocktail party or in a hearing room packed with hard-nosed newsmen—all faces would light up.

I wish I could claim that Kennedy's enormous personal magnetism did not affect my reporting in the fall of 1960 when I took turns covering his and Richard Nixon's election campaigns. It certainly did. One incident I am not proud of took place after one of the Kennedy-Nixon debates on television. As he was leaving the studio, the vice president hung back with a cluster of us reporters and suddenly bent over and pulled up his trouser to show us his bandaged knee. He had banged it against the door of a car, Nixon explained, and it was causing him considerable discomfort.

It was a typically awkward Nixonian gesture, an abrupt and embarrassing bid for our sympathy. Still, the man's injured knee added to the awful strain of a race for the White House, and that deserved a fair reflection before I wrote my file. Yet my sole reaction was resentment. My only thought was that Kennedy had never complained about his own health, though the campaign must have worsened the terrible backaches caused by his wartime injury.

In retrospect, my four and half years in Washington taught me some valuable lessons. One was that, given strong leadership, Congress could tackle an astounding variety of issues and dispose of most of them in a responsible fashion. A star example was President Eisenhower's Interstate Highway system. The enormous project had bilateral support although it was partly financed by funds from the defense budget, which was a very controversial issue at the height of the Cold War.

The Hill gave me also a standard for taking a measure of political leaders, which is one of the more critical and difficult tasks when reporting from abroad. The Czech Communists were stellar examples of qualities that did not inspire respect and following; now, the work on the Hill brought me close to the most impressive political leaders I was ever to meet. Some of them—Lyndon Johnson, John and Bobby Kennedy, or John McClellan—became my yardsticks for the personalities I later covered abroad.

And working in Washington also taught me about the power of the White House to shape public opinion. It was a phenomenon that puzzled me when I heard Bill White, Roscoe Drummond, and other top newspaper opinion makers criticizing—sometimes, severely—President Eisenhower's performance following his press conference. The next morning, what generally came across from their columns was that the country's business was competently managed, and that everybody liked Ike.

I first assumed that the columnists' about-face reflected the aura of respect that in those years shrouded the US presidency. But after I was assigned to cover Eisenhower's last three months in the White House, I found an additional explanation for this paradox. It was Jim Hagerty, Eisenhower's astute press secretary.

At first sight, Jim was a likable, unpretentious Irishman with the genial manners of one of the boys in the press room. But as I quickly learned, Hagerty's back-slapping arm was connected to an iron hand and his bonhomie disguised an accomplished spinmeister. Even in the lame-duck period of Ike's incumbency, Jim never relaxed his cardinal rule: he was the sole gatekeeper in the White House, and all paths to information in the building ran through his office.

For a newcomer like me in particular, all doors in the West Wing and the Executive Office building were locked unless Jim Hagerty deemed otherwise. Since I had to produce a weekly report on the presidency, in no time at all I found myself standing in line with most of the rest of the White House press, waiting for Jim's permission to see someone or for his handouts.

Hagerty handled everybody in the queue with an aplomb borne of his personal closeness to Eisenhower and fortified by nearly eight years on the job. For instance, he knew that both Anne Chamberlin, my *Time* magazine counterpart, and I had to write our main files first thing Friday morning. He therefore saw each of us for a half hour on Thursday afternoon—Anne at 6 and me at 6:30. The briefing he gave each of us was the PR equivalent of a complete baby formula fortified with iron and vitamins.

The spoon-feeding consisted of a week's overview of the most important presidential doings topped by a minor "exclusive"—a fact or two that had not appeared in the rest of the media. The other nutrients tossed in by Hagerty were several dollops of "color," as we called descriptive and anecdotal stuff. It was usually harmless tidbits about Eisenhower's private comments, conversations, or thoughts that made Ike sound both presidential and human.

Jim was such a pro that he even had different quotes and trivia for each competing weekly. What he gave Anne or me was the core of a perfectly respectable White House file that made each of us look good and kept the editors happy. There was only one thing wrong with the Thursday ritual. For Anne and me, two newcomers to the White House press, Hagerty was the top and closest-to-the-deadline source we had, and we had no time or way of checking his information. In my eyes—as well as in Chamberlin's—the Hagerty system was a travesty of journalism. It reduced us to note-taking factotums.

The pernicious effect of Hagerty's formula fully surfaced in November, when Eisenhower invited the White House media to accompany him on his last presidential quail shoot in Georgia.

The outing was one of those premium junkets that are short on work, long on fun, and let the White House press corps bask in the reflected glory of the presidency. The quail-rich Blue Plantation of W. Alton "Pete" Jones, a wealthy oilman and a member of Ike's small band of close personal friends, was a Hollywood-perfect setting for the outing. The plantation's rolling acres were covered with still-green, gorgeous grass and crowned by huge, serene oaks. Birds chirped overhead; there was no sign of man's polluting presence. And in the midst of this antebellum nirvana, all we did was follow Ike in two rubber-wheeled, horse-drawn buggies. We watched him aim and fire at the quail and ate steaks he personally grilled for us in a lush picnic spot. As Hagerty promised, the trip was a treat.

It was also a lesson in presidential image-making. My eyebrows first went up at the picnic when Hagerty let me snap pictures of Ike for my own album and the press photographers descended on me like angry hornets, hissing threats about dire consequences if one of my pictures should show up in print. It turned out that for eight years, Hagerty had maintained a ban on press pictures of the president hoisting, as was his want, a Scotch. I was doubly surprised because, according to the Washington rumor mill, the White House resident who allegedly imbibed was Mamie Eisenhower, not her husband.

My lunchtime surprise turned into shock before dinner, when Hagerty held an end-of-the-day press briefing. The first jolt was delivered by the senior wire service correspondent who, like the rest of us, had followed the president from morn to dusk. Ignoring the fact that for once we had actually witnessed what Eisenhower did, the UP reporter opened the session with the ritual inquiry about how the president had spent the day.

Jim officially announced what we all knew, namely, that Eisenhower had been quail-hunting, whereupon the AP correspondent looked up from his notebook and asked the follow-up question: "How did the president do, Jim?" This, after we had tailed Ike all day long and saw him bang away without ever hitting a feather.

I thought the AP guy was kidding and the room would break up with laughter, but the make-believe continued without a gasp from the audience. Hagerty, keeping a straight face, announced that "the President shot the day's legal limit in the State of Georgia," which led to a dumbfounding question number 3, how many quails was the day's hunting limit.

Jim provided the answer, which some of my colleagues actually wrote down in their notebooks, and on that fraudulent note the charade mercifully ended. Had it not been funny enough for *Alice in Wonderland*, the episode would have been scary.

Anne, who was as appalled as I was, joined me in swearing to expose Hagerty's sham, but I (and as far as I know, she also) never got around to it. For one thing, I was at least subconsciously aware of what would be Hagerty's vengeance if I'd write anything about his press control. And—I guess like the columnists—I also liked and respected Dwight D. Eisenhower, the great commander of the invasion of Normandy. I thought he was a man after my own heart: old-fashioned, straight shooting, and totally without airs. And as chance would have it, Ike confirmed my judgment during the same outing.

At the picnic lunch, Anne—who was very attractive and fashionable— seated herself opposite Eisenhower and engaged him in conversation. The meal done, she suddenly pulled out from her purse a robust Havana and, while the rest of us gaped, calmly clipped its tip. This was 1960, mind you, when men smoked cigars and women were still women. Then, as Eisenhower as well as everyone at the table watched her with mounting tension, Anne stuck the tobacco product between her lips, smiled, and with the aplomb of a brass monkey asked the president of the United States if he had light.

Pete Jones, who sat next to Ike, rapidly pulled out a cigarette lighter, leaned over, and lit the cigar, but Eisenhower would not let the incident go quietly. All red in face with indignation, he growled loud enough for all of us to hear, "This is really pretentious!" whereupon it was Anne's turn to turn crimson. Anne was one of us, a fellow trooper, but in my heart I applauded the former C-in-C of the European Theater. Eisenhower was too deserving a figure to be subjected to a playful dare fit for a boudoir.

This curious incident also remained unreported, primarily because the entire lunch was off the record. But deep down, I began to see what affected the columnists' views. I was therefore rather relieved when, after President Kennedy's inauguration, *Newsweek* was bought by the Washington Post Company. As part of the ensuing changes, Ken Crawford became the magazine's columnist; Ben Bradlee took over the Washington bureau; and I got a new beat—this time, the State Department. The area on which I was supposed to concentrate was Third World countries, foreign aid, and particularly,

Kennedy's program called the Alliance for Progress. "Alianza para el Progreso," as it was called in Spanish, was a signature JFK scheme and an ambitious aid project that the enthusiastic press rather recklessly hailed as "a Marshall Plan" for Latin America. As far as I was concerned, Bradlee's decision to send me to the Foggy Bottom was right on the nose.

I had greatly enjoyed covering the Senate and I continued to keep a foot in the White House by covering President Kennedy on weekends, but the switch to the diplomatic beat was just what I wanted. It was a step toward an assignment abroad. A foreign post in that era was a great professional distinction; moreover, working overseas had been my secret ambition ever since my junior year in college, when I wrote a paper on the Munich crisis in 1938.

The project, in which I compared the coverage of the historic sellout of Czechoslovakia by two big newspapers—the *Chicago Tribune* and the *Chicago Daily News*—was fascinating on two levels. It gave me an inkling of what the Munich crisis looked like from outside the eye of the hurricane, where I had lived through it as a frightened eleven-year-old. More important, the analysis heightened my appreciation of the role of foreign correspondents who, in those years before TV and cable, were the main reporters and interpreters of what was happening abroad. I had no quarrel with the coverage of the events by the liberal *Daily News*, but some of the stories in the affluent, right-wing *Tribune* made me livid: it was obvious that two of the Trib's correspondents in Germany admired Hitler.

My yen to work abroad did not abate even amid the glitter of the Washington press scene—if anything, it grew stronger. Watching the VIP traffic in Washington and going to fancy cocktail parties was sometimes ego-tickling fun, but the work that went with it was largely pack journalism. Even in those years, when the National Press Club had a fraction of today's hundreds of members, group reporting was a hallmark of the Washington news scene.

Covering Eisenhower's Wednesday press conferences as part of a crowd that included the wires and at least a dozen reporters from the *New York Times*, for example, made me sometimes wonder whether my presence in the packed room was really necessary. My editors could read what Ike said the same day in wire reports or the next morning's newspapers.

I had a similar sinking feeling whenever I joined the horde of newsmen who besieged the Kennedy compound in Hyannisport on weekends. Even my new job at the State Department was less than uplifting. Most of the time, I was merely filling holes in the files from abroad or quoting Foggy Bottom officials. After a couple of years of this routine I began to get restless. Real foreign coverage had to be done where the action was, and that's where I wanted to be.

My ambition only grew after I met Phil Graham, who shortly after the acquisition of *Newsweek* invited all of us in the Washington bureau for a get-acquainted lunch. When he was not suffering from one of his eventually fatal depressions, Graham was a man of captivating charm and magnanimity, and that's how we found him the day we followed Ben Bradlee into the *Washington Post*'s wood-paneled executive dining room. The fare was plain—hamburgers—but the conversation was memorable.

After the food was served Bradlee, who had known Graham for years, brought up a subject of exceptional sensitivity. It involved Tom Streithorst, *Newsweek*'s brand new Middle East correspondent, who had been arrested and was languishing in a jail in Turkey. Streithorst, Bradlee told Graham across the long dining table, had been recently hired by the magazine for the Beirut bureau and, to celebrate, bought himself a new Jaguar in London. While driving back to Lebanon, he had a head-on collision with a Volkswagen bus in Turkey in which Streithorst's Lebanese wife, who sat next to him, was killed. Under the Turkish laws, the minimum sentence for a fatal car accident was nine years in one of the country's abysmal jails. According to lawyers hired by *Newsweek* to defend the correspondent, it was almost certain that Streithorst would have to pay the penalty.

"Now," Ben told Graham, who was listening with obvious interest, "there seems to be only one thing we can do for Streithorst, and that's to hire a couple of former CIA spooks in Istanbul. They say they can get him out of jail and put him across the border to Greece."

Ben paused, crunched a potato chip, and resumed eye contact with Graham. "How much?" Graham laconically asked.

"At first, they were talking about $20,000," Bradlee left the figure hanging in the air while he scrutinized Graham's affable countenance, "but after they checked things out they say they need more." Ben's voice dropped, and there was a moment of silence.

"Thirty?" Graham asked, looking at ease as if they were discussing the menu.

By the time the back-and-forth ended, Graham had as good as promised to spend over fifty thousand dollars in valuable 1961 currency to help a brand-new staffer he had never met, and who had barely started working for a magazine Graham had just bought—all on the strength of Ben's shrewd pitch over executive hamburgers. I was hugely impressed, and even more determined to make a pitch for a foreign assignment: here was a man to work for in an environment that could turn risky.

As matters developed, Streithorst got out of Turkey without the former gumshoes. I learned that part of the story two years later, when I was based in Rio de Janeiro and was visited by vacationing Fritz Beebe, the chairman

CHAPTER 9

of the Washington Post company. Graham, he told me, was going to retain as the head of Streithorst's defense team Dean Acheson, the former secretary of state and author of the Truman Doctrine, who knew many top-ranking officials in Turkey. But before taking that step, Beebe flew to Ankara to see what he could do, and in the American embassy was approached by an employee, a Turkish lawyer, who said he knew how to get Tom out of the slammer. Beebe was at first unimpressed but eventually told the Turk to go ahead. A few hundred dollars and a couple of weeks later, Streithorst was out of jail and safely in Greece.

Meanwhile, back in Washington, I started taking evening courses in Spanish. Ostensibly, I was getting ready for a vacation in Yucatan, but in the back of my mind was a thought that working south of the border could be fun. I took on that vacation jaunt a typewriter and a camera, and I filed from Merida a feature with pictures about an interesting archaeological dig.

Bradlee was the last man for whom things had to be spelled out. When I got back to Washington, he told me to put my Berlitz lessons on the office expense account. Then, just before Christmas of 1962, he called me to his office and told me that Hal Levine, *Newsweek*'s correspondent in Mexico City, was about to be transferred back to the States. Bradlee had suggested to the New York editors that I take Levine's place, and they agreed. There was just one thing that could trip me up, Bradlee added, and that was if I dropped the ball on a cover story the magazine wanted to run early the next year.

"Cover on what?" I asked. Cover on João Goulart, the leftward meandering Brazilian president, Ben said. The magazine wanted to transfer the Latin American bureau to Rio de Janeiro, and I was to go there to report the Goulart story and get a feel for my new base.

All I could think about at the moment was that I had been learning the wrong language: Brazilians speak Portuguese. Aloud I only asked, "When do I go?"

"As soon as you get your visa," Ben said. He jumped out of his chair, thrust his chest forward, snapped his red suspenders, and added in his gravelly voice, "Go get 'em, buddy."

A few days later, on New Year's Day 1963, I flew to Rio.

CHAPTER 10

FRUSTRATED IN THE HEMISPHERE

I did my level best to heed Bradlee's warning and not drop the ball on my first foreign cover story, but the dreaded calamity almost came to pass during the effort's nerve-wrecking finale. After three hot and hectic weeks when I raced all over Brazil in pursuit of mostly elusive information, I retreated to Rio de Janeiro's old-fashioned Hotel Victoria, spent Sunday and Monday writing the main body of the story, and on Tuesday morning sent it by telex to New York. The following afternoon I flew six hundred miles to Brasília, the country's then-new official capital, to tackle the last but essential part of the cover package, an interview with Brazil's hard-pressed president. "Jango" Goulart, a wealthy landlord, was an inept and insecure left-leaning politician who shied away from foreign journalists, but I had a firm assurance from the Brazilian Foreign Office that he would "definitely" see me on Wednesday, two days before my deadline for my magnum opus.

That morning, when I showed up with a photographer in Brasília's strikingly beautiful, snow-white presidential palace, Goulart's chef du cabinet received us with elaborate courtesy. "Sim Senhor," he assured me, "the interview would take place on schedule. There is no need to worry."

With that reassurance, we were ushered into a large waiting room where important-looking Brazilians in immaculately pressed white suits and starched mint-green military uniforms drank tiny cups of thick *cafezinho*, smoked potent French cigarettes, and talked in whispers. I found it to be a most unnerving environment. The VIPs' faces and gestures were so somber and intense I felt sure something momentous was going on—possibly, they were plotting to overthrow Goulart's government—and I was the only person in the room who did not know about it. A few days before my story was due to go to press, it was a thought too painful to contemplate.

I watched the whispering plotters and drank my own cafezinhos with growing anxiety and impatience until one o'clock in the afternoon, when an aide of the chef du cabinet showed up and escorted the photographer and me to a smaller waiting room adjacent to the one we left. The interview would take place in a few minutes, he gravely announced. Feeling reassured, I re-read my prepared questions, re-checked whether my tape recorder was working, and sat back to survey the new cohort of my competitors for Goulart's attention.

This time, the coffee drinkers were fewer, talked less, and, arrayed in a row of chairs like a movie audience, kept their eyes on a high, massive door that I assumed led to Goulart's inner sanctum. From time to time the door opened and an aide in a dark suit, white shirt, and a silver tie momentarily broke the room's tensions by quietly motioning to one of the Brazilians to enter. Except for the silver-tied aide nobody ever returned through the same door: once the visitors walked through it, they were, as in a science fiction movie, off to another planet.

The disappearing act went on until half past two, when the chef du cabinet's aide appeared with the bad news that Goulart had been "unavoidably" detained and could not see me until the next morning. I returned to the hotel feeling both tired and worried.

Thursday morning the photographer and I went through much the same routine. This time, after a couple of hours' wait, I started pacing up and down in the first waiting room, more in order to signal my mounting impatience than out of any need to stretch my legs. The tactic achieved nothing beyond flustering the immaculately dressed plotters who lowered their voices each time I passed by—unnecessarily so, I might add, because my Berlitz Spanish was not a great help in making out their Brazilian-accented Portuguese.

By early afternoon, the photographer and I were again ushered into the advanced waiting room, only to be outranked for the second time by other door watchers. I was now so visibly upset by the snub that the aide skipped his usually blandishments and rushed out of the room ahead of me, looking sheepish. I demanded to see the chef du cabinet, but his secretary told me that he was out. I phoned him repeatedly from my hotel room during the afternoon, again with no success. I placed a call to the Foreign Ministry in Rio, but the switchboard operator could not get a connection. Or so she said. The pressure mounted.

I did not eat dinner that night. I had less than twenty-four hours to make my deadline, a task that in the case of the Goulart cover was all-important. In the early 1960s, when news magazines still had a strong preference for hard news, a feature cover—such as I worked on—could not compete for space with any late-breaking but important news story, and as such teetered on the brink of extinction until the very moment it went to press.

Getting a peg-less piece of reportage to run was like launching a space shot: the top editor's "Go" on Friday night was only uttered after a countdown that assured him of a perfect confluence of factors ranging from the absence of a major news development to the quality of fact-checked and fitted copy and availability of a cover picture that would look good on the newsstands. As I perspired in the hotel bed waiting for the dawn of Friday, I was acutely aware that the story, the cover picture, and my career as foreign correspondent all were in serious jeopardy.

There was no relief in contemplating my options. Given the chef du cabinet's track record, I couldn't bank on seeing Goulart before the week's deadline. The prudent strategy was to place an early call to my editor and, after a fulsome explanation of my mind-boggling difficulties, gently hint that the Goulart interview looked doubtful. But since the hotel operator could not get through to Rio, let alone New York, this sort of safety valve was out of reach.

My second option was to send the same warning by cable or telex. I weighed that course carefully and then turned it down. In those years of expensive communications, service cables from abroad had to be couched in a shorthand that made it difficult to fully explain how blameless I was for my grievous predicament. Moreover, I was on my first overseas assignment and my future hung on its outcome; I could not afford to sound like a failure, a quitter, or a crybaby. By the time I got up, I decided to go for broke and give Goulart another half-day.

A couple of hours later I gave the chef du cabinet a polite but stern lecture I had composed over my breakfast of papaya and rolls. Disregarding his darkening visage, I described to him the merciless nature of magazine deadlines. I warned that millions of *Newsweek* readers were going to be deprived of learning about Goulart and his great country if my interview with the president was late. And I made it clear that I found the repeated promises and postponements of the interview incomprehensible and bordering on a personal slight.

Talking like that to a distinguished-looking official who was many years my senior was, for me, not easy. I suspected that he was probably waiting for Goulart's go-ahead; moreover, I knew that courtesy is an important lubricant of social intercourse, particularly in cultures that put a high value on personal dignity. But I was under great pressure, and strong and direct language was my means of last resort. And it worked.

By noon, the silver-tied aide opened the big door and nodded to me to come forth. Trailed by my Brazilian photographer, I rushed into the next room with a "How-do-you-do-Sir" smile on my face only to discover that I was still not in Goulart's presence, but in waiting room number 3. This time, however, the aide did not avert his eyes and gave me a smile that, I felt, boded well for my enterprise. And indeed, a little after one o'clock in the afternoon the chef du cabinet personally ushered me into Goulart's office just as the president was about to leave for lunch.

The "interview" that followed was a farce. Goulart handed me typed and largely trivial answers to the questions I had to submit in advance to the Foreign Office. He flatly refused to elaborate on any of them or discuss any other political or economic subject I tried to raise. He also showed a tendency—unheard of among politicians—to keep his eyes pinned to the carpet, thereby driving the photographer nuts as he was trying to take the cover picture. But however little the three days of waiting contributed to the final shape of the cover story, it gave me the benefit of a personal encounter, which I always found extremely helpful in reporting.

Goulart and I sat side-by-side on a sofa for about twenty minutes, chatting—since he refused to talk politics—mostly about Brazil's beauty and history, while the chef du cabinet interpreted. My impression of Goulart differed from the Brazilian press, which painted him either as a dangerous leftist or as Brazil's populist strong man in the mold of Getúlio Vargas. Instead, I found Goulart surprisingly sympathetic, although seemingly out of place as the country's president.

Almost painfully shy, Goulart hesitated before answering even the most innocuous questions, never raised his voice, cracked a smile, or shifted his eyes away from his lame leg that he rested on a little cushioned stool. He stuck me as depressed—I found myself thinking about a recent story in *Manchette*, a major Brazilian picture magazine, about his very young and stunningly beautiful wife who was rumored to be divorcing him. When we shook hands before parting, I had the sense that Brazil had little to fear from Goulart except a lack of leadership, though that, in some circumstances, can be danger enough.

I left the palace on the run and, by three o'clock in the afternoon, was in the local office of Radiobrás, Brazil's monopolistic communications company, demanding immediate access to a telex. I was breathing hard and all sweaty from the hundred-degree heat, but I still had a chance to make the cover deadline. Instead of a cabin with a telex machine, however, I got another lesson about the differences between North and South America.

The Radiobrás manager first checked the length of my copy, estimated the time needed for its transmission, and politely inquired how I intended to pay for it. I gave him my credit card, and he spent several minutes checking in a dusty manual whether the card was accepted by his company. By then I was inwardly hitting the ceiling, but the man was still not done. Next, he pulled out another reference book and proceeded to double check the accuracy of the four or five telex numbers in the magazine's wire room in New York that I listed as my copy's destination.

Finally, the checks completed, the manager tidily arranged my copy and my credit card on the counter in front of me and, speaking with the grave courtesy that Brazilians reserve for foreigners and very wealthy countrymen, solemnly informed me that everything was in order.

I glared at him and struggled to keep my temper. "I know that everything's in order," I finally said, speaking very slowly to indicate to the manager that he was too dull-witted to be addressed as a person with a normal IQ. When sufficiently provoked, in my younger years I used to be capable of meanness. "Now can I use your telex?"

Looking profoundly embarrassed, the man sighed and shook his head.

"Infelizmente, O Senhor non pode, non," he replied. He had no telex connection, he explained. All commercial lines out of Brasília had been out of order for almost a week. Applying total self-control, I without a word grabbed my papers and ran out of the door.

I still refused to accept being drummed out of the ranks of would-be foreign correspondents and busted to the mail desk. I raced back to the hotel, grabbed my belongings, and took a cab to the airport where I caught the day's last flight to Rio. From the Galeão airport I went straight to the main Radiobrás office in town and managed to telex the interview to my editors before they went to dinner—late, but not outrageously so. The working schedule in the magazine headquarters on Friday, the day when most of the issue is put together, ran from morning until well past midnight.

Afterwards I repaired to Hotel Victoria, my Rio hostelry, collected my messages, and went to my room with a bottle of ice-cold Choppe, Brazil's very good Pilsner beer. It was then, at the merciful end of an awful mission that I discovered that my frantic scramble had been in vain. A message from the news desk that had been waiting for me since Tuesday, the day I left for Brasilia, said that the Goulart cover had been postponed for at least a week because of more pressing events somewhere else.

In fact, the cover kept sliding until the first week in March, when it finally ran under a headline concocted in a desperate attempt to boost the issue's sales on newsstands. It likened Goulart's wayward regime in Brazil, of all things, to JFK's New Frontier. When I saw it, well after my return to Washington, I gulped in disbelief and full of trepidation opened the magazine. In those years, the editors did not bother to send the edited material back to the reporter for final checking, and Dwight Martin, a creative writer who knew nothing about Latin America but ran the Hemisphere section, gave his imagination free rein.

Ignoring my hard-won facts and anxiously compiled analysis of Goulart's desultory flirting with the Left, he wrote a colorful piece based on a travel guide's description of Rio's carnival and the kites, goats, and voodoo on the

Copacabana beach. A brilliant wordsmith with a wonderful sense of humor, Dwight produced a breezy piece that was a vastly more fun to read than my earnest study of the convoluted Brazilian politics.

But despite this severe blow to my ego, I somehow passed muster. Two months later, in May 1963, I was back in Rio, setting up the bureau as the new chief correspondent for Latin America.

~

The frustrations of the Goulart interview were my introduction to the special problems of reporting in the Third World. At Medill we were taught that a story should be judged on importance, timeliness, accuracy, and style. After I started working south of the border, I put on top of these factors a fifth benchmark, which was the correspondent's obstacles in getting his work done. The Medill yardstick was OK for judging a feature about, say, gold mining in Colorado or folk dancing in Bavaria, either of which was just a piece of reporting and writing. But to use the same criteria for a similar article from some part of the Third World in those days was like assuming that the visible tip was the whole iceberg.

The hidden nine-tenths of the reporter's achievement was overcoming his or her biggest barrier, which was working to American standards in an environment devoid of any comprehension of what this meant. The obstacles I found most mind-boggling were cultural—the different meaning of such seemingly straightforward terms as "Yes" and "No," and the profound indifference to or disdain for the value that Yankees place on time.

Other crippling roadblocks included nonexistent, iffy, or primitive transportation, accommodations, and communications; inertia, ignorance, and occasional hostility of the host country officials; and barriers put up by the legman's own inadequate linguistics and overstressed physique. The latter peril in my case included such prodigious bouts of the south-of-the-border "touristá" that I kept a supply of anti-diarrhea pills in both my luggage and my wallet.

Most of the physical hurdles were an integral part of the underdevelopment, decaying infrastructure, and poverty that reigned, with rare exceptions, throughout the Southern Hemisphere. Outside big cities, hotels were scarce or nonexistent, and finding a place to park one's tired body at the end of the day could be a significant problem. Time and again, rattletrap vehicles fell apart on disintegrating roads, overloaded telephone lines refused to accept another call, and decrepit telex machines gave out just before the magazine's deadlines.

There was no margin for the unexpected, no fallback cushion. For instance, on several occasions I found myself in a hired car with a flat tire. Invariably, the tire that gave up its soul was smooth as a baby's face and years past what would have been its retirement age in the Northern Hemisphere. In almost every instance, it also turned out that the driver had no spare, and if it happened in the hustings, it would take a great deal of my time and his ingenuity to get us going again.

Once, in Rio, I asked my taxi driver why so many cabs in the country seemed to have no spare tires. The owner of an almost new, Brazilian-made Beetle Volkswagen, the cabbie told me that he had none either, because he'd sold it. With a net income of between two and three hundred dollars a year, having a fifth wheel was a luxury.

Underdevelopment fostered a mentality of underachievement. Since poverty was all there ever was and there was no visible way of getting out of it, it seemed pointless to work hard. With very few exceptions, between the Rio Grande in the north and Tierra del Fuego in the south there was no admiration for the gringo's sweaty pursuit of getting things done. On the contrary: hustling was an oddball behavior, unbecoming a gentleman. Frequently, the disdain for the Yankee work ethics went hand in hand with a deep resentment of the foreigner's higher standard of living.

There was a languid quality to the Latino culture that could be enchanting under the right circumstances, but they emphatically did not include deadline reporting. Arrangements were not binding, appearances meant more than substance, and procrastination was part of the lifestyle. Facts and figures, including those solemnly cited by senior officials, frequently were like poetry—they sounded good as long as their veracity was not scrutinized.

Even such appurtenances of modern civilization as airline reservations could be iffy: in Lima, the Peruvian capital, an airline office once sold me a ticket for a flight from Bolivia to Chile that did not exist. I was stranded in La Paz and almost missed my deadline. (In fairness I must add that Latin America held no monopoly on airline adventures. In the Middle East, my flight from Kuwait to Baghdad once left three hours ahead of schedule because a member of the Kuwaiti ruling family wanted to get to Iraq in a hurry.)

In later years and on other beats, I had the luxury of probing the news for hidden nuances and deeper causes and meanings. But particularly during my early years' tour in the Southern Hemisphere, when I was on the road practically all the time, my principal achievement was to get in and out of places, gather the essential information, and produce stories by deadlines. Even that barren output required an exhausting effort. In my four and a half years in the region, I took just three weeks of vacation, and I was rarely home in Rio for more than a week at a time.

CHAPTER 10

Reporting was not my only worry when my wife and I arrived in Rio one muggy day in May 1963, and I took on the mantle of the chief Latin American correspondent. First, I had to set up an office, and Romana, who was four months pregnant, had to establish a household. By promising to pay the rent in US dollars, we found a spacious apartment on Avenida Atlantica in the Rio suburb of Copacabana, and a fine office room in a high-rise building on downtown's Avenida Rio Branco. Brazilian inflation was running at the rate of some 100 percent a month, and landlords were eager to get stable currency. Even so, making the rented premises into a *Newsweek* bureau and a Kubic home took an effort of epic proportions.

To start with, I could not function as a journalist without a working phone in my office and at home. The apartment had a phone, a feature almost as attractive as its glorious view of the Copacabana beach. Getting the office phone, on the other hand, turned out to be one of my toughest assignments in South America.

The Rio telephone shortage was a classic illustration of the woes of the region. South of the border, everyone wanted a phone, and the populist governments responded by making the service charges ridiculously cheap. As a result, the state-run phone companies were invariably deeply in the red, their equipment was obsolete and in appalling condition, and new lines were rationed as strictly as shoes in wartime Prague. In Rio, for example, they were available only for top Brazilian officials and senior foreign diplomats. The advice I got from old news hands in Rio was to do what everyone else did, namely, buy the line for my office phone on the black market.

New to the ways of South America and naively determined to operate under the host country laws, I demurred. For one thing, the then-going black market phone price for Yankees was a stiff five hundred dollars, which I did not like putting on my expense account. Moreover, illegally acquired lines had to stay registered in the name of their original legitimate owner, who in most cases was long dead, and as a result the magazine's number could not be found in the Rio phone book. I later learned that the alphabetical telephone book was a sham, but I did not know that at the time. An uptight gringo, I declined to operate like a bookie under an unlisted number.

Long on dignity but short on wisdom, I submitted an official application for a new phone line and thereby triggered a period of complete inaction that lasted four solid weeks. After my home office inquired for the second time how they can reach me and what phone number should go on my new stationery, I wrote an indignant letter to the ministry of communications and sent a copy to the foreign office to which I was accredited. When nothing happened for two more weeks, I sent a reproachful cable to the Brazilian embassy in Washington and asked Ben Bradlee to take up my phone problem with the ambassador.

When even that did not work, I accepted the offer of Erena, my *carioca* (Rio-born) secretary, to accompany me to the hectic communications ministry where, after the ritual wait in a waiting room, I was allowed to plead my case to a portly bureaucrat. Somehow, this last-chance strategy worked. Whether thanks to my humbled presence in the anteroom, or the striking looks and charm of my pert assistant, I succeeded where all of my previous interventions had failed. To the astonishment and envy of the entire Rio-based foreign press corps, about three months after I filled out the application I actually got the line, legally.

My euphoria evaporated when I tried to use it. To begin with, the telephone system was so overloaded it took two or three minutes after the receiver was off the hook just to get a line. One could drink a cafezinho or hum a whole samba by the time the gadget emitted a buzz announcing a window of opportunity to communicate. The dial tone, however, was a mere teaser before the real hurdle, which was dialing.

Particularly during office hours, entering the first two of the number's six digits routinely changed the dial to the busy signal—evidence, I assumed, that people all over the town had their phones off the hook, waiting for a chance to dial. As for long-distance calls, they were almost out of the question. Once, when I insisted on placing a call to New York, the operator informed me that the waiting time was three days.

The vaunted listing of *Newsweek* in the phone directory turned out to be another phantom triumph. Since practically all of phone lines in Rio had been illegally traded, the alphabetical phone book that listed the names and numbers of the original (and usually long dead) owners was useless. The telephone company therefore put out a directory that listed each number not by name but by the address where the phone was installed—but since that book was updated once in a blue moon, there was no list of phones in new buildings, including the one where I hung *Newsweek*'s shingle.

Worst of all, I discovered that for all their love for the telephone, Brazilians would not use it for business. The most that could be accomplished with the help of this gadget was to set up an appointment. Answering questions by phone was regarded as unduly brusque, impersonal, and beneath one's rank and dignity. Official business, regardless of how trivial, had to be carried out face-to-face, over the inevitable cafezinho, and after a status-appropriate period of sitting in the waiting room.

CHAPTER 10

Setting up a household was another heroic exercise that bore no similarity to any such endeavor in the United States. In the early 1960s Rio, a city of about two million, was a housekeeper's nightmare. In contrast to its almost poetic beauty, it had a pathetically overburdened and jerry-rigged, slap-dash infrastructure that broke down with frequency and in ways that in the United States or Europe would have been regarded as catastrophic. The periodic disasters ranged from annual mudslides in the rainy season to monthly electricity blackouts and, in summer, almost daily water shortages. Rio's waterless periods, which could last a whole week at a time, had even greater impact on the cariocas' lifestyle than the laid-back culture and overtaxed telephones.

For newcomers like Romana and me, enduring a string of showerless days without air conditioning in a hundred-degree-plus weather invited comparison with some of our hardships in the DP camps. Fortunately, we were often helped by the indomitable cariocas, who were the most congenial and resourceful people I'd ever met.

As my secretary Erena and Jane Braga, *Newsweek*'s stringer in Rio, explained to us while we still lived in a hotel, our future comforts hinged on finding an apartment with a phone and in a building that possessed two all-important attributes: a big water tank on the roof and an alert janitor in the basement. The tank had to be big enough to hold several days' water supply for the whole house, and the janitor had to have the savvy and stamina of a Bedouin leading a caravan across the Sahara.

The janitor's most important job, we were told, was not to keep the lobby free of the omnipresent Copacabana sand, and not even to get the frantic house dwellers out of the elevator when the electricity went off, important as those tasks were. His main mission was to make sure that the house got the most of each meager water allotment that was supplied late at night by the Guanabara waterworks. To fulfill this critical chore, the janitor had to hold a nightly vigil close to the water pipes in the basement and listen for the sloshing sound that heralded the water rushing down the main. Then, at just the right moment, the janitor had to turn on a pump that sucked the precious liquid into the tank on the roof.

As we later learned, these nocturnal quests for water were filled with high tension. The Guanabara plant put out no schedule for dividing the water among the various sections of Rio; the bursts of water were excruciatingly brief; and there was no second chance to make up for a missed ration. Since everyone in our affluent neighborhood was using the same stratagem, the race went to the stronger house pump and the more alert janitor. For the losers, there was no water the next day for flushing the toilet or washing the dishes, let alone rinsing off the sweat of the tropical summer.

Thanks to Erena and Jane's sage advice, our top-floor apartment had a phone, and a competent water vigilante in the wrinkle-faced janitor, O Senhor Jorge. But we promptly ran into another problem, which was getting the customs' release of a crate we had shipped from Washington. It contained such personal effects as clothing and, most importantly, everything Romana needed for our expected baby. But extricating the crate from the Brazilian bureaucracy turned out to be as hard as getting the office phone line.

What brought upon us this new grief was my zeal to produce stories for *Newsweek*. About two weeks after we arrived in Rio, I flew to Belem, Brazil's equatorial port on the Amazon, to write a story about what was then the wide open and unabashed capital of the country's brazen contrabandistas. The reporting, for a change, turned out to be a snap: the economic section in the US embassy in Rio had some information on the subject, the archive of Manchette had great pictures of smugglers' boats loaded with cars, and the mayor of Belem was so proud of the town's key industry that he took me on a personal tour of the documents-laundering and product-numbers-changing establishments that gave new identity to the used Chevvies and Fords being shipped in, mostly from Florida.

I returned to Rio and wrote a sizable article about Brazil's thriving if illegal foreign trade, which then included exports of plutonium-rich sand to Europe. A yarn after Dwight Martin's own heart, he gave the piece generous play in *Newsweek*, which was fine. Unfortunately, the story was also picked up by the Argentine *Primera Plana* and several other South American magazines and newspapers, which triggered a panic in the Brazilian customs office. Undermanned or not really interested in stopping the car smuggling, the bureaucrats responded to the publicity by temporarily freezing the release of all imported goods—including my own household effects.

I again tried to live up to the Yankee code of honor by refusing to grease any palms, but about a month before my son Johnny was born, I bowed to the inevitable. I hired a *despechante*, an expert in a peculiar Brazilian survival technique described as *dar um jeito* (roughly, "put in the fix"), which Dwight Martin in his insightful cover story aptly described as "driving a Cadillac through an opening barely big enough for a Volkswagen."

For three hundred dollars in bribes and the despechante's own fees, by the wee hours of October 1, 1963, when I took Romana to the hospital, the crate with a year's supply of diapers was in our apartment. I went for a few hours to the office and at eleven o'clock in the morning drove back to the hilltop English-run Hospital dos Estrangeiros. As I stepped out of the car, I heard the cry of a baby that turned out to be my son. We gave him the Czech name of Jan. He was beautiful in the way of all babies, and I said a silent prayer for him to be strong, honest, and happy. Jan brought a new dimension to my life, though I was never wise enough to let him know that. When it came to revealing emotions, men of my generation believed it was manly to emulate cigar store Indians.

How Romana coped with her baby amid the vexations of Rio was always a mystery to me. Our janitor was not quite the insomniac he was supposed to be, and hardly a month went by when we were not without running water, sometimes for several days at a time. The blackouts-grounded elevator time and again left Romana stranded with the baby carriage ten floors below the apartment, and our first maid turned out to be a *macumbeira*—a voodoo practitioner. Fired, the woman came back at night to burn candles outside our door and cast a curse on Romana and the baby.

The madness that was Rio was best portrayed by a party for 120 guests that Romana and I threw for visiting Lilian and Fritz Beebe, the chairman of the board of the Washington Post Company. The day the event took place our building ran out of water at noon, and Romana had to organize a pail brigade to bring water bought from a nearby restaurant. At five o'clock in the evening, two hours before the party started, the electricity went off. We placed two dozen fat candles along the building's spiral stairs and throughout the apartment, bought more ice from the restaurant for the mounds of catered food, and braced ourselves for a fiasco.

Astonishingly, the party was a huge success. Accustomed to calamities of this sort, the caterer and waiters arrived with more ice, and did their job by candlelight without a murmur. The guests gamely climbed up the old-fashioned stairway flanked by a reeking garbage chute. Roberto Campos, the Brazilian minister of economy and at that time the most highly regarded South American technocrat, was among the first to arrive and almost the last one to leave. Nobody fainted from the odor, quit the stairs halfway in exhaustion, or came down with a heat stroke, and the Beebes were gracious and full of fun.

The gamely carioca spirit was only one of the marvels of living in Rio. Copacabana, in particular, in the early 1960s was an enchanting round-the-clock playground pulsating with bossa nova and other haunting rhythms. The beach was a kaleidoscope of fishermen peddling their morning's catch, vendors flying graceful handmade kites, kids racing among ice cream vendors, and nubile bikini-clad cariocas playing endless rounds of paddle ball. In the afternoon, the aroma of fried jumbo shrimp wafted from packed sidewalk cafés; at night, *macumbeiras* lit candles on the sand while insomniacs and skinny dippers came in for a swim.

During the annual carnival, masses of *favelados*—Rio's poor—descended on the city from their hilltop slums and put on a dazzling show of talent, beauty, and vitality that belied clichés about the destructive force of poverty. There was a rare magic to living in Rio.

～

But great as it was, the city had, for me, a major flaw: I did not get enough of it. The problem was the sheer size of my beat, which included everything south of Texas plus the Caribbean islands with the sole exception of Cuba, which in those years was almost inaccessible to American journalists. That left to my tender care more than twenty countries, including a few island possessions and colonies.

The physical demands of the job were formidable. The distances were enormous—to get to the foreign capital nearest to Rio, Montevideo in Uruguay, was a three-and-half-hour flight by jet. To reach the Caribbean islands or Mexico I usually had to take a connecting flight in Miami, which stretched the travel time to more than a day. Another hurdle was the climate, which ranged from steamy to freezing in different parts of my beat. Though it was always balmy around the Equator, it was always cold in the high Andes, and a hot summer in Mexico and Central America coincided with cold winter in Argentina or Chile.

Since I never knew where breaking news might take me—and since in those years I took pictures for most of my stories—my standard travel gear was fit for a safari. I lugged along a typewriter, cameras, radio, and both tropical and heavy clothing.

Moreover, to produce the weekly reports about the area, I had to keep on the move. I spent an inordinate amount of my time in hotels and airports, a schedule that was rough not just on me but also on my marriage and on little Jan, who once forgot what I looked like. That incident, which I'll never forget, took place when I returned from a nine-week-long trip. Johnny, who was then about a year old, scrambled to see who was at the door, but when I tried to hug him, he pulled away and cried. I almost cried myself. Had the wait for a phone call to New York been shorter than three days, I would have called my editor and told him I was quitting.

Professionally, the beat was also exceptionally tough because—except for Fidel Castro—it had no charismatic leaders and no strong running story that would truly interest American readers. This meant that, while I did my share of VIP interviews and coverage of military coups, I spent much more time grinding out features—flying in hired single-engine Cessnas in and out of gold-rush towns, jungle outposts, and remote bases where guerrillas were fighting the government or government troops were fighting the guerrillas.

CHAPTER 10

In those days, the junkets cost thirty dollars per hour of flight, the bush pilot's waiting time included. It was a fascinating lifestyle, the sort of adventure I imagined when as a school kid I read a best-selling book about a French boyscout called Fifi and his trip around the world. But it was also very iffy work, because my job was not done until I managed to get the pictures I had shot for the story to New York, and they had to be there by Saturday morning. In most countries I could deliver a pouch with the film to the airport freight office and get it on the first available flight. But in Brazil, where shipping by air was hopelessly tied up in red tape, the only way the film got to New York in a hurry was in the pocket of a kindly passenger.

Since the New York–bound flights left the Rio airport around midnight, I spent many Friday evenings scouting in the Galeão departure lounge for a dependable-looking traveler who would agree to hand my rolls of film to the *Newsweek* messenger at the JFK airport. In those years, with only one or two exceptions, the films got to the lab in time, but that still left me with a lot of other worries.

In the 1960s, the continent was seething with enough discontent, frustration, and anger to trigger an earthquake. The hemisphere's resources were hogged by feudal landlords, incompetent state enterprises, and greedy foreign companies; the countless have-nots shared only ignorance, disease, and poverty. The governments were corrupt and inept and the politicians were mouthing empty Marxist shibboleths. A sane and educated middle class was minuscule. And from one end of the continent to the other, the final political arbiters were strutting brass hats who commanded the best-equipped army units.

But while the big picture was clear, its all-important details were an enigma. The clannish military brass hats were so secretive that in most countries I found it impossible to size up how close they were to toppling the government. As a result, guessing was the endemic work style of both native and foreign journalists, and we suffered the unavoidable consequences. As my friend Nathan Miller, who worked for the *Baltimore Sun*, astutely put it, "anyone who covers the Southern Hemisphere and feels secure is, by definition, incompetent."

While I was squarely in the insecure category, I was far from proud of my coverage. *Newsweek*'s formula in those years was forward-tilted reporting, which was supposed to give the reader an inkling of events to come. My usual forward tilt was a limp "maybe." Even if I sensed that the country's politics might be overheating, the best I could do was to listen to the status quo–minded officials in the government and the US embassy, balance their platitudes with the bluster of the radicals, and have a lunch with one or two respected native newsmen or politicians to get their reading on the intentions of the generals. The resulting file had all the fiber of a tutti frutti yogurt.

After telexing my take on the country's problems and the requisite outlook of things to come, I frequently wished I could emulate a cabinetmaker in one of the short stories by Karel Čapek, one of the favorite authors of my childhood. When Čapek's craftsman finished a piece of furniture, he would run his thumb over the joints to check if they were smooth and solid and then he would nod, knowing that his work was good. Some Friday nights as I lay worried in the bed I yearned so much for the cabinetmaker's certainty that I could almost see his rumpled, stolid figure and hear him humming a contented tune as he examined the finished piece.

There was a beauty and strength to simple tasks, performed with skill and integrity, I thought. As a reporter, I never lost my admiration—and a tinge of envy—for that competent craftsman.

CHAPTER 11

MY QUARREL WITH THE *REFORMADORES*

On balance, my first foreign beat produced some of the best dinner stories I could have told if I had been good at telling stories. I'll get to the fun part of my job later, but first I must note that despite its many fascinations, covering Latin America was no sinecure. Far from it. The four and a half years I spent in the region were physically the most demanding of all my twenty-six years abroad; they were hard on my family; and although I worked my heart out and took barely any vacation, the results were never fully satisfying.

Moreover, it was in Latin America that I became involved in my only serious in-house controversy while working for *Newsweek*. The conflict absorbed more of my emotional energy than was prudent, earned me a stern summons from my bosses, and disabused me of my naive belief that as a journalist, I have the thick skin of a real professional.

What caused the quarrel was my skeptical view of much of the leadership of the countries I covered: the self-styled "reformers" who in the mid-1960s set the tone of public discourse and policies between the Rio Grande and Tierra del Fuego. As thick as flies, they comprised most of the region's ruling establishments and included professional politicians, government officials, labor union leaders, and most of the prominent native intellectuals, artists, and writers.

Enormously self-confident, they claimed to be the true champions of the poor—in those years, the vast majority of the South America's population. They had a one-size-fits-all list of malefactors—headed by the United States, foreign companies, and feudal landlords—and a sure-fire formula, called *reformas*, for fixing all of the continent's ills. After watching them for a while, I concluded that the Latino leftists were demagogues, as ruinous for the region as the Kremlin's apparatchiks who were at that time wrecking the economies in Eastern Europe.

I had two big problems with the *reformadores*. One of them was their knee-jerk attacks on the United States, which they blamed for all of their countries' woes. They did it with a viciousness that reminded me of Moscow's raging against the West. And while the temptation was to shrug them off as mere successors of the previous generation of South American populists, whose model were Italian fascists, I was covering the region during the coldest years of the Cold War. However impotent, their anti-Yanqui harangues served the goals of the Kremlin and Fidel Castro.

What angered me even more was that their solutions made no sense. The region had an important basis for economic development: it had sufficient population, plentiful natural resources, and a benign climate—the same conditions that had enabled North America to become the economic leader of the world. What the Southern Hemisphere lacked was responsible leadership and earnest effort to promote capital investment, education, social justice, and political stability. The quick-fix demagogues, instead of praising toil and perseverance, called for instant gratification through "revolutionary" violence and property seizures. And the region's influential *"pensadores"*—writers, academicians, and other intellectuals—applauded the ruinous policies and magnified the cant.

Any attempt by Washington to be of help received the same hostile treatment. During my years in the hemisphere, nothing drew more radical invective and fury than the crown jewel of President Kennedy's Latin American aid program called Alliance for Progress. The sober truth was that the much ballyhooed Alianza para el Progreso deserved to be criticized for too much bureaucracy and too little funds. To mention just one example, in the vast and terribly poor Brazilian Northeast, one of the world's most depressed areas, the annual US aid amounted to 10 cents per capita. It was preposterous to think that such a pittance could deliver any real economic impetus.

Adding insult to injury, much of the skimpy aid went for an army of American "experts" whose salaries far exceeded their contribution to the program. My favorite example of this boondoggle was the Alliance's office in Cuiabá, a small town at the edge of the Amazonian jungle, which was the capital of the Brazilian state of Matto Grosso.

The Cuiabá's Alianza office was staffed by two people. One of them was a contract consultant from Texas, whose job was to evaluate the region's economic resources. He spoke no Portuguese. The other person was his secretary, who was provided by the Brazilian government. She spoke no English. Almost symbolically, their office overlooked Cuiabá's only stoplight that was forlornly blinking at an intersection with no traffic. The two sat at their desks like ships passing at night until Saturday morning, when a bilingual Peace Corps volunteer came to town from his jungle outpost and helped them communicate with each other.

The operation reeked of waste of money; when I asked the Texan what developmental resources he had found in the area, he reached under his desk and pulled out a basket with some local fruit. Yet by the time I left Rio, in 1967, the USAID section of the US embassy was one of Brazil's largest employers with a payroll of over eight hundred, mostly Yankee, "experts"—and that was before the arrival of an Alianza-funded American mission to study, of all things, migratory birds.

Had the radicals lambasted this sort of aid nonsense, they would have been on target and performed a real service. But for them, the facts were not bad enough. Preposterously exaggerating the negligible impact of the program, they painted the Alianza as an economic version of the Allied invasion of Normandy, a Trojan horse for making the continent into a Yanqui "colony."

The radicals were on better grounds when tilting against their other Yankee bugaboo, the CIA, but once again, I thought they grossly overstated their case. There were three major political events on my beat that were widely attributed to the work of the agency, and not without justice. They were the 1964 overthrow of the populist Goulart by the Brazilian army led by Marshal Humberto Castello Branco; the 1966 military coup that brought down Victor Paz Estenssoro, the democratic president of Bolivia; and the CIA interference in the presidential race in which the moderate Eduardo Frei defeated Salvador Allende, the head of the Chilean Communist Party.

In both coups, what fed the charges of CIA involvement was the chummy relationship between the American military attaché and the brass that toppled the elected head of the government. I knew the US Air Force attaché in La Paz and there was no doubt in my mind that he was onto the plans of Bolivian Air Force general René Barrientos Ortuño, Paz Estenssoro's vice president, to send his boss into exile. But knowing about the planned coup was not the same as supporting or being responsible for it, as the reformadores (but not Paz Estenssoro, when I spoke with him in his exile home in Lima) charged. As far as I could find out, the moderate, US-educated former president had no enemies in Washington.

The story was different in Brazil, where the geopolitical stakes were much higher and the US military attaché was Colonel Vernon "Dick" Walters. I saw Walters, who later became deputy director of CIA, fairly often and regarded him as an excellent choice for the job. A brilliant linguist who had served as President Eisenhower's interpreter, Walters spoke Brazilian Portuguese so perfectly that even well-educated Brazilians took him for a native. He was witty, jovial, and a great storyteller, a quality much appreciated by the military brass. Best of all, as the former US Army liaison with the Brazilian expeditionary force in Italy during World War II, Walters was an old friend of many high-ranking Brazilian officers, including Castello Branco, who was the expedition's commander. The flinty general went on to become Brazil's top military leader and, following the coup, the army-appointed successor of Goulart.

I feel certain that Walters had played a part in the overthrow. After Goulart was toppled, Walters told me that just before the event took place he had a long conversation with Castello Branco in which he reported some of my observations about the similarity between the tactics of the South American leftists and the Moscow-led Czech Communists. Obviously, Walters was not trying to dissuade the staunchly anticommunist plotters from taking matters into their own hands.

As for Frei's first race against Allende, books have been written about the way CIA lavished funds to stop the Communist bandwagon. One example I remember was the CIA-financed publication on the eve of the elections of large chunks of the novel *Darkness at Noon*, Arthur Koestler's famous condemnation of the Communist tyranny. That particular use of US taxpayers' dollars to influence the electorate was a waste and a joke because the excerpts appeared in Santiago's *El Mercurio*, the Chilean counterpart of the *Wall Street Journal*. The well-heeled readers of this right-wing newspaper hardly needed additional persuasion to vote against Allende, and the poor didn't read it.

In sum, both the Peruvian and Brazilian coups and the Chilean elections carried Uncle Sam's fingerprints, and the Left had good reasons for raising Cain. Yet any close observer could also see that in any of these developments the CIA was far from the key actor.

Goulart, for example, was a decent man but a weak executive who endlessly zigzagged to avoid the law-and-order demands of the military brass while heeding the strident calls for "reform" from his radical-left brother-in-law Leonel Brizola. The vacillation encouraged ever growing provocations from the leftist radicals while infuriating the military brass and the other pillar of the Brazilian Right, the Catholic hierarchy.

Into this overheated atmosphere, Goulart on March 25, 1964, tossed a burning match by addressing an illegal rally of leftist noncommissioned officers of the Brazilian navy who had gone on strike, demanding better living quarters. After that brazen insult to his own military establishment, Goulart's goose was cooked, with or without Walters's input. The Catholic Church organized a protest march against the radicals, in which one million cariocas—overwhelmingly the poor favelados who were supposed to be Goulart's best supporters—packed the broad Avenida Rio Branco outside our office building. The same evening, Castello Branco's troops fanned out through the town and took over the government offices.

As for Frei's victory, there is no way of telling whether the CIA's contribution swung any votes. I visited Chile several times in 1963 and 1964 to check on the political atmosphere and took a tour through the most populated coastal region just before the elections. On each visit I looked for signs of the sort of widespread anger or discontent that Allende needed to put him over. I did not find it, or at least not enough of it.

Because the elections were on Sunday, when every minute of press time counted, I filed on Saturday two advance stories, one explaining why Frei won and the other why he lost, but I advised my editors that Frei was likely to win. He did, with a margin so comfortable that *Time* magazine brushed off the hotly fought elections with a one-column story. It was a tremendous letdown for my good friend and very able competitor Gavin Scott, whose election coverage ran a total of five hundred thousand words.

It was one of my basic conclusions in South America that its regimes were not made and unmade in Washington, regardless what the reformadores claimed and no matter how hard the CIA tried to make that claim true. Uncle Sam's real or suspected meddling was at most a contributing factor to developments that had much more to do with the reformadores' own incompetence and the generals' ambitions than with any designs in Washington.

In my memory, the inanity of the reformadores' crusade against the United States was best showcased in Georgetown, the capital of the equatorial British Guiana. In the mid-1960s the tiny country was on the brink of a civil war between the dirt-poor black plantation workers—who, ironically, were led by a right-winger, Forbes Burnham—and the better-off Indian peasants and merchants, who equally incongruously supported Cheddi Jagan, an Indian Communist.

The colony's bureaucracy was run from London, and most of the sizable enterprises (such as they were) were controlled by the British, a few Dutchmen, and a Canadian aluminum company. Unemployment was 20 percent, schools were a rarity, and the jungle was reclaiming the roads. Yet the most prominent sign that welcomed visitors to Guiana's independence celebration in May 1966 read, in huge white letters, "YANKEE GO HOME!" Ironically, it was spray-painted on the fence surrounding the barracks of the British infantry unit that was the main symbol of Guiana's colonial status.

I was reminded of the postwar jokes about Zdeněk Nejedlý, the Czech Communist minister of education, who was said to open his umbrella in Prague when it rained in Moscow. The one-track mind of the South American leftists allowed no deviation from the approved anti-Yankee cant, regardless of the reality.

What added to my disdain for the South American *reformadores* was their callous indifference to the price others paid for their excesses. One incident that took place before I came to the region was the cold-blooded execution of a half-dozen Bolivian soldiers who were captured during a skirmish with the radicalized miners of the nationalized tin mine Siglo XX. The miners—who, like the soldiers, were mostly impoverished and illiterate Quechua Indians— tied up the captives and blew them up with dynamite. Asked about this incident when I visited the mine, the union leader shrugged off the atrocity as a "revolutionary blow" against the "autarchy."

I found the same chilling attitude among upper-class Venezuelan radicals, who in the early 1960s were the spokesmen of *la guerra urbana*, a war against the government then raging in the streets and alleys of Caracas. On one of my visits, the *guerrileros* had left in the street, presumably to blow up a passing car, a bomb wrapped in a paper bag. What happened instead was that a mestizo shoeshine boy gave it a kick, and the next morning's newspapers frontpages carried the picture of two cops carrying the victim's arms and upper torso, which was all that was left of him.

I tore out the picture and took it to the campus of the University of Caracas, which the police were banned from entering under an old law designed to protect academic freedoms. As a result, the campus was the hub of the various "revolutionary factions," "liberation movements," and "guerrileros" represented by so-called students—frequently upper-crust young men who drove late-model Chevys and lived far from the city's slums.

I interviewed a couple of the salon revolutionaries and tried to shock them by showing them the picture of the dead shoeshine boy. "What do you think about this incident?" I asked, but they had no ready answer. This is nothing exceptional, one of them finally said with a dismissive shrug of his shoulders. "We take losses like this all the time." I left the campus feeling sick.

The hemisphere was by no means the only beat where I found myself in strong disagreement with some of the values and actions of the people I covered. That happened also in the Muslim countries, behind the Iron Curtain, and in Israel. But only on my first foreign beat did my emotions actually boil over.

The controversy started about a year after I moved to Rio and Dwight Martin was replaced with John "Tito" Gerassi, a New Leftist intellectual who admired the policies and oratory of the Latino *reformadores* as fervently as I abhorred their performance. We were a terrible fit. Democratic principles, which I regarded as essential for good governance, meant so little to Gerassi that, in one case I still remember, he elevated Brazil's Getúlio Vargas—a strongman who among his other sins suppressed the freedom of the press—into a model statesman. Using my story as a vehicle, he praised Vargas for allegedly giving "the workers the best standard of living in Brazilian history, even if he did it by taking away their freedom," and for developing "Brazilian industries, even if those owned by the government were mass-producing corruption." It reminded me of the wartime praise of Mussolini for making the Italian trains run on time.

In dispensing this sort of wisdom, Gerassi had me at an enormous disadvantage. Because long-distance communications were expensive as well as inadequate, those of us who in the 1960s reported from abroad did not get a playback of our edited articles. And since the top editors who reviewed the final copy knew next to nothing about Latin America and its history, Gerassi could write into, or take out of, my articles practically anything he wanted. Which he did. And I fought back by complaining to the top editors until Jim Cannon, who was then the chief of correspondents, called me on the carpet. My letters had been so intemperate that, as I flew to New York, I expected to be busted as bureau chief and transferred to a stateside bureau.

What happened instead was that I was given an hour and a half to defend my position to Osborn Elliott, *Newsweek*'s outstanding editor-in-chief who had made the magazine into a first-class competitor of *Time*. At first, the meeting only added to my dour expectations. Oz observed that Gerassi's recent book about South American politics was "a tour de force" that showed a great deal of knowledge about the continent. He went on to note that Gerassi was a hardworking writer who had recently received an eight-hundred-dollar bonus—big money in those years—for writing an exceptional number of foreign stories. Finally, Oz added that my tormentor was a family man with kids; and that he personally got along well with his colleagues in the magazine's home office. It was not an auspicious introduction to a session that was sure to be fateful for my career as a foreign correspondent.

I pulled out my files and with a sinking feeling began pointing out the twists and innuendos imparted to my stories by Gerassi's editing. The longer I talked, the more I worried whether I was getting my points across. Most of my objections to Gerassi's changes required considerable factual background, and I was not at all sure that my historic and political references were easy to follow. Still, Oz heard me out with only a few interruptions, and when my time was up, ushered me out without any comment revealing his thinking.

I returned to my hotel and a glum evening, expecting the worst. I was conscious of my status as a newcomer to the hemisphere, my angry letters, and my lack of a personal relationship with most of the New York brass, all of which bode ill for the outcome of the showdown. The next morning, to my great relief and surprise, I got a call from Cannon telling me to return to Rio, with no buts and howevers. I never heard another word about the affair, but several weeks later, Gerassi was transferred to another section of the magazine. He soon quit and went on to a prominent leftist career as an author and college professor.

It took me a while to live down the showdown with Gerassi. I had been aware all along that what fanned my outrage in South America were my memories of the sinister machinations of the postwar Communists. That was a part of my background with which I had no argument. What bothered me—and a lot—was the suspicion that my emotions had blinded me to the Latin American reality and distorted my reporting.

To put my mind at ease, I made an extra effort to seek out the leftists on my beat, listen closely to their arguments, and give them more play in my articles. But learning more about the reformadores did not change my views. As hard as I tried to be fair, I did not find them an admirable lot.

~

Not all of my Latin American impressions were negative. There were a few statesmen, such as Rómulo Betancour in Venezuela, Victor Paz Estenssoro in Bolivia, and Eduardo Frei in Chile, who I thought were honestly trying to do the best for their people. I developed a strong liking for the ordinary Brazilians who, unlike many of their Spanish-speaking neighbors, in those years had a civilized aversion to violence, a sense of national dignity, and great confidence in their own future. And I appreciated the muscle and flair of some of the big South American cities, such as São Paulo and Buenos Aires.

I wrote some stories that I believed were ground-breaking. One that I felt particularly good about dealt with racism in Brazil, a country that in the 1960s was reputed to have no color line. I found the reality to be just the opposite and described it in a story that came out months ahead of a massive report with similar findings by a UN agency. For example, a fancifully shaped office building on Avenida Rio Branco, one of Rio's main thoroughfares, was popularly referred to as "O Nego bebo ai" ("A nigger got drunk here"). Although the Brazilian army had a few black officers, there were no black or mulatto pilots in the air force, and the navy did not have even one dark skinned noncom. In a country where the dominant whites were outnumbered by people of African origin, there was only one tiny Brazilian organization dedicated to the advancement of people of color. It had no visibility, let alone clout.

But the stories I enjoyed most harked back to my childhood fascination with adventures in faraway and exotic places. One feature I particularly relished was about an isolated colony deep inside the Amazon forest whose population—the great-grandchildren of German immigrants—still spoke German, raised tapirs instead of pigs, packed holstered revolvers, and worried about hostile Indians who shot arrows at their flat-bottomed boat as soon as it ventured out of sight of the colony.

In the southernmost tip of Argentina's Tierra del Fuego, I spent a day with an Englishman, a third-generation native, who owned about one million sheep and untold hundreds of thousands of acres (he was not sure how many) of windswept pastures. My host's family at home spoke only English, sent the children to schools in England, and did their serious shopping in London. The ranch had its own seaport, which had no Argentine official presence and handled all imports as well as the shipments of wool it exported abroad. In that part of Tierra del Fuego, the rancher was the king.

I was not alone in being captivated by the continent's then still pristine wilderness, which included the Xingu National Park, a huge tract of land in the heart of the Amazon that was the home of eighteen stone-age tribes, only one of which had come in contact with civilization. A couple of decades later, this enchanted world was invaded by settlers and land-hungry profiteers who followed the crews blasting the trans-Amazonian highway, and according to news reports, killed the Indians on sight. But in the early 1960s the headwaters of the Amazon were still inaccessible, the land was not worth taking, and the Indians were at least formally protected by the Brazilian government. I reached the park's headquarters after a long wait for the government's approval and a two-days' flight, the second half of which I sat next to an open crate with an entire butchered cow. Spending three days with the stark-naked, friendly Indians was a fascinating reward for the travails of getting there. But the most unforgettable part of the trip was when I got off the plane, nauseous from the smell of the raw meat, and spotted a tall, erect figure at the edge of the landing strip.

Assuming that he was one of the brothers Villas Boas, the park's managers, and filled with the sense of historic occasion that must have inspired

Henry Stanley's famous greeting for the long-lost Dr. Livingston, I walked up to the dignified-looking stranger and executed a slight bow.

"How do you do, sir," I said gravely, conscious of the importance of my mission. "I am Mike Kubic from *Newsweek*."

The man smiled without a trace of awe and cordially pumped my hand.

"How do you do," he said in fluent English. "I am King Leopold of Belgium."

Which is what he was, the retired monarch of all the Waloons and Belgians, as well as an amateur anthropologist. My ego was never more memorably squelched, but the king turned out to be an excellent source for information about the park, which he visited often together with an anthropology professor from the University of São Paulo.

Another memorable experience was accompanying Robert Kennedy—then a senator from New York—on a trip to spotlight the flagging Alliance for Progress and help advance his bid for the 1968 presidential race. I had known Bob Kennedy since 1959, when he was the chief counsel of the Senate Labor Rackets Committee, and I was one of the reporters covering his battles with Jimmy Hoffa, the notorious head of the Teamsters Union. When in November 1965 I joined Bobby, his wife, Ethel, and a small group of his aides and friends upon their arrival in Lima, I was looking forward not just to reporting the colorful tale of a Kennedy abroad but also to taking his measure as potential presidential candidate. Over the next three weeks, I had plenty of opportunity to do both, and I was deeply impressed by Bob Kennedy as an American statesman and as a person.

Watching him make his way through presidential palaces, slums, mines, and university campuses brought to mind Bob's difference from his older brother. John Kennedy on his trips abroad was a true Camelot: a supremely self-confident leader of the free world and a polished symbol of the American Century. Bobby Kennedy in South America was all edges. He was ill-at-ease among dignitaries, disdainful of pomp, and bored by social chatter.

And yet, his trip was not a waste of his time or the US taxpayers' money. He had a message for the continent's leaders that by my lights was right on target—namely, that they needed less blame-shifting rhetoric and more reasoned and serious action. Essentially, he was advising the Latin Americans to stop their empty posturing and start making real reforms. Their political, economic, and social systems were not working; it was high time to replace them with something better—and, Bob made clear, this did not mean dictatorships of the Left or the Right.

Belgian King Leopold II was an amateur anthropologist who frequently visited the tribes on the Amazon to study their languages and culture. Here he is, in October 1961, with three members of the Camayuras tribe in Brazil's Xingu National Park. A friendly and generous man, Leopold gave me a half a dozen pocket knives so that I would have something to trade with the natives for their beautiful artifacts. All I had were American greenbacks and traveler's checks and Brazilian cruzeiros, which were worthless in the jungle.

King Leopold II taking more pictures of the Camayuras natives. The man striding behind him is Professor Harald Schultz, an anthropologist from the University of São Paulo, Brazil, who accompanied the king.

In a region whose politicians prided themselves on their *pronuncios muy emocionantes* (highly emotional speeches), Kennedy's sober message did not go over. The feudal elites fulminated because he called for real change, and the *reformadores* denounced him as yet another envoy of *imperialismo Yanqui*. His meetings in the presidential palaces—and some US embassies—were markedly cool. The slum dwellers were puzzled, and the university students whom he sought out with dogged persistence adulated Che Guevara and Fidel Castro. When Bob showed up they rioted, spat on him, and tried to prevent him from speaking.

What they failed to understand—and what impressed me—was that Bob Kennedy was not trying to win popularity, at least not in South America. He wanted to talk sense, and he pursued that goal with steely determination and courage. Against local police advice, he charged into auditoriums full of shrieking Yankee-haters, and he was unflinching in talking harsh facts with the ruling strongmen. There was no phoniness wafting from Bob Kennedy.

I have two other memories of Bob on the trip. One is about a brief visit I arranged for him—along with Richard Goodwin, who was then Bob's aide, Bonnie Angelo from *Time*, and me—to a British missionary couple who were transcribing the language of a small tribe deep in the Amazon jungle. The Hixkaryana had no idea who Bob Kennedy was, and he did not look much more physically impressive than Dick or I did. Yet as soon as we got off the hydroplane that landed on a river next to their village, the tribesmen instantly gathered around him as if he were a returning hero. The English couple were no more able to explain Kennedy's magnetism than we were.

For me (and, I felt sure, for Bob Kennedy) the highlight of his South American trip came the next day, when we were scheduled to fly back to Belém and from there to Caracas for a meeting with Venezuelan president Betancour. Instead, we left in a native dugout. Overnight, the water level in the river had dropped so low that the plane could not take off with the three of us, and it had to fly without us several miles downstream to reach a deeper segment.

Led by a young tribesman and accompanied by the missionary, we set out as soon as the plane took off, only to find out that the rarely used outboard motor would not start. We had to paddle, which ended all hopes of reaching Caracas in time for Bob's appointment. Without a word of complaint, Kennedy took turns paddling with the rest of us, swam in the piranha-infested water, tried out the bows and arrows of the Indians who were accompanying us, and helped navigate the boat through the rapids. It took us half a day to reach the plane, and Kennedy, to his regret, missed his appointment with Betancourt.

I was even more impressed by Bob Kennedy when I saw him cry real tears. On the eve of November 23, the anniversary of his brother's assassination, we spent the night in São Louis de Potosi, a lovely Brazilian coastal town that celebrated a local festival. Bob had been subdued all day, a mood we attributed to his memories of the shooting in Dallas. After dinner we sat around the table sipping drinks, and there was a sudden explosion of firecrackers just outside the windows.

In the most revealing moment of the trip, Bob curled up on his chair, covered his face with his hands, and cried like a deeply hurt child. I watched him with admiration and sympathy: it takes uncommon strength and honesty for a politician to cry in front of reporters. Later, when Kennedy ran for the nomination, I wondered if the story of his breakdown would surface and be used against him. As far as I know, it did not.

Senator Robert F. Kennedy delighted—and was delighted by—the Hixkaryana tribesmen, who instantly recognized that he was the real VIP when we disembarked from a small missionary hydroplane outside their village in November 1965. The rest of our party was all but ignored while they crowded around him. The Kennedy charisma worked even in the jungle.

Bobby Kennedy was pensive during the boat ride with the Hixkaryana tribesmen. The water level in the Amazon tributary where we landed the previous day had dropped so low overnight we had to take a boat to a point where the river was deep enough for the plane to take off with all four of us. Bobby knew that as a result he would miss his appointment with President Romulo Betancourt, "the Father of Venezuelan Democracy," one of the South America leaders he wanted to meet.

My Quarrel with the *Reformadores*

Bobby Kennedy did his share of the paddling and helping to steer the boat through the rapids.

CHAPTER 12

THE SIX DAY WAR AND ITS AFTERMATH

I was in Santiago in the middle of April 1967 finishing a story about the mounting troubles of Chilean president Eduardo Frei when the Saturday cable traffic brought a major surprise from the editors. Without any preliminaries, they offered me as my next post the Beirut bureau, the magazine's base for covering the Muslim world. If I accepted the assignment, the cable continued, I should pack up as soon as I could and hie to Lebanon.

The conditional tone of the message was mostly a reflection of the studiedly good manners that prevailed in communications between the magazine headquarters and the field. There was little chance that I would turn down the transfer. I had been covering South America for over four years, a year longer than what was then a routine tour in a foreign post. That was about two years longer than my predecessor or, for that matter, the correspondent who replaced me. I had done most of the basic stories I thought worth telling, and I was not looking forward to covering more anti-Yankee politics; it was time for me to move on.

Moreover, I was intrigued and flattered by the New York cable. The headlines from the Middle East clearly indicated that the Arabs and Israel were on the brink of their first all-out war in two decades. To be asked to take over an area at the onset of a major news event was a vote of confidence and a compliment.

I sent a cable to Romana asking how she'd feel about moving to Lebanon and set out on a tour of Santiago bookstores in search of recent books about the Middle East. The cable to my wife was also more a courtesy than a real question: both she and I were products of a culture where it was customary for wives to accompany their husbands wherever their jobs took them. In the evening, I had small bottle of a very good Chilean wine with my dinner. I was more than ready to take my leave from the reformadores.

It was my last relaxed evening for quite a while. By the time Romana, little Jan, and I managed to pack up and leave for the States it was mid-May, and the

Middle East crisis was heating up by the hour. We were about to depart from Rio when Egypt's president Gamal Abdel Nasser gave the world a jolt by ordering the UN Emergency Force out of Sinai and by mining the Straits of Tiran. The gambit imperiled the shipments of Iranian oil to Israel's port of Eilat in the Gulf of Aqaba and came as close to a casus belli as anything short of shooting.

The next escalation took place when I was in Washington getting briefed about my next beat and Nasser delivered himself of a crowd-pleasing chest-thumper matching the demagoguery of the Latin *caudillos*. "Under no circumstances will we allow the Israeli flag to pass through the Aqaba Gulf," Nasser blustered. "The Jews threatened war. We tell them: you are welcome, we are ready for war.... This water is ours." In the judgment of some Foggy Bottom Arabists, the Egyptian was merely blowing hot air, but to an outsider like me he sounded both reckless and serious. I could imagine that the Israelis did not share the State Department's confidence.

The day my family and I boarded a flight for Lebanon, the Arabs ratcheted up the tensions still higher. Iraq airlifted an army unit to join Egyptian troops that had occupied the heights above the Straits of Tiran, and most significantly, Jordan's King Hussein unexpectedly arrived in Cairo to sign a defense pact with Nasser.

Hussein was a pro-Western survivalist clutching on to a kingdom that, as the story went, Winston Churchill had carved out of the British mandate over a cup of tea. Nasser was a classic Third World *líder último* who followed the then fashionable Cold War policy of playing footsie with Moscow and promoting anti-Western, super-nationalistic pan-Arabism. King Hussein and al-rais Nasser had not been on speaking terms for years. The fact that the Jordanian monarch, an assiduous student of the complex Middle East wind patterns, felt compelled to embrace his enemy signaled that a hurricane-strength gale was gathering. As the headline in *Newsweek* aptly put it, "The Scent of War" in the Middle East was palpable.

When we arrived in Beirut, Romana and Jan checked into the seaside St. Georges Hotel while I flew on to Damascus to report on the war fever in Syria. That was Wednesday morning. I returned to Beirut late Friday to file: as I quickly learned, it was the standard practice in the Arab world to telex one's article about country A in country B—preferably, the relatively easy-going Lebanon—so as to bypass the censorship of the regime the story was dealing with. I spent Saturday and Sunday picking the brains of veteran American and British correspondents on the beat and getting to know my new office in the building of *Al-Anwar*, at that time the best Arab newspaper. Since the colleague I was replacing was already in Egypt, I decided to head fast for Jordan, the other Arab country that was likely to bear the brunt of the impending war.

CHAPTER 12

On Monday morning, June 5, I took the seven o'clock Middle East Airlines flight to Amman, the Jordanian capital. It was the emptiest commercial plane I ever flew: the only other passengers aboard the French-built Caravelle were a well-dressed Jordanian woman and her two children. What came to be known as the Six Day War broke out when we had been in the air about thirty minutes.

When we landed at the Amman airport, events took off at a hectic pace. Four visibly excited security men barged into the plane, barred my attempt to get off, and fell into a loud quarrel among themselves in Arabic. I surmised from their menacing gestures and occasional comments directed at me in broken English that they found my brand-new passport with a Jordanian visa issued in Washington a proof positive that I was an Israeli spy. The row was only settled by the arrival of a commanding-looking airport security chief in civilian clothing who quickly ruled in my favor. Speaking fluent English with a British accent, he apologized for "these idiots," as he referred to his subordinates and politely bid me to disembark.

The terminal was empty, and there was only one cab waiting outside. I got in and went straight to the Jordanian ministry of information at Amman's Third Circle to get the press credentials I assumed I'd need to cover the war. I was ushered into the office of a remarkably relaxed-looking director of the press section, who gave me an upbeat overview of the crisis and told me to come back after lunch to get my credentials and some assistance in getting to the front. Brand new as I was to the Middle East, I naively followed his instructions, picked up my valise, and checked into the Amman Intercontinental on the opposite side of the Circle.

Given the speed of events, I had already missed the war. Years later I found out that even before I landed in Amman, Ezer Weizman, the deputy chief of staff of the Israeli army, phoned his wife that Israeli Mirages had wiped out the Egyptian air force while it was still on the ground, which sealed the Arab defeat. As I also found out only later, by the time I met the press official—about an hour and a half after the war started—it was already too late to find a cab to take me to East Jerusalem and see the only action that involved Jordanian troops, which was the Israeli conquest of the Old City.

Blissfully ignorant of these developments, still unknown to the rest of world, I sent a telex to New York about my whereabouts, asked the concierge to get me a cab for a trip to Jerusalem, and sat down to a quick lunch. Meanwhile, history took several fateful turns. Golda Meir, the Israeli prime minister, sent a warning to King Hussein to stay out of the fighting; a Jordanian battery opened fire on Israeli troops advancing on East Jerusalem; and the Israeli army crossed the 1949 ceasefire line into the West Bank. Shortly after lunch, when that news reached Amman, the director of the press office showed up in the hotel and invited all foreign correspondents to the royal palace for a press conference with King Hussein.

There were about a dozen of us foreign correspondents arrayed around a big table at the head of which sat the handsome king. He wore the uniform of the Bedouin Desert Legion and, rather understandably, looked tense. Speaking in a deep voice interspersed with his characteristic long pauses, Hussein welcomed us to Jordan, apologized for not having seen us earlier, and informed us that the Arab nation was at war with Israel. He pledged that the Jordanian army would fight to the last man but said nothing about its disposition. He took no questions and concluded with a promise to see us as often as the war would permit.

Except for the honor of it, the encounter was a waste of time. We were hustled back to the hotel and told to wait for further word from the press office. By then the BBC was reporting heavy fighting in Jerusalem, all cabs vanished from in front of the Intercontinental, and over the suddenly deadly quiet Amman appeared six Israeli Mirages. Unchallenged by a Jordanian plane or artillery, they methodically bombed the runways of the Amman airport and the fuel depot of the adjoined Jordanian air force base.

As a bunch of us watched from the roof of the hotel, the Israeli planes flew so low that we could see the pilots as they turned around for each new sortie. Still, they were totally unchallenged except for a lone Jordanian soldier on the slope behind the hotel who was lying on his back and popping away into the air with a rifle. And by the time the raid ended, some thirty minutes later, the atmosphere in Amman and our hotel had dramatically changed.

When our group returned downstairs, we were met by unsmiling stares of the hotel staff, almost all of whom were Palestinian refugees from the coastal areas that Israel had seized during the previous war, in 1948. I still had no gut feeling for the multiple tensions of the Arab-Israeli conflict, but after a few minutes in the lobby even I could sense that the attitude of the hotel clerks and bellboys toward the foreign media people—the only guests left in the hotel—was getting worse by the minute.

Eagerness to please and earn a tip was replaced with disdainful looks or chilling indifference. By now I had given up on the press credentials and was anxious to head for Jerusalem. But when I asked what had happened to the cabs, the doorman who only a few hours earlier was obsequious just shrugged and walked away. The bell captain claimed he had no idea how to reach the managers of the two car rental agencies whose offices were closed. I tried to get help from the ministry of information, but the building was now guarded by armed soldiers who waved me off with gestures that were distinctly unfriendly.

CHAPTER 12

I was getting impatient. According to the BBC, the Israeli army was conquering East Jerusalem, an hour's drive from where I was, but I could not find any way to get there. What looked like my only break during that frustrating afternoon came around five o'clock, when I spotted in the lobby a Middle East luminary whose picture I had seen in stories about the crisis. It was Ahmad Shukeiry, the corrupt head of the Syria-sponsored Palestine Liberation Organization (PLO), who had just pulled up in a big black Mercedes, wearing starched combat fatigues and flanked by bodyguards.

I made a beeline for him in hopes of getting a few quotes, but while we were in plain view of the hotel help Shukeiry only stiffly motioned to me to follow him. Inside the elevator Shukeiry quickly mellowed and readily promised to see me "first thing" the next morning. As we were ascending toward his top-floor suite, Shukeiry was the Arab regime's designated spokesman of the hundreds of thousands of Palestinian refugees. His promise of an interview was, together with the Israeli air raid, the day's only antidote for my fast-growing sense that I was committing the worst sin in all journalism, being in the wrong place.

I returned to the lobby and eventually got hold of a cabbie who promised—for a hundred dollars (five times the usual fare)—to take me to Jerusalem. Only next morning, of course. I went to the dining room. It was dimly lit and empty except for a few worried-looking media characters like me. Every time the door to the kitchen opened we could hear a blast of martial music and excited radio announcers shouting in Arabic what I assumed were war bulletins. When the doors swung shut, grim-looking waiters served the food in heavy silence.

After dinner, handwritten signs appeared in the lobby and on the elevator urging guests to keep their curtains pulled and observe a blackout. I returned to my room and went on the balcony to listen for signs of war. The town was as quiet as an empty hospital ward. After a couple of minutes, a gruff voice in the courtyard below me barked out in broken English that nobody was allowed to stand on the balcony. I went to bed thinking there was history being made all around me, and I was falling down on my job.

The next morning, I indeed did see Shukeiry when I got up before seven o'clock. I pulled open the curtain over the glass door to the balcony and there he was, rushing out of the hotel in his salon fatigues (not, as was later rumored, in a woman's dress), getting into his big Mercedes, and speeding away with his entourage. The flight from Amman was Shukeiry's exodus from history: shortly afterwards he was replaced by a new PLO chief who had worked as an engineer in Kuwait and was called Abu Ammar. His real name was Yassir Arafat.

I listened to the BBC, the best source of news about the Middle East, as it announced Israeli advances both in the Sinai and in the West Bank of Jordan. When I came downstairs to look for the cab driver who was to take me to Jerusalem, I found that our glitzy hostelry had transmogrified, Kafka-style, into something resembling a compound for POWs.

The clerks and bellhops wore the Shukeiry-style PLO combat fatigues with naked pistols stuck behind their belts. No longer merely stern-looking, they eyed us, the hapless guests, with open anger and hostility. When I asked about my cab, the bell captain fixed me with a fierce glare and uttered a guttural sound so furious that I did not even bother to ask what it meant. My peers and I still could get breakfast, but the atmosphere was so strained we cut out all conversation and drank our coffee in silence.

The tensions burst into the open an hour or so later when I tried to use the hotel telex to send my editors a routine Tuesday advisory on the story outlook. As I approached the telex counter, the hotel cashier came running from behind his window, jerked the copy out of my hand, and began reading it while muttering something in Arabic. Still naive about the ways of the Middle East, I blew up, protesting that the text had been approved and stamped by the Jordanian military censor, and I tried to pull the advisory out of the cashier's hands.

The next thing I knew I was flanked by two hotel clerks and the cashier gave me a push, which I broke by grabbing the front of his fatigues. The scuffle was quickly over—the two guys pinned my arms behind my back—but it made me a marked man in a hotel that, for lack of a better option, became my Amman headquarters during the more than four years I was on the Middle East beat. In the eyes of the Palestinian employees I became a "Zionist," one of the worst things one could be called anywhere in the Arab world.

For the next three days, all of us in the hotel became de facto detainees of the Palestinian vigilantes. We could leave the hotel, but there was not a car in town that could be rented or hired for the twenty-five-mile trip to the Jordan River, which was quickly becoming the new demarcation line between Jordan and Israel. The airport was closed, which meant we could not leave the country. To add to our misery, as we heard on the radio, the Israeli conquest of the West Bank—the turf that was to be ours—was being amply covered by correspondents based in Israel. While we were stuck in Amman, they were roaming all over the place on the heels of the Israeli army. Frustrated and increasingly demoralized, we were reduced to useless phone calls to the Jordanian ministry of information, making equally unproductive daily visits to the few embassies in town that remained open, and to listening to the radio reports of our more fortunate colleagues.

For the Arabs, the news was unspeakably bad, and its coverage by the Arab media was even worse. In the first couple of days Radio Cairo kept exulting about fictitious military "victories," when in fact the Israeli air force controlled the skies and the Egyptian army was in full retreat across the Sinai to the Suez Canal. Ridiculous as it was, each time the Cairo bombast hit the Arab airwaves, the Palestinians in our hotel burst into shouts of delirious joy and their hostile glares at us became both triumphant and condescending. But by noon on Wednesday even they began to recognize the vast gap between the Egyptian communiqués and reality, and their attitude toward us became menacing.

There was only one brief respite from the tensions. Wednesday afternoon, as I recall, Radio Cairo triumphantly announced that an Iraqi expeditionary force had reached Nablus, a big Palestinian town in the northern part of the West Bank. Our hotel minutemen shrieked and jumped in ecstasy, but by the evening their euphoria collapsed into despair. The arriving troops turned out to be Israelis who had bypassed Nablus and entered it from the north, the direction from which the West Bankers expected the arrival of allied Syrian and Iraqi units. In cold fact, neither of those two armies had done any serious fighting, just like—except during the first day of the war in Jerusalem—their Jordanian peers.

As if that final blow did not inflame the Arabs enough, Nasser added still more heat. Casting for a scapegoat for his military debacle, he accused fictitious US warplanes of forming "an umbrella" over the attacking Israeli units. It was a blatant lie, but it gave Arab mobs additional reason for turning against the only "enemy" they could lick, the hapless, unarmed Americans and other Westerners trapped in their midst.

Some of the region's worst anti-Western riots took place in the "cosmopolitan" Beirut, where berserk mobs ransacked the fancy stores in the Hamra district, the favorite haunts of resident foreigners. The violence precipitated the evacuation of all Beirut-based Americans, including Romana and Jan, who were flown to Athens by planes chartered by the American embassy. On the way to the airport, the buses with the evacuees—almost all of them women and children—were attacked by throngs of howling bullies from Bourj al-Barajneh, a Palestinian refugee camp, who rocked the buses and tried to turn them over.

In our hotel, the vigilantes gave vent to their raw feelings by staging a "trial" of Louis Rukeyser, then an ABC television correspondent, who happened to be not only American but also Jewish. The kangaroo court took place on Thursday morning in front of the hotel, directly below the balcony of my room. I was listening to the BBC news when a bunch of the fatigues-clad waiters and clerks emerged from the hotel entrance with Rukeyser in their midst and marched him to a point where he could be seen from all the guest rooms facing the street. The vigilantes then arranged themselves in front of Rukeyser and proceeded to question him. This was well before the time when senseless murder of Americans became a signature Arab activity, but given the hotel atmosphere, I watched the kangaroo court with heart-thumping alarm and fear.

From where I stood I could not hear any of the exchanges but I could clearly see Rukeyser, and his response to the hatred of his captors filled me with admiration. Tall, slim, and handsome, he looked down at the tribunal with just the right mixture of disdain and dignity—the sort of bearing I only wished I had achieved in my own encounters with the minutemen. In that twenty-to-thirty-minute-long show trial, Rukeyser set my standard for a journalist's behavior when facing pressures far worse than deadlines.

To my great relief, the vigilantes eventually let Rukeyser return to the hotel. He was even allowed to go back to his work, such as it was, but whenever he left his room he was dogged by one or two of the hotel warriors. Rukeyser went through the motions of continuing his reporting, although there was no way he and his crew could get to where the action was—and if they did, they could not ship the film because the airport was closed. In fact, the fury vented by the Palestinians against us in Amman was entirely wasted, because none of us added anything to the war coverage. The stories about the Arab rout that so rankled the Arab world were written by our lucky colleagues on the other side of the Jordan River who basked in the glory of a triumphant Israel.

After the show trial of Rukeyser, the antics of the hotel staff were increasingly overshadowed by a new security threat, which was considerably more serious. The menace was a tidal wave of Palestinian refugees—many of whom had gone through similar experiences in 1948—who had been fleeing before the Israeli troops on the West Bank. By Wednesday night some of them reached the edge of Amman and the next day—in a mood the hotel help gleefully described to us as "very ugly"—they were reportedly headed for the royal palace. The main target of their anger was the pro-Western, British-educated King Hussein, who was a Bedouin by birth and as such was disliked and distrusted by most Palestinians. However, any American who might get in their way was believed to be a fair game.

When, following the Rukeyser event, a couple of us dropped in on the US embassy for our daily chat, the ambassador—whose name I've mercifully forgotten—emerged from his office in an obvious state of nerves. Sporting a several-days-old stubble and a threadbare sweater, he heatedly urged us to immediately leave the building, which, he said with rising panic in his voice, was at any moment likely to be stormed by the seething refugees. Nothing of the sort happened during the day, but in the afternoon we finally saw our first Jordanian army officer. Wearing a dress uniform, he came to our hotel lobby to warn us to stay away from the streets in order to avoid running into the vengeful West Bankers.

The influx of furious fugitives gave a jolt to the sulking Jordanian air force commander who had bought Nasser's line about the American "umbrella" and refused to accept any calls from the US embassy. Now, faced with the outlook for a hunt on Yanks in the streets of Amman, the general agreed to the proposal of an intermediary—the Italian ambassador, who was the doyen of the Amman diplomatic corps—to help with the evacuation of all foreigners. By Saturday night the holes in the runways were filled with dirt and the US press attaché, a plucky and affable guy whose last name was Butros, sent the word to all of us at the hotel to stand by in the lobby with luggage at three o'clock in the morning and wait for a ride to the airport.

Not long after the appointed hour practically all foreigners in town—with the notable exception of nine Russian diplomats who had signed up for the evacuation but at the last minute failed to show up—left Amman in a long convoy of private cars belonging to the staffers of the Western embassies. It was still pitch dark, and we took a roundabout desert road to the airport to give wide berth to Amman's Palestinian refugee camps and neighborhoods.

My most vivid recollection of the stealthy departure is of one of the Bedouin Desert Legionnaires, King Hussein's most loyal troops, who were posted along the road to protect the convoy. The soldier, a gaunt, erect figure straight out of Lawrence of Arabia was standing at an intersection wearing the red-and-white checkered kaffiyeh and long brown burnoose of the Desert Legion, keeping his rifle pointed in the direction we were supposed to take. Caught in the glare of the headlights of our car, the soldier waved to us and smiled. It was the friendliest Arab face I had seen since the start of the war.

We drove to the Jordanian air force base, left the cars close to the freshly patched up runway, and formed into groups according to a list prepared by our embassy. Minutes later, in the gray light of the dawn, we could make out the first of several Hercules coming in for landing. The cargo planes, which were based at the US Air Force base Wheelus in Libya—a country that was then still run by another pro-Western monarch, King Idryss—had to assume a disguise to be allowed into the Jordanian air space. Their air force insignia were covered with spray-painted red crosses, and the airmen wore overalls with similar markings scribbled with a ballpoint pen.

The evacuation was executed with a flair and precision that strengthened my long-standing admiration for the superb organization talents of our military.

The lead aircraft halted a few yards in front of the first cluster of evacuees, lowered the rear cargo gate without cutting the engines, and the evacuees, mostly women and children, ran inside through the cloud of dust and sand kicked up by the propellers. In seconds, the gate closed and the plane took off just as the second Hercules touched down at the other end of the runway.

The process was repeated without a hitch until I was picked up together with the fourth or fifth batch of evacuees. We were all flown to Tehran, then the capital of Shah Reza Pahlavi's kingdom of Iran. It took three kings and the US Air Force to get us out of harm's way—and for once, I found some sympathy for the State Department's cultivation of the Middle East's last, and increasingly obsolete, monarchs.

~

Changing a foreign beat is always akin to crashing a college course, but my first few weeks in the Middle East, a period when the Arabs were seething with fury and frustration over their rout in the war, were exceptionally instructive. The first and fastest lesson I learned from the explosive emotions in the streets, refugee camps, and hotel lobbies was about the basic difference between the anti-Yanquism of the Latinos and the anti-Americanism of many Arabs. The anti-Yanquism I had left behind was largely inane and baseless rhetorical scapegoating, and it never became personal.

By contrast, Arab anti-Americanism was borne of and fueled by a very real and deeply felt grievance—the US support for Israel. And unlike the fulminations south of the border, Arab hostility could be physical, vicious, and could readily turn against any American within reach, especially if he happened to be a journalist. In the wake of the Six Day War, American reporters trying to ask questions in the Muslim countries of the Middle East were regarded, prima facie, as spies for the CIA or Israel.

As a result, there was no way to do one's job without first easing the palpable tensions and distrust that invariably marked each encounter with a potential source. The approach I found to work best with any Arab, high or low, was to first impassively hear out an unavoidable tirade against the United States and the unfairness of its protection of Israel. Depending on the source's erudition, the philippic might eventually give way to a broader lecture on the history of the Arab struggle against Zionism, but in any case it would take at least ten minutes before the speaker would calm down.

Then, and only then, I could start asking carefully phrased questions. I decided early on to not let myself be drawn into arguments about US actions or positions. Whatever I thought about the Middle East policies of my government—and sometimes I thought of them very little—I had nothing but contempt for some fellow Americans (mostly, the Beirut-based representatives of American companies) who curried Arab favor by berating Uncle Sam.

The second most important lesson I learned from the Six Day War and its aftermath was how difficult it was to understand the motives and logic of Arab actions and to explain them to American audience. In the 1960s there was far less contact—and a huge disparity—between the Western world and the emotions-saturated Middle East. The readers for whom my colleagues and I were writing assumed at least a modicum of connection between an official pronouncement and reality; it was difficult to explain to them how enormously tenuous, if connected at all, this nexus could be in the Arab world.

A prime example of this reporting quandary was Nasser's bellicose speeches that kept pouring heat into the explosive atmosphere on the eve of the Six Day War. Until the war started, the old hands on the beat told me, officials in Cairo were delighted by the worldwide spotlight on the belligerent harangues of the Egyptian strongman when he demanded the withdrawal of UN peace-keepers from Sinai and threatened Israel. The attitude of Cairo's spokesmen was that the world had been long enough deceived by "Zionist propaganda," and that it was high time for the Western public to learn what the Arabs had to say.

After the bluster climaxed in a military fiasco, the same officials took a 180-degree turn and blamed the war, of all things, on the publicity given to Nasser's speeches in the Western press. The charge now was that the foreign correspondents had misread Nasser's intentions and thereby built up a phony crisis into a real one. As proof of Nasser's allegedly nonaggressive intentions behind his provocative oratory, Cairo officials harped on the fact that, while rattling his verbal bayonets, Nasser kept Egypt's elite army units fighting in North Yemen, hundreds of miles from Israel. And indeed, when the war broke out, forty thousand of Egypt's best troops were not on the battlefield: they were using mustard gas to convince Yemeni tribesmen about the wisdom of the pan-Arabism of Gamal Abdel Nasser.

The Egyptian ambassador to the UN who lectured me on my first visit to Cairo got so excited at the abysmal stupidity of the Western media that he lapsed into language not routinely used by diplomats. "If you think that Nasser intended to go to war against Israel while keeping his best troops in Yemen, you're as crazy as you think that we are," he shouted heatedly. The argument made some sense, but new as I was to the Middle East, I could not buy the idea that Nasser's threats were mere make-believe.

Official blame-shifting was also all the rage in Amman when I returned there a few weeks after the war. As I made the rounds of the senior government people, their analysis of the historic debacle invariably started with the emphatic assertion that, from the king on down, nobody in the government had had the least desire to fight Israel. The debacle, they said, was entirely Nasser's fault. When pressed about King Hussein's trip to Cairo and his rejection of Israel's last minute bid for Jordanian non-belligerency, the answer was that the monarch had to enter the war or else lose the respect of his own population.

Again, this was a good postwar line to feed to the Western press. Unfortunately for my informants, it clashed with my vivid recollection of the first senior official I met in Amman, a few hours after the hostilities started. I was sitting in the office of Ibrahim Azzidin, the director of the Jordanian Government Press Office, applying for press credentials and inquiring about the official Jordanian view of the war. Relaxed and in an expansive mood, Azzidin seemed to enjoy explaining regional basics to a brand new Middle East hand.

"Well, I'll tell you," he said, leaning forward in his chair. "For years and years, we Arabs have suffered nothing but humiliations and attacks from the Israelis. We were too weak and too disunited to strike back. But this time, we're all together and we've got Israel here—" Azzidin leaned back, stretched his left arm, and cupped the palm of his hand—"and now we're going to do this!" And with obvious relish, he slammed the cupped hand with his right fist.

King Hussein's leadership during the war reflected the same dissonance between facts and fantasy. On the first day of the war, after the Israeli Mirages bombed Amman airport, the king went on the air to assure his countrymen of his total resolve to press on with the fight. Speaking in his deepest voice and lapsing into dramatic pauses, the Oxford-educated descendant of Prophet Mohammed made Churchill's blood-sweat-and-tears prose of World War II sound like mere nursery rhymes.

"We will fight until we see the beard of God," the Hashemite monarch solemnly pledged. "We will fight until every grain of sand in the desert is drenched with our blood." He reminded me of the Jewish zealots on Masada swearing to die before surrendering to the Romans.

Yet less than thirty-six hours later, the same Hussein accepted a UN-brokered ceasefire that left in Israeli hands one-third of his kingdom, including East Jerusalem with its ancient Mosques of al-Aqsa and the Dome of the Rock. For Hussein to abandon the Dome of the Rock, the third holiest site in Islam— from which, according to Muslim tradition, Prophet Mohammed ascended to heaven—was said to have been excruciatingly difficult, and perhaps it was. But the actual fact is that the Jordanian army of fifty-five thousand well-trained and relatively well-armed soldiers stopped fighting before seeing "the beard of God." When Hussein threw in the towel, Jordan's total casualties were estimated at well below twenty thousand, including several thousand dead.

Our evacuation by "Red Cross" planes was another example of the chasm between Arab words and Arab deeds. It was a classical sleight of hand by a king who kept up his life insurance by making payments to all parties that mattered. His payoffs ranged from secret meetings with Israeli prime ministers and quiet tolerance of Israeli violations of Jordanian airspace, to highly publicized embraces with Egypt's Nasser, Iraq's Saddam Hussein, Syria's Hafez al-Assad and other belligerent anti-Israeli and anti-American radicals. In Western eyes, Hussein's leadership seemed meandering, but in the context of the Middle East, the Amman monarch pursued a straightforward course, which was doing whatever it took to stay in power.

There was one more fundamental opinion I began to form during my first few weeks in the Middle East, and that only grew more firm during the more than seventeen years when I covered the area. It had to do with the question as to whether the region's festering conflict, the Arabs' rejection of Israel, was capable of peaceful solution. This was the gut issue of the US-Arab relations and of Israel's survival, and it was clear that the answer would have to come from the Palestinians—the people who had lost their country, their homes, and their livelihoods to the Jewish state. The more I got to know this critical group of Arabs, the more skeptical I became about the long-term outlook for peace between the Palestinians and Israel.

I began forming this impression after I made my way back to Beirut and started covering one of the major results of the Israeli military triumph, a revolt of the Palestinian refugees. Since they had fled or had been expelled during the 1948–1949 war, more than one million of these illiterate former peasants and their families lived in abysmally poor UN camps in Lebanon, Jordan, the Gaza strip, and Syria. Politically and psychologically in limbo, they waited for Godot—that is, Egypt-led Arab armies—to destroy Israel and clear the way for their return to Palestine. When the Six Day War demolished these hopes, the refugees ditched Shukeiry, who was Nasser's puppet, and set on an independent course under Yassir Arafat, the new chief of the PLO.

Reporting on this new Middle East fault line in the summer of 1967 took me to several of the smelly, primitive refugee camps where I spent long hours sipping tea and listening to gruesome descriptions of the 1948–1949 exodus, laments about betrayals by the Western world and Arab governments, and fanciful plans for a PLO guerrilla war against Israel. I was profoundly skeptical about much of what I heard. But there was one impression I gained from little kids who could not be shrugged off as PLO mouthpieces, and which struck me genuine. It was their deeply felt Palestinian identity.

These were children who were born in the UN-run refugee camps and who had never set foot in the land of their ancestors. Yet when asked where they were from, each little refugee unhesitatingly named the village from which the parents and grandparents had fled two decades earlier. Many of those kids also pulled out a fading picture of a stone house they claimed had belonged to their family.

The village they called their home could not be found on any current map: more than 360 of them had been bulldozed and plowed over by the Israeli government. But every one of those hamlets existed in the minds of the little refugees. The Hebrew oath "If I forget thee, Jerusalem," had its own ironic echo in the Palestinian camps, and the refugees' mantra of a "return to the land" was just as fervent as the credo of the Zionists. A blind man could see that the Israelis had a problem on their hands that was not resolved by the Six Day War.

After this introduction to the Palestinian obstacle to peace in the Middle East, I got a glimpse of its equally formidable Israeli counterpart. It happened in the early fall of 1967, when I took my first trip from Jordan to the Israeli-occupied West Bank. After I crossed the bridge over the River Jordan, I was still technically in Jordanian territory, but the Israeli officer who motioned me into a makeshift security hut didn't see it that way. He carefully checked my typewriter, handbag, and passport and, as I was leaving, added a greeting that said volumes about the outlook for a Middle East compromise. "Welcome to Israel," he said. It made me wonder whether the six-day blitzkrieg had not been a defeat for both sides.

～

The working conditions in my new beat were both better and worse than in the Southern Hemisphere. One very important improvement was that, unlike in Latin America, I now spent most of my weekends at home in Beirut, which was a short flight away from most of the countries I covered and where, importantly, there was practically no censorship of outgoing press messages. Thanks to this loophole in the Arab-wide attempt to control the reporting, I routinely returned to Beirut Friday night to file an unexpurgated story for the magazine.

Another much appreciated advantage was that once postwar hysterics subsided and my family returned to Beirut, we set up a comfortable household on the sixteenth floor of a handsome modern building with a view of the gleaming Mediterranean on one side and the snow-covered Anti-Lebanon Mountains on the other. Johnny was enrolled in a nice American kindergarten, and there was no shortage of household help for Romana. Our neighbors were mostly prosperous Lebanese Christians and officials of the US embassy.

Travel from—and even to—this Western outpost, however, could be difficult. Immediately after the Six Day War, most of the countries on my beat—which included North Africa, Iran, Afghanistan, and Pakistan as well as the entire Arabian peninsula—closed their borders to US newsmen on the theory that we were all spies.

Even in Kuwait and Lebanon, the two Arab exceptions to the rule, an American who showed up after the Six Day War with a typewriter, camera, radio, and tape recorder got a frigid reception. I got a dose of this treatment when I returned to Lebanon after the evacuation from Amman. Instead of the usual customs officials, my luggage at the Beirut airport was searched by a young Lebanese air force officer who grew very excited when he found in my handbag a map of Jordan. As he told me, it confirmed his suspicion that I was spying for Israel. He gave me some very nasty looks and had a long consultation with his boss before letting me in the country.

Getting around the rest of my new beat in the weeks and months following the Six Day War required blithe disregard for rules that, if rigidly carried out, could have made me useless as a reporter. Egypt, for example, banned the entry not only of American journalists but of all Americans. About three weeks after the Six Day War, I decided to test that double barrier by flying to Cairo. That presented no problem for Lebanon's Middle East Airlines which, in a true free-enterprise fashion, took on board anyone who paid the fare. But when I showed my passport at the immigration counter in the Cairo airport, the official only shook his head and had me confined to the transit lounge.

I sat there on a sagging sofa between two husky and perspiring security men, expecting to be put on the first flight back to Beirut. Instead, late in the afternoon, a senior Egyptian officer showed up at the lounge and taught me something new about my beat, namely, that even Nasser's venom could not change the sunny nature of some of his countrymen. Instead of berating me for trying to sneak into the country, the officer treated me to a mint tea and gave me a three-week visa.

After that experience, I decided to ignore border regulations and follow the Middle East story wherever it took me. It turned out to be the only way to work as a journalist. Hafez al-Assad's Syria and Libya under Muammar Gaddafi, two of the most radical regimes on my beat, banished American newsmen throughout my years in the area. After the other countries lifted the ban, their consulates could be maddeningly difficult in handling journalists' visa requests. To get a visa for North or South Yemen, for instance, easily took

I am standing outside the UN guest house in Sanaa, the capital of (then) North Yemen. In the 1960s, this was the town's only place where a foreigner could get a room. The Yemeni government was almost constantly under attack by rebellious tribes, and it hardly ever let any visitors in the country. I was lucky—my visa application just happened to reach some official when he wanted to disprove reports that the rebels had overrun Sanaa and were besieging the presidential palace. The only hostilities I ran into was machine gun fire that may or may not have been aimed at the plane I was in, as it was trying to land at the Sanaa airport. The pilot circled the airport until the firing stopped.

six months. Saudi Arabia and some of the Persian Gulf emirates required a proof that the applicant was not a Jew.

Getting around some of these hurdles could require only ingenuity and brass. For example, since Syria banned American journalists but not American businessmen, some of my colleagues carried calling cards as salesmen of fictitious firms. I professed to be a representative of Intragrafia, a company I invented and claimed to specialize in "automated four-color lithography." Fortunately, I was never asked to describe that process or show the firm's catalogue, but the put-on was probably not necessary. I had no doubt that the Syrian intelligence services knew perfectly well what manner of American "businessmen" were calling on the Damascus headquarters of the Popular Front for the Liberation of Palestine and other Palestinian radicals. For reasons of its own—perhaps to give publicity to Syrian-sponsored groups competing with the PLO—the Mukhabarat let the border charade go on.

Entering other Arab countries could be more complicated. After King Idryss was overthrown and Gaddafi took over, his "Great Socialist People's Lybian Arab Jamahyria" became an irresistible feature for an American magazine. The problem was that Libyan consulates refused to give a visa to any US citizen, and the Tripoli government required airlines to check that the would-be visitors were authorized to enter the country before boarding the plane. What helped me to beat this system was that my passport was stamped in Washington with a pre-Gaddafi visa whose text and date were in Arabic.

Instead of trying to fly to Libya from Beirut, where all airline employees could read the stamp, I flew to Athens and presented my visa to the Greek agent of the Olympic Airlines who, predictably, could not make head nor tail of it. I then got off the plane in Benghazi, the relative backwater, where I assumed the officials would be less rigid about the rules than in Tripoli. The gambit worked and I got a tourist visa, but the customs official for some reason took me for a black marketeer. After thoroughly searching my luggage, he ordered me to empty and pull out the lining of all my pockets, the only time this ever happened to me at an airport.

The worst travel obstacles, however, were caused not by officialdom but by the violence that—then, as now—plagued the Middle East. North Yemen, for example, became practically unreachable while I was in Beirut because of almost permanent tribal warfare, and I only managed to get to Sanaa thanks to a rare break in the fighting.

It also took a considerable amount of luck in November 1967 to get into—and, also important, out of—the British colony of Aden when it was about to become the Republic of Yemen. The situation reminded me of Guiana: the British were getting out and were leaving behind an impoverished country with only one institution that—rather incongruously—worked, which was the telex office of the British Cable and Wireless. But unlike the Guianans, who celebrated the British departure with fireworks and rousing steel drum music, the warlike Yemenis were trying to accelerate the end of the colonial era by rioting. The fighting halted all commercial flights to Aden just as the Saturday morning advisory from my editors requested a coverage of the upheaval.

The only way to get there, I was informed by a British correspondent who was in the same quandary as me, was to get to a Royal Air Force base in the Persian Gulf and try to get on their mail run to Aden. I managed to track down the British consul; fortunately, she was on a tennis court in

Beirut, and gave me the visa for what was still the colony of Aden. Next, two British newsmen and I flew to Bahrain, took a cab to the RAF base, and threw ourselves at the mercy of the duty officer. This could have been the end of the trip but for a piece of luck: the last mail run to Aden was leaving the next morning.

The young, thoroughly bored-looking pilot officer who became our host couldn't have been nicer—he fed us dinner, gave us bunks to sleep in, and the next dawn we were put aboard a cargo plane for Aden.

We landed at a deserted airport and, there being no cabs or any other means of transportation in sight, the three of us set out on foot for the distant capital. After a mile or so we came to a stretch of the road that was flooded by crude oil pouring from a hillside tank farm that had been hit by mortar fire. We rolled up our pants and waded barefoot through the smelly, dark-brown goo expecting every second to step on a broken bottle.

Still favored by Lady Luck, we crossed the stream just as the American consul drove up from Aden to survey the damage. Ignoring the oil dripping from our legs, he gave us a ride to the old Crescent Hotel, Aden's finest hostelry. The hotel had a Victorian lobby done in pink marble, Indian staff in starched white uniforms, and a receptionist who checked us in without cracking a smile or raising an eyebrow. Equally poker-faced busboys ushered us to our rooms as matter-of-factly as if barefoot guests with rolled-up pants and reeking of oil were a daily occurrence.

Reporting the story was relatively simple. By Monday morning I was all cleaned up, equipped with a rented car, and getting briefed by the US consul about the fast-deteriorating situation. By midweek the British navy took us aboard for a last sail-by, and by Friday night my story was in New York, thanks to the intrepid manager of the local Cable and Wireless who kept his office open despite the shooting.

Leaving the now independent but still strife-torn republic, however, called for even more luck than getting in. The airport remained closed, and there were no more RAF mail runs. On Sunday morning I was contemplating hiring a fishing boat to take me to Djibouti in the Horn of Africa when I saw in the lobby an Italian family that had just paid their bill and were headed out of the door. They told me they were off to the airport to get on an unscheduled Alitalia flight that had been diverted to Aden to evacuate the staff of the Italian consulate.

I grabbed my suitcase, paid a fat baksheesh for a cab to the airport, and got there in time to be allowed to board the plane after I showed the purser I had traveler's checks. I paid the fare in flight and after we landed at the da Vinci airport in Rome, I flew to Paris to pick up a brand new Peugeot I had bought in May but never found time to bring to Beirut.

I drove the car to Livorno and caught a ferry that got me back to Beirut two weeks after I left. It was another just-in-time: Cyrus Vance, President Johnson's special representative, was arriving in Nicosia to try to resolve the Greek–Turkish feud over Cyprus, and *Newsweek* wanted coverage.

CHAPTER 13

ARAFAT AND THE RISE OF THE PLO

Getting in and out of the Middle East capitals was not my main job in the wake of the June 1967 Six Day War. My most important—and challenging—function was to explain to the American readers both the Palestinian side of the Middle East conflict and the rise of the Palestine Liberation Organization. As a journalistic assignment, it should have been a piece of cake, because the Palestinian Arabs had a compelling story. Their tragedy went back to 1948, when some eight hundred thousand of them fled or were expelled from the coastal area between Lebanon and Egypt's Sinai Desert by the troops of the new Jewish state

Whatever the circumstances of their mass exodus. the indisputable facts are that the fugitives were noncombatants, mostly poor, simple villagers, and that their homes and land had been taken away by a vastly superior adversary. On that ground alone, the refugees' grievances and calls for justice should have commanded strong Western sympathy, or at least interest.

Moreover, the 1948 events had a disastrous sequel in the Six Day War, which was spawned by the reckless leadership of Egypt's Nasser and other Arab caudillos. While the refugees waited, seethed, and grew in numbers in scores of camps run by the United Nations Relief and Work Agency (UNRWA), Nasser and his cohorts provoked Israel's preventive attack on June 6. The Israeli Defense Forces (IDF) won a quick victory and occupied the West Bank and Gaza, the last remaining enclaves of the Palestinians. The refugees from the coastal area were once again on the run, and their land was once again seized by an invader. It was the second act of an epic drama that cried for full coverage.

But compelling as it seemed, the drama had critical flaws that ruined its appeal to *Newsweek*'s audience.

In the first place, the Arab honchos who led the crusade against Israel fell considerably short of inspiring the admiration of Western readers. The best example of these nabobs was Gamal Abdel Nasser. The biggest celebrity on my beat, Egypt's al-rais was shown in the Six Day War for what he truly was—a big-mouthed rainmaker who could not make rain. In the war's aftermath, his reputation sank like a punctured blimp, but Nasser didn't even find the integrity to step down and let somebody else take over. He kept hanging on in the presidential palace, blaming the lost war on Americans and his generals, until his death in 1970.

Jordan's King Hussein, another Middle East figure with some name recognition in the West, was also not a man to conquer my readers' sympathies. The thrice-married Hashemite had a certain manly charm, but there was nothing certain about his policies, which rapidly adjusted to every change in the mood of the Arabs. There were also justifiable questions about the longevity of his reign. The only Arab head of state to grant the 1948 refugees automatic citizenship, Hussein wound up with subjects 60 percent of whom were of Palestinian origin and who deeply resented his Bedouin origin and Western connections. A classic example of the old maxim that no good deed shall go unpunished, His Majesty King Hussein bin Talal was sitting on a volcano.

The rest of the Arab chieftains were even less appealing. Syria's Hafez al-Assad, a former air force general who overthrew his predecessor after the Six Day War, was a classic military dictator who ran the country by terrorizing the opposition. The other major post-Six-Day-War upstart, the preposterous Muammar Gaddafi (whose titles included "The Guide of the First of September Great Revolution of the Socialist People's Libyan Arab Jamahiriya") was a mental case who fantasized about uniting the Arabs behind a mix of socialism and fundamentalist Islam.

The rulers of Iraq and Yemen in the late 1960s were vicious thugs without major regional importance. As for the absurdly wealthy Saudi monarchy and the emirs of the Gulf, they were medieval figures who shied away from publicity and shrank from overt involvement in Middle East politics.

And there was nothing on the region's horizon to please the Western eye. Human rights in most of the countries I covered were a joke. Popular elections were either unheard of or a fraud on the communist model. Assassinations, jailings, or expulsions of political opponents were rampant, and religious and tribal disputes were settled in blood. Even the relatively modern Lebanon was run by Christians although Muslims were the majority, and the country's religious and ethnic tensions were held in check only by the size of each group's arsenal. Latin America was a showpiece of tranquility and statesmanship compared to my new beat.

Another—and for my purposes even more ruinous—flaw in the Middle East drama was the Arab logic, which could be baffling to the Western public. Kipling's insight that "East is East, and West is West, and never the twain shall meet" is no longer apt after the brave Arab Spring, but it was true in the aftermath of the Six Day War, when the humiliating defeat drove some Palestinians out of their minds. A small but classic example was a spate of riots early in the fall of 1967 by refugees from the Israeli-seized West Bank who had set up an impromptu camp on the unoccupied side of the River Jordan. What triggered their violence was UNRWA's attempt to put dry floors under their tents before the rainy season.

The moment the trucks and cement mixer showed up, they were seized by the refugees and set on fire. The next day, UNRWA brought in more trucks and another cement mixer, and the same thing happened. After that I went to the camp and asked the refugees why on earth they fought an agency that was trying to help them. The reason, one of the camp leaders told me, was that "UNRWA is trying to make us comfortable so that we would stop fighting to liberate our land." He was referring to a "fight" of which at that time there was no evidence—and that presumably would not have been advanced if the refugees and their kids did not sleep on muddy ground during the cold winter. As I wrote the story, I could imagine the reaction of my fellow American taxpayers, who footed 90 percent of UNRWA's budget.

The Israelis liked to blame the enduring existence of the Palestinian refugee camps, most of which were already two decades old, on the Arab regimes' refusal to integrate the homeless people into their own societies. There is no doubt that the Arab governments wanted to keep the refugee problem alive as the centerpiece of their crusade against Israel. But it would be hard to overestimate the conviction of the refugees that if they left the camps and tried to improve their lot they would be giving up all hopes of returning to their old homes in Palestine.

Hard-to-fathom logic affected even the most sophisticated Arabs. One of them was Ghassan Tueni, the Lebanese publisher of *Al-Anwar*, who later served as Lebanon's ambassador to the United Nations. Educated in London and Paris, Tueni was thoroughly familiar with the ways of the Western world and sometimes helped me interpret the byzantine Arab politics. But when I asked him what he thought about the assassination of Robert Kennedy by the young Palestinian, Sirhan Bishara Sirhan, Tueni made no more sense than the illiterate refugees. To my utter astonishment, the publisher was jubilant: in his eyes, murdering one of the most popular leaders in America was a major Arab public relations victory.

"Finally!" Tueni exulted. "Finally, America will sit up and take notice of the Palestinian cause!"

I was so shattered by both Bob Kennedy's death and Tueni's abysmal reaction that it took me a while to say something to the effect that if the American people ever saw the murder as a PR act, the Palestinian cause was dead in their eyes at least as long as my generation was alive.

If the refugees and Tueni could be dumbfounding, the thought processes of the new PLO leaders were consistently beyond comprehension. To any Western observer, the most striking lessons of the Six Day War included that (1) Israel had a staggering military superiority over the Arabs; (2) the United States was Israel's most prolific and influential benefactor, protector, and ally; and (3) Israel's astute relationship with the Western media yielded reams of favorable publicity that gave the Jewish state a glowing image both in the United States and throughout most of the world.

Since the Palestinians in the late 1960s had utterly no military option against the superbly trained and armed IDF, their most promising strategy would have been to emphasize their moral case against Israel; appeal to the American sense of fairness and sympathy for the underdog; and last but not least, try to cooperate with, rather than antagonize, the Western media. Years later, some Palestinians adopted this approach, but during my time on the beat, the PLO charged in precisely the opposite direction.

The first counterproductive move was the choice of "Abu Amar" to replace the Arab League–anointed Shukeiry. Yassir Arafat was a traditional Muslim whose key leadership talent was flexibility in concocting alliances and strategies. As the PLO spokesman, however, he was an abominable choice: in the 1960s he did not speak a word of English, and in Arabic he seemed incapable of uttering anything but the most trite and worn-out clichés.

According to one of my better PLO sources, a Palestinian professor at the American University in Beirut, Arafat owed his elevation to a security fluke that made him the only member of the Persian Gulf–based, secret "revolutionary" PLO leadership, whose identity became known to the Mossad. Since his cover was blown, the embarrassed professor claimed, Arafat was the obvious choice for a public function.

Whatever the reason for his sudden prominence, Arafat quickly became a comic-strip stereotype of an old-fashioned Arab wheeler-dealer who could be relied upon to defy what in the Western world was regarded as common sense. Most astonishingly, instead of trying to drive a wedge between Washington and Tel Aviv, Arafat missed no opportunity to bring the United States and Israel closer together. One fundamental plank of his policy was to make the PLO yet another muddled Third World pinko and fellow traveler.

Rather than exploiting the unique nature of the Palestinian case, he spouted inanities from Chairman Mao's *Little Red Book*, rushed to embrace every leftist maniac who appeared on the world scene, and worst of all, ordered or condoned revolting acts of terrorism against Israeli and American civilians.

His preposterous strategy could not have been more self-defeating had it been scripted by Israel.

What made Arafat's cant about a Maoist-style "revolution that grows from the barrel of a gun" most unpalatable was that he tried to impose it on countries that wanted no part of it. In his afflicted view, the six to eight thousand fedayeen of Al Fatah—the military arm of the PLO—were the Middle East's version of the Viet Cong, and they had to be supported by what he called the region's "Hanois": Jordan and Lebanon, Israel's neighbors that were run by gingerly pro-Western governments. In effect, he demanded that the two countries give his militants sanctuary, abet their puny raids into Israel, and accept the massive IDF punishment that would invariably follow.

The predictable result was an explosive friction between the would-be "Hanois" and the PLO "revolutionaries," and their eventual expulsion from both countries. Arafat's pipe dream first collapsed in the early fall of 1970, when he grossly overplayed his hand by practically carving out a PLO state-within-a-state in and around Amman and launching a series of provocations, including the hijacking of three airliners to a deserted airfield in the Jordanian desert.

It was my luck to discover one of the PLO's shenanigans in the summer of 1969 when I walked onto the campus of King Hussein University in Amman, and ran into a group of German-speaking youngsters wearing US Army fatigues, then the uniform of European radical Left. I asked questions and they told me that they had been flown to Jordan by the PLO "to participate in the fedayeen experience," which turned out to be very brief. A couple of days after their arrival, they complained, an Israeli Kfir made a few low passes over the camp where they were staying, and the PLO organizers hurriedly brought them by bus to Amman—in their view, a most undignified end to their visit to the fedayeen front line.

I wrote a short piece about the ruined PLO caper and forgot about it until a couple weeks later when I returned to Amman to work on a takeout about the rise of the PLO. Instead of offering to help, Mohammed, the top PR guy in Arafat's headquarters, declared me a persona non grata and ordered me out of the building. Without a word of greeting, the burly official fixed me with his eyes and pointed at a copy of the offensive *Newsweek* article on the desk in front of him. He then reached into a drawer, pulled out a nasty-looking pistol, and placed it on top of the magazine. "Mr. Kubic," Mohammed growled, glaring at me with unblinking wrath, "the Palestinian revolution knows how to deal with this sort of writing."

What happened was that the youngsters had been flown to Amman entirely without the knowledge of the Jordanian authorities, and when Hussein saw my story, he raised hell with his underlings as well as with the PLO. It was one of the episodes of brazen PLO defiance of the king that climaxed a couple of months later when a fedayeen roadblock stopped the royal Rolls Royce with Hussein's mother in it. Upon that casus belli, the tanks of Hussein's Bedouins rolled into the PLO camps and sent the fedayeen fleeing across the River Jordan. The crackdown, remembered by the Palestinians as "Black September," was one of the PLO's worst military defeats, without a single shot fired by an Israeli soldier.

The fiasco failed to deter Arafat, who shifted his "revolutionary struggle" to the other "Hanoi," the militarily impotent Lebanon. With the tacit consent of the Beirut government, the fedayeen set up bases along the Israel-Lebanon border, and from there fired Russian rockets at Israel's Upper Galilee. This time it was the Israeli army that set out to get rid of the commandos, and the army did it so effectively that the Shiite and Christian farmers along the Lebanese border chose to ally with the IDF rather than be its target.

The strife triggered by these clashes tore up Lebanon, brought Syrian troops into the country's Bekaa Valley, and eventually prompted an IDF invasion that reached Beirut and sent Arafat and his troops packing all the way to Tunisia. It was only this second rout, which took place in the summer and early fall of 1982, that stopped Arafat's bombast about "Hanois." He knew that if he tried to put fedayeen bases in the two remaining neighbors of Israel—Egypt and Syria—their intelligence services would kill him.

What I found intriguing about Arafat's absurd leadership was not only that it made him a major Arab celebrity, but that he escaped the long arm of Israel's Mossad, an agency that rarely hesitated to aim for the enemy's jugular. I used to marvel at Arafat's curious immunity especially in the late 1960s, when I would see him time and again on my frequent flights to and from Cairo.

Arafat (like me) seemed to prefer Lebanon's well-run Middle East Airlines over the iffy schedules of EgyptAir, and he always sat in the front row of the first-class compartment flanked by two bodyguards. His only disguise was to take off his signature checkered kaffiyeh, thereby revealing his strikingly bald head. When we disembarked, Arafat was whisked past the immigration by a waiting Lebanese security man, but he still offered an easy target for anyone who wished him ill—and if I could see the PLO chief walking through the Beirut arrival hall, so could anyone else.

Reflecting on the deadly effectiveness of the Mossad, I at first wondered whether flying together with Arafat was the safest way to travel. But after watching his bizarre leadership, I concluded that Mossad had an excellent reason to keep Arafat alive. His vaunted "military operations" after the Six Day War were mere pinpricks; his unerring instinct for the wrong policy kept the Arab regimes in constant turmoil; his penchant for terrorism deprived the Palestinian refugees of the badly needed sympathy abroad; and his underlings' crass hostility toward Western reporters could not help affect their coverage. Arafat was manna from heaven for the State of Israel.

The most prominent exponent of the PLO's hostility to foreign media was the organization's chief press spokesman, a Palestinian poet named Kamal Nasser. He was a respected author, but as Arafat's top public relations man he was a joke. In my one meeting with him, shortly after he took the job, Nasser informed me that because I was an American correspondent I was ipso facto writing Israeli propaganda. That placed me on such an abysmally low moral plane that he, Kamal Nasser, could hardly bring himself to breathe the same air as I did, let alone address my questions. I was out of his office in about five minutes thinking at least as little of Kamal Nasser as he thought of me.

Nasser's arrogance memorably backfired at an Arab League conference in 1969 in Rabat, where Arafat made a big pitch for increased financial support for his "revolution." After the closed sessions were over, Nasser came to the hotel where most of us stayed, and held two separate press briefings, one in Arabic and one in English.

First, on one side of the hotel's swimming pool, he addressed the Arab correspondents. Speaking in Arabic, he delivered the standard PLO line for Arab audiences, which was a litany of complaints about the miserly handouts the PLO was receiving from the oil-rich sheikhs and other Arab rulers. Arab moneybags, the poet told our Arab colleagues, once again "tried to put off PLO with empty oratory" instead of providing the badly needed funds.

That part of his job done, Nasser crossed over to the opposite side of the pool to brief the Western press. Changing both the language and the spin, he gave us a glowing account of the purported generosity of "our Arab brothers, who demonstrated once again their solidarity with the Palestinian revolution." Perhaps Nasser thought that his psych warfare would sow fear into the soul of Israel. To me, it was yet more evidence of his insulting attitude toward us and our audiences, as well as a measure of his own limited candle power. It obviously never occurred to him that most of us would get the Arabic version of his spiel from our Arab stringers, who covered his "briefing" on the other side of the pool.

Personally, I found covering the PLO even more challenging than reporting on the South America's reformadores. One day, the Arabs in Palestine lived modest but reasonably ordered and contented lives. The next day their entire world was taken away from them. After the Jewish state was created, all but a few of the 360-odd Arab villages in the conquered territory were razed by bulldozers, deleted from maps, and plowed over into fields. The Israelis did it to grow food and assert their claim on their biblical homeland, but it was like dropping a piece of history into the Orwelian memory hole. I found it hard to take.

By the time I came to the Middle East, the refugees had vegetated for almost twenty years in reeking and decaying camps next to which our IRO barracks in Germany were showpiece lodgings. They were snubbed, ostracized, and feared by their fellow Arabs and ignored by the rest of the world. The final irony of their miserable existence was that they owed their sheer survival to the hated Americans. The United States financed almost all of the 10 cents' worth of food a day that UNRWA doled out to each refugee.

In some ways I felt sympathy even for the obnoxious PLO apparatchiks who in those years were hopelessly outclassed and outperformed by their opposite numbers in the Jewish state. In martial skills, political leadership, diplomatic ability, intelligence gathering, fund-raising, and PR abroad, the disheveled PLO trailed out of sight behind Israel, which was in every respect a modern, European-style state and thanks to Uncle Sam's generous aid, the regional military superpower. In the 1960s and 1970s, the Israeli-Palestinian conflict looked less like a duel than the thrashing of a small kid by an adult.

For instance, when the Mossad decided that Kamal Nasser was actually becoming an effective spokesman (on what grounds, I never did understand), Israeli commandos landed one night on a Beirut beach, broke into Nasser's apartment, and shot him dead in bed. Another refugee spokesman I knew, Ghassan Qanafani from the extremist Popular Front for the Liberation of Palestine, was killed by the Mossad in his Volkswagen in the garage of his Beirut apartment building. He turned on the ignition, and the car blew up.

These were surgical operations against unsavory targets, and as such drew little publicity and no disapproval in the West—if anything, just the opposite. By contrast all the PLO accomplished in those years was revolting hijackings and terror attacks that resulted in indiscriminate killings—time and again, of women and children—and reinforced PLO's well-earned reputation for savagery.

It was this bottomless capacity for hatred that, in my eyes, severely undermined the Palestinian claims to sympathy from the Western world. I got a glimpse of it one day in the early fall of 1967 in Amman when I ran into the funeral of one of the first fedayeen killed by the Israelis. It felt like watching a blazing lava spewing from the guts of the earth.

Up front, a tightly packed vortex of sweaty men pushed, heaved, and convulsed in a cloud of ocher dust, hysterically screaming "Allahu Akhbar! Biladi, biladi!" (God is great! My country, my country!) Above their heads, bouncing on their outstretched arms like a boat in rapids, was an open wooden casket wrapped in the Palestinian flag. Mourners not close enough to the shrouded body pressed frantically forward; in the rear of the procession, a phalanx of women piercingly ululated their grief.

From the balcony where I stood, the scene was truly breathtaking. I thought I had learned all about hatred during the German occupation, but the livid fury in the street below made my own wrath of those days look almost tame. My mind flashed back to the long-ago scene of the sealed, snow-covered boxcars on the siding in Horní Borek, and I was suddenly filled with a deeply personal anguish. What would happen, I wondered, if this frenzy ever swept over Israel? It was a horrible thought. They would kill not just the people, I thought. They would strangle the birds and crush the bricks.

Flying from one Middle East capital to another, I frequently reflected on my conflicted feelings about the Arab-Israeli conflict. I could not fathom the Palestinians' logic, I did not respect their leadership, and I was repelled by their passions. At the same time, I recognized that they had been grossly mistreated—and this really bothered me—that they had a point when they complained that the magazine's Middle East coverage was not even-handed.

The lack of balance was not something anybody wanted, but it was inherent in the difference between me and Mike Elkins, the magazine's stringer who covered Israel. Mike, who worked for *Newsweek* and BBC radio, was a native Californian and a man in some ways after my own heart: he was able, honest, and had a great capacity for moral outrage. But Mike was also an Israeli citizen who made no secret of his total loyalty to the Jewish state. As he frankly told me the first time we met, he would never report anything that could harm the Jewish state. I respected his position—Mike's devotion to Zionism predated the state of Israel—but since I had no such reservations about my reporting on the Arabs, it seemed unavoidable that *Newsweek*'s portrayal of the Arab-Israeli conflict would be unbalanced.

The upshot of my cogitations was the same as in the case of the Latino reformadores —I worried about my performance but I carried on. Banned by Mohammed from his headquarters, I hired a couple of stringers who felt as strongly about the Palestinians as Mike felt about Israel: one was the Arabic-speaking son of Glubb Pasha, the famed founder of Jordan's Desert Legion, and the other was Abdullah Schleifer, an American freelancer who had converted to Islam.

I swallowed the abuse of Arab spokesmen and sifted their stale clichés for a trace of new thought. I relied on Nabil Shaath and a few other PLO academicians at the American University in Beirut to fill me in on Arafat's zigzags and strategies, and I insisted that only attacks on civilians should be labeled "terrorism." When the fedayeen clashed with Israeli soldiers, they deserved to be called "commandos" or "guerrillas."

I took care not to make the mistake of my *Time* counterpart, who described a fedayeen base so well that the day the story came out, an IDF helicopter landed by the hideout and wiped out the whole Palestinian unit. I also drew the line on information that was mainly of value for the Mossad. An example was Arafat's assumed name and the number of his Moroccan passport that I once copied in my notebook when a Beirut immigration official left it open by his window. The data stayed in my notebook: I was an observer of the Arab-Israeli conflict, not a participant.

The payoff of my self-conscious labors came in an unexpected and yet ironically familiar fashion during the October War in 1973, which once again pitted the Arabs against Israel. Dispatched from Bonn, where I was then based, to help cover the Arab fronts, I went to the PLO press room in Beirut to ask for an opportunity to cover one of al-Fatah's "actions" along the Israeli border. Lebanon was then the second "Hanoi" of Arafat's "revolution" but, with my memories of Mohammed still fairly fresh, I did not expect to get very far. Instead, I got a reception fit for a celebrity.

As soon as I mentioned my name, the press officer stood up with a big grin, walked around his desk, and to my utter astonishment gave me a hug. He had just edited a collection of English-language articles about the early years of the movement, he explained, and my stories made up a substantial part of the publication. I couldn't believe my ears. Here I was, less than four years after Mohammed threatened to rub me out, being hailed as a valued historian of what the Palestinians called "The Struggle."

My reward was a VIP visit the same night to what the PLO called its "front" against the Zionist enemy. It turned out to be a classic example of the pitfalls of reporting in the Middle East. Late in the afternoon, an al-Fatah officer picked me up at the St. Georges Hotel, wrapped my head in a kaffiyeh, and put me in a Toyota jeep next to a similarly outfitted Tanjug correspondent from Belgrade. We crossed the Anti-Lebanon Mountains, passed two lax Lebanese army roadblocks near Chtaura in the Bekaa Valley, and from there took a southbound road that was so heavily used by the PLO that it was popularly known as "Arafat's trail."

At the foot of Mount Hermon, just north of the Israeli border, we joined another fedayeen who was driving, of all things, a fancy late-model Alfa Romeo. We followed him with the lights off on a dirt road that took us up a hill covered with prickly bushes and boulders of volcanic rock. Close to the top the fedayeen got out of his sports car, walked around to the rear, and in the glare of the stoplights took a reading of his compass.

Apparently satisfied that we were in the right place, he motioned the Tanjug reporter and me to follow him a short distance off the road to a cluster of trees beneath which loomed two fat 50 mm mortars. He and our driver then fetched about a dozen mortar shells from the two cars, and seconds later, the guns started belching projectiles toward the Israeli border.

Within minutes, the dark sky came alive with flashing lights and wheezing, buzzing, barking, and howling sounds of more weaponry than I could identify. Most of the cacophony seemed to be coming from the Israeli side of the border, although I thought I also discerned artillery northeast from us, which presumably was Syrian. As the crescendo rose, so did my earnest wish to get out of the place before the Israeli artillery zeroed in on the mortars.

To my growing discomfort, however, the feda and our driver kept hauling more shells from their vehicles and continued popping them off. Meanwhile, there was no response from the Israeli side of the border. How come, I wondered, that some of the ordnance in the air didn't come crashing on our hill? Where was the legendary mailed fist of the IDF?

A half an hour or so later the mortars spat out the last ammo, and the fedayeen signaled to my colleague and me to follow him to an opening closer to the top of the hill. There, under the panoply of strikingly bright stars, we could see in the distance the sharply etched silhouette of a hilltop village whose houses were being devoured by fires. "That's Metullah, Israel," the commando told us, a small town on the Israeli side of the border. The fires, he added, flashing a proud smile, were produced by his barrage.

I was back at the St. Georges Hotel in time for breakfast, and by noon I had telexed my story, but the lack of any Israeli response to the mortar fire would not leave my mind. After I filed the article, I sent a separate advisory to Rod Gander, the magazine's chief of correspondents, asking him to have someone in Israel write an on-the-scene report on the damage in Metullah. Rod did what I suggested, and the next day came back with an advisory that reminded me of Kamal Nasser's caper in Rabat.

Ron Moreau, a fellow *Newsweek* correspondent who had gone up to the border, found Metullah intact. The houses on which the fedayeen had rained destruction, Moreau was told, were in Marjayun, a small Lebanese Christian town that had refused to aid Arafat's commandos in their border raids on Israel. The shelling of Marjayun was part of the PLO's revenge. It was also my final exposure to the wide gap between Arab facts and fiction, but by no means my last encounter with the much-practiced art of deception in the Middle East. Two years later I was back in the area, this time reporting from Israel.

CHAPTER 14

COVERING THE LOSERS' BEAT

In all fairness I must note that Arafat and his coterie were not the oddest characters on the Middle East stage. In my jaundiced eyes that distinction belonged to various non-Arab admirers of the PLO who waxed so passionately against "American imperialism" that any Yankee-hater was OK in their book. Some of these ardent PLO fans were found among the Woodstock-generation wives of Beirut-based Americans who regarded the US support for Israel with the same rancor as the war in Vietnam. Their contribution to the Palestinian cause ranged from wrecking dinner parties by carping about US foreign policy to participating in anti-American demonstrations outside the US embassy.

Later, when I covered Israel, I sometimes marveled at the curious similarity between the fervent American anti-Israelis in Beirut and their opposite numbers in the West Bank and Gaza, the American-Israeli settlers. The former competed with the Arabs in their anti-Zionism and their Uncle Sam–bashing. The latter frequently outdid native Israelis in their Zionist fanaticism and their hatred for the Palestinians. In one important respect, however, the symmetry was incomplete: while the US-born settlers were fully assimilated in their new country and were appreciated as loyal Israelis, outsiders in the Arab world would never win the natives' trust.

I knew few Westerners who felt more strongly about the Palestinian cause than the two stringers I hired in Amman after my fall from Mohammed's grace. Abdullah (Mark) Schleifer and Faris Glubb were both not only capable young men but also remarkable personalities. Abdullah was a brilliant New York Jew who had married a very bright and beautiful American black Christian and moved with her to the Middle East. Somewhere along the way—in Morocco, I believe—they both converted to Islam and settled in the Arab Old City in Jerusalem, where Abdullah worked for an English language newspaper. After the Six Day War they felt so uncomfortable living under the Israeli occupation that they moved to Amman.

Faris, who had been raised in the Jordanian capital as the son of a famous warrior—Glubb Pasha, the British commander of the Jordan's Desert Legion—was a teacher of English poetry in London. After the Six Day War, he and his British wife, a physician, also moved to Amman—mainly, I gathered, out of sympathy for the Palestinian struggle.

Both Abdullah and Faris were well-educated, intelligent men who sacrificed promising careers and Western comforts to contribute to the Palestinian cause. I hired them following my banishment by Mohammed in the hope that as committed sympathizers they could cover the PLO better than I could. I soon learned that I had underestimated the profound suspicion that separated Arabs from Westerners—especially Westerners who were trying to be accepted. As far as I could tell, during my four years in Beirut, neither Abdullah nor Faris won the trust they vied for.

Abdullah—who wore a kaffiyeh and performed daily the Muslim prayers—was so distrusted that even the waiters at the Amman Intercontinental, who had me down for a "Zionist," would whisper to me that he was "a CIA agent." Eventually, Abdullah encountered so much Palestinian distrust and hostility that he moved with his family to the more cosmopolitan Beirut. As for Faris, he did not fare much better. He spoke fluent Arabic, fingered his worry beads like a native, and exuded youthful sincerity. Still, the PLO did not trust him any more than they trusted me. Shortly after I hired him, I asked him to get me the most unsecret sort of information imaginable, the lyrics of the fedayeen songs. Faris came back from the PLO office empty-handed: the Palestinian spin doctors, he told me, were suspicious of his motives.

In my experience nobody collided with the wall of Arab xenophobia more grotesquely than Timothy Leary, the high priest of the American drug culture. In the fall of 1970, Leary escaped from a California prison where he had been serving a drug sentence, somehow got a forged US passport, and in October arrived in Beirut accompanied by three groupies—Jennifer Dohrn and two Black Panthers, "Field Marshal" Donald Lee Cox and fund-raiser Martin Kenner. The incursion was supposed to be secret, as behooved self-styled antiestablishment revolutionaries, and Leary had even shaved his trademark long hair. But once he and his group landed at the Beirut airport, his odyssey became pure slapstick—a classical encounter between all-rules-be-damned Western iconoclasts and one of the world's most traditional societies.

The comedy began when Leary, who was obviously extremely well fixed for cash, displayed his lack of savvy by checking in with his group at Beirut's St. Georges Hotel. The seaside St. Georges was not only Lebanon's poshest establishment and one of the finest hotels in the Middle East, it was also the watering spot of the Beirut-based foreign correspondents. Worst of all for the

Leary junket, by staying in the hotel, his group came under the purview of St. Georges's Mansour Braidi, a six-foot, two-hundred-pound personification of all the virtues and skills that have made Lebanese concierges the pride of the world's hotel industry.

Braidi, a figure straight out of a John le Carré novel, was a reliable letter drop in a town of unreliable mail deliveries, and as such was on the retainer of several foreign news organizations, including *Newsweek*. Inevitably, Leary's sub rosa venture began to unravel the same night he arrived, and several American newsmen in Beirut—including me—were alerted by their home offices that the LSD guru was on the lam and might be headed for the Middle East.

The next morning, I called Braidi to ask him to be on the lookout for the counterculture characters, but he was already on top of the story. "He's here," he told me as soon as I described Leary. "He's registered under another name, but he is here." Half an hour later, I was squatting on the floor in a room adjacent to Leary's expensive seaside suite. Next to me was the sound man of a television crew (another Braidi client) who had slipped a pencil-thin microphone in the crack under the door that separated us from the foursome. The sound man was taping while I was listening on earphones and taking notes.

Leary, who came equipped with a list of Beirut and Damascus phone numbers, was calling PLO offices and representatives of the various radical Palestinian "popular fronts." His spiel was that he was a victim of American "political" persecution and was in need of refuge but not money, a point that should have earned him if not sympathy at least a respectful hearing. Instead, he was snubbed at every turn. None of the Palestinian groups would give him a hand.

When Leary got nowhere on the phone, Cox took a cab to Damascus to try his luck with the rabidly anti-American Syrian government. He came back empty-handed. The only members of Leary's group who that day had any fun were Kenner, who had brought along his racket and played tennis, and Dohrn. The sister of Bernardine of the Weathermen fame, Dohrn kept up her revolutionary spirit by placing orders with the St. Georges room service that included caviar and chocolate mousse for lunch. On Braidi's instructions, the waiter would stop in our listening post after each delivery, show us the bill, and report what he saw in Leary's suite.

In the evening, Leary compounded his misfortune by trying to sneak out of the hotel, which by then was besieged by a flock of American and British reporters. Unaware that we had overheard his plan for avoiding the media, Leary took the back elevator to the swimming pool, crossed over to the street, and jumped into a waiting car whose driver I recognized as the wife of Abdullah, my former Amman stringer. Three other reporters and I drove up to Abdullah's apartment ahead of Leary and when he arrived, we followed him into the living room. Leary, who look shocked, did not answer our questions but did not deny his real identity, either.

Had Leary checked a tourist guide, he would have learned that Lebanon's Bekaa Valley grew prodigious amounts of opium for export, but the natives themselves were too smart to use it. To such extent as the Lebanese—and the Palestinians, for that matter—had heard about Leary and his "turn-on, tune-in, drop-out" culture, they disdained both as decadent. Moreover, in those years Lebanon was still run by Christians who had great respect for Uncle Sam. To no one's surprise, the normally permissive Beirut government expelled the Leary group two days after they checked in at St. Georges.

The foursome's next folly was to try their luck in Cairo. At first sight it might seem likely that Egypt, which then was getting substantial Soviet military aid, would be friendlier to an American antiestablishment group than the pro-Western Lebanon. That, however, turned out to be another faulty application of Western logic to the Middle East. Leary and his groupies were kicked out from Egypt even faster than they were from Lebanon.

I witnessed the group's second fiasco thanks to Braidi, who made the foursome's airline reservation and gave me their flight number in time for me to book a seat on the same plane. My appearance in the Beirut departure lobby so infuriated Field Marshall Cox that he loudly announced to his companions, "I will deal with him," while casting an angry look in my direction. When we arrived at the Cairo airport, Cox ran to a senior Egyptian police officer who stood outside the arrival lounge and pointing at me, informed him in a loud voice that I was a "CIA agent." The officer gravely nodded, collected the group's passports, and took them to the transit lounge. He immediately came back and politely asked to me to follow him to his office in the terminal.

There, without asking any questions about my job, the Egyptian handed me the group's passports and asked me to examine them. I did what he asked. Leary was traveling under the name of William John McNellis on a US passport issued in Chicago on September 22, 1970, and Cox was equipped with an Algerian passport that had his correct name but listed his occupation as "Photographer." Dohrn and Kenner had genuine-looking US passports issued in their own names.

"Tell me," the policeman asked me after I jotted down the data, "which one of them is the big drug man?"

As I was leaving, the officer—who still showed no interest in what brought me to Cairo—assured me that he would not let the group into the country.

Leary and his entourage were put on the next plane for Algeria, the only country that would have them—at least for a while.

The Leary junket was a welcome break from the chaos, corruption, internecine warfare, and military defeats characteristic of the Islamic countries where I worked the 1960s and 1970s. The Middle East was not a happy place for the natives, and it was not a happy place for the foreign journalists who covered it.

The wars were a particular bane of the beat. They were unrewarding professionally, because covering defeats rarely puts a feather in a reporter's cap. Both during the fighting and afterwards, the big play in the newspapers and magazines goes to the victors, and the vanquished get only secondary treatment.

And adding insult to injury, Arab defeats were exceptionally hard to cover, because the Arabs blamed them more on the United States than on Israel. An American correspondent who tried to ask Arab officials questions in the aftermath of the IDF's triumphs ran into an angry tirade or stony silence; if he walked into a Palestinian refugee camp to check on the mood, he was risking physical abuse. And such was my luck, or lack of it, that I covered three Arab defeats—the Six Day War in 1967, the so-called War of Attrition in 1970, and the Yom Kippur (or Ramadan) War in 1973. As a footnote to this record of glory-less reporting, I should mention that I also covered the collapse of the East Pakistan rebellion against West Pakistan in 1971.

Rout and ruination became such a staple of my reporting that, years later, when I was transferred to Jerusalem I warned my Israeli contacts that the IDF's winning streak was over. I was trying to be funny but in fact, during my thirteen years in the Jewish state, IDF's two major military actions—both against the fedayeen in Lebanon—failed to accomplish their goals.

The first Israeli attack, in 1980, temporarily pushed the commandos away from the Israeli border, but it did not entirely stop their Katyushas and raids on the kibbutzim. The second Israeli invasion of Lebanon, in 1982, resulted in the expulsion of the fedayeen to Tunisia, but the IDF suffered serious casualties and the Sabra and Shatilla massacre, which it allowed to take place, contributed to Menachem Begin's decision to resign as Israel's prime minister.

Which is not to say that I found covering the defeats entirely without satisfaction. The stories lacked the upbeat exuberance of victories, but they had a somber pathos that appealed to the heroic in my Slavic soul. Some of the losers were inclined to be introspective, and those strong enough to bear their ill fortune well could be very impressive. It was easy to sympathize with them.

One gloomy tale I felt I had to report was the last stand of the American embassy staff in Amman in the late summer of 1970, when the PLO's control of the Jordanian "Hanoi" reached its peak. Already in the spring, armed fedayeen of the various Palestinian "fronts" had set up roadblocks in and out of the town and, depending on their whim, insulted and harassed the Americans. The tensions boiled over at the end of June, when the al-Fatah radio in Cairo issued a new "revolutionary" slogan du jour, "Death to the US agents!" Obediently, the Palestinian thugs in Amman went on a rampage.

In a series of night raids, they killed the assistant US military attaché, raped and robbed two embassy secretaries, looted the homes of three embassy staffers, and stole a total of twenty-two cars belonging to the American diplomats and their families. Since the State Department officials were not armed and the thoroughly intimidated Jordanian police looked the other way, the phony heroes of Arafat's "revolution" had fun. Beating up on defenseless Americans was almost as satisfactory as fighting Israel and—the beauty of it!—it was safe. The Yankees could not fight back.

As it happened, the havoc in Amman coincided with my sole transgression against my three tried-and-true rules for working abroad, which were (1) always carry an airline credit card and one thousand dollars in American Express checks; (2) never travel with more luggage than you can carry; (3) and above all, never get sick. In the late spring of 1970 I came down with a hemorrhaged disc that eventually reduced me to a cripple at the most inopportune time—just as the PLO and King Hussein were approaching a showdown.

By the end of July my left leg was useless, I was eating Robaxin like candy, and my orthopedist had me scheduled for an operation in the brand new American University Hospital in Beirut. The news about the rampage in Amman, however, gave me a big jolt. I was furious. Throughout the spring, as Amman became increasingly dangerous for foreigners, I was questioning the State Department's wisdom of keeping a presence in a capital where Americans took serious risks by just showing up in the street. And now a bunch of gutless, swaggering hoodlums—who wouldn't dare come near the Israeli troops less than an hour's drive away—were terrorizing the embassy skeleton staff, with complete immunity.

All I could do about it was write a story about a bunch of people who sat in Amman like ducks in a shooting gallery. Indignant to the eyebrows and hobbling on a cane and one good leg, I made it up the steps into a Middle East Airlines Caravelle, flew to Amman, limped into a cab, and rode to the American embassy. The flag was up and there were two visibly tense young Marines inside the entrance, but those were the only signs of normalcy. The building was almost empty.

Although I limped in without any advance notice or appointment, I was promptly ushered into the office of Morris Draper, the political officer in charge. To ease my back pain, "Morrie" let me ask questions while I was lying on the floor in front of his desk. When we were done, he brought in the rest of his minuscule staff to describe their life under siege.

Flat on my back and drugged with painkillers, I was in no shape to do more than scratch the surface of a drama that deserved much more nuanced and detailed reporting. But the fortitude and sangfroid of the embassy holdouts came through despite the shortcomings of my story. Draper, who had been held at gunpoint at one of the PLO roadblocks, was particularly impressive. With a humor one would not expect from a "US agent" under a PLO death sentence, Morrie cracked jokes about the 25 percent increase in salary—the same raise awarded to the embassy in Saigon—that he and his staff were getting for their hazardous duty. That, Draper dryly noted, "was an undeserved compliment for the fedayeen."

Draper also spoke with outward confidence about an unspecified "early warning system" that, he airily speculated, would enable "nine out of ten" of the embassy hands to survive the expected all-out assault by the guerrillas.

Since any rescue operation would have depended on a quick response by the Jordanian military, I did not believe these odds were anywhere near as high, and Draper probably had his doubts as well. But neither he nor his staff and the Marines with whom I talked that day let down their stiff upper lips. They reminded me of Hemingway's definition of courage: "grace under pressure."

The remaining staff must have been scared silly, resentful of the decision to keep the isolated and practically useless embassy operating, and they missed their evacuated families. But they soldiered on. They ate canned food, kept their curtains closed and their desks away from windows, never walked out in the open, and slept each night in a different house that had been emptied by their evacuated colleagues.

I spent the night with four of the diplomats sleeping on the floor in somebody's living room, and in the morning three Marines carried me on a stretcher while I took pictures of their flag-raising ceremony. If push came to a shove, the young Marines would have been the embassy's first (and probably only) very thin line of defense, and I very much wanted their picture in the magazine.

Afterwards, I took a cab to the headquarters of one of the PLO groups in town to get their version of the siege. Doubling again as a photographer, I also took a picture of a young thug in kaffiyeh holding the US coat of arms he'd ripped off the gates of the embassy. Alas, that was the picture the editors ran with the article.

Back in Beirut, I filed my piece about the "Sitting Ducks" and headed for the operating table. The explosion in Amman came a few days later, when Arafat's giddy followers brought down three hijacked airliners and tried to intimidate King Hussein's mother. When the Hashemite's army struck back, the vigilantes in the Amman Intercontinental took all foreign journalists hostage, but Arafat's "Hanoi" fell all the same. Best of all, the locked-up journalists and our embassy staff survived the rout without any additional harm.

Incidentally, I had one more occasion to admire Morrie Draper's professional composure and guts. It was during the Israeli invasion of Lebanon in September 1982, when he was based in Beirut and discovered that Christian Falangists were massacring Palestinians civilians in plain view of IDF tanks. Draper went ballistic. Dropping diplomatic niceties, he raised hell with every leading Israeli he could reach by phone or wire and demanded that the IDF troops surrounding the camp of Sabra and Shatilla immediately stop the mayhem.

When there was no response, Draper sent a blistering cable to Israel's defense minister Arik Sharon, the three hundred-pound rightist bully of Israeli politics, telling him, among other things, that "you should be ashamed of yourself!" Although Draper's furious protests failed to interrupt the slaughter of more than eight hundred Palestinian men, women, and children, I doubt anybody could have done more.

Another doomsday defeat I felt I had to cover took place in East Bengal, which was then called East Pakistan. The province, the smaller half of the divided Pakistan, in March 1971 embarked on an armed insurrection against the West Pakistan–dominated government, charging it with gross neglect and discrimination. Islamabad responded with a punitive expedition of seventy-five thousand heavy-handed troops. Practically unopposed, they roamed the impoverished East Bengal, burning houses and terrorizing villagers suspected of siding with the untrained and poorly armed rebels.

Since the uprising halted all transportation and most communications in East Pakistan, there was no truly satisfactory way to cover the story. For lack of better options, we in the foreign press kept tabs on the conflict from Calcutta (since then renamed Kolkata), the largest Indian city close to the East Pakistan border. In addition to its proximity to the rebellious province, Calcutta was the haven of many East Bengal refugees who were a prolific—if not always reliable—source of news about developments in the strife-torn province.

The drill that most of us routinely followed was to take a cab very early in the morning to the border of East Pakistan. Leaving the taxi behind, we would then set out on foot or in a rickshaw, if one could be found, in the direction of gunfire or black smoke. Because of the unequal strength of the adversaries, it was hard to witness any actual military clashes—most frequently, we'd find only destroyed villages or villages that were intact but whose population had discovered a new loyalty to the government in Islamabad.

CHAPTER 14

I happened to walk into a small village that was undergoing such transformation. Apparently forewarned about the arrival of West Pakistan troops, the villagers were frantically pulling down East Bengal flags and signs that read "Joi Bangla!" (Victory to Bengal!) when a West Pakistani army truck pulled in and the soldiers, swinging long bamboo sticks, started for the village square. Immediately, the houses began sprouting banners with the red crescent of West Pakistan, and a couple of clearly terrified villagers emerged into the open shouting, "Pakistan Zindabad!" (Long Live Pakistan!). Perhaps because of my presence, the village was considered sufficiently pacified. The soldiers climbed back in the vehicle and took off.

The place where I stayed—the Victoria Palace, at the time the best hotel in Calcutta—only added to the depressing experience. A relic of the age when only mad dogs and Englishmen went out in the midday sun, the hostelry's white-clad waiters served tea and crumpets to the incongruous strains of a quartet playing Viennese waltzes while, outside the entrance, begging lepers and sacred, mangy-looking cows blocked the sidewalk. An additional blow to my morale was attending a couple of parties where obviously affluent counterparts of the Latino *pensadores* pointedly ate food with their fingers while expounding on the "fascism" of American society.

It was against this dreary background that, toward the end of April, the first phase of the war finally acquired a dramatic focus—the last rebels-held area still unconquered by the West Pakistan troops. The enclave consisted of roughly a dozen villages near the border town of Dinajpur, a railroad junction about 240 miles north of Calcutta. For a reporter starved for a dramatic story, East Bengal's last stand was a natural. It was also a very long shot, because the trip to Dinajpur over West Bengal's roads could take a couple of days, which meant I could reach the area and find it full of Pakistani soldiers—more of the same story I'd been filing for weeks.

It was an iffy enterprise, but I had two reasons for doing it. One was my sympathy for the East Bengal rebels, who had a real grievance against Islamabad and were taking a terrible licking. The other, and possibly more persuasive inducement, was a swashbuckling feat performed the previous week by my opposite number from *Time*. He had managed to find a rickshaw and made it through the devastated countryside all the way to Dakka, the East Begal capital. His piece, which ran with a well-deserved fat byline, made it imperative that I try a similar derring-do.

Complications set in even before I left the hotel. The driver of the only jeep-for-hire that I could find spread the word about my trip among other potential travelers who would add to his fare. As a result, on the night before we set out, I got a visit from two exiled politicians of the rebellious East Bengal

Awami League who beseeched me, with tears in their eyes, to take them along to Dinajpur so that they could share the last stand with their people.

I was most reluctant to agree, knowing that the speed of travel diminishes with each additional person sharing the vehicle. But I reflected on the importance of the trip to the desperate-sounding exiles, and I gave in. Whereupon the driver the next morning arrived with not two but three somber-faced East Bengalis squeezed in the back of the car.

The vehicle was a Lend-Lease 1942 US Army jeep with the steering wheel on the opposite of where it should have been in India. Just outside Calcutta, the paved road narrowed down to one lane and every time we met another vehicle my driver, who was one-eyed, entered into a shrill argument with his opposite number over who was going to make way for whom. When we were not held up by other vehicles, we had to slow down to a crawl for handcarts and barefoot villagers trudging fresh produce and raw silk to markets.

The traffic was so interesting that I did not notice until we stopped at an inn for lunch that my passengers in the back had fallen into an agitated conversation, and one of them shed tears. After the meal he did not return with the rest of us to the jeep, and his companions explained that he had decided to return to Calcutta. Why, I asked? Because, one of the politicians explained with some embarrassment, his friend had second thoughts about the venture.

"If you run into the Pakistan Army, the colonel will invite you for a tea and politely send you back to Calcutta," the Bengali who only gave me his name as Farooq, told me. "If one of us gets caught, it means a bullet in the head, or at the very least many years in jail." Farooq was a serious-faced, slender man in his fifties who looked more like a college professor than the leader of an uprising, and I could readily see his point. There was no doubt that by returning to East Bengal the exiles were taking a serious risk.

We spent the night at an inn, and the next morning my two companions looked so glum I wondered if they would finish the trip. They did not. When we reached the outskirts of Raiganj, the last Indian town before we turned to the East Bengal border, one of the politicians shouted at the driver to stop at a roadside kiosk. The jeep slowed down, the man jumped off, and without lifting his eyes off the ground, mumbled something to the driver. We quickly resumed speed, leaving the exile behind. Not wanting to embarrass Farooq, the last holdout, I asked no questions.

We continued in silence until the road turned to a rice paddy beyond which a white boulder on a gently rising slope marked the East Bengal border. I told the driver to stop, gave him some money for food and an inn, and reminded him he was to wait for me in the same place every afternoon until I showed up, which I expected to do sometime during the next three days. I then grabbed my handbag and cameras and started sloshing across the paddy. Farooq trailed a few steps behind me until we reached the border marker. He stopped there and solemnly told me that he would go no further.

"Please do not think of us as cowards," he said, speaking with great dignity and fighting back tears. "It is a lost battle that's being fought here, and we all have families to feed. If I am dead or in jail, my children will starve." He thanked me for the ride and asked if he could ask my driver to take him to a bus stop in Raiganj.

We shook hands, and after a few minutes I came to a dirt road that turned away from the border. Less than a mile away was a sizable brick farmhouse in front of which stood a dark-blue Jeep with the markings of the Pakistan Air Force. I walked in and discovered that I was in the command post of the last rebel enclave.

My host was Major Najm Ali Huq, a thirty-four-year-old East Bengali who had deserted from the Pakistan Air Force and now commanded what was left of the militia of the secessionist Bangladesh (Golden Bengal), as the exiles in Calcutta had renamed East Pakistan. Huq was one of those solid, confidence-inspiring people that every reporter loves to have as a source. Athletic-looking, sober-minded, and self-assured, Huq readily agreed to take me along on what he described as his last round of the enclave before it would be overrun by the fast-approaching Pakistani army.

In the next two days we visited about a half-dozen palms-shaded villages that were hunkered down in expectation of the Pakistani troops. Most of the men and many women with children had joined the estimated million Bengalis who had fled to refugee camps in India. There was no economic activity in the area to speak of. The few small manufactories had ground to a halt weeks earlier, and almost all stores were closed. The sole pharmacy in the enclave stayed open, but it was running out of most medication, including aspirin.

The Awami League was trying to ration food and gasoline, but there was little of either. Food was particularly scarce because most of the farmers had fled and the rice harvest was slow. All that seemed to be left was a heavy sense of apprehension. In one of the villages the local youngsters gave me as a present their only handmade green-red-and-gold flag of Bangladesh. Nobody put it that way, but the gesture struck me as a symbol of their vanishing hopes for independence.

The only man who showed no loss of confidence in the future was Huq. His most urgent message to the villagers was to finish the rice harvest. "Do not give in to the temptation to flee before the harvest is in," Huq exhorted the remaining menfolk in each village. The revengeful Islamabad could not be expected to supply East Bengal with food, he warned, and if the rice was allowed to go to waste, the province would suffer "a terrible famine."

The second point made by Huq to the villagers was that they needed to get ready for the next stage of the war. In the coming weeks and months, he told a few cadres in each village, a way would be found to provide local youngsters with weapons and training in India. The struggle for independence would go on, but instead of open defiance, the fighting would be done by guerrillas and at night. Prolonged grassroots resistance, Huq believed, would wear down the resolve and resources of the West Pakistan government and might hasten a hoped-for Indian intervention on the side of the rebels.

Before Huq and I parted, I asked him what he intended to do before the Pak troops arrived: he was a military deserter, and if captured he was sure to be executed. Huq only told me to "come back four months from now, and I'll show you some action."

I recrossed the rice paddies to the same bend in the road where I had left my driver and his jeep two days earlier, and we made it back to Calcutta in time for my deadline. By the time the story ran in the magazine, four days later, the Dinajpur enclave had been overrun, exactly as Huq had expected.

Also in line with his forecast, by the end of the summer East Bengal guerrillas were harassing the occupying troops, and they struck back so furiously that some 150,000 Bengali civilians were killed and two million fled across the border to India. Early in December, Indira Gandhi finally put paid to the slaughter by ordering the Indian army to push the West Pakistani troops out of East Bengal, whereupon Islamabad threw in the towel. With the Pak army gone, the Bangladesh government in exile moved to Dacca and proclaimed the country's independence.

Neither Huq nor I were around to witness East Bengal's triumph. As his brother wrote me a couple of months later, Huq died in a car accident while training his guerrillas at a military base in India. The letter came shortly before I was transferred to Europe.

CHAPTER 15

WATCHING THE SOVIET SATELLITES

A few weeks before my trip to Dinajpur, the chief of *Newsweek*'s correspondents, Rod Gander, sent me a note on a subject that instantly commanded my attention: the transfer to my next post. After generously acknowledging that I had worked for eight years in difficult parts of the world, Rod asked me to "think for three days" and then write him what I would like to do next. He mentioned the option of my coming to the magazine's home office and "climbing the career ladder" and promised to do his best to fulfill my wish.

Just to be thorough, I briefly considered working in New York. Two foreign assignments plus a stint in Washington were a good base for getting one's name higher on the masthead, and before I went abroad it had been my ambition to become a senior editor. This was my chance to go for the brass ring.

Then I reminded myself that idly contemplating an upscale title was vastly more pleasurable than doing the job that went with it, which was packaging someone else's stories. After several short stints in the magazine's home office I'd seen enough of it to know that working abroad was, for me, the best job in journalism. I was a quintessential legman, and the thought of sitting in a New York office passed from my mind very quickly.

The next question I asked myself was where I should go next. Eventually I wanted to get a crack at the Vietnam War, the decade's top story, which was a feather in every correspondent's cap. But after four hectic years in the Middle East and another four in Latin America I had seen enough killing, hysterics, dirt, and exotic places that reeked of urine. My family and I needed a civilized break.

I also did not want a post with a demanding social scene. Dinner parties and small talk over cocktails were not my forte, to put it mildly. I loved London and Paris as places to visit, but not all the socializing that went with being the flag bearer of the magazine. I was even more leery about getting the West German bureau in Bonn, where—on top of the heavy diplomatic circuit—I knew I would be haunted by memories of World War II. Most of all—and this

I put in the lead of my letter to Rod—I did not want to go to Moscow, where I would cover and work under the watchful eyes of a totalitarian regime that had destroyed my parents.

I was, however, intrigued by the Eastern European story that kept knocking on my consciousness. The curious encounter in Cairo with Pepík, my Communist cousin, was still fresh in my memory. And before that episode, I was twice unexpectedly confronted with my past as a result of the so-called Prague Spring and the Czech experiment of liberal "socialism with a human face" under the maverick Communist Party chief Alexander Dubček.

When, in the spring of 1968, the Czech borders opened for travelers, my brother, Mirek, suddenly arrived in Beirut. I was down with my slipped disc, and this was the first time we'd seen each other—and could speak openly—in twenty years. Mirek sat at my bed and brought me up-to-date on the fate of our family.

Both Mother and Dad had died, Mirek told me. After their release from jail, they were assigned the worst and lowest-paying menial jobs: Dad, who was close to sixty years old, was ordered to go back to sweeping chimneys and Mother was sent to a factory as a cleaning woman. Both my parents were so shattered by their experiences that they broke down physically and mentally and died while in psychiatric care.

My cousin Míla, who had forged bank records to give me the German marks, was shortly afterwards fired by the Central Bank as a "bourgeois element" and was sent to a border region to work as a lumberjack. The work was so strenuous that he became severely ill and had to be discharged on medical grounds. My other cousins—except for Pepík—lost their professional jobs, became factotums in state enterprises, and moonlighted to earn a few Czech crowns.

Mirek was discharged from the army, more than a year after I fled, and was sent by the state employment office to dig ditches and mix cement at a construction site outside Prague. This was part of the regime's punishment of the whole family for Dad's stint in the anticommunist underground and, undoubtedly, for my escape. After two years of hard labor, Mirek came down with severe hepatitis and had to be hospitalized. When he recovered, he finally received permission to get a white-collar job. A talented writer, Mirek first worked as a reporter for a medical journal and later moved to a daily newspaper where he covered science and medicine.

In his spare time, he authored a dozen short stories, four novels, and three plays, but the government allowed him to publish only two books. The rest of his output, Mirek was told by one of the Communist overseers of literature, portrayed a Communist Czechoslovakia "in which nobody would want to live."

CHAPTER 15

Like other dissenters, Mirek continued eking out a living as a lowly reporter until the outbreak of the Moscow-defying Prague Spring in 1968. He then became the chief editor of a popular magazine called *Ahoj na sobotu!* (roughly, "Cheers for the Weekend!") that had been shut down after the Communist coup.

Mirek's new job filled him with optimism about the outcome of the then-looming showdown between Dubček and the Soviet Party secretary Leonid Brezhnev. "They'll box a few rounds, and then things will settle down," Mirek hopefully predicted. Things settled, all right, but only after Soviet tanks returned to Prague in August of the same year, this time to reinstall orthodox Marxism. Mirek's magazine was shut down, and he was once again reduced to a cipher, this time as an archivist.

The Soviet invasion resulted in another encounter with my past. A couple of days after the Red Army put an end to Dubček's experiment, my family and I left Beirut for a brief vacation in Abant, a Turkish mountain resort. As we checked in, the receptionist handed me a cable from New York: Bob Christopher, the foreign editor, wanted me to proceed as fast as I could to Vienna. The abrupt collapse of the Prague Spring caught thousands of Czechs and Slovaks vacationing in the Austrian capital, and they were now struggling with the agonizing choice between remaining in the West or returning behind the Iron Curtain. Bob wanted me to report the story.

Producing the article was the easiest part of the job; stories about truly dramatic events almost write themselves. Much harder was to watch the desperate vacationers, many of them young couples with small children, trying to decide what to do next. Only two or three weeks earlier, they had piled their rattling Škodas and Trabants with camping gear and happily set out on their first jaunt to a Western country. Now, suddenly, they had to choose between returning to their newly regimented, humdrum existence and the uncertainties of exile.

Some of the families I met while doing the story asked my advice. I had no easy solution to offer. Unlike my generation of refugees, the vacationers had lived under Communism for two decades. It seemed to me that if they still could contemplate going back for more of the same, they were not ready for the unavoidable stresses of exile. Several of my fellow DPs could not adjust to their new circumstances in the West and committed suicide. Not everyone had my luck.

The upshot was that I tried my best to describe the difficulties of creating a new existence, but I also emphasized the rewards, especially the prospects for their children. The vacationers usually listened with sagging faces. In most cases they knew they would choose the familiar misery over the risks of the unknown, and I only added to their frustration.

I returned to Abant and my interrupted vacation feeling pretty low. The distress of the young families was not the only reason: during those five days in Vienna I came to realize how much I—and my former countrymen—had changed in the two decades since I left Prague. In their eyes, I was a foreigner who spoke Czech. I felt the same way about them.

This experience was very much on my mind in the early summer of 1971 when I was mulling over Rod's offer. Perhaps I should get reacquainted with my roots, I thought. The visit to Vienna reminded me of the soothing familiarity of Europe—an environment filled with steeples instead of minarets, the sounds of familiar languages, and the aromas and flavors that had delighted my childhood.

I decided I needed a break from exotic cultures and there was no better place to do so than in Vienna, the splendidly civilized Old World city that was the magazine's base for covering Eastern Europe. I loved Vienna's magnificent landscape and imperial architecture. I could not get over the city's splendidly manicured rose gardens, and the world's only cab drivers who kept their radio tuned to classical music. Viennese food and wine were legendary. After years of labor in harsh and hardscrabble countries, Vienna's opulence and serene atmosphere had an almost magic appeal.

And the more I thought about the Eastern European story the more intriguing I found it. The Soviet satellites were classic examples of societies under pressure, which are awful to be a part of but fascinating to watch. It takes guts to function under pressure and in adversity; and gutsiness, next to decency, was a quality I have always greatly admired. Moreover, after years of avoiding any contact with the Communist nightmare, I was increasingly curious what, if anything, the Soviet-style "scientific socialism" was delivering on its grand promises.

Here we were, twenty years after the "progressive masses" had "swept away all reactionaries and class enemies," eradicated "exploitative capitalism," and brought up an entire generation on the Soviet model of the "New Socialist Man." Did the brave new world of Karl Marx work? This was, for me, a question raised by the many Prague Spring tourists in Vienna who opted for returning behind the Iron Curtain. Could it be that Marxism-Leninism was producing blessings that my brother, Mirek, did not mention and that went unreported by the hostile Western press? After years of indifference I suddenly felt that, personally and professionally, I needed to find answers to these questions.

Having duly cogitated, I asked Gander to send me to Vienna. Rod, as always, made good on his promise. In August 1971, just as the rows of grapes on the slopes of the lovely Viennese district of Grinzing were turning deep purple, Romana, Jan, and I moved into a pleasant old mansion overlooking one of the famed vineyards. The territory that came with the downtown bureau of the magazine included Albania, Yugoslavia, Poland, Hungary, Romania, Bulgaria, Czechoslovakia, Switzerland, and of course, Austria, which unconvincingly billed itself as a "neutral" nation.

I stayed in Vienna only a year and a half, but my early departure was no reflection on the quality of life in the Austrian capital. The town boasted some of Europe's most sumptuous and best-kept baroque architecture and palaces, gracious hotels, and a plethora of cozy little restaurants that abounded in light-as-air Wienerschnitzels, Apfelstrudls, and other delicacies of my youth. The wine cellars served Grinzinger to the tunes of gypsy music played by real gypsies; old-fashioned cafés emanated the soothing piano waltzes of Franz Léhar and Johann Strauss. Viennese neighborhoods were clean and neighborly, and street crime was practically nonexistent. The tap water came straight from an ice-cold lake in the Alps. Most impressive of all, the town was surrounded by a delightful wood called Wienerwald that was teeming with so much wildlife that the municipality kept statistics on deer and foxes killed by automobiles within the city limits. The only story I wrote about Austria was an admiring portrait of its remarkable capital.

As a Cold War listening post for journalists, Vienna reminded me in some ways of Beirut. Just as the Lebanese catered to Western journalists covering the Muslim world, Austrians made a business out of providing services for foreigners watching Eastern Europe. The Vienna airport vied with Frankfurt as the best departure point for the Warsaw Pact capitals, Viennese kiosks carried all major Iron Curtain newspapers, and Viennese banks bought and sold all Communist currencies. Another attraction for journalists were Vienna-based representatives of Western companies trading with Eastern Europe, some of whom knew more about the countries' economies than the Communists.

In addition, just like Beirut attracted hordes of fun-seeking Persian Gulf Muslims, Vienna was a potent magnet for Eastern European bigwigs who flocked to the nominally "nonaligned" Austria for a taste of the forbidden capitalist luxuries. As a result, Vienna was the base of an exceptionally large, though not exceptionally talented, group of Soviet bloc spies and diplomats, and it was frequently visited by senior Communist bureaucrats who came to talk business with the reviled capitalists.

Some of my peers in Vienna mined these news sources so adroitly they hardly needed to set foot beyond the Wienerwald. Armed with Radio Free Europe's daily summary of news from Eastern Europe, they made the rounds of the Vienna embassies, checked with the resident spies and Western companies' reps, added insights gained over an expense account dinner with a visiting apparatchik, and produced highly respectable copy. There was something to be said for the system because Communist officials always talked more openly in a Viennese Weinstube over a jug of wine than in their own grim, bugged offices. But for better or worse, I spent most of my time on the road. Covering countries long-distance was not my style.

Also, I found the Vienna-based Eastern European spies lacking. The first I met, a Romanian who said his name was Ion Popescu, was a sharp dresser, but as a news source he was as substandard as Russian automobiles. His "impressions"—that's diplomatic jargon for information—about happenings in Communist capitals were days behind the Radio Free Europe's summary, and while his English was adequate, he could not even read German.

I had better luck on some of my trips behind the Iron Curtain where, to my astonishment, I found it in some ways easier to work than in many non-communist capitals. For one thing, I was never subjected to the tongue-lashing and personal abuse that was a common experience in the Middle East, or to the anti-US tirades of Latino reformadores.

On a very rare occasion, I would run into a Communist official or journalist who would make a disapproving remark about the Vietnam War, but as a rule (with the significant exception of some of the post-Dubček's Communist Party brass in Prague), the people I dealt with were polite or even pleasant. In the Warsaw Pact capitals, where people knew real hegemony and where the Arab-Israeli conflict had no resonance, the United States was respected.

Covering Poland, Yugoslavia, or Hungary could almost be fun. The Poles in particular were so irrepressibly unregimented that I marveled how some of them managed to stay out of jail. On one occasion, I got lost in the building of the Polish Academy of Sciences in Warsaw and knocked on a door to ask for directions to my appointment. The man who answered, an elderly scholar of talkative disposition, inquired who I was. Upon hearing that I was an American newsman, he told me to sit down and proceeded to treat me to an incisive analysis of the blunders of his government. I heard similarly blunt criticism from ranking journalists in the leading Polish Communist publications, and they were among my best sources.

The situation was similar in Budapest, Hungary's beautiful capital on the Danube. One of my favorite Hungarian informants was a senior government economist who was invariably more pessimistic about the regime's performance than the State Department economist in the local US embassy. Once, upon rereading my notes on our conversation, I called him from Vienna and asked, as vaguely as I could, whether he was sure about his downbeat projections. "Absolutely," he said, knowing full well that the call was monitored by the Hungarian state police.

CHAPTER 15

None of which means that I found all of Eastern Europe an open book. The darkest—and most unimportant—place was Albania, which banned all Americans and foreign journalists. We'd cover it once every five years or so by sending in one of our correspondents who had a foreign passport. He'd take a PR tour put on by the government and write one story with a picture, just to remind the readers that the country was still there. Another dismal part of my beat was Ceaucescu's Romania, which reminded me of Iraq under Saddam Hussein. The only Romanians who were allowed to talk to visiting journalists were those who had to, because it was their job. And even these propaganda hacks had to fill out a report on every conversation with a foreigner.

Western embassies in Bucharest—with the sole exception of Israel's legation—had no more contact with ordinary Romanians than I did. Symptomatic of the atmosphere, the Bucharest Intercontinental was the only Iron Curtain hotel where I always got the same room with a big mirror fixed to the wall above the sofa—presumably, to disguise a monitoring camera. When it came to gathering the news, Romania, in short, was hardly worth the trip.

In personal terms, the most dismal experience during my stint in Europe was my sole working visit to the post-Dubček Czechoslovakia. It started with a surprise: after the Czech embassy in Washington turned down my visa request, I reapplied, expecting no success, at its counterpart in Vienna. In April 1972, out of the blue, I got permission for a two-week visit. As soon as I crossed the Czech border in my office Citroën, however, events took a more predictable turn. At the border station, stern-faced officials held me up for almost an hour studying my passport and inspecting the car and my luggage. The reason for the delay showed up in my rearview mirror a few minutes after I was finally cleared to go: hard on my tail was a big black Tatra sedan with four male figures.

They were an introduction to three two-sleuth teams that dogged me throughout the visit. Each team included one individual who stood out in every crowd. Most striking was a robust female figure whom I privately called "Mary" and suspected of being a male cop in drag. He/she was tall, stocky, wore low-heel loafers and a sack-like jacket, and had a canary-yellow mop of hair—presumably, a wig. There was no way of overlooking "Mary" within two blocks' distance. The second pair of gumshoes included an older guy with a pronounced limp, and the third one a youngster with the round, ruddy face of a heavy beer drinker.

Being tailed by security people in Eastern Europe was hardly unusual, but the six Czechs were so clinging they eventually got on my nerves. In the morning, "Mary" was pacing beneath my hotel room window, flanked by his/her male companion. During the day, the young guy and his partners stood behind me every time I looked into a store window. At night, the bad-leg guy and his husky partner—whom I pegged as the boss of the detail because he ordered the most expensive meal whenever I stopped somewhere for a bite—sat in club chairs in the hotel lobby.

By the end of my first week in Prague the sleuths' surveillance became so brazen that on Sunday I decided to punish them by climbing the 299 steps of the Petřínská tower, a Prague landmark high above the River Moldau. My assumption was that at least one of my tails would have to follow me to the top just in case I should be having there a clandestine encounter. To my great disappointment, my followers stayed on the ground. I took their picture as they craned their necks to catch a glimpse of me at the top of the tower, thinking that I would send it to their headquarters as a proof of their laxness. But after I returned to Vienna I decided not to bother.

Big Brother maintained its presence even when I was interviewing presumably trusted senior Communist officials: at the insistence of the press office in the ministry of information, I was accompanied on all my authorized rounds by a Czech-English interpreter whom I needed like a hole in the head. The guy robbed my conversations of the last semblance of spontaneity by taping every word on a bulky, 1950s-vintage tape recorder, and the ministry had the nerve to charge *Newsweek* sixteen dollars a day for his "services." It reminded me of the post–Six Day War period in Beirut, when *Newsweek* had to pay part-time censors for cutting out from each issue every mention of Israel.

When I griped about my escorts to Malcolm Toon, the blunt and savvy US ambassador in Prague, he emphatically warned me to be careful: "The State Security is the one bureaucracy in this country that works," he said. An experienced Eastern European hand, Toon himself took no chances: when we talked in his office, he wrote out sensitive names and facts on a piece of paper and wordlessly showed them to me so that they could not be picked up by hidden microphones. Even in darkest Bucharest, the American ambassador did not bother with such precautions.

The last evening before I left Prague I complained about the surveillance to a high-ranking apparatchik who was also the foreign editor of *Rudé Právo*, the official Communist Party daily. Over dinner, I described to him the brazen ways of "Mary" and his/her companions and asked, as matter-of-factly as I could, what was their purpose: "If they were trying to antagonize me, they've done O.K.," I said, "but if they were trying to intimidate me, they haven't done anywhere nearly enough."

The editor, who was a solid member of the post-Dubček pro-Soviet establishment, gave me an amused look and shrugged. "Maybe they just wanted to make sure that you don't do anything reckless—like fall off from high places," he said. The SOB obviously had seen the gumshoes' report on my climb up the Petřínská tower. Conscious that I still had to get out of the country, I dropped the subject.

One contact I did not make while in Prague was with my brother, Mirek. I almost bumped into him one morning as I was buying newspapers from a kiosk next to the hotel entrance and spotted him, from the corner of my eye, walking toward the building where he worked as an archivist. It was an emotional moment that gave me jolt, but I steered clear of him for his sake as well as for mine. The State Department had warned me that any contact with my relatives would jeopardize them, as well as my status as a foreign journalist. My visa was for a working—not a family—visit.

But I did call up several prominent dissidents and an old high school buddy, explained in full what I was doing, and asked them to call me back if they would feel comfortable about meeting with me. To my surprise, nobody I called turned me down, and while my guardians never lost track of me, they did nothing to interfere with this part of my research.

The dissidents—mostly former Communist writers and intellectuals who in the mid-to-late 1960s became disenchanted with their party—in a way were the least interesting people I talked with. Though one of them sounded contrite about his support for the 1948 coup d'état, what seemed to truly bother them was the punitive ban on the publishing of their books or plays, and the menial jobs to which they were assigned after they turned against their party. Since a far worse treatment had been inflicted on thousands of noncommunists, including my parents and my brother, I was not particularly moved.

Much more interesting and insightful were my sessions with ordinary Czechs of my generation who had never joined the party. After three decades under Communism, my high school buddy Pavel Mlčoch and his blue- and white-collar friends were living examples of the depressing existence—bleak but not outright unbearable—that characterized the system. For example, it took years for noncommunists to get tiny apartments in gray, dismal housing projects on the charmless periphery of Prague, but their rents and utilities were dirt-cheap, and healthcare was free. Scarcities and queues outside half-empty stores were commonplace, but even the lowest salaries bought whatever food and clothing the economy was capable of producing. There were no Western movies or literature, but everyone could get cheap tickets to well-performed operas and concerts. The system was fraudulent, but it offered a trade-off that Pavel's friends summed up as "They pretend to pay us, and we pretend to work."

Deep frustrations set in, however, when anyone outside the privileged Communist establishment tried to improve his or her lifestyle by making a foreign trip or by buying a second-hand Škoda 1000, a Czech subcompact so full of bugs and squeaks it was popularly called "1000 small pains." Attaining such elusive goals was a major long-range project that called for sustained effort.

Mlčoch, who was forty-five years old, married with two children but still without a car, worked all day as a draftsman (as did his wife) in a state enterprise. In the evening, he kept the records of a sports club and performed odd jobs for older couples who lived in his apartment building. In winter, for example, he hauled coal for them from the basement. A friend of his, a mother of two, spent evenings sewing clothes. (My brother, Mirek, I learned later, moonlighted as cabinetmaker while working as archivist. He built simple furniture for himself and his friends.)

To get the necessary foreign currency and permit for a trip abroad required shrewd planning. My friend Pavel, for instance, was doing the paperwork for a scull racing club not only to earn an extra income but because the scullers were occasionally permitted to compete outside the Communist bloc. His goal was to become one of the club's senior functionaries who were allowed to accompany the athletes. In the West, an effort of this sort would be a labor of love. In Eastern Europe, it was a few days' escape from the dreary routine and a chance to snatch a bit of the "good life," as Mlčoch called it, from the jaws of their humdrum existence. Pavel's crowning achievement, he told me, was a trip with the club to West Germany and Austria.

The hunger for more than a barren livelihood affected millions of people in Communist countries, but I concluded, nobody felt it more acutely than members of my own generation who were not craven enough to join the party. Their formative years were seared by the war, and when that nightmare ended, their future vanished in the Soviet vortex. The three best decades of their lives sank in the bottomless pit of fictitious five-year plans, cheap sloganeering, and brazen official lies. By the early 1970s, all that the future held for them was to see their growing children being swallowed by the same dreary miasma.

Throughout my visit, the sights, smells, and sounds of Prague left me curiously indifferent, but the fate of Mlčoch and his friends affected me a great deal. They were uppermost on my mind when I described the post-Dubček Czechs as "a benumbed nation, without leaders, without illusions, without the strength to even hate its oppressors."

When my two weeks were up and I saw my gumshoes and the Prague skyline in my car's rearview mirror I felt no surge of emotion other than a sense of relief. My story pulled no punches, and I was gratified when the party hacks in the Prague press office informed our embassy in Vienna that I was a persona non grata and should not bother applying for another visa. As far as I was concerned, they did me a favor.

CHAPTER 15

Although I stayed in Vienna only a year and a half, I continued covering Eastern Europe from my next post and watched the dismal story of Soviet-style socialism for a total of four and a half years. My many visits to the area bore out what I had thought about Communism when I fled after the 1948 coup: the system was rotten to the core and alien to human nature.

In every country, the public discourse consisted of brazen lies about the past, present, and future. In former concentration camps in East Germany, for example, the memorial displays glorified the executed Communists and downplayed the millions of Jews who were gassed. The Warsaw regime insisted that the wartime execution of Polish officers at Katyn was the work of the Wehrmacht, despite incontrovertible evidence that it was carried out by the Russians. The Czechs and Slovaks were told that Tomáš Masaryk, the country's first president, was a bourgeois reactionary and that the real founders of Czechoslovakia were obscure Stalinists who lived much of the time in Moscow.

The present was falsified by bureaucrats who put out phony figures showing every five-year plan outperforming the previous one while the stores remained empty. In Bulgaria, my official briefers bragged that the party chief Todor Zhivkov personally kept abreast of the output of all key state factories. The statistics produced by his computers were glowing, but the reality was far from it—the plant managers were putting phony production figures in the system.

As for the official hoopla about communism's glorious future, it flew in the face of the total alienation of Eastern European youth. Even during their darkest hours in the spring of 1945, the Nazis were able to enlist fourteen- and fifteen-year-old German kids as *Wehrwolfen*—guerrillas who were to fight for their Reich behind the lines of the advancing allied armies. But the Eastern European Marxists managed to lose their youth even while firmly in control of their regimes and propaganda, entirely on the strength of their incompetence and inane doctrines.

The youngsters I met in Poland, Hungary, and Czechoslovakia were agog over the American lifestyle, blue jeans, and Elvis Presley; Marxism bored them beyond words. What kept the Communist cliques in power was the threat of Soviet intervention; their own state security systems, which were well provided for; and the apathy of the populace. Fifty years after the great bolshevik revolution, the party's true believers were either dead or disenchanted, the workers were oblivious to the crap about socialist paradise, and students and young intelligentsia were openly antagonistic. From Poland in the north to Yugoslavia in the south, Communist parties as mass movements were a joke.

The system was hollow and barely plodding along, like a piece of wheezing machinery with just enough steam to keep the wheels turning. It had one achievement to its credit, which was the cradle-to-grave assurance of basic food, austere shelter, and mediocre medical care in return for no back talk, grudging obedience, and very little or no work. But the regimes' enormous mismanagement and misreading of human nature carried an unacceptably high cost by alienating the talented and the able who could have made a difference.

Economic incentives were banned on ideological grounds—under socialism, everyone was supposed to do his or her best according to their abilities. And political power, the key to obtaining anything above average, was zealously hoarded by the fourth-rate dimwits that made up the party apparat. The price for admission into the ruling circles was such slavish acceptance of their caprice and idiocy that eventually it gagged even such Communist enthusiasts as my cousin Pepík.

By the time the postwar Eastern European regimes were two generations old, they were drowning in their own backwardness and mediocrity. As I made my rounds in the world of Marx and Lenin, I could not help marveling at the self-deception of the Soviet prime minister and Communist Party leader Nikita Khrushchev when he told a group of Western ambassadors, "We will bury you!" The brazen little muzhik must have been full of vodka.

~

For a citizen who experienced twice the defeat of decency, watching the decay of East European Communism was both a saddening and a satisfying experience. As a journalist, however, I found the process so slow and barren of drama or news that I soon started getting restless.

After a little over a year in Vienna, I wrote Rod Gander that we should close the Eastern European bureau and I should go somewhere else. When I finished the note I slept on it for several nights, knowing I was courting a potential disaster. Tactically speaking, sinking one's own boat before having another one to leap into is a piece of bravado that can end in drowning. But as had been the case when I reached other crossroads, I found future risks no antidote for my present discontent. I crossed my fingers and mailed the note.

As it turned out, Gander had an idea so urgent he replied not by mail but by jet cargo. Appraised by a cable that he was sending me an important parcel, I rushed to the airport and spent half a day extricating from the Austrian red tape a big brown envelope that contained a small white envelope with a brief

CHAPTER 15

letter. The gist of it was that I had landed on all fours, but in a place I would have much rather missed.

What my chief of correspondents proposed was to add Eastern Europe to the West European beat covered from Bonn. That was step number 1, which made sense. Step number 2 was Gander's suggestion that I take over the enlarged territory as the new Bonn bureau chief—a job I had repeatedly said I did not want because of my memories of the Nazis.

As Gander later told me, he and Ed Klein, the new foreign editor, had been frequently discussing how to make me accept a transfer to Germany. Now, I handed them a solution: Bonn was the only overseas bureau that needed a new boss, and since I spoke German I was the logical person to take it. I still could turn Bonn down, but the alternative would have been a return to the States, probably the New York headquarters of the magazine.

With a sigh I reminded myself of one of the prime lessons I had learned in my youth, which was that life was not meant to be fun. The choice between the New York's office politics and work in Germany left me unenthused, but I found comfort in the hope that my tour in Bonn was bound to be busier than it was in Vienna, and it would not last more than two or three years. Most important of all, I would still be meeting real people, and doing reporting.

In February 1973, my family and I left the vineyards of Grinzing and moved into another rented family house, this time in the shadow of *der lange Eugen*, the high-rise West German parliament in Bonn.

CHAPTER 16

MEETING THE NEW GERMANS

My assumption that West Germany would be a busier beat than Eastern Europe came true sooner than I thought. The week I took over the Bonn bureau the US dollar dropped against the German mark so disastrously that we did a cover story about the realignment of world currencies. To say that I was unprepared for the task is an understatement. The next week, the dollar dropped again, and the overseas editions went into another cover. By the time the exchange rate settled at a more or less stable level, the magazine had run four major stories on a complex subject I had to learn from scratch in a matter of days.

The hectic first weeks in Bonn had one silver lining—unlike in Vienna, I didn't need to worry about getting space for my stories in the magazine. But on the whole, covering the tanking of the almighty dollar (which took a big bite off the purchasing value of my salary) was not an endearing welcome. Especially to a country I was trying to avoid in the first place.

The new environment in which I worked was another mixed blessing. On the one hand West Germany was the very opposite of the slothful morass in East Europe: it was a stellar showpiece of modern technology and orderly achievement. The "economic miracle" whose birth I had watched in the DP camps at the end of the 1940s had rebuilt the country's devastated cities from underground garages to church steeples and created an infrastructure that bristled with efficiency.

German trains were particularly impressive: they were clean, plentiful, on time, and took passengers straight to the heart of town—almost any town. The communications were first-class. Lufthansa service was exemplary. The famed Autobahns had no speed limit, and the office Mercedes Benz was built to take it. The West German bureaucracy was so alert that its IRS hit me for taxes the very first year I lived in Bonn. Compared with Latin America, the Middle East, and Eastern Europe, West Germany worked like a Swiss watch.

CHAPTER 16

And if there was anything more impressive than the country's steel, concrete, and all-round competence, it was the cornucopia in West German shopwindows. Produced by thousands of small entrepreneurs rather than by a few giant chain stores, the variety of some consumer products bested those in the United States. The West German bakers, for instance, made dozens of kinds of bread and rolls, every one of which was superior to the soggy, plastic-wrapped cotton sold by 7-11s in the States.

But the glistening Wirtschaftswunder carried a very big ecological tag, and the price was paid by everyone who lived in Germany. Traveling around the country I soon came to understand why the Germans were such passionate vacationers in faraway places. In some parts of the country, including resort towns in the Alps, the developers did not rest until they poured concrete over every inch of ground that could sprout a blade of grass. The legendary River Rhine, which rolled like a broad, gray, overworked highway a few hundred yards from our windows, was so polluted with dumped chemicals that in one test its water developed an exposed camera film. The freight boats were so thick and noisy they would wake me up in the wee hours of the morning.

And it was not just my eyes and ears that were offended by some of Germany's postwar achievements. When the wind blew from the direction of the twenty-two-mile-distant Bayer chemical complex in Leverkusen, the stench was strong enough to spoil our Sunday picnic. It did not take long before our family joined the natives in driving to Amsterdam for a Sunday lunch and renting a vacation apartment on the Adriatic.

The job was not real fun, either. The dollar slide was followed by the sort of news doldrums that are the hallmarks of stable and prosperous societies. Since my foreign editor demanded features when there was no hard news, I wrote potluck stories about everything from ethnic discontent in Lapland to West Germany's thriving sex industry, honky-tonks in the Alps, and the "in" inn in Bonn. The stuff was published—largely, I thought, to provide some balance in the magazine to the grim running story in Vietnam—but it did not make me feel at the top of my form.

And while the news was slow, the Bonn dinner circuit, as I had feared, was hyperactive. The foreign diplomatic corps, underworked but fat with entertainment budgets, laid on an endless round of dinner parties whose attendance was one of my least cherished duties. Instead of reading, playing with Jan, or watching the superb German TV, Romana and I would shuttle between Bonn and Bad Godesberg, the diplomatic suburb, to assume our places at formal dinner tables.

The events were billed as fun and relaxation, but they were run as rigorously as the German railroads. Forty-five minutes for drinks, ninety minutes at the table, from thirty to forty-five minutes for after-dinner liqueur and coffee.

After three hours, the conversation suddenly ebbed and everyone headed out the door. Under the unwritten but carefully adhered-to rules, one had to circulate during the before- and after-dinner drinks, and no in-depth one-on-one discussions were encouraged. During the meal, one chatted alternately with the lady on one's right and the lady on the left. For a man with utterly no store of small talk—that is, me—the main course was a form of torture. The only people who suffered more were the bored women who sat next to me.

But my biggest problem, predictably, was caused by my memories of World War II. I had experienced some difficulties of that sort already in Austria, whose population in the 1970s included three hundred thousand known ex-Nazis. Sometimes I'd be sitting in a Viennese Weinstube, picking the brains of some diplomat, and suddenly find myself wondering what the guy at the next table had been doing during the war.

But Vienna was only my bedroom, and at any rate, Austria was not Germany. The Austrians did not occupy Czechoslovakia in 1938, and Bruno Kreisky, the savvy and personable Austrian chancellor, was an anti-Nazi who had spent the war in exile. In other words, Austria did not automatically conjure up for me the brutality and humiliation of the Nazi occupation. But in Germany, the problem was up front and center. Here, the monsters of my youth and I were eyeball to eyeball.

Fortunately, the Germans I worked with or met socially were not the Germans of my memories. By 1973 every German under the age of twenty-eight was born after the death of Hitler, and even Germans in their early forties were untainted by Nazism. This distinction proved to be all-important: as I found out, my aversion to Germans was age-dependent. A contact with any German male of my age or older made me tense up; Germans younger than me triggered no emotional response traceable to the war.

Professionally, this was a blessing because once I got to know a cross section of well-placed, youngish German officials and politicians, I could do my job quite well. One of my sources, a thirty-something political planner in the Bonn headquarters of the Social Democratic Party, became my regular lunch partner. There was no German problem or development that Uwe Janssen and I could not or would not talk about.

Another youngish German, a savvy Kremlinologist in the Bonn foreign office, became an excellent diplomatic source as well as a frequent dinner guest. My relationship with the three young German women who worked in my bureau could not have been easier if they had been Americans. Truth be told, they were among the most reliable and conscientious researchers and assistants I had ever worked with. Even without the Nazi dictatorship, thoroughness and dependability were traits admirably imbedded in the German culture.

To satisfy my own curiosity as well my foreign editor, I did a feature on the Bundeswehr, the successor of Hitler's Wehrmacht. Naturally, I saw only a very small piece of the new army, but the tactical missile unit near Koblenz, which I visited for three days, left me with a very favorable impression. The atmosphere in the barracks was even more informal and unmilitary than it used to be in my own basic training unit in Kentucky. Relations between officers and soldiers were so relaxed there was hardly any saluting. The soldiers, who were all volunteers, talked about the Bundeswehr as an employer rather than a symbol of Teutonic superiority, and they showed no trace of the disdain toward civilians that had been the hallmark of the Wehrmacht. It was hard to believe these were the sons of the heel-clicking, arrogant praetorians who used to strut around Prague.

Another eye-opener was the West German high schools. The first surprise came when Heidi Witt, my assistant, called the ministry of education to ask if I needed permission to visit some of the schools in Bonn. The answer was that I should stop by the principal's office to introduce myself. After that, I could drop in on any class not taking a test, and ask any questions I liked.

I visited one junior high school in a blue-collar neighborhood in Bonn and another one in the chichi suburb of Bad Godesberg, and in both I had access to any classrooms I picked. The teachers waved me right in, the kids talked a blue streak and made very good sense. Asked how they felt about their country, for example, the youngsters would talk about the Bundesrepublic (the postwar Federal Republic of West Germany) as a part of Europe rather than the ancestral redoubt of Germanic Aryans. Considering the long history of wars between Germany and its neighbors, these teenagers—only one generation removed from the ultra-chauvinistic Hitlerjugend—displayed a striking sense of kinship with their peers in the rest of Europe.

Listening to them gave me a new appreciation for the postwar denazification campaign conducted by the Western Allies. In the late 1940s, the view often heard in Germany was that the program was a flop. For example, it was prominently reported at that time that German audiences laughed at a documentary film showing dead bodies and gas ovens in the concentration camps. Whatever happened then, I found no hint of the Nazi virus in the kids born from ten to fifteen years later, at least not in those I spoke with. When I wrote the story, I felt pretty certain that in the western part of their "Thousand-Year Reich," Adolf Hitler and his Brown Shirts had lost much more than a war: their era was rapidly fading from memory.

I was much less confident that the same transformation had taken place in East Germany, which in those years was frozen solidly in the Stalinist mold.

From what I saw, the only time Erich Honecker's regime gave me a working visa, young Germans east of the Berlin Wall were still marching in a lockstep very similar to that of the Wehrmacht.

I was issued the rare visa to attend a Communist World Youth Festival, one of those contrived pseudo-international affairs the Communist regimes periodically laid on in an attempt to persuade their youth that growing up in a police state was fun. For this particular weeklong event in the mid-1970s, the entire center of East Berlin, including the huge, barren Alexandersplatz, was closed to all vehicular traffic. The ban, executed with the traditional German thoroughness, had only one noticeable flaw: the traffic lights throughout the temporary pedestrian zone stayed on.

It was in this almost eerily noiseless echo chamber that the East German teenagers, some two hundred thousand strong, would remind me of their peers during the Third Reich. The kids would be roaming in bunches among the gray blocks of Stalinist architecture searching for socialist entertainment when, suddenly, a streetlight in front of them would turn red. Mind you, the whole area was off-limits to vehicles: there were no cars, trucks, or streetcars anywhere within sight or hearing, and even the ever-present East German cops were gone. Yet, the youngsters would freeze like Pavlov's dogs. They'd stand on the sidewalk, gazing at the empty cobblestones that separated them from the other side of the street, until the light changed to green.

It was a depressing sight. "Befehl ist Befehl!" (An order is an order!), the Nazis used to shout. East of the forbidding Berlin Wall, that iron rule still held.

That is not to say that I found West Germany to be free of echoes of my wartime years. For all my upbeat encounters with young West Germans, my old loathing of Nazi Germany was by no means gone—for my generation, it never will be. Thirty years after the war, my anger was submerged enough to let me go about my business, but it was there, alert and ready to burst forth at the slightest provocation. For example, the first time I sat behind the wheel of the Bonn bureau's car, I froze: staring at me across the hood was the trademark star of Mercedes Benz, the same emblem that had topped the hoods of the Wehrmacht jeeps and combat vehicles roaming the Nazi-occupied Prague. When someone broke off the ornament soon after I came to Bonn, I never replaced it.

I also received a jolt every time I passed the German railroad crossing signs, which were identical to those the Nazis had installed in the occupied Protectorate, and I tensed up whenever I saw German firemen, who wore World War II Wehrmacht helmets. I found it hard to even bring myself to buy a Krups coffeemaker. Krups used to be one of the biggest names in Hitler's military-industrial complex.

CHAPTER 16

At one point, my feelings almost boiled over. It happened after a cop outside the presidential palace in Bonn pulled me over, charging that I had cut into the traffic. He did not claim I broke any traffic law but, in a classic display of German priggishness, called my driving *unhöfflich* (impolite). This alone irritated me because, when I had changed lanes a couple of blocks up the street, I had had plenty of room to spare, and because I was not an impolite driver. It was always one of my basic rules that foreign correspondents abroad should behave like good guests, and that included defensive driving.

What escalated the episode was the cop's reaction when he saw my Austrian driver's license. He first closely scrutinized my place of birth—he even read out loud the word "Tchechoslowakai," as if there were something incriminating about it—and then, lifting his head, he slowly examined my high, unmistakably Czech cheekbones. Feeling my blood pressure rising, I gave him an equally hard look in return. I noted that he looked about five years older than me and had a ruddy complexion with prominent red veins on his nose. I also let my eyes pause on his potbelly and his collar insignia, which reminded me of the chevrons of Wehrmacht's noncoms. When we finished examining each other, the cop and I glared at each other in a silence.

"So, what do you want?" I finally asked the cop in English. I meant to sound nasty, but I was so excited my voice turned husky. The cop's neck grew red as a slab of fresh beef and his lips moved as if he was about to speak but he said nothing. We kept glaring at each other for a few more angry seconds until he mumbled something about "Vorsicht" (Watch out!) and handed me back my driver's license. I got back in my car and drove off.

Years later, when I watched Israeli troops throwing teargas and shooting at protest rallies in the occupied West Bank and Gaza, I frequently wondered about the mark these clashes would leave on the Palestinian demonstrators, who were kids about the same age as I was during World War II. Hard as I tried to control my emotions, the bruises inflicted by the Nazis never really healed, and they influenced my work.

For instance, I had a professional admiration for Helmut Schmidt, the personable Social Democrat who in the early 1970s succeeded Willy Brandt as German chancellor. Schmidt was a first-class politician—"a good actor," as he liked to admit with his characteristic candor—and an impressive prime minister who knew how to hold his ground even to Uncle Sam. A good example was his response when Watergate-scarred President Nixon suggested a photo-op stopover in Bonn on the way to visit Egypt. Schmidt refused to meet him. "I was appalled by the idea," Schmidt told me, knowing fully well I had my tape recorder on and I was going to quote him. "Here I am, a brand new chancellor trying to win some popularity among my own people, and Nixon expects me to shake hands with him on television!" I only wished our own politicians were as forthright.

But despite my appreciation for some of Schmidt's qualities, I never proposed writing his profile for the magazine, although profiling politicians was something of my specialty. I couldn't bring myself to add prominence to a man who as an anti-aircraft officer during World War II fought so hard for the Thousand Year Reich that he was awarded the Iron Cross.

Another example of my wartime hangup was my dogged refusal to appear on *Frühshoppen*, a popular Sunday morning talk show on German TV that featured foreign correspondents. Much as I was conscious of my obligation to carry the flag for the magazine, I could not abide the thought of aging veterans of Waffen SS sprawling on their living room sofa and chortling over my garbled syntax.

Of course, I soldiered on, and not only because it was my livelihood. The longer I worked abroad the more I was impressed by the fact that there were three million people all over the world—almost a million of them outside the United States—who spent hard-earned cash to read what my colleagues and I had to say. The audience was paying us a compliment, and it deserved a fair return on their time and money. The old lady in Duluth that Medill's Jacob Scher had taught us to keep in mind was entitled to the best-informed and most fair-minded reporting and analysis that I could muster.

Part of my attitude was an esprit de corps. Although some of my foreign counterparts were outstanding, on the whole no one covered the world's events faster, more fully, and more straight than mainstream major American newspapers and magazines. This was not my view alone. In the early 1970s, when *Newsweek* and other major American publications introduced their international editions, millions of foreigners—many of whom struggled with the English language—joined our audience. Within a few years, the circulation of *Newsweek*'s international edition shot up from thirty thousand a year to close to eight hundred thousand. *Time* did even a bit better, and the Paris-based *International Herald Tribune* was on every respectable newsstand anywhere outside the Iron Curtain. At a time when the biggest General Motors dealer in West Germany barely managed to sell six Cadillacs a year, it was good to work in a field where America still set the standard.

I tried to live up to it as much on my European rounds as I had done in Latin America and in the Middle East. I gave the Communist regimes credit for a job well done if I could find it, and I protested to my editors when, while I was on leave, *Newsweek* published an article about German *Hitlerwelle*—an alleged Nazi renaissance of which at the time there was next to no evidence. But I also wanted to cover the Vietnam War, and soon after I came to Bonn I launched a campaign to get a Far East bureau. In the summer of 1974, while in New York on home leave, I hit pay dirt. After Gander okayed my transfer to Hong Kong the following January, I returned to Bonn with a stack of books about China and the Viet Cong.

A few weeks later the Hong Kong decision was scrapped: the magazine's projected ad revenue for 1975 unexpectedly dropped so low that all transfers were put on hold. The ban was lifted the next summer, but by then the Vietnam War was over, American interest in the Far East had taken a dive, and Gander decided he wanted me back in the Middle East. This time, to cover Israel.

One of the qualities that made Rod Gander such a formidable chief of correspondents was that he always thought at least one move ahead. Even before my Hong Kong transfer fell through, he had started sending me from Bonn to cover stories in Israel, either to fill in for the vacationing Jerusalem bureau chief or to lend a hand during such crises as the resignation of prime minister Golda Meir and the "Mount Hermon War" between Israel and Syria.

I welcomed the trips as a break from the routine in Europe, but as the crafty Gander undoubtedly planned all along, the junkets gave me a basic working knowledge of Israel's politics, which were vastly more exciting than Europe's. Even more seductively, I was introduced to the special magic of what was then the most unique of cities, Jerusalem. In other words, deep down, I was almost hooked even before Rod proposed that I go back to the Middle East.

Still, when on my next home leave he offered me the Israeli bureau, I almost panicked. I had no premonition of the personal upheaval that was awaiting me there, but I had plenty of objections as a journalist. "Good heavens, no!" I told Gander when he first raised the subject while I dropped in on him in New York. I had had it with the interminable Arab-Israeli conflict, I argued, and I was fed up with the hatreds of the Middle East. Besides, I pointed out, I was used to bigger beats. Israel was so small just staying there would give me claustrophobia. "Please, Rod," I earnestly asked him, "think of something else."

What Gander thought of was to invite me for lunch to his house in Vermont, about three and a half hour's drive from my own summer cottage I had built in that God's country a few years earlier. After we ate in apprehensive near silence, Rod asked me to join him for a walk in the surrounding woods. Then, as we slowly strolled down a logging road, Gander returned to the subject of my transfer with a skill that reminded me of the legendary persuasiveness of Lyndon B. Johnson.

First, he massaged my ego. My judgment was solid, he said, and that was the most important reporting requirement for the complex and explosive issues in the Middle East. He also dwelt for a while on my familiarity with the Arab side of the story and my experience over the years in covering fast-moving developments and military conflicts. After we turned around and started walking back, Gander smoothly segued to his second theme, which was the iffy future of the Hong Kong bureau. As part of the post-Vietnam syndrome, he said, most Americans didn't want to read or hear anything about that part of the world, and there was a question as to how long the Hong Kong bureau would remain open.

In contrast, Gander pointed out, the Arab-Israeli conflict was a major foreign story, it showed no signs of flagging, and it had a big and deeply interested American audience. Hardly a week went by, he said, without the magazine running a Middle East story. Knowing my workaholic ways, Gander added, he thought that I not only would be the right man for the beat, but that I would enjoy covering it.

He saved his most telling point until we reached his house, and then dropped it disguised as a footnote. Of course, he said in a seemingly offhanded fashion, if I found another Middle East assignment too hard to take, I could always stay in Bonn or come to the magazine headquarters in New York.

As Rod knew perfectly well, he was activating my alarm system. Over the years, I had made no secret of my lack of enthusiasm for editing and space-fitting stories instead of reporting them, and I was on record that I wanted to get out of Bonn. Still, I gave Gander no answer and returned to my hideaway in Vermont's Northeast Kingdom to cogitate on his proposal. The Czechs tell a story about a fictitious medieval prisoner named Dalibor who had no musical training until he somehow got hold of a violin and discovered that if he played a good tune, people would gather outside the prison and throw him food through the window. As I pondered what to do next, I perceived the wisdom of the Czech maxim that "Dire need taught Dalibor to fiddle." Out of dire necessity, I had to seriously consider a transfer to Jerusalem.

The beat was indeed puny—by far the smallest foreign area covered by any bureau of the magazine. It consisted of Israel within its 1948–1949 cease fire lines plus the Palestinian West Bank and Gaza, the Syrian Golan Heights, and the Egyptian Sinai Desert that IDF overran during the Six Day War. In the mid-1970s, the population of Israel was 3.5 million Jews and about 0.5 million Israeli Arabs, and in all of the occupied territories lived about 1.0 million Palestinians, Druze, and Bedouins. Except for the easternmost part of Sinai, there wasn't a place in the whole beat that could not be reached within a few hours' drive from Jerusalem. The claustrophobia that I worried about was more than a figure of speech. So was my aversion to a return into the cauldron of raw emotions stirred by the Middle East conflict.

But after the walk in the woods I had to decide whether Jerusalem was a worse assignment than Bonn or the story-editing and picture-selecting operation in New York. My back thus against the wall, I began to see that Gander's proposal was not as bad as I had thought. He was certainly right about Jerusalem's importance as a news capital, which by far exceeded the country's physical size. American Jews were fascinated by whatever was happening in Israel, and it was common knowledge that they were the most avid and discerning readers. Big audience was a plus factor number 1. And of course I knew that, unlike Europe, the Middle East was never dull. The place was in a more or less permanent state of war, and to be completely cold-blooded about it, war made for excellent copy.

Plus factor number 3 was that the Arab-Israeli friction was pregnant with serious consequences for the Cold War, which was then still the dominant news story. Washington regarded the Jewish state as a strong and stable ally in an unstable region—a part of the world where Western presence was essential because the Persian Gulf oil was vital for the economies of the United States and other noncommunist countries. For the same reason, the Soviets were hostile to Israel, and they vigorously courted its Arab enemies.

Next to Berlin, the Arab-Israeli conflict was the prime East-West flash point: during the October War in 1973, President Nixon put the US armed forces on nuclear alert to preempt Soviet intervention. Finally there was a plus factor number 4 in the unique shape of the Israeli beat, which straddled both the Jewish state and its core adversaries, the occupied Palestinians. Covering both sides of a conflict is one of the most professionally satisfying but relatively uncommon assignments in journalism. In the Jerusalem bureau, it was a major part of the job.

The more I thought about working in Israel, the better it looked. With China still closed to Western reporting, Hong Kong would have been yet another bedroom outpost for flying from country to country for short stories without much, if any, depth. In Jerusalem, by contrast, I'd report on two societies under relentless, mutually generated pressures. In-depth coverage was something I had sorely missed everywhere except in Germany, a country that was stable, unexciting, and redolent with bad memories. In Israel, the outlook was just the opposite.

Last but by no means the least, there were the implied creature comforts: Jerusalem would be the first post since I had left Washington where most of the time I could stay put. The thirteen years of almost constant travel had turned me sour on the world's airports and hotels, all of which I came to classify as "bad" or "worse." Just not having to lug luggage, spend weekends alone, and worry about airline connections was going to make a marked improvement in my quality of life. Speaking of which, I would be also leaving Bonn's dinner parties for the enthralling narrow alleyways, hidden courtyards, and fragrant jasmine wafting from behind the ocher walls of the Old City of Jerusalem.

I was still vacationing in Vermont when I called Gander and told him that he won. Five months later, in February 1976, Romana, Jan, and I moved to Jerusalem.

~

There is a footnote to my reporting from Germany that I might as well include here, although it happened years after I left Bonn. It is the story of my biggest journalistic goof, a tale when my instincts and sources failed me and I fell for a momentous hoax. Of course, it had to happen to me in Germany. Where else?

It started one evening in April 1983 when Maynard Parker, the magazine's executive editor, called me at home in Jerusalem with intriguing marching orders. Without any explanation, he asked me to take the next morning's Swissair flight—he even gave me the flight number—to Zurich, go to Hotel Bauernhof on the lakefront, and at half past eleven in the morning meet him and Bill Broyles, *Newsweek*'s new chief editor, in the lobby. That Parker said nothing about the purpose of the trip was not surprising, because he knew my phones were bugged by Israel's nosy security establishment. Obviously something of substance was cooking, and Maynard did not want to give an advance notice to the Israeli Shinbet, the FBI of the Jewish state.

The next morning I took the suggested flight and at the appointed hour was duly ensconced on a sofa in the very small lobby of the Bauernhof, waiting. The receptionist had told me he had no reservation for Broyles, Parker, or me, which was a bit surprising but at first not really disquieting. It gradually became so as time dragged on and Parker and Broyles were not showing up.

At 12:30 a.m.—a brutally early 5:30 a.m. New York time—I felt sufficiently unsettled to call Mike Ruby, Gander's successor as the chief of correspondents. Reflecting on how frequently I was getting calls from the headquarters at even more ungodly hours, I pulled Ruby out of bed and asked him if he knew what was holding up our two top editors.

I drew a complete blank. Ruby did not even know that Parker and Broyles were out of town, and nobody had told him I had been summoned to Switzerland. Whatever the three of us were supposed to be doing was obviously a top secret even for the senior managers of the magazine. Ruby took it in good style, considering the hour, and tried to sound matter-of-fact when inquiring if I was sure that the guy who had called me was Parker. I stifled an offended groan, grunted "Yes of course!" and returned to the sofa, conscious

CHAPTER 16

of being by now the subject of discreet scrutiny by the eminently polite but concerned-looking receptionist.

Around one o'clock in the afternoon, the door to the lobby was suddenly flung open and Parker walked—no, barged—in, looking like a man who is having a whale of a time. Without mentioning a word about the purpose of our expedition, he made a quick phone call to Ruby to tell him not to worry about his and Broyles's whereabouts and then asked me to walk with him "around the corner." Parker even carried my suitcase, not a routine gesture of executive editors toward their underlings.

A block from the hotel, we entered the branch office of a big Swiss bank and were promptly ushered into a private conference room inside the vault. Sitting in the windowless cubicle was Broyles and two other men to whom I was introduced by Parker. One of them, a relaxed and affable-looking executive type in his early forties was Wilfried Sorge. Sorge was the publisher of the *Stern*, a major West German magazine. The other man was Professor Gerhard Ludwig Weinberg of the University of North Carolina. Weinberg was a leading American expert on the Nazi era and documents left behind by Hitler, and he looked serious, almost grim, as well as excited.

On the table between Weinberg and Sorge was a stack of old-fashioned hard-cover notebooks of the type I remembered using in high school during World War II. The notebooks, Parker had told me during the short walk from the hotel, were alleged to be Adolf Hitler's diaries—potentially one of the biggest historical finds (and magazine stories) of the postwar era. The allegation was so startling I did not fully grasp it until I saw the pile on the desk. I stared at it, trying to think straight.

"Go ahead and take a look at them," Parker told me, nodding toward the notebooks. Parker, of course, was not asking me to become an instant authority on Hitler's memorabilia. In addition to the one-thousand-dollar-a-day fee for Weinberg, *Newsweek* was paying big bucks for expert evaluation of the diaries by two other leading American authorities on Hitler's documents and handwriting. But as a former correspondent, Parker understood a reporter's yen for sizing up the evidence, regardless of how arcane.

The notebooks were slightly larger than standard office stationery and well-preserved, though obviously old. Some had a ribbon attached to the cover that could be tied to keep the notebook closed. Rather gingerly, I reached for the diary closest to me and opened it.

The first thing that hit me was the familiar pungent aroma of old papers kept in a slightly damp, poorly ventilated place. I knew the musty smell so well that in my mind's eye I suddenly saw the two bottom drawers in my grandmother's bedroom closet. It was the treasure trove of her correspondence, mostly postcards and letters sent to her during World War I by one of her sons who died on the battlefield. Grandma let me peel off the stamps for my collection. The stamps showed the well-fed but rather pained-looking profile of Austro-Hungarian Emperor Franz Josef. The venerable emperor reputedly prayed so hard for the troops who were getting killed for his greater glory that, poor guy, his knees hurt.

I snapped out of the reverie and looked again at the open pages in front of me. In the sharp light of the vault's ceiling lamp the edges looked ocher and the ink was rusty brown, the same colors I remembered from grandmother's correspondence. My mental association of the notebooks with my dead uncle's Feldpost cards by now was so strong I could almost smell the onions cooking in Grandma's kitchen.

I began gingerly turning the pages and reading the hastily scribbled, sometimes nearly illegible entries. There would be one or two on every page, in straight declaratory sentences, frequently alluding to events or facts that to the author were commonplace and therefore required no explanation—just the sort of shortcuts one would expect in the diary of a very busy person without literary pretensions.

My German was not sophisticated enough to pick up stylistic subtleties, but as far as I could tell, there was nothing phony about the notebooks in front of me. I remembered, or had read about after the war, a few of the events mentioned in the entries, and again, nothing struck me as suspicious. Moreover—under each day's entry was a wiggly, obviously rapidly executed signature. It was a very peculiar autograph, shaped like a short and wide ice cream cone, and it looked like Adolf Hitler's signature I once saw in a German magazine.

As I turned the pages I could feel the excitement tightening my chest. The thought, at first distant, was gaining volume like "The Marseillaise" in Tchaikovsky's *Overture of 1812*. Could I, I began to ask myself, an erstwhile slave laborer of the Third Reich, be holding in my hand a personal record of that monster, that incredibly evil mind that stained the twentieth century? I took off my coat; suddenly, the room felt too warm.

I was not the only one whose face was flushed with excitement. So was Weinberg, a native of Germany, who had devoted his professional life to lecturing and writing about Hitler and his era. Here was a savvy historian who was a walking encyclopedia on the Thousand-Year Reich, and he was going through the notebooks in front of us with the fascination of an archaeologist who had stumbled on an unplundered grave of an Egyptian pharaoh.

Weinberg's excitement, of course, was on much more solid grounds, one of which was his initially profound skepticism about the diaries' origin. He'd agreed to accompany Parker and Broyles only after warning them that despite thirty years of effort by hordes of researchers, there wasn't the slightest indication that Hitler had ever kept a diary. Moreover, Weinberg said, it was well known that Hitler hated to write in longhand. As far as the professor was originally concerned, his job was going to be debunking the authenticity of the alleged find—and to that end, he came prepared to compare the journal's entries with his own data about some of Hitler's most obscure decisions and meetings.

It was a task in which he and Sorge had been engrossed for more than two hours by the time I came, and to Weinberg's great surprise, the diaries were holding up—and then some. Regardless how arcane the event, the diaries had a comment on it—most of the time mundane, sometimes surprising, but never patently false—at the appropriate date. The scribbled remarks sounded so unfailingly authoritative that after a while I had the impression that Weinberg was checking his own data against the diaries, instead of vice versa.

A few of the entries I saw struck me as odd. For instance, the diary's reaction to the Kristallnacht, the notorious anti-Jewish rampage by the Nazis in November 1938, was an exasperated sounding complaint about, of all things, "the damage caused to Germany's reputation abroad." As if Hitler would have cared, I thought. But the few eyebrow-raising oddities of that sort were more than outweighed by seeming evidence that the diaries were genuine.

One of them was the marked deterioration of Hitler's alleged handwriting after the generals' attempt to assassinate him in July 1944. From that date on, the jottings started sloping downward across the pages as if sinking with the writer's spirit and physical condition. Another touch that I found convincing was the despairing simplicity of the last entry, of April 16, 1945. "The long-expected Russian offensive has begun," the note read, referring to the Red Army's final assault on Berlin. "May the Lord help us all." It was not an immortal statement from a man staring at an utter catastrophe of his own making but, like the rest of the entries, it was not inappropriate for the occasion.

What struck me as oddest of all was that Hitler's funny signature was under almost every one of the hundreds of entries. For one thing, it was certainly strange that Hitler, despite his dislike for writing in longhand, would bother to sign every blurb he wrote. Moreover, as Weinberg explained, signature is the hardest part of anyone's handwriting to plagiarize. That being the case, I wondered, why would a forger take so many unnecessary chances to be found out?

By the time Broyles, Parker, Weinberg, and I left the vault to catch a flight to Hamburg, Weinberg, a historian of Nazism and a Jew who had fled Germany in 1938, seemed to be as excited as I was. Ever the scholar, Weinberg during the flight withheld his final judgment of the diaries. But in the careful analysis he later wrote for the magazine, he expressed his "preliminary feeling" that the documents "looked genuine."

As far as I was concerned, the story looked even better after Broyles, Parker, and I met in Hamburg with the brass of the *Stern* magazine. The big question, at this point, involved the diaries' origin, and the explanation we received sounded entirely plausible.

Stern, we were told, had been secretly buying the notebooks from smugglers who had brought them out of Communist East Germany. According to the magazine's employee who was running the operation, the diaries had been stashed in a trunk aboard a Luftwaffe cargo plane that was shot down during the last days of the war. The person or persons who found the plane and searched its wreckage hid the notebooks and eventually sold them to a smuggler who brought them piecemeal to West Germany and sold them for a stiff price to *Stern*.

The German publisher now offered to sell the diaries' English-language publication rights to several newspapers and periodicals, including *Newsweek* and American and Australian dailies owned by Rupert Murdoch. Both Murdoch and Katherine Graham, the owner of the Washington Post Company and *Newsweek*, were interested, and so were Broyles and Parker, who returned the next day to New York.

I was told to stay in Hamburg and learn all I could about the notebooks while a squad of Murdoch's and Graham's lawyers would negotiate the proposed deal. If Graham decided to spend a million dollars on *Newsweek*'s part of the package, it was to be my job to help write the magazine's own series of stories based on "Hitler's diaries."

Over the next few days, I was poring over the transcript of the journal's entries and talking at length with two bright young staffers of *Stern* who had spent a whole year quietly checking the accuracy of every word in the notebooks. Thomas Walde and Leo Pesch—the former was *Stern*'s expert on the West German intelligence services, and the latter the magazine's top writer—struck me as studious, serious, and straight. They only strengthened my growing belief that the notebooks were no hoax.

Secluded in an inconspicuous office several blocks away from the *Stern* headquarters, and surrounded by a whole library of books about the Third Reich and Hitler, Pesch and Walde had lived with the diaries for so long and so intimately they could cite entire passages by heart. They were equally at home with much of the historic evidence bearing on the veracity of the entries. And they both were convinced that the diaries were genuine.

As Pesch told me, it was not just the accuracy of even the most obscure entries and asides that had sold him on the diaries. He and Walde had also scrutinized the diaries for contents that could have served the interests of West Germany's ex-Nazis or the Communist regime in East Germany, the two major groups that were suspected of possibly being behind this potential historic find. Their analysis revealed nothing suspicious. "What rings most true is that when you read the whole thing, it does not carry water for anyone," Pesch told me.

Despite a few surprising comments such as the criticism of the Kristallnacht, Pesch thought that Hitler did not come out of the totality of the diaries looking any better than the heinous villain the world knew him to be. Since they found nothing politically suspicious, then why, Pesch and Walde asked themselves, would anyone have tackled the giant task of forging fifty thousand historically accurate words, not to mention hundreds of Hitler's signatures?

The answer I should have immediately thought about, of course, was "money": *Stern* had given Gerd Heidemann, its staff photographer who had allegedly bought the notebooks from a "smuggler," 9.9 million German marks. But hard-nosed skepticism was not among the tests to which the notebooks were subjected, at least not by me, and for a while not by anyone else. On the contrary: for a few weeks after *Stern* announced the "diaries" existence, they were widely hailed as genuine.

Three of the world's most prominent handwriting experts—a German, a Swiss, and an American, all of whom had authenticated Hitler's documents before—had weighed in with bulky certifications that *Stern*'s hoard was the Führer's handiwork. Laboratory tests confirmed that the notebooks were manufactured in the early 1940s. Assays of the ink were inconclusive; the age of ink, according to forensic experts, was almost impossible to determine with certainty. As for the text, prominent scholars rushed to endorse its origin. Hugh Trevor-Roper, Britain's foremost historian and author of the famous *Last Days of Hitler*, was one of several heavyweights who examined the notebooks and publicly vouched for their origin. Trevor-Roper was so sure of it he told a reporter that he "staked his reputation" on their authenticity.

Most of the brouhaha was fortunately ignored by the brass of the Washington Post Company, who in the end declined to buy into the *Stern* lode. I returned to Jerusalem, only to read a few days later that a laboratory test performed by West Germany's version of our FBI showed that the ribbons attached to the notebooks contained nylon, a substance that did not exist in Germany in the early 1940s. Shortly afterwards Heidemann confessed that the diaries had been forged by a West German accomplice.

All of which would have made a much better dinner conversation if I, too, had not fallen for the hoax. I felt thoroughly abashed. Never again, I swore to myself, would I put my faith in my instincts, in my childhood memories, and in experts.

PART III

CHAPTER 17

MY LAST BEAT

Israel

I took over the Jerusalem bureau in mid-February 1976 and promptly learned why Israel was such a fascinating country to watch as a reporter. It was the enormous combativeness of Israel's politicians, which stood in sharp contrast to the country's other striking characteristics: its palpable ethnocentrism, cohesiveness, and highly developed—and enviable—sense that all Jews are one family. I was introduced to the political battlefield while working on my first story in the new post, which was about Israel's prime minister Yitzhak Rabin's return from an official trip to Washington.

I thought that Rabin's visit had gone very well indeed. Foreign aid seekers were not exactly America's preferred visitors after the ruinously expensive war in Vietnam, but Rabin was given a red-carpet treatment. President Gerald Ford and Secretary of State Henry Kissinger endorsed his refusal to deal with the PLO or to give up all the territories occupied in the Six Day War. Congressional leaders assured Rabin of continued and generous economic and military assistance. Heads of American Jewish organizations, the pillar of Israel's support in the United States, were adoring and eager to be of help, as always. Bringing home this sort of bacon was a feat for which any leader deserved applause. To deliver it as the head of a tiny country surrounded by 120 million enemies—and not just any enemies, but enemies whose oil production was vital for the economy of the West—was an achievement that, I thought, rated particularly warm kudos for a prime minister and the head of Israel's nation-builder, the Labor Party.

What he got instead was abuse. In the Knesset, the Israeli parliament, right-wing hecklers accused him of surrendering to some unspecified US pressures and demanded his resignation. Yuval Ne'eman, Israel's leading nuclear scientist and a prominent superhawk, went several steps further and accused Rabin of making Israel "a vassal" of the United States. And *Ha'aretz*, the leading Israeli newspaper, added insult to injury by running an article questioning

Rabin's sobriety and mental endurance. John Kennedy often mused that life is unfair, but what was happening to Rabin, it seemed to me, was a bit too much.

Obviously more was going on than met the eye, and it took the excellent Israeli newspapers only a couple days to put the hubbub into a more understandable light. It turned out that the crisis was linked with yet another clash between Rabin and Shimon Peres, his perennial Labor Party rival. Peres, whom I came to regard as Israel's most manipulative and conniving politician was then the defense minister in Rabin's cabinet. The issue that triggered the attacks on Rabin was a lengthy arms request Peres had sent to the Pentagon—behind Rabin's back—on the eve of the prime minister's visit to Washington.

Informed about Peres's sleight of hand after he arrived in the United States, the stiff-necked Rabin exploded, as he had every right to do. In the first place, US relations were so vital for Israel that traditionally all major Israeli aid requests had been vetted and, usually, delivered personally by the prime minister. In the second place, Rabin was a lifelong soldier, the chief of staff of the IDF during the Six Day War, and a former ambassador to the United States. He was correct in regarding himself as far more competent in dealing with both military matters and the administration in Washington than Peres, who had never worn a uniform, had never served in Washington, and who in those years wouldn't have known his way from the Treasury Department to the White House.

To make Peres's blunder complete, his list, which included top secret weapon systems that were still in the design stage, raised the blood pressure in the Pentagon. The requests were blatant evidence of Israel's penetration of the US military's innermost sanctums, a serious problem that later surfaced with the Jonathan Pollard espionage scandal. Even Israel's friends in the Defense Department regarded Peres's move as more than a mere monumental chutzpah.

In my experience, if a similar multiple faux pas had been committed in the United States or any Western democracy, either the perpetrator would have been fired or his misdeed would have been hushed up. Neither happened in Israel. Rabin denounced Peres's request in an off-the-record briefing for Israeli correspondents in Washington. Peres retaliated by charging that Rabin had promised President Ford to press ahead with Rabin's old formula for resolving the Palestinian issue by trading a "piece of land for a piece of peace." This, in turn, raised a bugaboo that terrified the opposition Likud Party and other hardliners.

The result was a public uproar that filled rows of newspaper columns and hours of excited debates in the Knesset, and in the end produced no change. A few days after Rabin returned to Israel, the rightists' attacks ceased as suddenly as they had started, the arms list affair vanished from the newspapers, and the political atmosphere calmed down.

Contrary to the savagely critical editorials, blustering oratory in the Knesset, and my own story that cautiously hinted at a possible government change, Rabin kept riding the political rapids until December, when he called for an early election. He then fought off Peres's bid for the Labor Party nomination for prime minister, only to lose the contest after *Ha'aretz* reported that he and his wife kept in Washington a bank account that was illegal under Israeli law. That caused Rabin's chances for another term to take a dive, and he relinquished his candidacy to Peres. It was the first time they passed power from one to the other, an exercise they went on to perform time and again until Rabin's assassination by a religious zealot.

The arms list kerfuffle was my first lesson about the deceptive nature of the interminable political fulminations the Israelis called "Jewish wars," a spectator sport they ranked in popularity right after soccer. It was the start of a learning process that eventually destroyed my preconceptions based on adulatory books and movies about Israel. But I also learned that some of Israel's reality was more solid than its hyped PR and the lore.

I was greatly impressed by Israel's success in creating a thriving Western society and nation. The country was in many respects a triumph of European values—a stable democracy that coddled its Jewish citizens with well-functioning institutions, cradle-to-grave welfare, and modern, industry-based economy, all of which had been created in an amazingly short time despite hostile neighbors and a complex population mix. The country was living proof of the wonders that can be accomplished by highly motivated people with sophisticated culture and the right skills.

But however positive, my early impressions were soon followed by some sobering surprises. For example, I came to Israel ready to admire the savvy of its legendary intelligence services. It was a reputation based on such events as the embarrassing experience of *Life* magazine's Middle East correspondent when I was based in Beirut. Shortly after the Six Day War, he accompanied a squad of PLO fedayeen on what he was told was a raid from Jordan into the Israeli-occupied West Bank. A couple of days after *Life* ran the story as a major exclusive, the reporter was instructed by his editors to proceed as soon as possible to "Dixie"—the term we used for Israel, which in those years was unmentionable in the Arab world—for a meeting with the brass of the Israeli military intelligence.

When my hapless colleague arrived at the defense ministry in Tel Aviv, he was escorted to a room with a mockup of the Jordan Valley. Surrounded by chuckling intelligence officers, he was shown in detail how instead of crossing the Jordan River to the occupied West Bank, he and his photographer had been taken by the fedayeen from the Syrian to the Jordanian side of the Yarmouk, a tributary that joins the Jordan River south of the Sea of Galilee. The "raiders" had not set foot on an inch of land held by the Israeli army.

Stories of this sort, on top of the legendary worldwide exploits of Israel's Mossad, made all of us in Beirut marvel at the Israeli penetration of the Arab world. But within a few weeks after I settled in Jerusalem I realized that the seemingly all-knowing Israeli intelligence establishment had a huge blind side—incongruously, in the very territories the IDF had occupied and administered since the Six Day War. Eventually, this strange flaw resulted in the incomprehensible failure of the IDF to anticipate and control the *intifada*, the massive Palestinian uprising in the late 1980s. But there was plenty of evidence of this intelligence gap already in the spring of 1976, when the Israeli government called its first and only municipal elections on the West Bank.

Even to me, who had been in Israel only a few weeks, the Israeli decision defied reason. Israel was under no pressure to allow Arab voting. The West Bankers had elected some municipal leaders four years earlier, the territories were quiet, and there was no tradition of elections under the Jordanian rule. Most puzzling of all, it was abundantly clear to anyone who talked with the occupied Arabs that the elections would produce a landslide for the "nationalist" candidates of the various factions of Arafat's PLO.

This was not just my conclusion; it was the tenor of most of the preelection coverage in the Israeli and foreign press. Yet, shortly after the first predictions came out, no lesser authority than defense minister Shimon Peres held a background briefing at which he challenged our reading of West Bank politics. Citing his intelligence experts, who had watched the area closely for almost nine years, Peres produced a four-point list of concerns that, he told us with his customary air of self-assurance, were going to be "uppermost on the minds of the Arabs" on election day.

The top consideration, which I had never heard mentioned by a single West Banker, was "whether the candidate would make a good municipal administrator." It sounded like something out of a civics textbook, but it had absolutely nothing to do with the situation on the ground. The Arabs didn't give a damn about sewers, which most of their towns didn't have anyway. They hated the occupation and could hardly wait for an opportunity to make that clear.

The next two concerns that Peres's sleuths had attributed to the occupied Arabs were each candidate's standing in his *hamula* (extended family) and in the eyes of King Hussein. Hamulas were indeed of importance, but the notion that King Hussein could sway Palestinian voters was preposterous. Such loyalty as he had ever commanded among the West Bankers was limited to the "notables"—officials and town and village elders—who were on his payroll. Even that tie was severely weakened by the poor performance of the Jordanian army in the Six Day War.

Most dumbfounding of all was the final item on Peres's list. Speaking about the candidates' relationship with the PLO, Peres said his experts rated it as the "very last" factor in the election. In Peres's condescending aside, the voters were supposed to think about the PLO only "if they still had any room left in their head" after taking account of all the previously listed factors. The PLO leadership, Peres assured us with aplomb, "was disconnected from the West Bank."

It was obvious that unless Peres was giving us an incomprehensibly foolish spin, IDF's election scouts and their paid Arab informers were not worth an inflated Israeli pound. I was so amazed by the briefing that I couldn't believe Peres meant it, and I checked whether he was dispensing the same line when briefing Israeli newsmen. He was; Israeli officials, I learned over the years, did not share Kamal Nasser's disdain for the foreign media. But the best proof of Peres's confusion about the situation on the West Bank came shortly after his background briefing, when he tried to give the voters in Hebron, West Bank's second largest city, the sort of anti-PLO candidate he thought they wanted.

First, Peres summarily expelled Dr. Ahmed Hamzeh, who was by all accounts Hebron's most popular nationalist candidate, to Lebanon. The quiet-spoken physician was simply grabbed in the middle of a night, put in a helicopter, and flown across the border. It was not a move to improve Israel's image abroad: Dr. Hamzeh's wife, an articulate and energetic French citizen, made the rounds of the foreign embassies and media and saw to it that the illegal and unexplained expulsion got wide publicity abroad.

Next, Peres abruptly postponed the West Bank elections for a couple of weeks while trying to persuade Mohammed Jaabri, Hebron's wealthiest, oldest, and most conservative notable, to replace Hamzeh as the PLO's candidate for mayor. It was another example of wishful thinking. When I saw Jaabri, a couple of days after Peres's briefing, the old sheikh was sick in bed, but he vehemently denied that he could be forced or persuaded to run in the elections. Jaabri called the PLO slate "Communist" and made no secret of his dislike of Arafat and his followers. But he was above all a Palestinian, he knew his people, and he told me he had no illusions that it was useless to challenge the nationalists at the polls.

The predictable upshot was that Peres and his expert Arabists fell flat on their face. The PLO slate swept not only Hebron but every one of the twenty-three municipalities holding the elections, including the affluent and conservative Bethlehem, whose Christian mayor Elias Freij was reelected on a nationalist platform.

In addition to embarrassing Peres, the intelligence blunder had long-range consequences: it saddled the Israeli government with the unsavory job of getting rid of the elected mayors, who at Arafat's urging promptly launched vociferous protests against the occupation. Their removal was accomplished by hook or by crook: two of the mayors were assassinated by Jewish terrorists, and by the time I left Israel, the only elected mayor still in office was Freij, who had influential friends in the United States.

Another of my preconceptions that crashed soon after my arrival was about the government's genius for press relations. What gave me that mistaken impression was Meron Medzini, the director of Israel's government press office when I was based in Beirut. I saw him whenever I visited Israel, and I regarded Medzini, who was a former spokesman of Prime Minister Golda Meir, as the best press official I had ever met. He answered all questions and was knowledgeable, witty, outspoken, energetic, and friendly in the jovial, informal way that made working with many Israelis a pleasure. When he was not briefing visitors on subjects ranging from the Dead Sea scrolls to the intricacies of Ashkenazi-Sephardic relations and Israel's political feuds, Medzini was churning out commentaries for Kol Israel, the Israeli radio, lecturing at the Hebrew University in Jerusalem on Far Eastern cultures and languages (which, he maintained, was his real specialty), or picking the brains of his countless contacts in the government for inside dope to be passed on to news junkies.

The very choice of such an affable and cerebral greeter of visiting journalists was, as far as I was concerned, evidence of a superior PR aptitude. And I was not all wrong. Most of the time, the Israeli Government Press Office did indeed coddle foreign correspondents with a plethora of accurate and highly useful information that influenced our coverage and did the Jewish state's image a whole world of good. But a major story that broke out soon after I came to Jerusalem was so memorably bungled that I never again took Israel's PR IQ for granted.

The event was the daring raid in July 1976 on the airport at Entebbe, in which Israeli commandos killed seven German and Palestinian terrorists and freed more than a hundred passengers of a hijacked Air France airliner. The lightning strike, executed two thousand miles from Israel, became an instant object of enormous admiration and curiosity all over the world. It was precisely the sort of story that had given the Israel military their swashbuckling, larger-than-life image in the West and that in the Arab world had the deterrent value of several armored divisions.

Yet when more than two hundred journalists from all parts of the globe descended on Jerusalem to find out how the fabulous rescue was carried out, Major General Mordechai ("Motta") Gur, the IDF chief of staff, told them in effect to get lost. Addressing a news conference in a packed Jerusalem auditorium, Gur simply repeated a previously released curt announcement that the raid had taken place, and then he stonewalled all attempts to dislodge additional information. When pressed for operational details that were the real flesh and blood of the story, he merely said that "these were tricks that we may want to use again" and called for the next question. As if that was not bad enough, whatever descriptive material some of us managed to get from unofficial sources was mercilessly excised by Israel's military censors. The upshot was that the story did not get the detailed coverage it merited.

At first I was among the most painfully injured parties, because in addition to doing a *Newsweek* cover story, I had agreed to write a four-thousand-word piece about the raid for the Japanese magazine *Shimbun*. Fortunately, my disappointment did not last long because Don Pattir, Rabin's press aide, quickly arranged for me a meeting with the prime minister. Rabin personally briefed me on the details of the operation, all of which were—at least for the moment—officially censorable "military secrets."

If this was not evidence enough that Gur's gag order made no sense (and that I was right in smuggling Rabin's details to New York without showing my file to the censors), the next proof emerged a few months later, when a full description of the Entebbe raid—together with on-scene photographs taken by an IDF photographer—appeared in an Israeli paperback that had been cleared by the censors. I admired the two Israeli authors to whom Gur had given a monopoly on the alleged secrets, but by the time the book came out, the story had lost its news value.

Another Israeli reality I found out of sync with the country's image was the uneven quality of its political leadership. When I arrived in Israel, the ruling Labor Party was still widely reputed as the dominant political force. It was basking in the shining reputation of its founding fathers, the great historic figures of the *Yishuv*, the pre-state Jewish community in Palestine. Many of those leaders were still running the country.

Yitzhak Rabin, Moshe Dayan, Yigal Allon, Haim Bar-Lev, Lova Eliav and Shimon Peres, to name some of the key figures in the Labor Party, were among the most remarkable nation-builders of the twentieth century. They were the best and the brightest of a generation that had established kibbutzes, smuggled into Palestine hundreds of thousands of survivors of Nazi concentration camps, fought against the British in the underground Hagana, and won the War of Independence against the combined Arab armies. Then, led by David

Ben Gurion, they created Israel's successful economy, established strong ties with Europe and the United States, and built the IDF that triumphed in the Six Day War. Collectively, these Israelis—although still relatively young—had shaped four decades of history.

But as I soon learned, the Labor Party these men represented was far from the irresistible voting machine that used to be synonymous with the State of Israel. Outwardly, the party was still riding high, firmly in control of Israel's state-run industries, the trade union movement, and the entire government machinery from the presidential palace to the smallest post office. It had the support of most of the media—including Israel's only television channel—and of the Ashkenazi intellectuals, bureaucracy, and the entrepreneurial middle class, as well as a pantheon of retired IDF brass. But its leadership was in bad disarray, and as a grassroots political force, it was in deep trouble.

Some of the Labor leaders were still very impressive. My favorite member of the older generation was Haim Bar-Lev, the minister of commerce in Rabin's cabinet, who as a former IDF chief of staff had built Israel's defense system on the Suez Canal. The Bar-Lev line did not hold in the 1973 war, but the problem was a lack of man- and firepower, not the integrity and skill of its author. Bar-Lev was the salt of the earth, an example of the sterling qualities that I imagined had distinguished Ben Gurion. He was unpretentious, thoughtful, rock solid, and he exuded common sense and decency.

I was of a more divided mind about Rabin, the prime minister, whom I saw quite frequently. Rabin had an admirable inner steel that served him well on the eve of the Six Day War, when he was the IDF's chief of staff. He collapsed from exhaustion and from smoking too many cigarettes, but he had the strength of mind and character to turn over his command to his deputy Ezer Weizman. Stepping aside before a battle for which he was preparing for years must have been a wrenching decision. Fortunately, he quickly recovered and went on to lead the army to its historic victory.

Another example of Rabin's integrity was his memoirs in which he recounted how during the War of Independence, Ben Gurion instructed him to evict the population of the Palestinian town of Lydda (now called Lod). By the time I came to Jerusalem, few Israelis had the nerve to seriously repeat the official line that the roughly eight hundred thousand Arabs who fled from Palestine in 1948 and 1949 had acted of their own free will. Still, even fewer Israeli leaders were ready to admit that what had enforced the mass exodus were the Jewish troops. Rabin, who was by no means a conventional dove, deserved double respect for telling the truth.

As the prime minister, Rabin had the solid support of Labor's important kibbutz movement and, as a former military hero, some sympathy even among the Israeli right-wingers. But as a politician and the titular head of the Labor Party, Rabin was not even a middling performer. He was almost painfully introverted, socially awkward, humorless, and too honest to disguise his dislikes. Horse trading to reach consensus ran counter his stiff-necked nature. On top of it, Rabin tried—in on-record interviews and other public pronouncements—to break down any political or military issue into its components and come up with an irrefutable solution.

This was intellectually brave but, as any pol would instantly recognize, almost guaranteed to backfire. In the inner Labor Party councils, the ever-scheming Peres ran circles around the prime minister, and Rabin was time and again compelled to fight back after the damage was done. As he admitted to me when I interviewed him after Labor lost the 1977 election, he had not known how to work with his sprawling party. The upshot was that he failed to make inroads into Peres's following, and the party was hobbled by a chronic leadership contest.

Moshe Dayan, the legendary Israeli warrior and Establishment figure was another symptom of the malaise at the top. In the spring of 1976 he was formally still one of Labor's leaders, but he seethed with resentment toward critics who had accused him of not responding fast enough to Egypt's surprising attack across the Suez Canal in October 1973. To get even, Dayan advertised his disaffection from what he called his "political home" by tossing off maverick ideas like a kid dropping stink bombs. For instance, Dayan told me—speaking on record—that the United States should invite the Soviets to help negotiate a peace agreement between the Arabs and Israel. With the Cold War in full swing, it was a clearly unrealistic notion that was rejected out of hand by Rabin and vehemently opposed in Washington. For a good measure, Dayan added in the same interview that Israel should announce a policy of atomic deterrence, a proposal that flew in the face of denials by all Labor governments that Israel had the A bomb. When I reminded him that only a few months earlier, when he was the defense minister, he had shown no inclination to depart from the official line, Dayan merely shrugged his shoulders. "I guess I've changed my mind," he said.

Dayan's alienation cost the Labor Party dearly after it lost the 1977 election to its traditional bitter rival, the Likud bloc of right-wing parties. Despite his open disaffection, Labor had put Dayan near the top of its ticket, and he was elected as member of the party's greatly diminished delegation to the Knesset. But when Labor's lifelong foe, the prime minister-elect Menachem Begin, offered Dayan the ministry of defense, the one-eyed ex-general promptly crossed Israel's most forbidding political divide and joined Begin's cabinet. Under the rules, he took with him his Labor-won Knesset mandate, thereby adding to Begin's majority and depriving Labor of a sorely needed vote in the parliament.

But the man who for me personified the Labor Party's disarray was Rabin's perennial rival. Shimon Peres was a man of many talents, of which the greatest was for advancing projects that couldn't stand the light of the day. As a young, hardworking aide of David Ben Gurion and Golda Meir, Peres helped arm the Hagana with surplus tanks smuggled into Palestine as "tractors"; launched Israel's military aviation industry with the help of stolen blueprints for the Mirage, the French fighter plane; created (disguised as a "textile plant") Israel's atomic bomb facility at Dimona; and negotiated the secret Anglo-French support for Israel's 1956 raid to seize Egypt's Suez Canal. These and other underground exploits earned him the reputation of a *bitsuist* (achiever), which he tried to live up to, by similar methods, in politics.

For example, as a leading Labor MK (member of the Knesset) and Rabin's defense minister, Peres was formally committed to the government's ban on Jewish settlements in the occupied areas that were densely populated by Palestinians. The main aim of the policy was to keep away from the West Bank and Gaza religious-nationalistic fanatics of the rapidly growing Gush Emunim—the "Bloc of the Faithful." The Gush's announced goal was to Judaize the entire West Bank and Gaza, expel the native Arabs, and incorporate the areas into "Greater Israel," a term that encompassed biblical Israel stretching all the way from the Euphrates in Iraq to the Nile in Egypt. It was a program that symbolized the aggrandizing tendencies that the Arabs cited as their reason for rejecting Israel as a legitimate neighbor.

The Labor Party was officially opposed to this messianic concept. To the extent that the party defined its occupation policy, it was spelled out in a plan drawn up in June and July 1967 by Yigal Allon, who was then the deputy prime minister. It called for keeping the densely populated Arab areas free of Jewish presence, so that one day they could be returned to Jordan in exchange for a peace treaty—or, in Rabin's often repeated mantra, to trade "a piece of land for a piece of peace." According to the Allon Plan, the only permanent Israeli acquisition in the West Bank was to be the high ridges overlooking the Jordan River and the East Ghor Valley where fortified IDF outposts could detect and stop any hostile activity from Jordan.

The Allon Plan was in short order violated when Dayan authorized the construction of Kiryat Arba, a major Jewish outpost outside Hebron, but the final nail to the peace plan was hammered in by Peres, who in 1975 helped the Gush Emunim establish Ofra, the first illegal settlement in the heavily Arab populated region just north of Jerusalem.

Working behind Rabin's back, Peres first gave the settlers a pretext to move into the off-limits area by giving them a defense ministry contract to put up a fence around a cluster of former Jordanian army barracks. Next, he ordered the IDF to bring in a field kitchen to feed the fence builders, and after they brought in their families, Peres had the army pipe for them water from the wells of the nearby Palestinian town of Ramallah.

While this went on in defiance of the policy of the government of which Peres was a leading member, the rabbinate converted one of the barracks into a synagogue, and the ministry of education organized a school for the settlers' kids. Peres flew in periodically in a helicopter to check on the settlement's progress and to assure the Bloc's leaders that, as one of them told me, "You'll get everything you need, as long as you keep it out of the press." The Ofra settlers—all Likud voters—who in the spring of 1976 gleefully described to me Peres's double-dealing did not admire his character, but they enjoyed the way he sabotaged his own party's and the government's program.

Peres's alliance with the religious ultranationalists was a classic example of his devious ways and of the contradictions that in the mid-1970s characterized the policies and deeds of the Israeli government. For example, when I interviewed Peres after Rabin stepped down as the candidate for prime minister, early in 1977, Peres, now the standard-bearer of the Labor Party, was formally committed to an election platform that called for an exchange of most of the occupied territories for peace with the Arabs.

Yet at the same time, Peres was promoting the so-called functional division of the occupied territory, under which Israel would keep the control of the West Bank and of the government-subsidized Jewish settlements and Jordan would be administratively responsible for the Palestinians in towns and villages. As for the official Labor Party commitment regarding the settlements, Peres in effect told me that the policy was wrong. Speaking on record, he argued that, "since the Jews have the right to live in Brooklyn and the Bronx, I cannot see why they can't settle anywhere on the West Bank." I couldn't believe that his equation of the Bronx with Palestine was serious, but he insisted it was.

And while not as devious as Peres, Dayan—who was called the Labor Party "dove"—was another key Israeli figure with a muddled occupation policy. As Prime Minister Levi Eshkol's defense minister, Dayan immediately after the Six Day War issued an order prohibiting Israeli civilians from spending the night anywhere in the occupied territories. Yet a few months later, he permitted the construction of Kiryat Arba, the first religious-nationalist settlement on the West Bank. It rose like an alien space station on the rocky outskirts of

Hebron, a traditional Muslim stronghold, and in time became a major source of violence between the IDF and the Palestinians.

The double-faced occupation policy had ample precedent in the way the State of Israel treated the Arabs who did not flee during the 1948–1949 war and accepted Israeli citizenship. After World War II, there was no greater champion of minorities than was the Israeli government and the Labor Party. Any discrimination against Jews—whether in the Soviet Union, Syria, Argentina, or Ethiopia—triggered loud and urgent demands from Jerusalem for intervention by the Socialist International (where Peres, in particular, played an active role) and the Western powers, primarily the United States. At home, however, the government's treatment of its own minority was reminiscent of one of the most shameful period of our history, the Jim Crow era in the South.

When I came to Israel, its five hundred thousand Arabic-speaking Muslim and Christian citizens accounted for 15 percent of the country's population, but they had no school of higher learning and almost no presence in Israeli universities. Their share in the country's power structure was reflected in official statistics showing that of the 1,839 senior officials in government service, only 16 were Arabs. On a per-capita basis, Israeli Arab towns received one-half of the government subsidies provided for their Jewish counterparts.

Because the Israeli Arabs did not want—and were not allowed—to serve in the IDF, they were automatically denied hiring and promotion preferences and most of the advantages of Israel's welfare state, including cheap housing loans. They could not hold any supervisory positions: even in Nazareth, the heart of the Israel's Arab community, the head of the local post office was a Jew. Arab political parties, although they were all headed by leftist Jews, were kept outside both opposition and government coalitions, which rendered them powerless. The pariah status of the Arabs was maintained openly and without any sense of opprobrium. As Gershon Avner, Rabin's top aide, emphatically told me when we first met, "In the Jewish state, the laws are stacked in favor of the Jews."

The ugliness of the system was best depicted in a lengthy document that surfaced in an Israeli newspaper about six months after I arrived in Jerusalem. Written by Yisrael Koenig, the district commissioner in the predominantly Arab-populated Galilee, the report warned his boss, Interior minister Yosef Burg, that the improving education and high birthrate of Arabs posed "a threat to our control of the area."

Koenig, who had been running the Galilee for ten years, recommended several Draconian measures to hold the Israeli Arabs in check. Three of them struck me as particularly outrageous. Jewish employers, Koenig proposed in his memorandum, should be forbidden to give more than 20 percent of their jobs to Arabs; Jewish firms should be encouraged to compete against Arab businesses; and the government should urge young Arabs to study abroad and then make it difficult for them to return, "thereby encouraging their emigration."

The last proposal in particular summed up what struck me, a former immigrant, as the fundamental difference between Israel and the United States. While America was all-inclusive; and at least in its policies honored its motto of *E pluribus unum*, Israel was by design and in practice all-exclusive. The most openly and intensely ethnocentric society I ever encountered, Israel made no bones about keeping non-Jews far outside its mainstream.

After the document was published Koenig declined to meet any newsmen, but I drove to Galilee to talk with Jewish farmers who lived there side-by-side with the Israeli Arabs. The Jews I met had nothing but praise for Koenig's proposals. My stock question was whether the country would not be better served by making Galilee a showpiece of Jewish-Arab cooperation and thereby possibly encouraging the neighboring regimes to make peace with Israel. Most of the people I talked to thought I was wildly naive. In Tabor, a prosperous Jewish settlement, a *moshavnik* (collective farmer) answered my question with a query of his own. "You want my children to sit next to Arabs in school?" he incredulously asked. "Next thing you know, they'll get married. Would you want your daughter to marry an Arab?"

The last time I heard this sort of talk was in the spring of 1960, when I was working on a story about Virginia rednecks who had closed down public schools in Prince Edward County to prevent their court-ordered integration. But while the American racists acted in opposition to the law and the federal government, in Israel there was not a word of official disapproval of Koenig's proposals.

The only Israeli leader to address the issue directly was Yigal Allon, who was then the foreign minister and reputedly one of the most dovish members of Rabin's cabinet. Allon merely expressed his "regret" that the Koenig report was "ever written, and even greater that it was published." Rabin's reaction to the international hubbub over the document was to declare that "discrimination has no basis in the Israeli reality," which was blatantly untrue. Koenig was still the Jewish tzar in the Galilee almost thirteen years later, when I left Israel.

The racist insensitivity of Israel's and Labor Party's Establishment, which then was almost totally of Ashkenazi—European—origin, had devastating consequences for both the party and the state. It gave birth to the patronizing attitude toward the Sephardic Jews who had immigrated to Israel from Iran and the Arab countries in the 1950s, and who eventually ended the Labor's political dominance. Originally, the Labor Party had treated the Sephardic immigrants just like the American Democrats had treated the European newcomers in the late nineteenth and early twentieth centuries: it gave them basic jobs and housing, and they gave Labor their votes.

For almost three decades, the Israeli system worked, but unlike in America the Sephardi children were not moving into the mainstream. By the time I arrived in Israel, they were the fastest-growing part of Israel's Jewish population, but they were still undereducated, still living in slums, and still did not share in the political power and economic progress of the Ashkenazis. The Labor Party, the Sephardis complained with increasing rancor, treated them like poor cousins—good enough to serve in the polling booth and the IDF, but not much else.

The grapes of wrath that grew out of this bitter soil ripened slowly, but from the mid-1960s onward, they were increasingly sweetening the election results of the Labor's traditional competitor, the rightist-nationalist Likud. When I arrived in Israel, the Sephardis accounted for almost one-half of the electorate, but they made up only one-third of the voters of the Labor Party, and their support was shrinking. As Labor pols worriedly acknowledged, practically every Ashkenazi obituary meant one vote less for their party, and the eighteenth birthday of most Sephardis translated into a new vote for Labor's right-wing opponents.

But as I saw it, the crowning fault of Israel's ruling Establishment was its refusal to come to grips with its most momentous problem, which was the disposition of the occupied Arab territories. In the nine years between the Six Day War and my transfer to Jerusalem, the only serious Israeli attempt to resolve this problem was the Allon Plan, which, Allon told me, was discussed by Golda Meir's cabinet but was never voted upon, "so as not to commit Israel to a specific policy." Instead, Moshe Dayan—who was regarded as Israel's most astute Arabist—made cracks about "waiting for a phone call" from Egypt's Nasser and other Arab potentates with offers of a peace settlement. After the Arab League in the summer of 1967 voted in Khartoum for "no peace, no negotiations, and no recognition of Israel," successive Israeli governments effectively let the issue fester.

I thought it was a huge blunder. By the mid-70s, the religious-nationalistic settlement movement bestrode Israel, corroding the country's institutions and monopolizing its public agenda. It fueled the Israelis' deepest existential fears as well as their most passionate expansionism. It inflated extremists and demagogues who otherwise would have been political footnotes. It corrupted Israel's moral standards, tied the hands of its government, and embarrassed its spokesmen abroad. It was a toxic, metastasizing cancer that weakened Israel while strengthening the hatred of the Arabs.

Officially, the Labor Party still claimed readiness to trade "occupied territories" (not "the" occupied territories, a term that would have implied the totality of the Six Day conquest) in return for peace. In reality, the genie of irredentism was out of the bottle within weeks after the war, when the IDF looked the other way while the zealots erected settlements in the occupied territories in an undisguised effort to prevent their return to the Arabs. Some of these outposts—on the Syrian Golan Heights, in the Jordan Valley, and in Egypt's Sinai—were sponsored by the Labor Party and sanctioned by the government. Others were officially labeled "illegal" or "unauthorized" while (like Peres's Ofra) being protected by IDF and subsidized by the Israeli treasury and, indirectly, by US aid to Israel.

By the time I moved to Jerusalem, the Zionist policy of "creating facts" on seized Arab land became Israel's barely disguised foremost mission, and settling Jews in the occupied territories was the country's biggest growth industry. The monumental land grabs were protected as a military secret: the settlements, it was officially claimed, were Israel's first line of defense in case of an Arab attack, and therefore any publicity about them was subject to military censorship. But there was no disguising the enterprise because almost every month, another West Bank hilltop would sprout an IDF-guarded construction site bristling with Israeli flags and barbed-wire-protected prefabs on cinder blocks. Some of the *garinim* (collectives that moved into the settlements) were formed in the United States. To me, who grew up under the Nazi occupation, the determined conquest of the Palestinian patrimony echoed Germany's *Drang nach Osten* to provide its Herrenvolk with greater Lebensraum. Most puzzling to me were the American Zionists who flocked to the West Bank as if to prove, as Peres argued, that they could live on Arab land as well as in the Bronx.

Whether or not the Israeli leaders recognized their blunder, they defended it vehemently, at least to this journalist. In May 1976, when I interviewed Allon about his post–Six Day War peace plan, he spent a good thirty minutes denouncing the critics who opposed the settlements and charged that their military value was discredited in the 1973 war. Allon did not deny that, in that war, Golan Heights settlements had added to the IDF's burden because it had to evacuate women and children instead of fighting the advancing Syrian army. But he gave me a long lecture on how Jewish settlers had fought the Arabs in the 1940s.

Eventually, perhaps realizing that he sounded like yet another Maginot Line general, Allon fixed me with a hard, in-your-face look that some Israelis reserved for non-Jews who asked difficult questions and informed me that the West Bank morass was not really Israel's fault. "The greatest responsibility for Middle East peace," Allon emphatically concluded the interview, was "on the shoulders of the rest of the world."

~

I can't leave the subject of my early years in Israel sounding disappointed and wallowing in bad memories. In fact, I was delighted by much of what I found in Israel—above all, by the people I dealt with as a journalist. I could not get over some of the country's elites. The Israelis I met and worked with were hyperactive, extraordinarily sharp, and personally the friendliest folks I had encountered anywhere. The senior bureaucrats, columnists, military officers, academicians, and politicians on whom I came to depend for much of my reporting were almost invariably well informed, intelligent, outspoken, and frequently refreshingly iconoclastic. In my opinion, the fact that Israel in the mid-1970s had such glittering image abroad had less to do with its actions and policies than with the high caliber of Israelis who made themselves accessible to foreign newsmen.

To mention just one example, a few weeks after I came to Israel, a group of foreign correspondents were invited to a briefing by Shmuel Toledano, a former Mossad agent who served as Rabin's Israeli Arab affairs adviser. The middle-aged, ruggedly handsome Toledano was barely five minutes into his briefing when he dropped a broad hint that the Israeli Arabs were seething with anger, and that there was going to be trouble in Arab-populated parts of Israel, especially in the northern mountains of Galilee.

When we started asking questions, Toledano readily admitted that the Arab citizens of Israel—the heirs of the Palestinians who did not leave the country in the late 1940s—had been, and were being, mistreated. He told us that the State of Israel, which had already confiscated fully one-half of their land, was in the process of seizing another five thousand acres, to be used by the IDF and several government agencies. Toledano went on to add that the Israeli Arabs had had their fill of these dispossessions and were going to fight back. He knew whereof he spoke: a few days later, on March 31, 1976, there were bloody riots in the Galilee and in coastal areas called Arab "triangles," during which six Israeli Arabs were killed.

Washington, I believe, has had only one top bureaucrat—David Stockman, Ronald Reagan's director of the Office of Management and Budget—who could hold a candle to Toledano's defiance of the official line. In Israel, outspoken government sources were legion. When searching for opinions, trends, and insights, for example, there was no better place to visit than a squat pseudo-Greek building above Jerusalem's Valley of the Cross: the Knesset, Israel's parliament.

During important debates, the Knesset was filled with the entire *Who's Who* in Israel—from the prime minister, top IDF brass, leading rabbis, heads of the security services, and trade union chiefs to the newspaper editors and columnists. When not orating on the Knesset floor, the entire Establishment was in the Knesset restaurant sipping weak tea, chatting, and enlightening buttonholing journalists.

And any day, Members of the Knesset were eager to be quoted. One of them, Abba Eban, was memorably eloquent. Some were well-informed and ready to share even unflattering facts with the foreign media. Loquacious and effervescent, the Knesset reminded me of the House of Representatives in Washington, but with a difference: its edgy partisan strife was tempered by the allegiance, and sense of kinship, of a closely knit tribe.

I soon came to know and greatly admire a number of Toledano's kindred spirits, special elites I privately called "Righteous Israelis." Their backgrounds varied—they included retired IDF generals as well as politicians, academicians, and journalists—but they all had certain traits in common: they were loyal and patriotic Israelis; they were intellectually honest; and they were forcefully outspoken, although their views could be far out of the mainstream and could outrage many of their countrymen. There was, for example, Shulamit Aloni, an outstanding MK who knew no cause of decency too small or too controversial to pass over in silence. Like most of the Righteous Israelis, she regarded Israel's treatment of its Arab citizens unworthy of the people of Old Testament. She rose on the Knesset floor time and again to protest the mistreatment of even Bedouins and Christians, two Israeli minorities that had no champion in the mainstream Jewish parties.

Another formidable dissenter was Meron Benvenisti, a scholarly historian and former deputy mayor of Jerusalem. Benvenisti was an intellectual (and physical) powerhouse who refused to tolerate fraud regardless how important it was to the legend of Israel. The author of a particularly revealing and brutally honest book about the "unification" of Arab and Jewish Jerusalem, Benvenisti spent most of the late 1970s and 1980s producing meticulously documented studies of the legal and moral wrongs committed against the occupied Palestinians. Despite his vehement criticism of the settlement enterprise, Benvenisti's facts were unquestioned not only by the government but even by Gush Emunim, the organization of Israel's most extreme settlers in the occupied West Bank.

And there was Zeev Schiff, the most respected Israeli military analyst and leading columnist of *Ha'aretz*, the *New York Times* of Israel. "Wolfiq" Schiff, who became a cherished personal friend, fought countless battles with the military censors in order to tell his readers unpleasant truths about the practices of the Mossad and the Shinbet, Israel's secret services. The Righteous Israelis—and the highly salutary fact that the rest of the Israeli society tolerated them—had much to do with my long tenure in Israel.

I liked them personally and I admired them professionally as public figures. They withstood the disapproval of their own people, fought inner wars between loyalty and conscience, and voiced their dissent without venom or bitterness. Speaking in anguish rather than anger, they lit up their country's moral landscape with probing flashes of truth and decency. The privilege of knowing them and adding to their resonance was one of my greatest satisfactions as a journalist.

Another bright discovery of my new post was the charm of West Jerusalem, the Jewish half of the city. On my previous visits from Beirut or from Bonn, I had always stayed in East Jerusalem and reveled in the exotic beauty of the walled Old City and the Oriental ambiance of the Palestinian part of the town. The Jewish West Jerusalem used to leave me cold. It looked like a small, shabby Central European borough that rolled up the boardwalks at two o'clock in the afternoon on Friday and after the rabbi blew the shofar to start the Shabbos, did not stir again until Saturday morning. Compared with its Arab counterpart, West Jerusalem seemed incongruously out of place, an ersatz shtetl perpetually overrun by package tourists and rich Americans throwing expensive bar mitzvahs at the five-star Hotel King David.

But when my family and I settled in an old Arab house next to a monastery in the German Colony, a pine-shaded neighborhood hard by the walls of the Old City, my attitude toward West Jerusalem began to change. The more time I spent in the well-worn Jewish sections, the more I savored the atmosphere that the early Jewish immigrants brought along from my part of Europe. The echoes of the Old World went beyond the sedate turn-of-the-century apartment buildings, some of which would have looked just right next door to where I grew up. Religious rites apart, there was a haunting familiarity in the West Jerusalem lifestyle and encounters that gave me a sense of comfort.

Part of it was human contact of the sort that has all but vanished from the American urban scene. There were, for instance, two good non-kosher butchers in town, one (Jewish) close to my office and the other in the Arab quarter of the Old City. Their supply of meat was unpredictable, and just like in Prague, it was advisable to have a friendly chat with the butcher to improve the chance of getting a certain cut of meat. Buying bread also required personal contact. I favored two Jewish bakers, one of whom sold dark, crusty loaves of the farm bread I used to love as a kid. The other baked excellent naan, Iranian flat bread. Both spoke some English. The European baker extolled his wares; the Iranian immigrant complained about high taxes.

For newspapers and books I went to Mrs. Meir's shop on Jaffa Street, a main West Jerusalem thoroughfare. Mrs. Meir's life abounded with small incidents that usually happened on her way to work. She recounted them in Hebrew and in English with equal fluency and the relish of an accomplished raconteur. A short walk from Mrs. Meir's establishment, at the top of Bezalel Street, there was a well-stocked hardware store whose salesmen—all Orthodox Jews— spoke no English but were fluent in German. At first they made me feel discriminated against because they always seemed to wait first on plumbers and handymen in skullcaps. My distrust lasted only until I came in to buy a new faucet, and one of the salesmen talked me out of it. He showed me how to fix the old one, for just a few pennies.

Hard by the Zion Square, in a house no bigger than Winnie-the-Pooh's, a tweedy pipe-smoker ran a tiny rubber shop whose prolific inventory was stacked in confusion along the walls and hung from wires suspended from the ceiling. The owner spoke with a British accent and exuded the polished and somewhat aloof manners of country gentry. But he went out of his way to satisfy every customer and always knew where to find the right size of whatever piece of rubber was needed.

And in the residential Gaza Street, the home of Jerusalem's upper crust Ashkenazis (to whom the lesser Ashkenazis sneeringly referred as *bessere Gesellschaft*, "better society"), an old electrician once gave me a long lecture about the problems of Israel's economy and the meager salaries of average workers. The reason he told me all of this, he added, was so I would understand why he charged me so much less for fixing my heater than it would cost in the States.

For me, these were sounds and sights from other places, other times, and they cushioned the sense of being different, a feeling no non-Jew or non-Muslim can escape in the Holy City.

Best of all, this delightful piece of old Central Europe was just a short stroll from the pungent colors, noises, and aromas of the Arab world I loved—precisely because it was so utterly different and it made no claim on my sense of belonging or sympathy. On weekends, the profusion and chaos of the Old City and its ancient souk became my favorite hideaway. My son, Jan, was preoccupied (or so I thought) with his adolescence, school, and friends; Romana and I had over the years drifted apart and lived in separate spheres. Saturday, the Jewish Sabbath, was my loneliest day of the week, with nothing to do except answer a few checking queries from the magazine's New York researchers.

That job done early in the morning, I would walk from my office in West Jerusalem's Independence Park to the Old City's ancient Damascus gate, sit down on one of the stones on the sidewalk and savor the kaleidoscope of humanity surging under the Ottoman walls. Deeply suntanned, sturdy-looking Palestinian women vendors in embroidered costumes pushed their way through the crowd, their heads crowned by carefully balanced baskets with freshly picked figs. Skinny, dark-faced Coptic priests in gray tunics darted forth on mysterious urgent errands, clutching plastic bags with groceries. Religious Muslims, resplendent in white flowing robes and skullcaps, haggled with vendors who hawked freshly baked pita, green almonds, and mulberries. And weaving like a plain ribbon through an exuberant fabric, pale-faced pilgrims from Denmark and Germany dutifully followed their priests and tour guides, half intimidated and half thrilled by the Oriental face of the place where Jesus had died for their sins.

The garish show would go on and on; and just when Israel would seem to be planets away, the throng surging through the gate would swell with a group of Orthodox Jews from Jerusalem's Mea Shearim neighborhood. Incongruously dressed in white stockings, knickers, shining black coats, and magnificent fur hats, they seemed to have stepped straight out of the shtetls of nineteenth-century Poland. Oblivious to the heat of the Mediterranean sun and the profane extravaganza of the souk, they would frantically rush to pray at the Western Wall.

I would crunch a bag of freshly roasted almonds from a nut shop on Salaheddin Street, inhale the tempting smell of coffee with cardamom, and listen to the Egyptian love songs of Oum Khaltoum wafting from a shop behind the gate. There was a soothing magic in the cacophony of cultures, the brilliant light on ocher stones, the azure of the cloudless sky, the dry breeze from the desert. I would feel alone and yet less lonely, searching and yet not quite lost. And time and again, I would give a grateful thought to Rod Gander, for making me come to Jerusalem.

CHAPTER 18

MENACHEM BEGIN AND THE RISE OF ISRAEL'S RIGHT

I interviewed Menachem Begin for the first time in May 1977, three days after his Likud bloc crushed the previously undefeated Labor Party, the founder of Israel, by an astonishing margin of eleven seats. It was a historic triumph, and getting to see its author so soon was a distinction that, in my case, had a long incubation period. It went back to a curious scene on July 5, 1976, when Begin showed up at an Israeli military airport outside Tel Aviv to welcome the Israeli hostages freed at Entebbe. As it happened, many of them were Sephardic Jews, and their numerous relatives and friends came to welcome them at the airport. The place was packed and filled with festive mood, and when Begin arrived, it exploded with fervor rarely encountered even at campaign rallies.

There was something incongruous in that encounter. Physically, Begin was the very symbol of the Ashkenazi elites whose dominant role in Israel was increasingly resented by the Sephardis. Gaunt, frail-looking, and strikingly pale under the blistering sun, Begin looked like a Polish pensioner rather than a rightist leader of Jewish immigrants from Iran, Maghreb, and other Arab countries. He had nothing to do with the rescue operation, which—as far as politicians could claim credit—was a feather-in-the-cap of prime minister Yithak Rabin and defense minister Shimon Peres. But while the two Labor Party biggies got barely a round of applause, Begin's arrival triggered a roaring ovation. Swarthy men hoisted him on their shoulders and exuberant rabbis blew shofars, the ceremonial ram's horns. There were shouts, ululating, and fervent clapping of calloused hands. The air was so full of unbridled emotions it reminded me of an Arab wedding.

Thus alerted that something was happening that my Labor Party sources had failed to mention, I asked for an appointment with Begin. He turned me down twice, complaining that too many American correspondents had taken up his time without publishing his views. Undoubtedly, that was true. Begin was Israel's hawkish icon, a former head of the Irgun terrorist underground, and for many years a political outcast. He did not make good copy for articles projecting a favorable image of Israel, which was what most editors wanted.

Still, when the 1977 election campaign started, my memory of the airport episode was a strong warning not to bet on another Labor victory. I made the rounds of the leading Labor candidates, but I also covered several Likud rallies, got to know the bloc's program, and interviewed Ezer Weizman, the former commander of the IDF Air Force, who was Likud's campaign manager. About two weeks before the elections, I had a long talk in the Knesset restaurant with Yehiel Kadishai, Begin's veteran aide and close personal friend. The meeting foreshadowed a surprising experience I later had with other Israeli arch-nationalists and hardliners: I had no use for their politics, but personally we got along well.

Kadishai, a former impresario-turned-politician, was an example of this unexpected relationship. He was an arch ethnic who regarded all goyim—non-Jews—me included, with a barely disguised mix of disdain and suspicion. He was far from alone: some Israelis openly disliked Gentiles at least as much as some Gentiles disliked Jews. But Yehiel had other qualities, which I found both admirable and helpful. He was a walking encyclopedia on Likud's and Begin's political history and, as I learned later, a highly reliable source on the prime minister's actions and thinking. Moreover, Yehiel was a congenial raconteur whose wit and delight in the gab were so reminiscent of my father's that I found it easy to ignore his barbs against the goyim.

As we parted at the end of our first meeting, I asked Kadishai to arrange for me an interview with Begin if he should win the election, and he readily promised to do that. Two days after the history-making results were in, Kadishai was besieged by a horde of diplomats, leaders of American Jewish organizations, and journalists who were trying to get to see the new man-of-the-hour in the Middle East. Yehiel, as good as his word, called me up and told me that Begin would see me in time for my deadline.

And so it happened that on the first Friday afternoon following the elections, I was sitting in the lobby of a seaside hotel flanked by Leesa, my brainy and increasingly indispensable Hebrew-speaking assistant, waiting for Begin to come down for the interview. As I waited, I was growing uptight.

The most immediate reason for my discomfort was professional. I was under the gun to wrap up *Newsweek*'s cover story, aptly entitled "The Day of the Hawks," in which the Begin interview was scheduled for two full pages. Friday is a late day in the newsweekly's universe; my telex machine was in Jerusalem, almost sixty miles away; and the quality of Begin's answers was anyone's guess. I was sure my editors had some other material if the interview did not pan out, but failing to deliver on a major story was serious business.

Less nagging, but also in the back of my mind, was uncertainty about the chemistry of the encounter. Begin had the sort of record that made my skin crawl. His fame as an extremist went back to the 1940s when he commanded an underground group known as Irgun Zvai Leumi, whose symbol was an arm clutching a rifle superimposed over the map of an "Erets Yisrael" that included all of Palestine, the entire Kingdom of Jordan, and a hunk of Syria, Lebanon, and Egypt's Sinai.

Irgun was a gang of unabashed terrorists who, among other outrages, smuggled a bomb into King David Hotel in Jerusalem and blew up one wing of it, killing ninety-one civilians and British soldiers. On another occasion, Begin's gunmen drove into the Palestinian village of Deir Yassin, massacred in cold blood anywhere between 100 and 254 villagers (the exact number is disputed)—mostly old men, women, and children—and threw their bodies into a well. Begin's fanaticism and brutality revolted even the rest of the Yishuv's anti-British underground, and at one point (known, in the Likud lore, as "the Season") the Labor Establishment collaborated with the British police in trying to put the Irgun out of business.

After the state was created, Begin switched from extreme violence to extreme politics as the head of the Herut, a small party that later became the nucleus of the Likud bloc. As a political leader, Begin continued to shock most Israelis by his penchant for violence—for example, he led a stone-throwing assault on the Knesset after it accepted German reparations—and by his single-minded dedication to the Greater Israel doctrine of Vladimir Jabotinsky, the radical guru of Zionism. Even after the Irgun was disbanded and Begin became an MK, Ben Gurion refused to pronounce his name and referred to him as "the deputy sitting next to" whoever was Begin's neighbor in the Knesset. Israel's new prime minister, in short, had been for many years the country's most notorious Jew beyond the pale, and I felt that's where he belonged.

Mixed in this morass of grim thoughts was my personal resentment of Begin's penchant for blaming all goyim for Hitler's crimes against the Jews. The prime minister, who had lost many relatives in Nazi gas chambers, was mesmerized by the Holocaust. This was entirely understandable; but what made me angry was that, time and again, Begin would insinuate in his speeches that the guilt for the genocide was shared by the entire goyish world. Whenever I read that line I would mentally growl, "Brother, don't you put *me* in the same bag with the Nazis." On his record, Begin was an expansionist, a zealot, a terrorist, and a bigot of first magnitude—the epitome of a leader the Middle East did not need.

My unsettling reverie was only interrupted when Begin, accompanied by his wife, Aliza, and a bodyguard, showed up—exactly on time—for the interview. I stood up to shake Begin's hand, all keyed up for an adversary encounter, and promptly sensed something was wrong: Begin's unsmiling but polite expression and his restrained body language did not exude the alpha male personality I had expected. As he and his equally unassuming-looking wife sat down on the other side of a small cocktail table, Israel's sixty-three-year-old prime minister looked distinctly nonthreatening—he seemed to be even more frail than he did on the campaign trail.

As I began to relax, I grew conscious of the afternoon sun glowing through the orange curtains behind my back, and of the little silences in the big hotel lobby signifying the approach of the Jewish Sabbath. From the corner of one eye, I could glimpse the wiry figure of Begin's Shinbet bodyguard, the first overt sign of the Likud leader's new status.

I asked questions from a list I had brought along and listened to Begin's carefully formulated answers that, I noted with satisfaction, would neatly fill the reserved space in the magazine and needed very little editing. Relieved of my most pressing worry, I began to focus on the man who was calmly facing me across the cocktail table. There was a private side to this pale, starchy wisp of a politician with high cheekbones and thick glasses that clashed with what I had thought of him.

One surprise was his careful, almost precise English. There was something strangely reassuring about Begin's respectful use of the language of an enemy he had fought during his years in the underground. Another striking characteristic was his austerity.

The Knesset was full of stories about Begin's personal modesty, but it was not until our meeting that I realized how truly unpretentious he was. Begin wore a nondescript gray suit that was meticulously pressed but so old that it shined at the elbows and the cuffs of the sleeves were threadbare. The collar of Begin's white shirt was about a size too big, a sign that it had been bought years earlier, when he was less skinny. And even as prime minister, Begin could not bring himself to rent a suite, which was the reason for holding the interview in the hotel lobby.

I also did not expect him to show up with his wife, Aliza. It was a puzzling gesture because in Israel, wives of high officials were not regarded as public figures and were kept out of the media spotlight. Aliza, a particularly retiring person, sat through the entire interview without saying a word. I could think of no other reason why Begin had brought her along except as a courtesy to the American public. In the United States, First Ladies were a legitimate object of media attention. It was another subtlety that did not square with

Begin's extremist reputation. I began to understand why his opponents in the Knesset called Begin only half-jokingly *Polski shlachtic* (Polish nobleman). Form and dignity, old Eastern European style, seemed to be an important part of Begin's persona.

In that introductory interview I asked Begin predictable questions, and he almost always gave me expected answers. Two of his responses, however, surprised me. In one of them, Begin defended the Israeli occupation of the West Bank, Golan Heights, Gaza, and Egyptian Sinai Desert on the patently ludicrous grounds that a pullback from those area would result in the establishment of "a Soviet base" at the crossroads of three continents. By refusing to return to its 1949 ceasefire lines, Begin claimed, Israel was preventing "Communism from taking over this part of the world." It was a spurious argument, but it was clearly meant to sound more acceptable to the American ears than Begin's standard claim, which was that Jews had the unquestioned "right" to claim all of Palestine because it was their only "homeland." I couldn't help thinking of Helmut Schmidt's observation that all politicians are actors.

Begin was still the unrepentant prophet of Greater Israel, still determined to hold on to all of the occupied territories, but without the harsh, the-world-be-damned attitude that had marked his oratory when he was in the opposition. Less than a hundred hours after he won the race, Begin the True Believer was assuming the role of Begin the Statesman.

Begin's other surprising answer was to my question as to how he felt about his terrorist past. Abruptly reverting to his customary defiance of goyish morality, he not only defended Irgun's terrorism as a legitimate struggle for Jewish "national rights." He insisted that had he acted otherwise, "I would now be deeply ashamed."

This startled me. In his memoirs, Begin defended the indiscriminate killing of Deir Yassin civilians as a major contribution to the founding of the Jewish state, on the grounds that the shock waves from the massacre had swelled the massive exodus of Palestinians who had outnumbered the Yishuv at least two to one. But as Begin must have realized, *Newsweek*'s audience regarded similar Nazi atrocities during World War II as crimes against humanity. Moreover, it was now more than thirty years since the deed was done and Begin was at the zenith of his political career. Why could he still not allow himself the slightest doubt about his outrageous past?

Something did not quite add up, I thought. An average politician would have blamed the Irgun excesses on Arab provocations or mistakes of his subordinates; an exceptional politician would have admitted to second thoughts or some remorse for the butchery. The total, blunt defiance of Begin's reply, however, was clearly not only over the top—it was out of character with his earlier answer, when he avoided repeating the Likud's historic claim on the occupied Arab territories. I could think of only one explanation for Begin's shocking answer: he could not allow a drop of doubt about his actions as the Yishuv's legendary terrorist.

For Israel and the Middle East, Begin's election was rife with implications, none of which were good. His success in the polls proved that Israel was leaving its secular, semi-socialist moorings built by the labor unions, kibbutzes, and most of the Ashkenazi intelligentsia and was heading for the perilous rapids of ultranationalist-religious irredentism.

It was a future that Begin foreshadowed after joining the government of Levi Eshkol on the eve of the Six Day War. On the third day of the fighting, Begin called Dayan, the defense minister, at five o'clock in the morning to warn him that the UN Security Council was about to call for a ceasefire. Since King Hussein was sure to agree to it, Begin argued, the IDF had to capture Jerusalem's Old City right away, before the war was over.

When that was accomplished, Begin immediately agitated for the annexation of the "liberated Judea and Samaria," as he called the West Bank of Jordan, and its Judaization by settlements. And in November 1967, when Eshkol reluctantly agreed to the UN Security Council Resolution 242 calling for an Israeli withdrawal to the ceasefire lines in exchange for peace with the Arabs, Begin furiously denounced the decision and left the cabinet.

Now he was in power, and with more than a hundred Jewish settlements already on the West Bank and Golan Heights, Begin's crusade for Greater Israel was ready to take off. It was not a pretty picture, but it promised to be a great story.

~

The fact that I was a goy who had spent more than four years covering the Arabs was not exactly the most propitious background for reporting from Israel. A few months after I arrived in Jerusalem, a senior *Ma'ariv* columnist informed me that he had read "all" of my articles about the Palestinians and did not like any of them. My writing, he said with a frown and his eyes fixed at his feet, was "not just anti-Israeli—it was anti-Semitic." In Israel, a label like that was the equivalent of a leper's bell. If more Israelis had come to share this view, my stay in Jerusalem would have been much, much shorter.

In retrospect, there were several reasons why the columnist remained an isolated case, and why I worked in Israel for almost thirteen years, made friends, and did some of my best reporting. In the eyes of surprisingly many Israelis, one of my virtues was my Czech origin. In the Jewish experience in pre–World War II Europe, the Czechs and the Prague government stood out in a favorable light.

Czechoslovak president Tomáš Masaryk, who as a university professor volunteered to defend a Jew accused of ritual murder, was the first head of state to visit the Yishuv, the Jewish community in pre-state Palestine, and one of the oldest Israeli kibbutzim was named after him. Jews held high positions in the governments of both Masaryk and Beneš and were prominent in the new country's academy, arts, and economy. Until Munich, Zionist organizers in Czechoslovakia—one of which was Begin—never encountered the official hostility that was their lot in Poland and elsewhere in Eastern Europe. I sometimes wondered whether the affinity for the Czechs was a reason that Israel's anthem "Hatikva" (The Hope) unmistakably echoes Smetana's symphonic poem "Moldau"—the river the Czechs call "Vltava."

Some of this positive image rubbed off on me. On one of his frequent flights to Washington, Begin let down his usual starchy reserve to tell me about his work in Czechoslovakia before World War II as the leader of Betar, a rightist Zionist youth movement that provided recruits for the Irgun and its political arm, the Herut Party.

Begin's interior and religious affairs minister Yoseph Burg, who had also lived in prewar Prague, insisted on talking to me in Czech. Since the extent of his Czech vocabulary was about a dozen words, Burg never became one of my more productive sources. But I had better luck with two Czech-born Israelis who called me a "landsman" and conversed with me in English: one was a brigadier general in IDF and the other the prime minister's adviser on terrorism.

On my part, what helped bridge the distance was my sense of a common bond—the shared abhorrence of the Nazis—with Israel's European immigrants. In time, I was able to form personal friendships or at least comfortable professional relationships across the country's political spectrum. These congenial contacts gave me some sense of ease in a country where most non-Jews were sometimes regarded as nonpersons, and helped me do a much better job as a journalist.

The longer I stayed, the wider became the circle of people on whom I could depend for information or views. I even had a favorite Orthodox rabbi. Adin Steinsaltz, the brilliant translator of the *Jerusalem Talmud*, was not only an erudite scholar and an insightful social critic, but a wise and genial man who showed none of the strain that frequently affected Orthodox Jews when talking with a Gentile. I called on him from time to time for the sheer pleasure of listening to his astute and frequently maverick views.

Another unlikely Israeli I came to like was Ezer Weizman, an ebullient veteran of Israel's wars and the IDF's air force commander and deputy chief of staff during the Six Day War. I first interviewed him when he was managing the Likud campaign in 1977. Trying to earn a senior cabinet post if Begin should win the race, Weizman sprinkled his comments with the most hawkish sentiments he could summon.

"The West Bank should be made part and parcel of Israel, and the sooner the better," he told me with his customary rapid-fire delivery. When I wondered how the annexation would play out abroad, Weizman came back with the disdainful brush-off that Israeli hardliners loved to fling at non-Jews. "The world will always look for an excuse to make the Jews look like a bunch of bastards," he snapped.

Weizman loved to debunk the Labor Party's pretensions to superior morality. Addressing students at Beersheva's University of the Negev, he urged them to pay no attention to the goyim. "Jews should decide what they want, and then go ahead and do it," he said. He paused before slyly adding that that's what Yigal Allon, the Labor Party's so-called "dove," did in 1949 as the head of a Hagana unit that conquered Beersheva and the Negev, "even though there were no Jewish holy places here." Weizman, whose uncle was Israel's first president (and who later became president himself), knew all the skeletons in the Labor Party's closets.

What Weizman was peddling was fourteen-karat Likud ideology, but I could not believe he really meant it. A garrulous and witty extrovert, he had a breezy openness about him that did not jibe with his xenophobic politics. He was just too handsome, too successful, and too self-confident to really think that the world was out to get the Jews. I made a point of seeing Weizman periodically, just because I liked the guy and because I wondered about his real views. And sure enough, about three years after the Likud victory, Weizman made a complete political about-face and became one of Israel's most outspoken proponents of peace with the Arabs.

The personal chemistry did not work with everybody. One notable exception was Yitzhak Shamir, Begin's successor as prime minister and a Polish-born Zionist who during the 1940s was a top figure in Lehi, an underground group even more extreme than Begin's Irgun. Lehi—which was better known as the Stern Gang—carried out several revolting political murders, including the assassination in Cairo of Lord Moyne, the British Resident in the Middle East, and of Count Folke Bernadotte, a prominent Swedish diplomat who during World War II had negotiated the release of more than thirty thousand Jews from German concentration camps. Churchill denounced Lehi as "a set of gangsters worthy of Nazi Germany." Shamir, who took part in the planning of the killing of Moyne and was the head of Lehi when Bernadotte was murdered, never denounced those crimes or denied his share of responsibility for them.

In exploring Shamir's past I learned that he was the Lehi's chief in Tel Aviv when, early in World War II, the underground group sent two emissaries to German embassies in Ankara and Beirut to propose an alliance to overthrow the British rule in Palestine. I found the idea of Jews seeking Hitler's help against the British so outlandish that I made a special effort to check out the story with a couple of surviving Lehi old-timers. They confirmed that Shamir indeed had supported the bid for an alliance with the Nazis, although he apparently had some doubts that they would accept the proposal. On that, at least, he was right.

After the war, Shamir dabbled in business and in politics without distinction in either and eventually spent some time in Europe as a Mossad agent. His activities there remained a secret, but I was told that he was killing ex-Nazis who had escaped the Allied retribution. One story I heard in the Knesset had Shamir dispatching one of the war criminals by pushing him from a speeding train in Switzerland.

Shamir's only recorded political activity in the early days of the Jewish state was a 1949 speech in which he discussed the Cold War. This was the period of Stalinist executions of "cosmopolitan" Jews in the Soviet Union and its satellites, but according to a contemporary report in an Israeli newspaper Shamir had advised the audience to "pray for the victory of the anti-imperialist camp," which was then the shorthand for the Communist countries.

After Stalin died, Shamir became an admirer of Mao Zedong and praised him as a "political genius." And true to his extremist record, Shamir was the only top Likud figure to vote against the Jimmy Carter–brokered Camp David agreement that paved the way for the historic Egypt-Israel peace treaty.

I disliked Shamir so much I could hardly bring myself to talk with him, and he heartily reciprocated. On one occasion we sat next to each other on the plane from New York to Tel Aviv. The nonstop flight lasted more than ten hours during which we were served three meals. Our entire conversation amounted to about as many sentences.

Another Likud figure I stayed away from was ex-general Ariel ("Arik") Sharon, Israel's legendary blood-and-guts caudillo who in the 1973 war led the IDF's attack across the Suez Canal and routed Egypt's Third Army. I met with Sharon—who was by then out of active military service—twice before the 1977 elections, only to conclude that the chemistry between us didn't work. For one thing, Sharon was full of the phony bonhomie affected by out-of-office politicians who need the media to keep their name before the public. A more weighty reason I had no use for Sharon was because he lied to me (as well as to everybody else in the media) so much that I decided that seeing him was a waste of time.

Except that he could be truly dangerous, Sharon reminded me of Borees, a 1950s TV cartoon character who constantly skulked around plotting mean tricks and ambushes. The first time we met, for instance, Sharon made a big point of telling me how happy he was to be just an ordinary farmer in the Negev instead of putting up with the disgusting Israeli politicians in the Knesset. Why he wanted *Newsweek* to print that particular piece of fiction was beyond me. The very reason I went to see him was his widely reported maneuvering to get back into the political limelight.

Then, as soon as the 1977 campaign started, Sharon dropped his farmer's dungarees and unfurled the flag of his own political party, which he poetically called Shlomzion, or "Peace of Zion." It was the start of a power drive with more twists than a Swiss highway. Sharon's "peace" program called for the settling of "one, two million Jews" on Arab land between the Syrian Golan Heights in the north and Egypt's Sharm-el-Sheikh in the south, a scheme far more aggressive and aggrandizing than anything that was then advanced even by Begin's Likud. At the same time, Sharon was privately promising "surprising" concessions to Lova Eliav and Yossi Sarid, two genuine doves in the Labor Party, if they would broaden the Shlomzion's appeal by joining his ticket. Both turned him down.

After the elections Sharon accepted Begin's offer to become the minister of agriculture in charge of Jewish settlements and I decided to watch Sharon's zigzags from a distance.

Shamir and Sharon aside, I had good working relationships with a cross section of hardliners, including a couple of leading figures in the Gush Emunim settlement movement and a whole flock of right-wing deputies in the Knesset. I had no sympathy for their hawkish views, and I never pretended—to them or to anyone else—otherwise. But as long as the conversation stayed clear of the Palestinian issue, most of my right-wing sources and I could swap jokes and talk Israeli politics in a congenial atmosphere.

Geula Cohen, the firebrand leader of the far-right Tehiya Party, once volunteered a comment on my relationship as a non-Jew with most Knesset members. "We are comfortable with him," she told Peter McGrath, *Newsweek*'s foreign editor who was visiting Israel. From almost anyone else, I would have regarded the remark as patronizing. Coming from Cohen, who was one of the most mercilessly honest and straightforward Israeli politicians, it was a compliment. Geula, as everyone called her, was an ideologue and a fanatic who could create such scenes on the floor of the Knesset that she'd be evicted by the ushers. Away from the well of the turbulent parliament, however, she had many admirers in all political parties as the soul of integrity who never hesitated to talk truth as she saw it—in broad daylight and in public. Except for her ideology, she was the polar opposite of Sharon.

∼

Begin, too, had a private side of decency that stood in sharp contrast with his record as a terrorist and a zealot. Despite his strong partisan feelings, Begin could be astonishingly considerate of his political adversaries. For instance, as the new prime minister he kept almost all the appointees of his predecessor, including Dan Pattir, Rabin's press secretary. It was a model nonpartisan gesture if I ever saw one.

Another quality strikingly out of character for the "butcher of Deir-el-Yassin" was Begin's capacity for compassion. For example, out of his own pocket he quietly paid for phone calls to Moscow by Avital Sharansky, the wife of a prominent Jewish dissident who was in Soviet jail. It was by no means an easy gesture: Begin's salary was meager, he had no slush fund, and overseas calls were expensive. Yet, as far as I knew, neither this nor his other charitable deeds had ever been leaked to the Israeli press. There was a warm, avuncular Begin underneath the stiff veneer of the "Polish nobleman." Officials who worked with him most closely were not always admiring of his spur-of-the-moment work style and his hawkish policies, but they were very fond of Begin the person.

I also recognized Begin's supreme skill in courting the votes of the Sephardi Israelis, who felt they were disrespected and taken for granted by the Labor politicians. Instead of the khakis and shirtsleeves of his opponents, Begin delivered his campaign speeches—even in the sweltering heat of the summer—wearing an immaculately pressed dark suit, white shirt with cuff links, and a necktie.

He always appeared alone on an elevated platform or the marquee of a movie house, and with his dark silhouette sharply etched against the blue-and-white Israeli flag and his pale face gleaming in the spotlights, Begin put on a political theater that had no match in Israel. He reminded me of Haiti's Papa Doc, who delivered his "vibrant" orations dressed like a voodoo priest in a black double-breasted suit. A polished orator who spoke entirely from memory, Begin knew how to address the unspoken concerns of many Israelis about the long-term survival of the Jewish state. He peppered his remarks with references to Israel's biblical greatness and never finished a campaign oration without swearing to perpetuate the Jewish rule in Palestine "forever and ever, and all eternity."

He appealed to his constituents' sense of the melodrama to heighten their respect for the state, which was a matter of some concern in a young country with many new immigrants. For example, before departing on each of his missions to the United States, Begin would carry out an elaborate ceremony at the airport. He would stand on the runway at rigid attention while the IDF band played Israel's national anthem. He would then review an IDF honor guard by stiffly marching, Sandhurst-style, with clenched fists held firmly against his sides. Next, he would stop in front of a pole with the Israeli flag, pause for a dramatic moment, and execute a solemn bow. Finally—still alone—he would climb up the stairs to the plane.

And Begin was very effective in using the power of his office. His 1981 reelection campaign, which he entered during an economic slump, a soaring inflation, and with popularity rating of 20 percent, was a political masterpiece. First, Begin rallied the country around the flag by ordering the Israeli air force to shoot down Syrian planes that had repeatedly tried to curb IDF flights over Lebanon. After the Damascus government lost two planes, the attacks on the IDF overflights stopped. Next, Begin briefly embraced supply-side economics and drastically cut Israel's sky-high import taxes on cars and major household appliances, thereby triggering the biggest consumer shopping spree in Israel's history. For the grand finale, just three weeks before the voters went to the polls, he sent IDF's US-supplied F-16s to bomb Osiraq, the unfinished nuclear plant in Iraq. The grateful voters, feeling patriotic, prosperous, and protected, chose Begin over Peres despite an inflation that was hitting 100 percent a year.

But much as I admired Begin as a political pro, I never felt—as did one of his biographers—that he was a "great leader." In my judgment, any competent politician can ride the tide of history, but it takes an exceptional individual to make one, and Begin was not the author of the sweeping changes that took place on his watch. The Sephardi electoral shift to the Likud had been in the making for years, driven by their anger at their misery and the arrogance of the Labor Party. Their switch to the Likud was bound to reach critical mass with or without Begin.

As for the peace with Egypt that Begin signed in 1979, after the Camp David conference, the man who—next to Jimmy Carter—did by far the most for the breakthrough was Anwar Sadat. Sadat's trip to Jerusalem, which started the process, was an act of spectacular statesmanship that challenged public opinion not only in his own country but in the entire Arab world. His November 1977 visit to Jerusalem and his speech to the Knesset defied the region's greatest taboo, the recognition of Israel. His signing of the peace treaty was the equivalent of abruptly turning around a battleship despite the passionate protests of its crew, and he paid for it with his life.

To accomplish a comparative feat, Begin would have had to end the occupation of the West Bank and Gaza and recognize a Palestinian state. He was utterly incapable of anything of such magnitude: his policy was to absorb the seized territories, not give them up. As for his agreement to pull out of the Sinai, it was, for Israel, an enormous bargain.

Economically, the withdrawal did not cost Israel anything, because Uncle Sam made up for the Sinai oil that Israel had given up and replaced the two Israeli air bases in the Egyptian desert with state-of-the-art facilities inside the 1949 ceasefire lines. There were no Jewish holy places in the evacuated area, and to compensate Israel for the loss of the desert's security value, President Carter agreed to turn it into a huge US-monitored buffer zone between Egypt and Israel. As for the few abandoned Jewish settlements, they cost Begin no votes because they had been founded by the Labor Party and held no Likudniks. Except for Shamir, Arens, and a handful of other way-out hardliners, the agreement had wall-to-wall support in the Knesset.

In return for giving up the seized Egyptian territory, Begin got a previously unthinkable recognition of Israel by the leading Arab country; a US-guaranteed protection against an attack by Israel's strongest enemy; and, as a bonus, worldwide acclaim and a Nobel Peace Prize. It was a fantastic deal, and it was practically delivered into Begin's lap by Sadat and President Carter.

Incidentally, Sadat's magnanimous rapprochement with Israel did not change a whit Begin's own total rejection of any similar accommodation for the Palestinians. For one thing, Begin was so shattered by the Holocaust that he could not bring himself to accept the security risks he believed were inherent in an Israeli withdrawal from the West Bank and Golan Heights. At least equally important was his utter conviction of the righteousness of the Zionist cause and the insignificance of the Palestinians. I don't believe he met a single one of them during my nearly thirteen years in Israel, and they certainly did not figure in his speeches.

This was not the case with some of Likud's Israeli-born up-and-coming leaders—such as the then-MKs Ehud Olmert or Dan Meridor—who were much more confident of their Middle East roots and much more realistic about Israel's need to make peace with the Arabs. But for Begin, to deal with the Palestinians would have lent validity to their claim to areas that he believed belonged exclusively to the Jews. As in the case of the Deir Yassin massacre, he could not admit, to himself or to others, that there could be another side to his truth.

After Sadat's historic visit and peace offer to the Knesset, it still took thirteen days of haggling at Camp David, relentless pressure from the president of the United States, and a phoned assurance by Begin's favorite general, Arik Sharon, that the Sinai Desert was not essential for the defense of Israel to overcome Begin's rejection of any compromise. When he finally relented, Begin found the strength to comply only with the part of the historic agreement that neutralized Egypt as Israel's enemy in exchange for Israel's relinquishing the Sinai Desert. When it came to delivering on the other major Camp David commitment, which outlined the steps toward Palestinian autonomy and possible self-determination, Begin dug in his heels and stonewalled.

In my interview with him in New York and again when we talked on the plane returning to Israel, Begin was almost panicky about two concessions that Carter and his state secretary, Cyrus Vance, thought they had won in return for the Egypt-Israel peace treaty. Begin insisted that he had agreed to suspend the construction of new Jewish settlements "for only three months," and not until the peace treaty was signed, as Carter and Vance believed to be the case. And he was almost apoplectic over the agreement's reference to the "legitimate rights" of the Palestinians.

During a twenty-minute tape-recorded conversation I had with him before we landed in Tel Aviv, Begin would not be dislodged from rehashing his differences with Carter and Vance. The word "legitimate" bothered him in particular: Begin told me he had accepted it only because it was "meaningless." He said he had researched the term in an English dictionary and was satisfied that, as he put it, "a right per se is legitimate." When I asked him what was the extent of Palestinian "rights," legitimate or not, Begin only answered, "We shall see about that." His entire mental machinery was in reverse: consciously or otherwise, he was determined to prevent that part of the Camp David agreement from working.

Begin's visceral attitude reduced subsequent attempts to resolve the Palestinian problem to empty posturing. Dayan, who saw what was happening, resigned as foreign minister soon after the peace treaty was signed, charging that Begin wanted to annex the occupied territories. Weizman quit his job as defense minister a few months later.

True to his colorful style, Weizman departed with a bang, not a whimper. He tore down a peace poster in Begin's conference room, heatedly accused the prime minister of sabotaging Israel's relations with Egypt, and stormed out of the building into a new career as one of the country's leading doves. Not long afterwards the Israel-Egypt talks on Palestinian autonomy collapsed, precisely as Begin had wanted.

Begin's readiness to fool the non-Jew—including the one who lived in the White House—belied his pretensions to moral stature. Lying to the goyim might have been a necessary survival strategy in the shtetls of Poland and the Ukraine, but it was small-minded and badly out of place for a "Polish nobleman" and the prime minister of the State of Israel. Begin, for instance, had the nerve to personally assure Vance that Shilo, a Gush Emunim settlement that was set up on the West Bank a few days after the Camp David accords were signed, was an "archeological camp." The Shilo settlers, most of whom held white-collar jobs in Jerusalem, were the first to protest Begin's attempt to distort their true status as the "returning children of Israel."

Another example of the demeaning trickery of Begin's government was the Potemkin's villages that Sharon, then the defense minister, had built in Sinai during the Camp David talks. The empty plywood barracks, hastily nailed together in the stealth of the night, were a cheap attempt to strengthen Israel's bargaining hand in negotiations with Egypt by inflating the number of Jewish outposts in the desert.

In fairness to Begin, the attempted fraud had ample precedents: by using similar stage props, Labor's early Zionists had successfully persuaded UN arbitrators to allocate to Israel chunks of Palestine where there was no real Jewish presence. Begin and Sharon, however, overreached themselves by pulling the stale old trick at a time when Uncle Sam's earth satellites readily spotted every move in the desert.

When the failed subterfuge broke in the open, I asked Kadishai what went wrong. How, I said, could Begin allow Sharon to do a dumb thing like that? Kadishai, who was Begin's true alter ego, usually loved to be asked an accusatory question because it gave him an opportunity to lecture the critic on how non-Jews were ignorant of Israel's history and unmindful of the country's security problems. But this time, Kadishai was at a loss: he saw nothing wrong with the scheme except that it did not work. "Why," he told me with a genuinely perplexed look, "Arik was only trying to make for us some chits for the negotiating table!" By his lights, "pulling the wool over goyim's eyes," as he called it, was OK.

What I found hardest to take was Begin's obsessive drive to fill the occupied West Bank and Gaza with settlements populated by the Gush Emunim and other religious and nationalist fanatics. Though the process had started already under the Labor governments, Begin gave it an enormous boost by making the Judaization of the Arab areas his top domestic priority.

When Likud came to power in 1977, the settlers in the occupied territories and their *garinim* in Israel were about 35,000 strong, or 1 percent of

Israel's Jewish population. With Begin's leadership and support this relatively tiny group of ultras became a significant political force that dragged the country into the pit of expansionism, even after Labor temporarily regained its plurality. By the time I left Israel, the settlers claimed to have 150,000 residents on the West Bank alone, and their settlements were multiplying like cancerous tumors.

Begin, who for a time hero-worshiped the Gush Emunim, inaugurated the new settlement era on the morning after his first election victory. Followed by a convoy of TV crews and newsmen, he rode to Kedumim, an illegal outpost not far from Nablus, the West Bank's biggest Palestinian city. The reason for that visit, the only one Begin as prime minister paid to the West Bank, was obvious. Kedumim's unauthorized existence was—like Ofra's—a classic example of the fraud that was characteristic of the entire settlement project.

Kedumim had been established in 1976 by the Bloc of the Faithful with the help of Arik Sharon who was then Rabin's military adviser. When Rabin learned about the illegal venture and tried to shut it down, the settlers and their religious allies put up an enormous ruckus in the Knesset, invoking the sacrosanct rule of Zionism that Jewish settlements, once established, must never be given up. Rabin caved in and placed Kedumim under IDF protection, but he never made it legal.

Begin's post-election elevation of Kedumim to a model of his settlement policy was another showpiece of his talent for ceremony. The scene took place in the hilltop settlement under the glare of brilliant late-spring sun. Israeli flags encircling the community flapped defiantly in the wind; rabbis blew ram's horns and sweaty, skullcap-wearing settlers danced the hora for the benefit of the cameramen. Begin, visibly buoyed by the fervent emotions in the air, solemnly pledged "the energy and treasure" of Israel to the construction of "many more Kedumim." Before leaving, he turned excitedly to the accompanying foreign newsmen and exhorted them to stop calling the West Bank an occupied territory. "It's liberated Judea and Samaria," he shouted, using the area's biblical names. "Can't you say it? Liberated Judea and Samaria!"

In Begin's eyes, the religious-nationalist settlers were the rightful successors of the secular kibbutzniks who under Labor's leadership had carved the Jewish state out of Palestine. The vast majority of the new settlers were young, suntanned Ashkenazi sabras wearing the knitted yarmulkes of Israel's religious colleges. Many of them had served in IDF's commando and other elite units, which lent them additional prestige. They were bright, articulate, and except for their loaded assault rifles as wholesome-looking a lot as I had seen anywhere.

They acted their role of the new elites of Zionism to perfection. They prayed hard, worked hard, and on Saturday mornings they jogged to the Old City's Western Wall in tight formations, singing nationalist songs and lustily dancing the hora just like the sabras in Hollywood movies. They married sturdy-looking child-bearers who could be seen strolling around the settlements, frequently with a toddler in a baby carriage, an infant on the back, and a third offspring in the belly.

I used to tag along on Gush Emunim's annual trek in March across the West Bank which they performed to demonstrate their claim on the entire occupied territory. The young families that made up the bulk of the procession were picture-perfect. Exuding zeal, purpose, and self-righteousness, they looked like latter-day Puritans.

Their pioneering role-playing was a full-time job. Though most of the settlers were urban-raised professionals who worked in Tel Aviv, they affected—particularly when calling on Begin to demand more subsidies—the looks of dirt farmers by wearing IDF fatigues and heavy boots. Their wives were picture-perfect homemakers who served cakes and coffee to the IDF troops guarding the settlements. And to a man and a woman, the Gush Emunim minions were conspicuously cheerful in the presence of foreign journalists, happiness being a ritual part of The Return to The Land.

Toward their Arab neighbors, they were ruthless. Certain of their sole right to Greater Israel, they usurped the occupied land as if its inhabitants were of no consequence. They sounded virtuous even when shooting up Arab villages because the local kids had thrown stones at the settlers' cars. Under their pious God-invoking surface, these young Israelis were hard-bitten racists and bullies. They reminded me of my Dad's "poseurs"—behind their make-believe front was a fraud.

Begin at first praised them fulsomely as the new generation of Zionist idealists, but he grew much less enthusiastic as time went on. Bolstered by their fast-growing numbers, the settlers during my years in Israel made it increasingly clear that they regarded themselves as morally superior to the Jews who lived outside the occupied territories. Begin couldn't accept that. After his one trip to Kedumim, he never visited another settlement or set his foot on the West Bank.

I was by no means alone in loathing the settlers. By the time Begin stepped down, David Grossman, a brilliant young Israeli writer, described the Torah-quoting Zionists as Israel's "hollow men" who "have created their ... spiritual Sparta on the [West Bank] mountain tops" and who "allow history to stuff them, and then they are dangerous and deadly."

Another Israeli who by the mid-1980s saw through the settlers' pious facade was Abraham Achituv, a former commander of Shinbet, Israel's FBI. He called the settlements "a hothouse for Jewish terrorism," a distinction the fanatics earned by assassinating elected West Bank mayors and trying to blow up the Old City's Dome of the Rock, the third holiest shrine of Islam.

Begin never uttered a critical word about the settlers in public, but after he signed the Camp David accords, the settlers were rarely seen in his office. For one thing, the Gush and other extremists accused the prime minister of selling out to Israel's enemies. Even worse, they deserted the Likud for Geula Cohen's Tehiya and other way-out parties that demanded not only the annexation of the West Bank but also the expulsion of the Palestinians.

The upshot was that Begin avoided the settlers—including those whose outposts in Sinai were dismantled under the terms of the Camp David agreement. The violation of the historic Zionist oath to never abandon a Jewish settlement almost demanded that Begin should personally explain his decision to the few score of affected Israelis, but he could not bring himself to do it. He left it to Sharon to meet with them and defend the withdrawal from Sinai.

Begin's hot-cold attitude toward the settlers had a parallel in his relationship with Sharon. On the one hand, Begin was fascinated by the hawkish warrior: he addressed him, sometimes with a slight bow, as *mon général*, and in founding the Likud bloc he specifically accommodated Sharon's political demands. But at the same time, Begin distrusted the general's authoritarian tendencies, and for four years refused to make him defense minister. Even after the resignation of Weizman, who had held that position during the peace treaty negotiations with Egypt, Begin took the critical portfolio himself rather than entrusting it to Sharon. As Kadishai told me, Begin did not want to take the chance on finding one day his office building "surrounded by tanks."

Begin only relented after the 1981 election campaign to which Sharon made a major contribution by organizing free bus tours to the newly constructed settlements. The excursions were very effective with American visitors—even my friend and colleague Sam Shaffer, a staunch liberal on US issues, came back from Sharon's West Bank tour praising "what the stiff-necked Jews can accomplish."

Sharon's venture was believed to have brought so many votes and campaign contributions for the Likud that Begin felt obligated to finally give the ex-general the post he wanted. It turned out to be a huge mistake that in June 1982 brought about the IDF invasion of Lebanon and, the next year, Begin's resignation and retirement from politics.

The Lebanon campaign was a good example of the naiveté and overconfidence that characterized Israel's dealings with the Arabs. Sharon's stated goal for the invasion of Israel's northern neighbor was to destroy the camps of Arafat's fedayeen and thus, in Begin's words, give Israel "forty years of peace." Sharon's own promise was that the attack would "reshuffle the cards" of the Arab-Israeli conflict. But as described to me on the eve of the invasion by Moshe Arens—then the chairman of the Knesset foreign affairs committee—the general's real goal was to reshape the map of the Middle East.

According to Arens, Sharon hoped that the IDF assault on the "Hanoi" in South Lebanon would trigger the fedayeen's flight to Jordan, where they would again clash with the king's Bedouins. In contrast to the Black September rout in 1970, this time, Sharon predicted, the PLO's commandos would be joined by Jordan's Palestinians in a civil war that would unseat King Hussein and lead to the establishment of a Jordanian republic run by Arafat. The hoped-for bottom line was that Israel would have a potent argument for keeping the West Bank and Gaza on the grounds that the Palestinians had a state of their own in Jordan.

What happened instead was the final proof that I was not fated to cover military victories. The invasion of Lebanon became Israel's most unproductive military venture since the 1956 capture of the Suez Canal. The IDF got bogged down on the outskirts of Beirut; many fedayeen, instead of fleeing to Jordan, were evacuated to Yemen and Morocco; and suicidal attacks by South Lebanese Shiites bled the IDF so profusely that it eventually beat a retreat. In between, Begin took more blows than he could stand.

One major disaster struck in September 1982 when Sharon allowed the Lebanese Christian militia into the Palestinian refugee camps of Sabra and Shatilla and the Falangists massacred eight hundred unarmed men, women, and children while IDF troops looked on. The mass murder triggered such outrage abroad that Begin—though feeling wronged: "the goyim are killing goyim and everybody blames the Jews," he complained to me—agreed to the appointment of a commission of inquiry headed by Yitzhak Kahan, the chairman of the Supreme Court.

An even worse personal tragedy followed in November when Begin's beloved wife, Aliza, died. The prime minister, already overstressed and dejected, was now also without his closest companion. Adding to his emotional misery, his body seemed to be giving out: he fell in the shower and broke his hip.

As 1983 got under way, things continued to deteriorate. Even the Israelis who used to be at Begin's feet became increasingly rebellious against the Lebanese quagmire. IDF reservists swamped the prime minister with petitions protesting the invasion. Dovish and hawkish Jews fought fistfights in the streets, and a rightist fanatic threw a hand grenade at a peace march outside

Begin's office, killing one of the demonstrators. Six months after he promised the country "forty years of peace," Israel's first Nobel Peace Prize laureate found himself presiding over a calamity that was ripping apart his people.

The last nails to the coffin of Sharon's grand scheme were Shiite ambushes and bomb attacks that harassed the IDF's pullback from Lebanon. By the time the invasion was one year old, the Israeli army had suffered more casualties than it had in the entire Six Day War, when it defeated three Arab armies and conquered an area several times the size of Israel. For Begin, this was more than he could bear.

In September 1983, he told his cabinet that he could not "go on" and abruptly resigned as prime minister, letting Shamir, his deputy, take over. Afterwards, in a gesture of almost Wagnerian doom, Begin secluded himself behind the shuttered windows of his apartment on the outskirts of Jerusalem. He only emerged to commemorate the anniversary of Aliza's death.

I last spoke with Begin three months before his resignation, after the Kahan commission of inquiry released its report on the Sabra and Shatilla massacre. The commission denounced the event as Israel's version of the anti-Jewish pogroms in Eastern Europe and called for Sharon's resignation as the top official responsible for the tragedy. The report also recommended punishment for several IDF senior officers who had failed to prevent or stop the bloodshed.

Begin emerged uncensured, but the released transcript of the closed hearings disclosed a curious discrepancy between his and Sharon's testimonies on an important point of the inquiry, which was who in the Israeli government knew that the massacre was underway without trying to stop it.

Speaking under oath, Begin testified that he had first heard about the massacre on BBC news on September 18. This was some thirty-six hours after the mayhem was first reported by IDF units stationed around the camps, and after the State Department's Morris Draper tried to stop it from his Beirut outpost by frantically calling every Israeli official he could reach.

Sharon, also speaking under oath, contradicted Begin's testimony by telling the commission that Begin had called him some twenty hours before the BBC's September 18 broadcast and asked about an "American report"—presumably, one of the urgent messages sent by Draper—of killings that were taking place in the vicinity of the Sabra and Shatilla hospital. What made Sharon's statement even more striking was that he volunteered it, without being asked, toward the end of his testimony.

The commission of two Supreme Court justices and an IDF general did not explore who spoke the truth and who lied: the picture of Begin that emerged from the testimonies was that during the invasion he was already so feeble, physically and mentally, he could hardly follow what Sharon was doing, let alone control it. But I found Sharon's claim so intriguing that I sought out Begin in the Knesset and asked him whether it was true. Begin, standing next to Kadishai, leaned on his cane, looked down at his feet and vigorously shook his head. "*Lo!*" (No!), he said emphatically in Hebrew. He had made no such phone call to Sharon, he insisted, but he made no other comment.

Shortly after Begin resigned, I asked Kadishai, who visited him daily, how the former prime minister felt in retrospect about letting Sharon send the troops to Lebanon. According to Kadishai, his former boss continued to believe the invasion had been eminently justified. Begin, he told me, was convinced that he had preempted a fedayeen offensive from South Lebanon that would have been followed by a combined assault on Israel by the armies of Egypt, Jordan and Syria.

The scheme was totally illusory—among a great many other problems, the Egyptian army would have had to overrun the US peace observers in Sinai—but it echoed Begin's self-righteous rationale for his terrorism: "Had I done otherwise, I would have to be deeply ashamed of myself."

I knew no one in Israel who shared his delusion, and I wondered whether it gave Begin any comfort. As I saw it, by resigning from his office, Begin silently bowed to the moral standards he had so shockingly defied as a young leader of the Irgun. It was a formidable gesture—perhaps, I thought, an act of self-punishment. I still could not forget the bombing of King David or the butchery at Deir Yassin, but what I felt most for the former prime minister was compassion.

CHAPTER 19

ISRAEL'S SECRET KEEPERS—AND LEAKERS

Begin's departure from the scene ushered in one of the infrequent periods when Israel took on the countenance of a reasonably relaxed society and country. The peace process that had captivated the world after Sadat came to Jerusalem stalled and withered, deprived of oxygen by Israel's refusal to stop settling the occupied territories. The ruinous invasion of Lebanon was over, and Shamir, Begin's successor, had no stomach for overt military adventures. In the West Bank and Gaza, Palestinian protest demonstrations continued, but produced no major incidents. Inflation remained a problem, and restitution to the settlers who left Sinai cost a fortune, but the three-billion-dollar annual aid from US taxpayers helped keep the Israeli economy on an even keel.

Of course, Israel was never dull—some of the Knesset skirmishers were fierce, and even the dour and profoundly uncharismatic Shamir gave the country something to giggle about: he publicly suggested that, as a cure for inflation, Israel should drop the shekel—currency that had replaced the old Israeli pound—and adopt the US dollar. Coming out of the same fertile mind that had tried to make a World War II alliance with the Nazis and, after the war, admired Mao Tse Tung, the notion was recognized as way over the top and quickly died amidst the chuckles of columnists.

In this relatively calm period, there were several events in the public arena that were well worth the telex fees to New York. One of them was the July 23, 1984, elections in which the Peres-led Labor Party recovered enough from its drubbing by Begin to cobble together a bloc in the Knesset that matched the strength of the Likud-led coalition. The electoral toss-up gave birth to an unprecedented power-sharing arrangement in which the Likud and the Labor parties each got half of the seats in the cabinet, with Rabin running the defense ministry and an obscure Likudnik the country's finance portfolio. The most unorthodox part of the agreement was that Shamir and Peres would each take a two-year turn as a "rotation" prime minister and serve the rest of his four-year term as minister of foreign affairs. Peres was first to take over the PM's office.

In addition to this exemplary political compromise and creativity, the two halves of the government also worked hand in hand on projects of such moment that they had to be kept secret. Peres and Shamir, although ostensibly at odds ideologically, turned out to make perfect partners in pursuing both schemes, which were known and supported by their defense minister, Yitzhak Rabin. As a result of these hushed-up activities, I had frequent run-ins with Israel's military censorship.

I should add that jousting with the secrecy bureaucrats was not something that weighed heavily on my conscience. Breaking official taboos comes easy given a visceral disdain for any attempt to control the press, an attitude I had developed during my first Nazi- and later Moscow-dominated formative years. Although I personally got along quite well with most of the Israeli censors, I had utterly no respect for the part of their mission that went far beyond the understandable maintenance of Israel's genuine military secrets.

What made my defiance less gutsy than it sounds was that I was far from alone: in fact, many highly placed Israelis shared my contempt for the official gag rules that had been in force, in war and peace, since 1948. What rallied these potent allies to my side was that by the time I came to Israel, the country's censorship became a class A exhibit of a bureaucracy gone amok. It was a farce that cast the censors, who personally were not a bad lot, in the demeaning role of comic strip grave diggers frantically trying, but never quite succeeding, to bury the shenanigans and hanky-panky of their government.

For example, in November 1978 *Ha'aretz*, the best and most respected Israeli newspaper, appeared one Monday morning with several column inches of white space on page 1, courtesy of the military censor. The "security information" that the censor deemed unfit for the eyes of the Israeli readers consisted of two items that had been taken up by Begin's cabinet in its regular meeting on Sunday morning. What made them unpublishable was the prime minister's ruling that the ministers were meeting as "a committee on security." One of the two unprintable secrets was that seven of the twenty-odd ministers in that meeting had the nerve to vote against Begin on a technical question dealing with the peace talks with Egypt. The other suppressed item was that the negotiations about the future of the West Bank and Gaza were scheduled to start within a month after the signing of the Egypt-Israel peace treaty.

This was by no means an extreme example of what passed for "security information" during the years I covered Israel. I was so frequently officially reprimanded for revealing phantom "security information" that, on one occasion, I asked the chief censor in the Jerusalem Government Press Office for a clear definition of what constituted unprintable news. The censor, who was a lieutenant colonel in IDF intelligence, reached into the drawer and read to me a list of seventeen categories of prohibited news items. In addition to such obvious subjects as the identity of Shinbet and Mossad agents and the location of IDF installations, the list included any news that "brought disrepute on the State of Israel," "injured the prestige of the IDF," "endangered the public morale," or disclosed anything about the cabinet when it was meeting as "a ministerial committee on security." It was an umbrella big enough to cover half of the Mediterranean. The last item on the list, which even the censor could not read with a straight face, was any reference to the fact that the censored article had been censored.

As if this were not inane enough, the censorship was enforced in a fashion that was nothing short of schizophrenic. Had *Ha'aretz* ignored the censor's blue crayon and printed Begin's two treasured "secrets," the publisher would have been open to prosecution on charges of "aggravated espionage." The newspaper could have been shut down or, at a minimum, it would have been fined. But if the same story had been printed abroad—especially in a country where Israel aspired to the image of a liberal democracy—the censors would have applied a completely different standard.

If I had regarded the two banned items as worthy of space in *Newsweek* (which they were not), I could have sent them to my editors quite easily. As an accredited foreign correspondent, I was obligated to show the censors only stories that contained "security information," a term I quibbled about every time I was called on the censor's carpet. In theory the duty censor, who monitored my (and everybody else's) telex and, later, electronic mail filings, could have stopped the transmission the moment he'd spotted the "security" leak. In practice, this rarely happened because the censors' English was not good enough to follow the fast-moving copy, and they did not like to advertise their surveillance by stopping a transmission just to reread what it said.

Had I thus broken the censorship, I would have been held accountable, but my "punishment" would have been a far cry from that of *Ha'aretz*. Following the appearance of the "secrets" in the magazine, the chief military censor would have called me and politely complained that I had filed censorable material without submitting it to his office for clearance. I would have equally politely asked for an explanation as to how my report detracted from Israel's security or image.

The colonel, of course, could not admit that Begin had made the outcome of the meeting censorable merely to cover up his political setback. He knew—and he knew that I knew—that the prime minister wanted to hush up a cabinet revolt prompted by his acceptance of the Camp David accords. The upshot would have been that, instead of meaningfully communicating, the censor and I would have hemmed and hawed, and after several awkward sentences our desultory conversation would have ended with neither of us giving ground.

Theoretically, the censor could pull my accreditation and, in an extreme case, have me expelled from Israel. But that would have smacked too much of the treatment then accorded to foreign newsmen in Moscow and Beijing and would have raised a stink in the State Department and the publishing circles in the United States. Moreover, the censor fully realized that no security harm had been done, and he probably resented as hell the way politicians abused a system of which he was a guardian, and which did play a legitimate role in wartime. He would therefore write out a short report that I had been reprimanded, and the matter of yet another offensive item in *Newsweek*'s Periscope section would have been closed.

Closed for the IDF censor, but not for *Ha'aretz* and the rest of the Israeli newspapers, which could hardly wait for my item to come out. Under the nutty Israeli rules, most of the censorable information, once printed abroad, could be reprinted and developed by Israeli newspapers with considerable latitude—which meant that *Ha'aretz* and its competitors could enlarge on the Periscope item and run editorials and columns about the political implications of the revolt in the cabinet. Any half-wit could see why the system cried out to be violated, and how Mike Kubic got many of his scoops.

What made the Mickey Mouse censorship doubly excessive was that it was hardly ever truly necessary, because of the extraordinary security consciousness of the Israelis. In a country that repeatedly fought shooting wars; a country that drafted even young women and where every man and his son, brother, father, and cousin, time and again, risked their lives in battle, real security information did not leak. Safeguarding information of a truly military nature was in Israel everyone's personal business and was taken very, very seriously.

Perhaps the most bizarre aspect of the absurd censorship was that it was both sanctioned and violated by some of the most exalted members of the country's Establishment. The briefing Prime Minister Rabin gave me on the unpublishable "secrets" of the raid on Entebbe was one example of this baffling phenomenon. Another, perhaps even more incongruous, was the attitude of Israel's top newspaper executives who belonged to an institution called the "Editors' Committee."

The Committee, which dated back to the founding of the state, was a classic old boys' club. It was exclusive: magazine and broadcasting executives were not admitted. It was secretive: its meetings and decisions were never publicized. And it was highly status conscious: the editors huddled almost without exception only with Israel's prime minister, the defense minister, the foreign minister (usually after he returned from a mission to Washington), the IDF chief of staff, and the shadowy commanders of the country's secret services. Most outlandish of all, considering the Committee's membership, was the group's function: it was to keep the lid on important stories in exchange for the privilege of hearing about them from the country's top insiders.

This scandalous arrangement was still in force when I was in Israel, although the country's most respected publisher—Gershon Shoken, *Ha'aretz*'s founder and chief editor—on occasion walked out of the briefing rather than accepting some of the more abusive requests for secrecy. But since the security rationale was usually threadbare, and since the aging publishers and editors sometimes sent to the meetings their younger and less docile deputies, the "Editors' Committee" was porous. For the Israeli press, the stories remained off-limits, but under the screwy rules of censorship, politically motivated "secrets"—of which there were many—leaked to the foreign media like a sieve.

Efficient or not, the secrets' bureaucracy thrived throughout my stay in Israel. Its minions operated on several levels, only one of which—the GPO censors in Tel Aviv and Jerusalem—was visible. The next, less visible mode of supervision was done by official eavesdroppers who monitored the foreign correspondents' phone calls, both at home and in the office. Their main prey were radio reporters who ventured beyond a censored text when calling in their stories, but even print media types like me were routinely monitored, without any particular attempt to disguise the operation.

For example in 1980, when I moved into a new apartment, my phone rang the first evening I settled in and a British-accented male voice inquired, "Is this *Newsweek*?"

"No," I answered, "this is Mike Kubic," thereby trying to indicate that this was my home, not my office.

"But you work for *Newsweek*, right?" the voice on the phone insisted.

"Right," I said, whereupon the man came back with a peevish, "Well, I'm just trying to sort out the wires," and hung up.

What manner of wires the man was sorting out I later learned from a senior aide of prime minister Shamir who wanted me to publish an item that would have done the government a double service, both by rattling bayonets at Syria and showing the folks at home that Shamir, though a rightist ultra, was enjoying the support in Washington. The censorable news—which the aide could not get into Israeli papers without laundering it through a foreign publication—was that the IDF was about to receive a big shipment of American F-16 and F-15 fighter planes.

It sounded like a Periscope—after all, American readers deserved to know where Uncle Sam was shipping its premium military hardware—but I needed more detail, including the number of each type of planes. Since the aide did not have the figures when we had lunch on Friday, I suggested that I'd publish the story the following week, but my source would not hear of it. To make sure I got the story to New York on time, he promised to phone me the necessary details from his home on Saturday morning. But first, he said, we needed a code. For what, I asked? To avoid triggering the censor's tape recorders that, he explained, were activated by the sound of preselected words.

Instead of talking about F-15s, the prime minister's aide suggested, let's use the word "ants," and instead of F-16s let's talk about "antlers." Both grown men and nearly fifty years old, that's what we did. I don't know about the official, but I felt silly.

Conversations tapped by the monitors were transcribed and passed on to the censors, which on one occasion gave me an opportunity to score a mean little triumph. It happened one Monday morning when the censor called me up to read to me yet another censorable item that, he complained, I had sent by telex without clearance from his office. He was wrong, and by then I had been on his carpet so many times I was not about to do him any favors.

"Colonel," I told him when he finished, "you have reached into the wrong basket. What you're reading is not my file, but the transcript of my telephone conversation with one of my editors." I let that sink in and then added, just to stay on the safe side, "Incidentally, I was merely backgrounding him, and none of the stuff we discussed was for publication." There was a flourish in my voice, because "background consultations" between correspondents and their editors were not supposed to be any of the censor's business. After a short pause the censor said "Oh!" wished me "Shalom" (peace), and hung up.

The surveillance by Shinbet, Israel's FBI, was by contrast extremely professional and discrete. The only time I thought I encountered evidence of its interest in my doings was when I returned from my sudden trip to Switzerland and West Germany in pursuit of the "Hitler diaries." I walked into the bachelor pad I was then renting, turned on the light in the kitchen, and saw something that I was meant to see.

On the floor, neatly placed in the middle of the room, was a plastic ring. There was no furniture or fixture anywhere near or above it from which it could have fallen and, much like the yellow wig of the Prague cop I called "Mary," there was no way I could have overlooked it. Brown, fairly thin, over an inch in diameter, apparently unused. The sort of an item an electrician might have in his kit, though I had no idea for what.

My wife and I had separated and I was living alone. The apartment had been locked during my absence, and the only set of keys I knew about was in my pocket. The ring on the floor stared at me, I thought, as Shinbet's silent reproach for Maynard Parker's guarded phone call and my hurried departure the next morning.

The evidence that my phones were bugged was by no means new, and I accepted it as part of the Israeli reality. After all, *Newsweek* had broken enough stories some Israeli officials did not like to generate their interest in who were my sources. But the thought that occurred to me as I gazed at the ring on the floor was that my overseers were now curious or angry enough to wire my apartment for sound and, moreover, wanted me to know about it. It was a whole new dimension of fish bowl living that I did not find easy.

I did not change my lifestyle, but the perceived lack of privacy exerted a pressure. How much and what kind I found out later when three senior Shinbet agents staged an in-house rebellion following an incident in which one or several of their colleagues and superiors brutally killed a Palestinian prisoner. While working on the story I learned that one of the dissenters was in charge of surveillance of the foreign press. I couldn't resist: I got the agent's home phone number and called him up in the evening.

When the man answered I suddenly realized that the Shinbet story was not the main reason for my call. What I really wanted to find out was my standing in the eyes of somebody who, I assumed, knew all about my personal life. About topics of much greater moment than *Newsweek* scoops, matters that I—uptight and aspiring to a veneer of dignity—had not discussed with anyone: the failure of my marriage, the terribly painful estrangement from my son, Jan, and my studiedly low-profile but intense courtship of Leesa, my Hebrew translator and assistant. It was a preposterous notion, but I wanted to know what the Shinbet guy thought about me as a person.

Of course, I didn't breathe a word about that on the phone, and as I half expected, the agent declined to see me to discuss the Shinbet turbulence. But our brief conversation was not a complete loss, either. As I eagerly noted, the man on the phone was very cordial, and his assurance that there was "nothing personal" in his turning down my request for a meeting sounded sincere. Such was the wretched state of my mind that I hung up with something approaching a sense of relief: here was someone who knew all about me and, erring as I was, did not condemn me.

∼

My description of Israeli censorship would be misleading if it portrayed the institution as completely toothless. Some important Israeli events remained unmentionable inside the country, regardless of how innocuous in security terms and how well-known abroad. The best example was the so-called

Lavon Affair, which was the code name for a hare-brained Israeli attempt in the summer of 1954 to cause a crisis in Western relations with Gamal Abdel Nasser. The plan was to firebomb US and British installations in Egypt and make it look like the work of Nasser's secret service. An enormously tangled boondoggle, the operation was "authorized" over a forged signature of Pinhas Lavon, Ben Gurion's defense minister, and involved thirteen Israeli agents who were quickly rounded up by Egyptian security. Two of them were sentenced to be executed, and most of the rest spent years in jail.

The "Lavon affair" threw the Israeli government into one of its worst and longest-lasting political crises and triggered street protests against Ben Gurion, Moshe Dayan, and the man whom Lavon accused of concocting the bungled plot, the ever-skulking Shimon Peres. But although widely publicized abroad, Israel's military censors consigned the entire event to the Orwellian memory hole. Any discussion of the scandal was rigidly kept out of the Israeli press, school textbooks, history books, memoirs, and any other public communication until 2005, when the surviving bombers were released from jail, received Israel honors, and the sordid tale was finally taken out of the censors' wraps.

Another fact that for many years was widely publicized abroad but could not be mentioned to the Israeli public (as well as inquiring members of US Senate) was the existence of Israel's nuclear bomb facility, which was officially described as a "textile factory." For thousands of well-read, sophisticated Israelis, all of these official "secrets" were nothing of the sort. For example, I was told about the nuclear facility within a month of coming to Jerusalem, which raised the question of why the Israelis—an intelligent, open, and garrulous folk—continued to tolerate the useless censorship when the country was not in a shooting war.

Some of my Israeli colleagues believed that the annoying censors were protected by a combination of turf politics and bureaucratic inertia that affects every government. In their view, the IDF wanted to hold on to the unit's budget and the brigadier general's slot in the censor's Tel Aviv headquarters, and the politicians did not want to do anything that might look like weakening the country's security.

My own Macchiavellian take on this issue was that the censorship was maintained because it actually promoted Israeli *hasbarah* (official propaganda) by whetting the journalists' interest in information that would otherwise be of limited news value. Leaks had a far higher gee-whiz potential than government press releases, and Israeli "secrets" published abroad were sometimes useful in psych warfare against the Arabs. In other words, stories camouflaged as secrets delivered more bang for the buck.

The ants-and-antlers story volunteered by Shamir's aide was one example. Another censorable item that was passed on to me for similar reason was the June 1988 decision of the Israeli cabinet to put into orbit the country's first satellite. There was no doubt in my (and my source's) mind that the leak was part of Israel's response to the then-current reports that Iraq was receiving Chinese Scud rockets capable of reaching Tel Aviv. The only truly baffling aspect of that *Newsweek* Periscope item was that—as I was told afterwards—it was news to the US embassy in Tel Aviv.

Planted leaks present a reporter with a dilemma that requires a careful weighing of their perils and benefits. There were several officials and politicians in Israel whose "exclusives" I would not touch. They included, most emphatically, the extremely well-placed but mendacious and devious Arik Sharon. After he lied to me a couple of times, I would not go to see him even after he complained about it to visiting *Washington Post* publisher (and my ultimate boss) Kay Graham.

The factors I regarded as decisive for using or dropping the item were whether it was true and of interest to *Newsweek*'s readers, the leaker's likely motivation, and—and this was critical—whether the publication would cause anyone undeserved harm. I was also conscious of the rule of no-free-lunch. Informants—especially those in high places—invariably try to get something from news people, just like news people try to get something from informants. This is a fact of life in journalism, and what truly matters is whether the value received by the reporter (and therefore the reading public) is a fair trade-off for the benefits derived by the source from the resulting publicity.

This is not to say that every leak I filed made my chest swell with professional pride. New as I was on the beat, for instance, I realized that by briefing me about the raid on Entebbe, Rabin was giving the finger to Peres, his political nemesis who, as then the defense minister, presumably approved Motta Gur's no-information policy. I filed what the prime minister told me anyway because there was no question about his access to the facts; and the operational details he described—which is what I was after—were fascinating.

Another time I carried someone's political water was when Gur, the IDF chief of staff and Labor Party member denounced Begin's agreement to give up Sinai in exchange for a peace treaty with Egypt. The Labor Party apparatchiks were so eager to get the story out that I was offered not one, but two copies of a tape recording of Gur's supposedly "secret" briefing to a closed meeting of senior IDF brass.

Gur's links with Labor were hardly news—after his retirement, he became one of the party's MKs—and the motive behind the offered tapes was obvious.

Labor needed to get Motta Gur's views out of the censors' clutches in order to rattle Begin's image as the hard-nosed guardian of the country's security. I ran the story anyway because the top general's opposition to the Camp David accords was a significant development that deserved to be known to the American as well as Israeli publics.

One scoop that was legitimate but caused me no joy was an item that led to the resignation of Andrew Young as President Carter's ambassador to the UN. In August 1979, as I routinely scanned a transcript of Moshe Dayan's colloquy in the Knesset, I was struck by the exceptionally irate language he used when referring to Washington. Since there was no hint in his remarks as to the source of his anger, I called a couple of sources who were close to the then-defense minister and asked them to find out what made Dayan so mad. On Saturday morning one of the minister's aides called back.

Dayan, he said, was infuriated by a report from Israel's New York consulate that Young had secretly met with Zehdi Labib Terzi, the PLO representative at the UN. This was censorable news in Israel, but an obvious story for *Newsweek*. The meeting was not only a blow to Israel's efforts to isolate the PLO; it also violated President Carter's pledge to Begin that the United States would have no contact with Arafat's organization. After getting a confirmation from a second source, I sent the tale to my editors, expecting that it would run with Young's denial that any such meeting had ever taken place. When he admitted that the report was true and resigned his UN post, I was far from pleased. I wished Young had stayed on the job.

On the whole, however, I still believe that scoops were among my best reporting from Israel. Such stories as the boondoggled development of the Lavie, Israel's super-expensive, US-financed fighter plane; the smuggling to Israel of US-made triggering devices for atomic bombs; Mossad's kidnapping in Europe of Mordechai Vanunu, the Dimona technician who had revealed Israel's atomic secrets; and examples of Israel's shady military cooperation with the apartheid regime in South Africa; all were solid, legitimate news which were well worth breaking Israeli censorship and which deserved the attention of *Newsweek*'s worldwide audience.

And the most remarkable—and gratifying—aspect of these scoops was that their sources were patriotic Israelis. Mostly middle-aged and senior-ranking, these professionals, government officials, and politicians leaked to me the country's shenanigans because they considered them inane or because they insulted their sense of decency. Morally, we were on the same wavelength. For example, my source agreed with me that it was indecent for Shimon Peres to lie to State Secretary Shultz who, as Begin's treasury minister told me, had arranged for Israel to receive its annual aid of three billion dollars at the beginning—rather than the end—of the fiscal year, a change that earned Israel an additional fourty million dollars in interest.

Yet however close and cordial my relationship with the leakers, it was always clear to me that it had very definite limits. I was a foreign goy whose allegiance was to the United States. They were an integral part of their society, sharing the serious risks and responsibilities of their compatriots.

Without ever exchanging a word on the subject, there was not the slightest doubt in my mind that if I knowingly published information that could jeopardize Israeli lives, my sources would instantly evaporate, and I might as well ask *Newsweek* for a transfer. As it happens, I've never believed that any story was worth the loss of an innocent life, and I've always drawn a distinction between journalism and espionage. Thanks to these standards, I got the cooperation I needed when covering the three biggest Israeli stories in the 1980s that the powers-that-be—both in Labor- and Likud-run governments—tried very hard to keep secret.

CHAPTER 20

POLLARD, IRANGATE, AND BUS 300

The three clandestine misadventures that rocked Israel between April 1984 and November 1986 contained several illuminating lessons, the most obvious of which (though hardly novel) was that corruption does not thrive only in dictatorships. Even democratically elected, ostensibly respectable high officials—in this case, Likud's Yitzhak Shamir and Moshe Arens, and Labor Party's Yitzhak Rabin and Shimon Peres—if allowed to operate without the scrutiny of the free press can act with the moral abandon of hardened mafiosos. Another telling lesson, which made me particularly uncomfortable, concerned the limits of Israel's "special relationship" with the United States.

Two of the signature affairs that defined the period started less than three months before the elections of July 23, 1984, and ushered in a new Israeli political phenomenon: an evenly divided "national unity" government in which Peres and Shamir "rotated"—changed places—after each of them served two years either as the prime minister or as the foreign minister.

The first scandal grew out of an incident one sunny afternoon in the middle of April when four teenage Palestinians, armed with toy guns and knives, hijacked an Israeli bus with passengers and ordered the driver to head for the border with Egypt. The terrifying ride ended when an IDF commando unit caught up with the speeding vehicle south of Ashkelon and shot up its tires. In the ensuing fight two of the hijackers and a woman passenger were killed. The other two hijackers, who were captured alive, were interrogated and beaten to death. The killings were covered up by all four top Israeli leaders, and the censorship remained so tight it took almost two years for the "Affair of Bus 300" to fully emerge into the open.

The second scandal started less than six weeks after the hijacking of the bus. The curtain-raising event was a message sent by Arens's defense ministry to Israeli Air Force colonel Aviam Sella, a senior member of the IDF mission in New York. It authorized Sella to accept the offer of Jonathan Jay Pollard, a US Navy intelligence analyst in Washington who had volunteered to spy for

Israel. The go-ahead was issued by Rafi Eitan, a former Mossad officer and the director of LEKEM, the defense ministry's scientific intelligence agency that (like Mossad, Shinbet, and the rest of the country's secret apparatus) was supervised jointly by the incumbent prime and defense ministers—at that time Shamir and Arens, and later Peres and Rabin.

Sella's meeting on May 29, 1984, with Pollard, a fervent Zionist, launched a sordid enterprise that according to unconfirmed reports enabled Israel to trade some of America's most closely guarded secrets for the Kremlin's permission for Russian Jews to emigrate to Israel. At the very minimum, the venture violated a no-spying agreement between the United States and Israeli intelligence establishments, and it was a slap in the face for the country that subsidized Israel, supplied it with sophisticated military equipment, and in effect guaranteed its very existence.

By September 14, 1984, when Arens turned over the defense ministry to Rabin, and Peres took over as prime minister from Shamir, Sella had met with Pollard at least three times and had given him the first payment of two thousand dollars for the purloined documents. The base skulduggery continued running full steam ahead under all rotating ministers until November 18, 1986, when the FBI arrested Pollard and his wife outside the Israeli embassy in Washington.

The third top-secret Israeli venture began early in May 1985 (less than a year after the start of the Pollard affair) when Peres raised the subject of violating a US ban on arms delivery to the participants in the Iran-Iraq war. He asked visiting Michael A. Ledeen, a consultant to the National Security Council (NSC), whether the White House would approve a shipment of artillery or ammunition to Iran. Two months later, on July 3, 1985, David Kimche, the director of Israel's Foreign Office and a former Mossad agent, took the next step in a meeting in the White House with Robert McFarlane, the head of President Reagan's NSC. The Iranian government of Ayatollah Khomeini—then in the fifth year of its exhausting war against Iraq—was so desperate to buy embargoed American arms, Kimche told McFarlane, that to gain access to them it had signaled its willingness to arrange the release of seven American hostages held by pro-Iranian terrorists in Lebanon.

Since the arms could not be sold by the United States, Kimche had a proposal to make. If the Pentagon would provide Israel with appropriate replacements, Israel would facilitate the arms-for-hostages trade by selling Tehran US arms that were in Israel's arsenal.

Encouraged by the White House interest in Kimche's scheme, in January 1986 Peres sent Amiram Nir, his former campaign manager and NSC liaison, to Washington with another creative idea. Meeting with NSC's gung-ho Lieutenant Colonel Oliver North, Nir suggested that part of the profits from the overpriced arms sold to Tehran could be diverted to the Nicaraguan Contras.

The resulting Iran-Contra affair surfaced on November 3, 1986—two weeks before Pollard was arrested outside the Israeli embassy—when *As Shiraa*, a Beirut newspaper close to the Iranian regime, revealed that McFarlane (accompanied, among others, by Nir) had paid a secret visit to Tehran. The purpose of that bizarre trip was to repair the damage caused by an Israeli attempt to unload on Iran Hawk missiles that were obsolete.

The most striking common denominator of the three secret enterprises—aside from the fact that they all backfired—was their truly bipartisan nature. Historically, the semi-socialist Labor and the ultra-nationalist and religious parties of the Likud bloc were bitter ideological and political opponents. But when it came to covering up Israeli secrets and pulling wool over Uncle Sam's eyes, Peres and Rabin—both regarded as liberal-minded "doves"—sang from the same hymnal as Shamir and Arens, the rigid hawks at the opposite end of Israel's political spectrum.

Given his long record for shady operations, Shamir's disregard for laws, agreements, and common decency came as no surprise. I also had no illusions about the ethics of Peres, a former kibbutznik. By the time I came to Israel, he was known to his peers to be an able and hardworking but also shifty and conniving operator who readily double-crossed both allies and adversaries. In Israeli political circles, the word was that John Le Carré's Karla had nothing over Peres when it came to skulduggery.

What I found harder to take was the low blow delivered to Uncle Sam by Arens and Rabin when they authorized Pollard's stealing of US secrets. Arens was brought up and educated in the United States and kept his American citizenship until early in 1983 when Begin sent him to Washington as Israel's ambassador. Even then, he turned in his US passport only when asked for it personally by Sam Lewis, our envoy in Tel Aviv.

Arens had the seemingly open demeanor of a secular aeronautical engineer with degrees from the Massachusetts and California Institutes of Technology, and during his stint in Washington he became a social friend of Kay Graham, the publisher of the *Washington Post* and *Newsweek*. In fact, under his smooth surface, Arens was a rigid ideologue and a hardliner. For example, as the chairman of the powerful Knesset committee on foreign affairs and security, he was one of the few Likud members who voted against the Camp David agreements and Israel's peace treaty with Egypt. And as defense minister,

Arens allied himself with Israel's religious-nationalists led by Rabbi Moshe Levinger and helped them expand the Jewish quarter in the heart of Hebron, a major Arab town in the West Bank.

Most disheartening, as far as I was concerned, was the deep involvement in all three miserable undertakings of Rabin, a native sabra with a reputation for personal integrity. I saw Rabin fairly often, liked him, and had a lot of respect for him, but his role during the Pollard scandal was a big letdown. As a former IDF chief of staff, ambassador to Washington, and defense and prime minister, Rabin knew firsthand about the importance and generosity of the US diplomatic, military, and economic aid for Israel. Yet when he learned about Pollard's activities, Rabin emphasized only the need for "caution" and asked to see the originals of some of the stolen documents.

Pollard continued getting his retainer on Rabin's watch; he and his wife were dined and wined by LEKEM's chief Rafi Eitan in Paris and Tel Aviv; Pollard's wife was presented with a diamond ring; and Pollard was issued an Israeli passport with a new name. And Pollard was not the only illicit operation run by LEKEM in the United States while Rabin was defense minister. In the spring of 1985, US customs agents intercepted a shipment to Israel of more than eight hundred "radio tubes," which were in reality krytrons, devices for triggering an atomic bomb. The alleged recipient of the embargoed shipment was a LEKEM-rented mailbox of a nonexistent firm.

While all four rotating principals were involved in the scandals up to their ears, Peres, in my mind, was the top villain. The group's most senior and most experienced Israeli bureaucrat and politician, Peres must have recognized the affairs' perilous nature and could have easily and quietly prevented or stopped all of them. Instead, he added to these scandals another one in October 1986—just before he was rotated out as prime minister—by authorizing the Mossad to kidnap in Italy Mordechai Vanunu, an Israeli citizen and former technician in the Dimona plant that manufactured Israel's atomic bombs. Vanunu, who had embraced Christianity and leaked the country's nuclear secrets to a London newspaper, was smuggled back into Israel and sentenced to eighteen years in prison, eleven of them in solitary confinement.

After the Pollard affair blew up, Peres did most of the lying. On November 25, 1986, one week after Pollard's arrest, Peres testified before Abba Eban's intelligence subcommittee that nothing improper had taken place because Pollard had delivered the intelligence documents as an authorized "back channel conduit" between the US Office of Naval Intelligence and Israel. And two nights later, at eleven o'clock at night, Peres called on Ambassador Thomas Pickering, Lewis's successor, to give him a letter for Secretary of State George Shultz that elaborated on the same brazen lie. "Our examination" of the affair,

Peres wrote in that urgent note, "brought out that Mr. Pollard presented himself as an official representative of a US Government Intelligence Office dealing with counter-terrorist activity. He claimed that he was authorized to establish contacts with a number of countries, including Israel, on matters of counter terrorism outside the frame of routine inter-service exchange in order to assure maximum discretion."

Working hand in hand with Shamir, Peres later escalated his thumbing of his nose at Shultz and Uncle Sam by stonewalling a State Department mission that came to Israel to find out who else had figured in the spy affair. I was amused to see the top fact finder, the State Department's chief legal counsel Avraham Sofaer, hugging Israeli VIPs in the dining room of the King David Hotel. Despite his obvious closeness to Jerusalem movers and shakers, my Israeli sources told me that Sofaer was told little, if anything, about Sella and about the Washington, DC, apartment with a copying machine that was provided for the operation by a wealthy American collaborator.

Peres also turned down Sofaer's requests to interview the embassy secretaries who had used the apartment to copy the stolen documents and who, together with Sella, fled the United States the same day Pollard was arrested. As a sop to Washington, LEKEM was formally dismantled, but after Pollard blew the whistle on Sella and Eitan as his spy handlers, Peres and Rabin gave Uncle Sam the finger.

Peres made Eitan the chairman of the board of Israel's Chemical Works, one of the country's largest state-run industries. As for Sella, he was promoted by Rabin to the rank of brigadier general and was put in command of one of two brand new IDF air bases that were wholly financed by the United States to compensate Israel for the withdrawal from Sinai. Only a threat of some furious US Air Force brass to stop cooperating with their Israeli counterparts persuaded Rabin to transfer Sella to a less exposed post. The final touch of official cynicism was a press conference called by Peres after *Newsweek* published his letter to Shultz. Peres did not deny my story but charged that *Newsweek* had acted "irresponsibly" by publishing it.

~

The Bus 300 scandal started, literally, in front of Defense Minister "Misha" Arens. On April 12, 1984, he and his spokesman Nachman Shai arrived at the scene shortly after the commandos overwhelmed the hijackers, and stood next to a photographer from *Hadashot*, a Tel Aviv tabloid, when he snapped a picture of two Shinbet agents walking with one of the surviving Palestinians to an interrogation van.

By the following morning the state-run radio Kol Israel announced that all of the hijackers had "died of wounds suffered in the fighting," and the military censor prohibited *Hadashot* from printing the snapshot of a surviving and seemingly unharmed hijacker after the fighting was over. The official version crumbled after David Shipler broke the story in the Sunday *New York Times*—one day ahead of my own report in *Newsweek*, which came out on Monday—that at least one of the two surviving hijackers was actually beaten to death.

But this did not deter both Labor and Likud leaders from doing their utmost to keep the lid on the affair's details and its furious aftermath. When *Hadashot* broke the censorship by publishing the snapshot of the surviving hijacker, Arens shut down the newspaper for three days. Afterwards, he ordered an IDF inquiry into the affair, but this attempt to identify the killer ground to a halt in a maze of procedural obstacles, perjured testimonies, switched fingerprints, and forged forensic documents.

The brazen fraudulence of the process prompted three senior Shinbet officials to accuse Avraham Shalom, the agency director, of orchestrating the chaos that wrecked the inquiry. Shalom denied any involvement and ordered all three accusers off active duty. The rebels took their case to Prime Minister Shamir, but he rejected their charges out of hand. After Shamir was rotated out, the three Shinbetniks called on Peres, the new prime minister. He fully endorsed Shamir's decision that there was nothing to investigate, denounced the trio as "putchists," and ordered them to resign from the agency.

There was an interesting contrast in the way the Israeli public reacted when the underground ventures of their leaders broke into the open. The revelation of Pollard's spying had virtually no negative fallout. On the contrary, there was strong public support for the vigorous campaign launched by Pollard's American supporters for his release from jail. The Iran-Contra affair also generated very little, if any, criticism. Only the attempt to squelch the Bus 300 affair after a long gestation backfired, thanks to the guts and decency of a few individuals.

At the top of the short honor list, together with the Shinbet trio, was one of my sterling "Righteous Israelis," the country's attorney general. Yitzhak Zamir, the hero of the piece, was an unassuming, pleasant-looking man with the low-key, thoughtful demeanor of a middle-aged law professor. Behind the bland exterior, however, was a strong-willed, top-notch judicial official who had a long and distinguished record for intellectual courage and sterling ethics. Long before the Bus 300 affair, for example, Zamir had fought government seizures of Bedouin land, investigated charges of torture by Shinbet's interrogators, and had the nerve to demand prosecution of Knesset members for traffic offenses. At one point in his career, Zamir even overruled the chief rabbinate's ban on excavations in the Old City of Jerusalem, a step that called for exceptional guts because it encroached on the suzerainty of Israel's powerful religious establishment.

Another height of defiance of the powers-that-be was Zamir's insistence on putting on trial thirty-five Jewish terrorists—whom Prime Minister Shamir publicly praised as "good boys"—for assassinating West Bank mayors and trying blow up the Dome of the Rock, one of the holiest shrines in Islam. In the Bus 300 affair, Zamir lived up to his maverick reputation. He took on the Likud-Labor Mafia, and he won.

The attorney general pursued the Bus 300 case, mostly alone and against heavy government resistance, for almost two years. He first stepped in after the collapse of the military inquiry, by ordering a new investigation, this time by the ministry of justice. This probe, conducted also behind the thick wall of secrecy, lasted a whole year before it bogged down in phony statements and bogus evidence concocted by the top brass of Shinbet. Zamir's response was to put the IDF brigadier and the five Shinbet interrogators of the hijacker on separate secret trials, in which everyone was acquitted for lack of evidence. Still not ready to throw in the towel, Zamir made a last-ditch personal appeal to Shalom to reopen the investigation. After the Shinbet chief turned him down, pleading a duty to protect "his people," Zamir announced his intention to resign.

His impending departure prompted the three Shinbet rebels, who had remained silent after Peres ordered their resignation, to give Zamir their evidence of Shalom's cover-up. Zamir withdrew his resignation and, despite a stormy protest by Peres, ordered a new probe of the affair. By then, the three Shinbet dissenters told their story to the Israeli media, and the military censor—mindful that the charges cleared the IDF general—allowed the story to be published. In the ensuing uproar, Peres tried to have Zamir fired, but several ministers in his cabinet refused to cooperate.

Soon afterwards Shalom and ten other Shinbetniks involved in the Bus 300 affair resigned from the agency and received—again, in secret—presidential pardon. The last Periscope I wrote about the discredited Shalom was that he had applied, under a different name, for a security contract at New York's JFK airport.

My files on the Bus 300 affair include two wire service stories. One of them is a July 25, 1996, wire service recap of a *Yedioth Ahronoth* interview with Ehud Yatom, a retired Shinbetnik, in which he confessed to the 1984 murder of the two hijackers. "I received instructions from Avraham Shalom to kill them, so I killed them with a big stone. I crushed their skulls," Yatom told the Israeli newspaper. Yatom added that he was proud of his actions, and that he was "one of the few people who emerged emotionally fit from the affair." The other story, from the office of the then Israeli prime minister Benjamin Netanyahu, denied that Yatom had made any such comments to the newspaper.

~

There was no Zamir in the Israeli government fighting against the arms shipments to Iran because, as State Secretary George Shultz testified before Senator John Tower's committee, the only injured party was the United States. "One of the things Israel wanted," Shultz told the president's Special Review Board after the Irangate and Iran-Contra debacles surfaced, "was to get itself into a position where its arms sales to Iran could not be criticized by us because we were conducting this Operation Staunch [which sought to prevent arms shipments to both sides in the Iran-Iraq war], and we were trying to persuade everybody not to sell arms. That's what all that is about."

Shultz's statement merely touched on an issue that, for Israel, was of major significance. Arms trade, indeed, was important. Iraq's invasion of south Iran in September 1980 triggered Tehran's frantic search for spare parts and weapon systems that during the Shah's regime were provided by the Pentagon, and no country was in better position to reap the big bucks than Israel.

Israel's armories had a surplus of most of the sought-after hardware, either in Pentagon-supplied originals or in knock-offs made in Israel, and—with the connivance of top officials in Khomeini's entourage—it had been supplying Iran in roundabout ways with military hardware since at least 1981. The trade was carried out by SIBAT, a defense ministry agency that was selling Israeli-made or captured Soviet bloc arms to China and Third World countries; it had twelve hundred licensed, globe-trotting salesmen, mostly retired IDF and Mossad brass, who were expert at arms trafficking. Undermining the pesky Operation Staunch, as Shultz pointed out, therefore was an essential Israeli objective.

Dollars and cents, however, were not likely the only consideration behind Israel's arms-for-hostages proposal. In the early and mid-1980s, the ebb and flow of the Iran-Iraq war was accompanied by a vigorous debate in the IDF and Israeli strategic think tanks about which side presented a greater threat to Israel. While some Israeli academicians argued that the religious fervor of the ayatollahs was a more serious long-range menace than the anti-Zionism of the strongman in Baghdad, this was not the majority view. The military establishment, mindful that during the Six Day war Iraq sent an expeditionary force to Jordan, regarded Saddam Hussein as the greater threat. To help Iran batter Iraq's formidable war machine gave the arms trade a strategic dimension.

Next, I suspect, there was the weighty factor of the Pollard operation, which was running at full tilt while the Reagan administration was anxiously casting for a way to free the Hezbollah-held American hostages. Peres, an old hand at covert activities, must have been conscious that one day, the Pollard spying could be discovered, in which case helping to free the Americans would be an important plus on the balance sheet of US-Israeli relations. Finally, I feel quite certain that on the operational level, there was genuine sympathy for a bunch of Americans in very serious trouble. This was particularly true about the more senior government employees who had done tours of duty in the United States.

Having said that, I must add that, after the operation collapsed, two of my best-informed, directly involved Israeli sources separately volunteered the observation that greed was the main reason for its undoing. The critical event each of my sources cited was a meeting in November 1985 in Savyyon, Tel Aviv's fancy suburb, in the house of Alfred Schwimmer, who at that time held the title of special consultant to Prime Minister Peres.

Al Schwimmer, an American engineer and Peres's longtime close personal friend, was the former head of the Israeli Aviation Industry and, after his retirement, a major Israeli arms dealer. The purpose of the meeting, which was attended by the small Israeli team running the arms sales to Iran, was to plan the shipment of eighteen improved Hawk surface-to-air missiles. The hardware was urgently sought by the Iranians to combat the Iraqi air force, and it comprised one of the bigger single payloads of the entire operation.

The transaction was regarded as critically important because the Iranians had promised to pay in cash and on top of it release two of the six Americans held in Lebanon. For the Israelis, this would have been the first successful exchange since September 15 when the Hezbollah had set free Reverend Benjamin Weir, one of their American prisoners, outside the gates of the US embassy in Beirut. Since all subsequent exchanges were repeatedly snarled by double-dealers in Tehran, the Israelis were anxious to show Washington that their Iranian connection still produced results.

My sources told me that, despite the importance of the deal, an Israel Air Force brigadier general at the Savyyon meeting suggested that SIBAT should ship to Tehran an obsolete version of the Hawks instead of the latest, high performance missiles ordered by the Iranians. If successful, the sale would have resulted in upgrading Israel's own stock of Hawks because the Pentagon would have replenished it with the latest hardware. Haim Carmon, the head of SIBAT who was also at the meeting, was immediately receptive to the idea. Schwimmer, according to my sources, emphatically warned SIBAT against any shenanigans, but Carmon shipped the old Hawks anyway. The Iranians test fired one of them, and when it failed to reach the altitude of Iraq's warplanes, they dumped the remaining seventeen crates in plain view next to one of the runways of the Tehran international airport. Furious about the attempted fraud, the ayatollahs also suspended all negotiations for the further releases of the hostages, thereby setting the scene for McFarlane's futile conciliatory visit to Tehran in May 1986, and its prompt disclosure by *As Shiraa*.

In the opinion of one of the Israeli officials engaged in the operation, the attempt to fool the Iranians was "the worst screw-up of the whole affair." Following the flop, Peres tried to improve his image in the White House by replacing Kimche with Nir and sending him to Washington to discuss the idea of diverting part of the Irangate profits to the Nicaraguan Contras.

Shultz's testimony before John Tower's Special Review Board contained one statement that was incorrect. Discussing his suspicion that the Israelis wanted the shipments to compromise the US arms embargo, the secretary said that "Israel would have an interest in leaking such a deal.... I had been told that [while the Irangate was in progress] *Newsweek* had the story of the Kimche-McFarlane meetings but did not run it. I noted that Kimche may have leaked it deliberately."

Shultz's information was incorrect. Strictly speaking, *Newsweek*'s editors did not know about Irangate until the story became public in November 1986. I knew about the operation, but I did not report it for fifteen months for the simple but very important reason that I did not want to do anything that would in the least jeopardize the possibility that the trade of arms for hostages might work. I knew enough about Arab brutality to shudder at what the Americans—who included AP's Terry Anderson, a fellow journalist—were going through.

Shultz was also wrong in naming Kimche as the person who told me about the shipments. I was tipped off about the operation in September 1985, a few days after I returned to Jerusalem from my annual vacation in Vermont, by one of my government sources. We were already parting, following a conversation about what had happened in Israel during my absence, when he mentioned that there was afoot a joint White House–Israeli operation. The idea, he said, speaking as casually as if he were talking about a cultural exchange program, was to sell Iran US-made arms in the Israeli arsenal in exchange for the release of Hizbollah's hostages in Lebanon.

I gave him a long look, but that was all my source either knew or was ready to say. I felt like standing in front of a big white canvas with a fascinating silhouette sketched out in charcoal. All I had to do was fill in the details.

If the picture did gain some clarity, it was because I had worked in Israel for more than nine years and knew most of the country's movers and shakers, including some who operated out of the limelight. Thanks to this background, while I was still driving to my office, I mentally identified several Israelis who, I felt certain, were involved in the barter.

Peres, Israel's craftiest backroom performer, was the first on my list. At the time I knew nothing about the Pollard case or about Zamir's campaign, but Peres's passion for secret schemes ran like a fat red ribbon through Israel's history. There was no force on earth that could keep him out of a hush-hush operation involving arms, Iran, and Washington.

The second name that quickly came to mind was Yaakov Nimrodi, an Israeli arms dealer whom I had met while working on another story. Nimrodi was an Iranian Jew fluent in Farsi who, as the Mossad's chief agent in Tehran, used to be Israel's main liaison with the Shah's generals. After leaving the Mossad, Nimrodi used his Iranian contacts to become one of SIBAT's most prosperous salesmen—"a multimillionaire," as he told me. Nimrodi had a mansion in Israel and offices in Tel Aviv and London, the international headquarters of most death merchants.

The third obvious name was that of the American Al Schwimmer. He was an Israeli legend—an aviation engineer and fervent Zionist. Peres visited him in California soon after the Jewish state was born and recruited him to organize and run the Israeli Aviation Industry (IAI). After his retirement from IAI, Schwimmer—who (like Arens, and all American Israelis I knew) had kept his US citizenship—became one of Israel's most discreet arms salesmen to regimes that publicly ostracized the Jewish state, including the various African potentates and the Saudi Arabian royal family. It was clear to me that Schwimmer must be another key player in the trade with Iran.

I paused before including Kimche's name because to my best knowledge he had no Iranian or arms-trading experience. As a former Mossad agent, Kimche worked mainly in Africa and, more recently, was Israel's liaison with Christian leaders in Lebanon. But as I tried to pick the best men that Peres would likely choose for the operation, there was no way to leave Kimche out. For one thing, Kimche, as the director of Israel's Foreign Office, could shuttle between Jerusalem and Washington without raising any eyebrows. Second, Kimche was a Likud appointee and as such was the right man to brief Shamir, who was now the foreign minister, and had to be kept in the picture under the rotation formula. Finally, I knew that Kimche qualified for the job because he had the qualities that enabled 3.5 million Israelis to defy 120 million Arabs. Slender, wiry, and sharp, Kimche was an Israeli d'Artagnan, a highly able, hardworking adventurer at heart.

CHAPTER 20

The fifth person I also decided to sound out early on about the Iranian operation was Amiram Nir, who had an office in the Tel Aviv defense ministry. Nir was a former Israel TV military correspondent who had worked for Peres during the 1984 election campaign and became his terrorism adviser after retired IDF general Gideon Machanaimi (one of my Czech "landsmen" in Israel) died of a heart attack. It was Nir's job to know everything about Hezbollah and its hostages. He was another likely member of the core team.

With this list in mind, I set out to find out who would talk—and how much—about what was clearly a very closely held operation. Considering the stakes and the involvement of the White House (an institution no Israeli government in those years wanted to antagonize), I was at first skeptical about getting much help. It turned out that I was wrong. Once my sources learned that I was onto the Tehran operation and was not about to blow it up, picking up pieces of information became easier than I expected.

By the end of 1985 I had collected a respectable amount of detail about the operation and its principal figures, but I was increasingly concerned about where the whole enterprise was headed. For one thing, the arms shipments were not followed by the promised releases of hostages, a repeated foul-up that my Israeli contacts blamed on corruption and double-crossing in Ayatollah Khomeini's office. I also kept hearing from the Israelis that Shultz and Defense Secretary Casper Weinberger vehemently opposed the operation, and it seemed only a matter of time before someone on their staff would leak the story in order to kill the project.

Another nagging worry of those months was my very scant knowledge about the American end of the operation. My sources gave me the names of the Americans they dealt with, but with the Shinbet monitors on the phone, there was no way I could approach them from Jerusalem. At the same time I did not dare tip off my colleagues in New York or Washington for fear of a leak for which Terry Anderson and the other hostages might pay a bitter price.

My tensions eased somewhat doing my home leave the following summer. I tried to get a meeting with McFarlane, but he turned me down. I was more successful in getting to see Ledeen, the NSC's consultant who had met with Peres in 1985, and he gave me some understanding of the administration's side of the operation. But still afraid of a possible leak, I returned to Jerusalem without briefing my colleagues at *Newsweek*, a mistake that backfired in the fall, when the magazine—without checking with me—ran a big story about the hostages whose main point was that nothing was being done to secure their release.

After *As-Shiraa* broke the story of McFarlane's madcap flight to Tehran, I knew it was a mere matter of hours before my editors would start sending voluminous queries. There was nothing for me to wait for. Ignoring the censor, I filed my ready-to-send chronology of the affair to my home office and took the first flight to London to resend it over an uncensored line. I also interviewed Nimrodi about additional details of the operation, but it was wasted effort. The brand new editor of the magazine's foreign section—who had never met me and was skeptical about the details in my files—did the safe thing: he devoted the cover almost entirely to the Irangate and Iran-Contra stories coming out of Washington.

The tale of my unheralded scoop had several footnotes, only two of which are worth retelling because they still give me a chuckle. One happened while I was in London and staying at the old Ritz, one of the town's aging but still prestigious (and expensive) hostelries. I was on the phone with my colleagues in New York and waited to be switched to another editor when the hotel operator suddenly cut in and, in a voice that brooked no dispute, informed me that "Mr. Nimrodi wants to talk to you." With that, she disconnected me from my editors and turned me over to the Israeli arms dealer. Having seen earlier in the day Nimrodi tipping a waiter the equivalent of twenty dollars after a fifty-dollar lunch, I could appreciate the telephone operator's readiness to respond to his bidding, and I began to understand why London is the preferred base of global death merchants.

The other footnote is about the response of the Israeli military censor to my Irangate file, which I had sent on purpose from Jerusalem rather than waiting until I got to London. It was the longest and most official secrets-filled story I had reported from Israel without showing it to the censor, and when I returned from London I was curious about the aftermath.

There was none. No Monday morning phone call, no formal letter of complaint, no summons to appear in the censor's office. There were a couple of possible explanations for the Big Brother's strange lapse. One was the theory suggested by Secretary Shultz—namely, that Peres had intended all along to use *Newsweek* to leak the story, and the censors were instructed to leave my copy alone.

Another, more realistic hypothesis was that the secrecy bureaucrats realized that Irangate was a story of such a resonance in the United States that it would be most unwise, as well as ineffective, for them to try to censor it. Whatever the case, I worked in Israel for more than two more years, without a single unpleasant encounter with the military censor.

CHAPTER 21

MY QUARREL WITH ISRAEL

If the military censor bothered me less in my final years in Israel, my conscience was a different story. The scoops were a massage for the ego, but they did not blind me to my shortcomings in covering the most momentous and dramatic event in Israel, a story that was nobody's secret. The disastrous Israeli occupation of the West Bank and Gaza was a process of far greater importance than the scandals of Irangate, Bus 300 affair, and the spying of Pollard all rolled into one, and it was unwinding day after day in front of everyone's eyes, frequently with a stunning sound and fury. I was one of the few American reporters in the Middle East who had followed the saga since it began in the wake of the Six Day War, two decades earlier. And I knew that my coverage of this history-making process was not doing it justice.

The occupation was an epic tragedy that all of us in the media chronicled as closely and fully as each violent explosion and turn of events called for—yet I, at least, did not tell the real tale. What was happening was far more than Palestinian kids throwing stones at Israeli soldiers and settlers, and Israeli soldiers and settlers shooting back. Hijacked airliners and military invasions made the headlines and the cover stories, but they were mere flashes of the heat caused by the friction between two deadly antagonists.

What was really taking place in the West Bank and Gaza was an inexorable contest between two societies that, I became convinced, would be fought for a long time and change both Israel and the occupied Arabs.

For the Palestinians, the stake was nothing less than their very identity as individuals and their home as a people. Their aspirations were the mirror image of the goals of the founders of the State of Israel: an assertion of their timeless culture, religion, and ownership of the land to which they felt anchored. The greatest terror that animated the occupied Arabs was to be permanently displaced, eradicated like their villages, and scattered to relive the fate of the ancient Hebrew tribes.

I saw these sentiments first taking root in the refugee camps in Lebanon and Jordan after the shock of the Six Day War roused the Palestinians from their soporific expectations of salvation by Arab armies. By the time I came to Jerusalem, it was plain as day that self-reliance and *sumud* (unyielding rejection of the occupation) was the abiding faith of the Palestinians; and Arafat, although personally disdained by many young West Bankers, was their iconic leader. In 1979, when Sadat signed a peace treaty with Israel, the Palestinian inward-turning was hardened by their awareness that they—like the Czechs and Slovaks after Munich—faced their prodigious nemesis on their own.

For Israel, the triumphant Six Day War presented a historic opportunity for achieving the Jewish state's ultimate goal: its acceptance by the millions of Arabs as a legitimate member of the Middle East nations. Yet none of the Israeli leaders I met after the war seemed to give it a thought. Moshe Dayan was "waiting for a phone call" from Cairo. Yigal Alon was waiting for "the rest of the world" to settle the Arab-Israeli conflict. Israel's foremost agenda, Rabin's aide Gershon Avner told me, was to make sure that "the needs of the State of Israel are met." When in the fall of 1967 I asked Ron Medzini, the government spokesman, what Israel planned to do with the occupied Arabs, his answer was "what really matters is that I can drive along the Old City walls and nobody shoots at me."

The reaction of ordinary Israelis to the sea change created by the war reminded me of Golda Meir's famous claim that when she came to Palestine (where, at that time, native Palestinians were estimated to be twice as many as the Jews), "there were no Arabs here." After June 1967 Israelis by the thousands drove to the West Bank to buy the cheaper food and consumer goods or to hire the low-paid Palestinian laborers, but they did not see them as a people.

With some honorable exceptions, there was no recognition of Palestinian grievances and no sense of obligation arising out of Israel's economic exploitation of the captive Arabs and the seizure of their scarce water and their lands. As Weizman told the students in Beersheva, the Jews were calling the shots in the Land of Israel. When stones-throwing Palestinian kids started giving the settlers heartburn in the mid-1970s, they were still perceived as a temporary nuisance, not a threat that could grow and challenge the existence of the Jewish state.

With their eyes averted, the vast majority of Israelis left the occupied territories to the mean-spirited care of nationalist politicians, religious zealots, Shinbet, and IDF's occupation brass whose sole concern was to keep the Arabs quiet. The dreadful job they did created frustrations and anger so searing that a simple car accident in December 1987 triggered a furious outburst of Palestinian violence called *intifada*. It was a foretaste of more savage warfare to come.

~

"Beware of phonies!" my Dad used to say. Watching the Israeli occupation I could only add, "and phony language, Amen." The Israeli craving for Palestinian land spawned fraud, but to me nothing captured the quest for the Likud's Greater Israel better than the occupation newspeak that Begin introduced within a couple of days of his election in 1977.

"Don't call this 'occupied West Bank!'" Begin shouted at the foreign newsmen who accompanied him to the Jewish settlement of Kedumim, at the time still officially disguised as an "encampment of IDF."

"This is 'liberated Judea and Samaria!'" His face flushed with emotion, the Likud prime minister glared at the reporters with a mixture of anger and disdain: "Come on! Can't you make yourselves say it? 'Liberated Judea and Samaria!'"

It was the beginning of a Kafkaesque change in Israel's official terminology for the occupied territories. An area that hadn't been under Jewish sovereignty for almost two millennia became the "legitimate homeland" of thousands of Jewish immigrants. Wholesale land seizures, diversion of water from the West Bank aquifer, and economic exploitation of the natives ceased being predatory and became part of "the return of the rightful owners to their ancestral home."

On any West Bank hill, two rows of prefab modules brought in the stealth of night instantly became "Jewish villages." Generations of Arabs born, raised, and buried in the rugged hills of Palestine became "Arab residents in the Land of Israel," a status only marginally more permanent than foreign tourists.

Under the Israeli laws, the "returning rightful owner" could be any Jew who disembarked from an El-Al Boeing 747 at the Ben Gurion airport and thumbed a ride to a West Bank settlement. I ran into one of these new arrivals, a seventeen-year-old kid from the Bronx, in Kedumim about two weeks after Begin visited the settlement. The youngster was so recent to the Middle East, he didn't even have a suntan, but he felt very much in charge. "Man," he told me, waving his arm expansively toward the hills all around that had been laboriously terraced by generations of Arabs, "this is my homeland."

The corruption of language was only one part of the web of official falsehoods designed to rob the Palestinians while pulling the wool over the eyes of the rest of the world. The process started soon after the Six Day War when the old guard of the Labor Party began seizing chunks of the occupied territories and putting up settlements. When the Likud took over in 1977, it made only one major change: while the Labor's style was to seize Arab land as secretly as possible, Likud was publicly proud of it. Shamir, Begin's successor as prime minister, defended land fraud on the West Bank as a patriotic mission.

What prompted Shamir's indignant comments was a 1983 report by the Israeli Comptroller General that 71 percent of the acquisitions of land in the West Bank that were privately arranged by Jews were marred by "irregularities." The illegal practices of Israeli land dealers and lawyers identified by the Comptroller included the following: hiring of thugs who forced Palestinian peasants at gunpoint to sign away their holdings; use of forged powers of attorney to sell to Jews assets of absentee Arab landowners; and hiring of Arab straw men to buy Palestinian properties that were immediately resold to the government at tenfold the purchase price.

Outright theft was so brazen that in one instance cited by the Comptroller, a West Bank settlement continued to sell lots despite formal complaints by 109 Arabs that the land in question was registered as their property. When Israeli newspapers responded to the report by demanding a police investigation, Prime Minister Shamir decided that the time had come to call a spade a spade. Addressing a Likud meeting, Shamir insisted that the Israeli police "must consider national interests. Sometimes tricks and schemes were needed and unconventional methods were used to purchase land," he said, referring to the Labor Party's practices in the 1940s, and it was "intolerable that a witch hunt should try to block this Zionist mission."

"This Zionist mission," of course, was in no danger of being blocked. In fact, it had been steadily advancing ever since the Six Day War, seventeen years earlier.

The first step of that mission was the IDF's takeover of the so-called Crown Land, a rough equivalent of the New England commons, which for centuries had served as the communal grazing grounds for the sheep and goats of the West Bank villagers. Formally, the Crown Land belonged to whoever was the sovereign in Palestine. But as the Palestinians angrily pointed out, neither the Ottomans, the British, nor the Hashemites ever deprived the villagers of the use of the land, much less settled it with their own people.

The Israelis were the first conquerors to do that. For a while, the IDF would use the confiscated areas as shooting ranges or training grounds but eventually, practically all of the Crown Lands were turned over to Jewish civilian settlements.

After the Crown Land, the Israelis seized the so-called rocky—untilled— land without registered owners, and the land of "absentee landlords," most of whom had fled to Jordan during the Six Day War. When the acreage in these categories was exhausted, the occupiers simply took over Arab land they wanted, regardless of its status. The seizures were almost invariably carried out at night: the villagers would wake up in the morning to find big parcels of their land fenced off by coils of barbed wire and guarded by IDF troops.

What I found most infuriating was the Labor Party's (and later, Likud's) pious insistence that the land seizures had been carried out for "security purposes," and that unauthorized settlements were being "dismantled" by IDF. In fact, the opposite was true: time and again, IDF was the forerunner and the shield of the religious and nationalist extremists who purposely put up their settlements in the most densely populated Arab areas.

The earliest example of this collusion was Kiryat Arba, the first Jewish settlement on the West Bank, which was built after Defense Minister Moshe Dayan lifted his ban on overnight Jewish civilian presence in the occupied territories. That policy lasted from the Six Day War in June 1967 until Passover in April 1968, when an orthodox rabbi, Moshe Levinger, called on Dayan and asked him to allow a small group of religious Jews to pray in Hebron, the second biggest town in the West Bank. Hebron's conservative Muslims were regarded as exceptionally ill-suited for hosting Orthodox Jews, but Dayan recognized the reasons for Levinger's request:

The town's mosque held the tombs of three Jewish biblical patriarchs, including Abraham, the reputed founder of both the Israelites and the Arab people. Almost as important for the Jews was the memory of Hebron as the site where in 1929, raging Arab mobs murdered sixty-nine members of the local Orthodox Jewish community. Recognizing that Levinger's plea stirred some of the deepest Israeli emotions, Dayan told the rabbi to go ahead.

Permission granted, Levinger moved with his flock into Hebron's modest Hotel Park and refused to leave after the holiday ended. When Fayegh Kawasmeh, the hotel owner, asked the IDF to remove his unwanted guests, the local commanding officer, instead of escorting the group back to Israel, put up Levinger and his by then eighty followers inside his own headquarters in the Hebron military compound.

The group stayed there, fed, cared for, and protected by the same soldiers who were supposed to keep Israeli civilians out of the territories, for more than two years. As time went on, the army helped the would-be settlers set up inside the post a makeshift synagogue and a school for their children. Eventually, so many religious zealots and their families moved to the military post that it no longer could hold them. In 1970 Dayan, an Arabic-speaking sabra who was regarded as expert at dealing with the Palestinians, scrapped his own rules completely and authorized the construction of a high-rise Jewish town on Hebron's outskirts.

Rising out of the barren ground like fata morgana in the desert, the government-financed settlement was given the biblical name of Kiryat Arba, and the Levinger's group that moved in became the nucleus of the infamous Gush Emunim, the "Bloc of the Faithful."

His base secured, Levinger set out to Judaize Hebron, a 5500-year-old town populated by 140,000 Muslims and a small group of Christians. In 1979 Miriam, Levinger's American-born wife, led in the middle of a night a group of Kiryat Arba women to the gates of Hadassah, one of the six buildings in the heart of the town that in the 1920s were owned by Jews. IDF soldiers—who supposedly were guarding the mansion against precisely such an invasion— helped the women unload their truck and get settled.

In the morning Begin's defense minister Moshe Arens ordered a beefed-up IDF detachment to set up more outposts around the building and to keep the seething Palestinians at bay. In quick order, the process was repeated with the rest of the formerly Jewish buildings, and within a year, the Gush had established a Jewish quarter in the heart of Hebron that had to be protected by barbed wire and IDF troops stationed on surrounding rooftops.

The next step was the takeover of Hebron's massive, centuries-old Mosque of Abraham. The Orthodox settlers, who were supposed to pray in a small part of the mosque, kept increasing their presence until February 25, 1994, when—while the IDF security guards were helpfully absent—a US-born medical doctor and Gush Emunim settler walked into the mosque during Muslim prayers and opened fire, killing 29 Palestinians. In the ensuing melee, more than 120 other Muslim worshippers were injured before they overcame the assailant and beat him to death. Following that massacre, the Hebron settlers built for the assassin a shrine.

The settlement mania started by Kiryat Arba proved unstoppable and was pursued with equal ardor by practically all Israeli governments. In the early years of the occupation, Labor governments put up most of the settlements on the Golan Heights, a territory belonging to Syria, and in the Jordan Valley. The official justification doggedly repeated by Rabin and other Labor Party leaders was that these were "security" settlements that "would not be an obstacle to peace," a statement that sounded good in Washington but had few, if any, believers in Israel.

The settlement construction became frantic under Begin, who at least did not bother claiming that the shtetls in the territories increased Israel's security. Arik Sharon, as Begin's settlements czar, put the Judaization of the West Bank and Gaza into high gear by promoting private acquisition of Arab land in the hook-or-crook fashion later defended by Shamir, who eventually linked the mushrooming Jewish outposts with highways that bypassed Arab population centers.

By the end of the 1970s the Likud-led West Bank land grab was so rampant that it incurred the public displeasure of President Carter, who called the settlements "illegal," as well as of the Reagan administration, which referred to them more politely as "ill-advised." But tongue-clucking in Washington did not stop the annual US grants to Israel, which then covered 10 percent of the country's budget and, indirectly, freed Israeli funds for the settlements in the occupied areas.

Not to be completely outshone by the Begin government, in 1981 the Labor Party delegation in the Knesset launched a campaign to extend Israeli laws, jurisdiction, and administration to the occupied Syrian Golan Heights, which amounted to their annexation by Israel. The prime minister who signed the decree was Begin, but the roughly seventy-member Knesset "lobby" that pushed through the measure was headed by Avraham "Katzele" Katz, a senior Labor deputy, and included more MKs from the Labor Party than from the Likud.

In December 1982 the IDF was bogged down in a bloody and highly expensive invasion of Lebanon; Israeli inflation was pushing toward 100 percent a year; and the nearly one hundred West Bank settlements already in place were running out of religious and nationalist settlers. Still, the Begin government felt so secure in its support from Washington that it authorized $830 million for the construction of another thirty-five West Bank outposts.

After Shamir stood up for "tricks and schemes" in the territories, the creative Peres—the rotation government's 1984–1986 prime minister and a latter-day Nobel Prize–winning "peace maker"—made the West Bank communities more attractive to secular settlers by giving them special tax breaks and direct subsidies. Thanks to this policy, in the fall of 1986, a typical new two-bedroom apartment in a West Bank settlement sold for forty thousand dollars, less than half of the going price for similar housing in Israel.

By the time I left the country in November 1988, the Levinger-launched crusade in the West Bank had succeeded beyond his wildest dreams. In Peres's two years at the helm alone, construction started on 5,000 new West Bank apartments, and the Jewish population in the territories increased by 13,000. The population of Ariel, a big settlement not far from Nablus, increased from 2,500 when Peres took office to 6,000 two years later.

The skullcap-wearing religious-nationalist fanatics were still the dominant element among the more than 120,000 Israelis in the territories and the new Jewish suburbs of Jerusalem, but the term "settler" was no longer synonymous with membership in Gush Emunim. In fact, the Labor Party had so many members and sympathizers in the occupied areas that it opened a branch office in Ariel. According to a newspaper report Maale Adunim, a major settlement between Jerusalem and Jericho, was the home of two members of the "Peace Now!" movement, the most vehement Jewish group opposing the settlements and the continued occupation.

The uncrowded environment and ersatz pioneering spirit of the Jewish outposts attracted to the West Bank so many American supporters of Israel that Tehiya, Geula Cohen's far-rightist party, in 1984 tried to use their political clout to defeat the long-standing US ban on tax-deductible donations for the settlements. The mission was entrusted to Yisrael "Winkie" Medad, an American-born Tehiya spokesman in the Knesset, who traveled to Washington to argue that the ban hurt the interests of nine thousand dual US-Israeli citizens in the settlements—all of whom, he pointed out, were registered to vote in the upcoming US presidential elections.

In my years in the Middle East, it was one of the rare Israeli missions to Washington that didn't succeed. For one thing, President Reagan was riding so high in the polls that the nine thousand votes in Israel did not matter. And more to the point, the GOP probably knew that Medad could not deliver them for Reagan, anyway. Curious as it sounds, the Americans settlers voted in Israel for Tehiya and other far-right parties, but in the US races they predominantly cast their absentee ballots for the Democrats. Like the alleged dovishness of the Labor Party, the American settlers were another example of the deceitful reality in the Middle East.

~

If the Israeli "tricks and schemes" to seize Arab land were arrogant and shameful, the way the IDF, the security agencies, and Israeli courts controlled the occupied people was unworthy of a country pretending to democratic values. The most widely and indiscriminately used mechanism—particularly by the purportedly "liberal" Labor Party governments—was the so-called administrative detention. A legal lacuna as big as the Mediterranean, the policy enabled the Shinbet to warehouse thousands of Palestinians behind bars without charging them with anything or putting them on trial.

Theoretically limited to six months, the detention could be and was repeatedly reauthorized for another half a year by helpful judges on the agency's say-so. Ironically, the only prime minister who during my years in Israel objected to administrative detentions was the arch-hawkish Begin, who had been a political prisoner himself. He ordered the practice stopped, but Shamir and Peres brought it back after the Likud leader stepped down in 1983.

The next most favored control mechanism was secret trials based on so-called voluntary admissions of guilt that were almost invariably obtained under duress. Israeli governments kept denying the use of torture for many years, but by late 1980s the evidence was so overwhelming that even the military censors stopped excising the reported incidents in Israeli newspapers.

According to scores of testimonies, Shinbet's favorite (and least labor-intensive) method for breaking down prisoners was to put heavy hoods over their head and keep them standing against the wall day and night. In winter, the interrogators added to the fatigue and sensory deprivation the intense discomfort from cold showers and lack of heat. After several days of this treatment, most exhausted prisoners signed whatever was put in front of them. The Shinbet was so confident of the judges' blanket acceptance of the agency's charges that the signed "confessions" were frequently written in Hebrew, which most of the interrogated Arabs couldn't read.

The third method of keeping the Palestinians in check—and the one most feared by the Arabs—was expulsion, which was done by simply putting the victims in a jeep or a helicopter and dumping them across the border in Lebanon or Jordan. Theoretically, expulsions were supposed to be authorized by a court. But although most Israeli judges were cooperative, the military government or Shinbet frequently expelled the undesirable Arabs first and took care of the paperwork later. This shameful system, incidentally, was aided by scores of West Bank and Gaza Palestinians who had been blackmailed or bribed to become Shinbet and IDF informers.

After the flop of Peres's naive attempt in 1976 to elect subservient West Bank mayors, the Israeli occupation authorities focused on controlling the Palestinian towns by manipulating their elected new leaders. An important victim of this policy was Karim Khalaf, the mayor of Ramallah, a town that competed with the nearby East Jerusalem as the Palestinian political capital. A Christian lawyer and an affluent landlord with a penchant for loud vests and natty suits, Khalaf was by no means an easy man to control—if anything, he was a strong-willed rogue who did things his own way. After the Six Day War, while the PLO's resources and influence were low and King Hussein's prestige in the occupied West Bank was high, Khalaf hewed to a pro-Jordanian course and repeatedly defied Arafat's bidding.

In the fall of 1967, for example, Khalaf, a lawyer, refused to stop defending Palestinians in the occupation courts despite a PLO-ordered strike by West Bank attorneys. He defied the PLO's call for a boycott again in 1972, when he ran in the Israeli-supervised municipal elections and was elected mayor.

But after Arafat's PLO won in November 1974 the Arab League's recognition (and multi-million-dollar subsidies) as the "sole representative" of the occupied Palestinians, Khalaf swung around. In 1976, when he ran for reelection, he wooed his constituency by denouncing the occupation, mouthing Arafat's anti-American slogans, and bragging about his ties with the PLO. The star example of the folly of Peres's confidently predicted "conservative landslide," Khalaf won more than 80 percent of the votes.

Khalaf liked to talk big, but he was not a mere windbag. A couple of months after his reelection I watched him march with an open Koran in his arms at the head of a massive funeral of a five-year-old local boy who had been shot dead by an Israeli soldier. The killing of a small child who had thrown stones at the settlers infuriated Arabs all over the occupied territories, and the IDF only made things worse by sticking to its routine claim that the soldiers had fired only "over the heads of the demonstrators." As the angry slogans-shouting and ululating funeral procession wound its way through the heart of Ramallah, it seemed only a matter of time before the mourners would charge the IDF jeeps trailing the procession.

Khalaf, aware of the explosive atmosphere, halted the march outside the house of the boy's parents, handed the Koran to an *ulema* (a learned Muslim), and climbed to the balcony where he made a short speech. What he said was unexceptional—he merely asked the town people to save their anger for another day, and let the boy's family bury their son in peace. What astonished me was the response of the crowd of several thousand highly emotional Arabs. Within minutes, some began drifting away, and the mood of the funeral changed from nasty to somber. It was obvious that, among his own, Khalaf, like most of the 1976 crop of West Bank mayors, was a leader.

But as Khalaf soon found out, commanding personality was not enough for surviving an occupation that above all required steely nerves. The first blows he suffered after his reelection were delivered by the most loathsome creature in Israeli politics, the American-born rabbi, political leader and Knesset member Meir Kahane. Whether because of Khalaf's religion, his newly discovered admiration for Arafat, or simply the town's proximity to Jerusalem, Kahane picked Ramallah as the prime target of small pogroms carried out by the followers of his party called Kach! (Thus!) Kach! was an openly racist group whose program, symbolized by a clenched fist, was to expel all Arabs from Greater Israel. The treatment visited by Kahane's thugs on the partly Christian Ramallah and Al-Birreh, its Muslim twin town, was worthy of the antisemitic rampages in Hitler's Germany.

Kahane would wait until some incident involving the IDF would raise the tensions in the territories. Then, late at night, he would assemble a squad of his armed young goons in yellow T-shirts and drive them in a big van to Ramallah. With a roof-mounted loudspeaker at full blast, the violent band would cruise through town screaming that the West Bank belonged to the Jews, and that all Arabs must get out. While the rabbi shrieked, his hoodlums would imitate the infamous Nazi Kristallnacht by smashing the windows and windshields of parked cars.

The assaults would inevitably extract a stiff price beyond the broken glass. The first to pay was Khalaf who would run to his office and call the local IDF command post to demand intervention to stop the mayhem. No help ever came, and the mayor, who had a short temper and a bad heart, would spend the rest of the night chain-smoking Marlboros and pacing his office in an apoplectic rage.

In the morning, the Ramallah school kids would add to the frenzied atmosphere by holding an especially noisy stone-throwing demo, which the Israeli troops—now ready to enforce law and order—would stop with real bullets and teargas, and sometimes slap a curfew on all twenty-five thousand people in town. As if that were not punishment enough, the next time Kahane pulled duty as an IDF reservist, the colonels in IDF's Beit El headquarters would assign him to a street patrol in the heart of Ramallah, the Tel-al-Zaatar Circle. The idea presumably was to teach the Arabs who was the boss.

Israeli settlers whose cars were frequently stoned by the kids while driving through Ramallah also singled out the town for their vengeance. For example, in the late 1970s a group of armed Gush Emunim types invaded Ramallah at night and systematically thrashed more than a hundred cars parked in the streets. Not long after that excursion, Israeli TV showed memorable footage of several settlers in knitted skullcaps shooting at the town's demonstrating kids. The most striking part of the footage was the deliberate, unemotional way the vigilantes aimed and squeezed off their rounds, as if they were duck-hunting or on a rifle range. Next to official fraud, brutality—both of the red-hot Kahane variety and of the racially superior kind of many religious-nationalist settlers—was a hallmark of the Israeli occupation.

For all the harassment that preceded it, Khalaf's worst fate followed the Camp David meeting in October 1978 where Carter, Begin, and Sadat agreed to conduct negotiations for autonomy for the West Bank and Gaza. Just before the three leaders met, Khalaf, to his great surprise, received permission from Ramallah's Israeli military governor to visit the United States for a PLO conference whose purpose was to denounce Sadat's policy of making peace with Israel. Considering the nature of the gathering and Khalaf's radical politics, the governor's leniency was, to say the least, puzzling.

The plot thickened the morning after the Camp David accords were signed in Washington. As Khalaf later told me, he got a phone call in his hotel room from the same military governor who had let him take the trip, this time ordering him to return immediately to Ramallah. Upon his arrival, the IDF officer gave Khalaf the even more mind-boggling news that the occupation authorities had authorized the formation of a new leadership body for the occupied territories, called the National Gui Council (NGC). The group was to be composed primarily of the West Bank and Gaza mayors—and Khalaf, the military governor added, was free to become a member. It was an astounding proposition: it was clear on the face of it that the new body would be a proxy of Arafat's PLO.

Khalaf's first theory was that the IDF authorized the creation of the Council so as to give more prominence to local leaders and thereby undermine Arafat. The twenty-two members of the NGC shared Khalaf's brand of ambitious activism, and their emergence as spokesmen for the occupied Arabs was likely to cause Abu Ammar some worry. But long before posing any threat to Arafat, Khalaf and his colleagues went on perform an even more essential service for their occupiers: they made mincemeat of the Camp David autonomy proposal, which Arafat had rejected and Begin was determined to sabotage.

Excited by the unprecedented Israeli tolerance for his inflammatory oratory, Khalaf and the rest of the Palestinian mayors went on a rhetorical binge to denounce the Camp David accords as a Zionist-American plot to continue the occupation and deny Palestinians their own state. Echoing Arafat, the NGC warned that any Palestinian who'd agree to take part in the negotiations called for by Camp David would be a traitor. As the Israelis undoubtedly planned, the unleashing of Khalaf and his peers buried whatever chance there might have been for the success of the Camp David agreements. The results again confirmed Abba Eban's observation that the PLO "never missed an opportunity to miss an opportunity."

While the autonomy talks limped along in a rapidly deteriorating atmosphere and with only US, Israeli, and Egyptian participation, a special Knesset committee worked out an elaborate catalogue of injunctions that would have reduced the Palestinian self-rule to little more than an authority for garbage collection. The preemptive legislation, however, was hardly necessary. Without Palestinian cooperation, the Camp David formula for gradual dismantling of the West Bank and Gaza occupation regime became a dead letter. Begin's nagging worries about the meaning of the "legitimate rights" of the occupied Arabs were over.

To compound the self-inflicted injury, the NGC's rhetoric so enraged the Gush Emunim vigilantes that they launched a series of violent attacks on Palestinian targets. Before the Shinbet finally rounded them up, the Jewish terrorists had tried to place demolition charges around the Dome of the Rock, the third holiest shrine of the Muslims; gunned down students in broad daylight on the Hebron university campus; and—long before Palestinian terrorists did this to Jews—put bombs on Arab buses in East Jerusalem. Their most significant assault, however, was on the Palestinian leadership.

One morning in April 1980, as Khalaf started his aging Oldsmobile to go to work, a bomb under the hood ripped apart the front end of the car and tore off his foot. At just about the same time, similar explosions blew off both legs of Bassam Shakaa, the mayor of Nablus. The mayors of Al-Birreh and Hebron, whose cars had also been booby-trapped, did not drive to work that day and escaped injury, but the bomb in the car of the Al-Birreh mayor blinded an Israeli bomb demolition expert who tried to defuse it.

The assassinations ended the career of Khalaf and the NGC. After several months in Jordanian and American hospitals, both Khalaf and Shakaa returned to work, but with the autonomy talks safely buried, the Israeli military administration dismantled the Council, banned all public meetings, and put the mayors back on a short leash. Silenced, dispirited, and rendered ineffectual, some of the elected mayors resigned and some lingered on until March 1982, when the last holdouts—with the single exception of Elias Freij in Bethlehem—were summarily fired by the Israeli military administration. Khalaf, who never fully recovered from his injuries, died three years later while still in his fifties.

By then the West Bank IDF command introduced the most despicable control scheme of my years in Israel. Called the Village Leagues, it consisted of bands of Israeli-armed and -financed Palestinian criminals, thugs, and quislings who were rightly regarded by the rest of the Palestinians as the scum of the earth. According to the IDF reserve intelligence colonel and Hebrew University professor who invented the stratagem, the Leagues were supposed to represent the allegedly "apolitical silent majority" of the West Bank peasants. What they really represented was the professor's colonial mind and the dismal depths to which Israel had sunk by trying to dominate an entire people.

Propped up by the military governors and Beit El's IDF brass, the hand-picked hoodlums for a while became the sole address for any mukhtar who wanted to repair a road in his village or a peasant who tried to get his son out of an Israeli jail. But although the Shamir government funded the scheme with several hundred thousand dollars, the West Bankers rejected it utterly.

Ignored and isolated, the Leagues vanished within two years, whereupon their author applied for a sabbatical as an "international scholar" with the Woodrow Wilson Center in the Smithsonian Institute in Washington. The nefarious saga, however, had a deadly footnote after the outbreak of the intifada less than four years later. The "apolitical" peasants rounded up many of the former Village Leaguers and summarily executed them by hanging.

If the collapse of the Likud-bred Village Leagues held any message for the occupiers it was lost on Peres, who shortly afterwards took the helm of the government as the first rotation prime minister. Still searching for Palestinians opposed to the PLO, Peres resumed the traditional secret Israeli huddles with King Hussein, which the king had declined to hold when Begin was in power.

Meeting in the king's palace outside Amman, Peres and Hussein worked out a scheme far more ambitious than the Leagues. It was based on the same idea Peres had expounded at length at a background briefing shortly after I came to Jerusalem: divide the West Bank between Israel and Jordan. The so-called Israeli-Jordanian condominium was to return the West Bank population under Jordanian administration and sovereignty while leaving Israel in physical control of the occupied area.

The plan enjoyed a brief flowering in 1986, mainly thanks to the support that Peres gave to Hussein's last-ditch attempt to win the allegiance of the occupied people. Under their proposed "condominium," King Hussein was to boost the West Bank economy with development aid worth $1.3 billion. Peres's role was to authorize the reopening of the Nablus branch of the Bank of Cairo and Amman—which used to be the West Bank's main financial link with the rest of the Arab world—and to permit the king's emissaries to call on the West Bank mayors and mukhtars to discuss how the money would be spent.

There was a brief flurry of excitement, but the whole scheme collapsed when Arafat denounced it as a "Zionist plot," the Persian Gulf sheikhs refused to donate any money, and worst of all, the delegations of West Bank notables who were supposed to troop to the king's palace to proffer their fealty had failed to materialize. The IDF still tried to keep the "condominium" alive by appointing to it nine West Bank mayors selected by the king, and by permitting the publishing in East Jerusalem of *An Nahar*, a Palestinian newspaper that was subsidized by and reflected the views of the king's palace. Both measures failed to weaken the Palestinian sumud.

When Peres stepped down as the rotation prime minister in the fall of 1986, the total failure of the condominium was confirmed by the first respectable opinion poll ever conducted in the territories. Designed by an American-educated Palestinian professor and carried out by university students in Nablus, the survey found that 93.5 percent of the West Bankers regarded the PLO as their "sole representative," 71 percent supported Arafat, and only 3.4 percent professed loyalty to King Hussein of Jordan The IDF occupation bosses in Beit El were so incensed by the findings that they refused to renew the work permit of the survey's author, a naturalized US citizen who taught at the Nablus University. The professor had to leave the territories, but nobody—including the king—contested the results of the poll.

Although the following year king Hussein secretly hosted Shamir for dinner in London (a puzzling honor the monarch had never extended to Begin), the Hashemite made no further attempt to cobble another Israeli–Jordanian Palestinian control system. In July 1988, he publicly renounced his promise of the never-delivered $1.3 billion aid to the West Bank and—except for his guardianship of the al Aqsa mosque and Dome of the Rock in Jerusalem—officially ceded the responsibility for the West Bank to the PLO.

Which was just as well. By then the occupied Palestinians had undergone a change so profound that they were beyond the control of not only the king and the Israelis, but even Arafat.

CHAPTER 22

THE WEST BANKERS

In the 1970s and 1980s, Karim Khalaf's Ramallah, a former summer haven of desert Arabs not rich enough to vacation in Switzerland, was one of the most charming spots in the West Bank. From afar, the town looked like a painting in subtle watercolors. It was gracefully spread out over a gentle hill, and on most sunny days its ochre stone walls, green pines, and faded red tile roofs exuded peace and comfort. In Ramallah's Tel-al-Zaatar Circle, a star-like junction of five dusty streets, squat, look-alike houses defied order by flaunting a profusion of grocers, furniture makers, butchers, and machine shops flanked by pushcarts piled high with green almonds and freshly baked pita. Further up the hill, away from the pungent aroma of spices and coffee with cardamom, out of the earshot of the cacophony of banging hammers, shouting shopkeepers, and honking cars, a cluster of missionary-run schools, the town's pride, overlooked campuses of shady trees and well-kept lawns.

Beyond Ramallah, a sweeping landscape of timeless hills not quite high enough to be called mountains bewitched the visitor with two alternating images. In the spring, for less than four orgasmic weeks, their slopes exploded with lush green grass, fiery red poppies, and a wondrously dense carpet of tiny, vividly blue, white, and yellow desert flowers. Then, as if by magic, the exuberant show abruptly vanished and all that met the eye were gray outcroppings of porous volcanic rock, bushes of bright-yellow thistle, and hawks circling silently in the sky. To the east, air trembling with summer heat gave way to the haze over the Dead Sea; to the west sparkled the Mediterranean.

Along the road from Ramallah to Nablus, rows of stone terraces and gnarled olive trees cradled somnolent valleys with bone-dry wadis dreaming of the winter rains. A flock of sheep would come into view, dutifully trotting behind a bell-jangling goat and an old peasant straddling the rump of a curiously tiny donkey. Otherwise, silence and eternity beckoned beyond each twist of the road. When I worked in Beirut I used to marvel at the fervent longing of the refugees to reclaim their country because, as the wife of a Palestinian professor tried to explain, "Palestine is special." Standing outside Ramallah, I thought I understood.

Ramallah was founded four centuries ago by Christian Arabs from Karnak in Jordan who moved to the West Bank to get away from their Muslim neighbors. Over the years, they made their town an important hub of Palestinian commerce; they welcomed American missionaries who founded in Ramallah the West Bank's best schools; and in the late 1940s, they helped their twin town Al-Birreh and thirteen nearby UN refugee camps to absorb tens of thousands of refugees from the coastal plains conquered by the Yishuv's army, the Hagana. In the 1970s and 1980s, Ramallah was no longer an all-Christian enclave, but its atmosphere still differed from the rest of the West Bank: it hinted at the possibility of peace between the Israelis and the Palestinians.

The key exponent of this goal was one of the early coastal refugees who settled in Ramallah. Aziz Shehadeh was a courtly, gentle-mannered lawyer who became my Palestinian counterpart of Israel's Rabbi Steinsaltz: a man on whom I called for the pleasure of his thoughtful mind and his insight. He was the living symbol of the brave, arduous, and ultimately frustrated early attempts of some Palestinians to find a peaceful answer to the enormous upheaval in their lives caused by the birth of Israel.

Shehadeh was a gentleman, a maverick, and a man of great integrity and without an ounce of pretense. He was short and slight and his round, boyish face gave him the looks of a prematurely aged child. What the air of frailty disguised was a steely backbone that enabled him to withstand the pressures of his community and keep a mind of his own. The lawyer showed his mettle already in 1949, the year after he fled to Ramallah from his family home in the Hagana-occupied seaside town of Jaffa. The exodus plunged most of the refugees into convulsive hatred of Israel, but Shehadeh drew from it a different lesson. He recognized that the Palestinian tragedy would not be reversed by the Arab armies, which were no match for Israel's IDF.

He also realized that under the authoritarian rule of the Jordanian King Abdullah, the grandfather of Hussein, Westernized Christians like himself would have no future. Showing remarkable courage, Shehadeh organized in Ramallah a congress of Palestinian notables and put before them a radical proposal: the creation of an independent West Bank entity that would be loosely linked with Jordan and sign a peace treaty with Israel.

Decades later, Shehadeh's idea became the holy grail of Western diplomats, but in 1949 it was far too advanced for both the Arabs and Israel. The European-born founders of the new Jewish state wanted to deal only with established Arab regimes. The West Bank peasants had more confidence in the Hashemites than in an urban, non-Muslim, suit-and-necktie-wearing lawyer.

And in the eyes of the Amman regime, Shehadeh was a dangerous Palestinian nationalist. Instead of independence, in 1950 the West Bank notables voted to accept the Jordanian rule, whereupon Shehadeh's forebodings came true. He was twice arrested by the kingdom's security agency, the Mukhabarat, and exiled for thirteen months to Egypt.

A less spunky man would have learned his lesson, but not Shehadeh. When I first met him on a visit from Beirut, barely two months after the Six Day War, he was back to his old tricks, once again trying to make peace between Israel and the Palestinians. This time, Shehadeh wanted to put before his people his old proposal in a more elaborate form: in exchange for IDF's withdrawal from the occupied territories, the West Bankers would establish their own demilitarized entity, sign a peace treaty with Israel, and enter into a federation with the Kingdom of Jordan.

Unlike in 1949, Shehadeh was no longer alone. Impressed by Israel's armed might, a group of prominent West Bank professionals and businessmen joined him in petitioning Israel's prime minister Levi Eshkol to allow them to submit Shehadeh's plan to a West Bank plebiscite.

His plan should have been Israel's dream come true, but once again the timing was wrong, and all Shehadeh got was a high-level runaround. Defense minister Moshe Dayan asked Shehadeh six questions focused on whose side the Palestinian state would take in the Cold War. Foreign minister Abba Eban wanted to know who would be the leaders of the new entity. Only the third Israeli who met with Shehadeh, Prime Minister Eshkol, seemed to the lawyer to be sympathetic to the proposal. But even Eshkol, who two years before the Six Day War called for an Arab-Israeli mutual security pact within the 1949 ceasefire lines, was not ready to authorize the plebiscite.

By the time Shehadeh finished his rounds in Tel Aviv and Jerusalem, the occupation was more than six months old, and the Arab-Israeli conflict began picking up new momentum. It was not toward peace. In Israel, descendants of Labor Party settlers who in 1948 had fled from three kibbutzim near Hebron were demanding the right to return, and Begin, Shamir, Rabbi Levinger, and other right-wingers were lobbying for the Judaization of all conquered areas. In August 1967—two months after the war—the humiliated members of the Arab League met in Khartoum and adopted the policy of three No's—no peace, no negotiations, and no recognition of Israel. It was a senseless gesture, but it slammed the door on the peace plans of both Shehadeh and Eshkol.

In November, the UN Security Council poured fuel into the Arab anger by adopting Resolution 242, which did not require Israel to withdraw from all of the occupied territories in exchange for peace, and referred to the Palestinians as mere "refugees" who would not be a party to the proposed settlement. This prompted the resolution's rejection by the Arab governments. Levi Eshkol was able to accept the UN formula only after months of wrangling with right-wingers in his cabinet and Begin, the champion of Greater Israel, quit in protest as Eshkol's deputy.

In the winter that followed, clashes between the PLO's fedayeen and the IDF along the River Jordan began to create the first Palestinian fighting legends, and Shehadeh realized that in the new atmosphere his plebiscite, even if authorized, would probably fail. A new window of opportunity briefly opened during the "Black September" of 1970 when the Jordanian crackdown on the fedayeen so embittered the occupied Arabs that, Shehadeh believed, they would have accepted his proposal just to get even with King Hussein.

By then, however, the Israeli government had lost all interest in the project. Levinger's group was in Hebron, Dayan had authorized the construction of Kiryat Arba, and for many Israelis, the heady vision of Greater Israel looked better than Shehadeh's two-state idea. His peace plebiscite was definitely buried in 1974, when the Arab League's summit in Rabat made the PLO "the sole representative" of all Palestinians. Happy with that promise of self-government, the increasingly nationalistic West Bankers and Gazans rallied behind Arafat's Maoist slogan of "revolution" that "grows from the barrel of the gun," and his illusory call for armed struggle against Israel.

The next ten years taught Shehadeh still more lessons about the hazards of Middle East peace making. His son Raja, a lawyer and a writer, displeased the IDF colonels at Beit El by publishing in the States *The Third Way*, a book arguing that the Palestinians could outlast the Israeli rule by simply staying on their remaining land, regardless of the hardships. The occupation authority punished him by ignoring his request for permission to publish a law review to help sort out the mind-boggling mix of Jordanian and Israeli rules in force in the occupied territories.

Aziz Shehadeh had also an unfriendly official encounter, this time with his old nemesis, the Mukhabarat. While he was visiting Amman, the king's enforcers seized Shehadeh's Jordanian passport and sent him back to the occupied territory without a document he needed for his occasional trip abroad to escape the West Bank pressure cooker.

Worst of all as the years went by, any departure from Arafat's writ became punishable by a brutal beating or worse at the hands of the PLO goons, and Shehadeh's peaceful message became a Palestinian anathema. In the mid-1970s, when he refused to join in the adulation of Abu Ammar's "revolution," Shehadeh became the target of viciously threatening calls but—since Shinbet encouraged strife among the occupied Arabs—had no protection. "People like me," the lawyer once told me, "live in a jungle."

Following the Camp David agreement, Shehadeh further infuriated the PLO by ignoring Arafat's ban on any exploration of the proposal for a West Bank autonomy. Braving menacing messages from the PLO underground, he discussed the issue with visiting presidents Jimmy Carter and Anwar Sadat. He also became the spokesman of a small group of West Bank mayors and notables who tried to keep the autonomy option alive by meeting with American and Egyptian diplomats even as the proposal withered from PLO and Israeli hostility.

Radio broadcasts from Damascus called Shehadeh "a traitor" and accused him of trying to "sell the Palestinians' birthright," but the West Bank radicals held back until mid-1980s, when rumors swept Ramallah accusing Shehadeh of participation in a bitterly contested land deal. In December 1985, at the age of seventy-three, Aziz Shehadeh was attacked outside his house, knocked to the ground, and repeatedly and savagely stabbed to death. A year later, the PLO underground killed Nablus mayor Zafer al-Masri, another Palestinian patriot I knew who refused to tow Arafat's line. Neither the all-knowing Shinbet nor the impotent West Bank police apprehended the murderers.

Savagery was Arafat's increasingly common approach as he cast around in the 1970s and 1980s for ways of punishing Israel and its ally and protector, the United States. The mindless terrorism during those years added hideous bloodshed and grief to an atmosphere already contaminated by the hatred-driven terrorism of "red armies" and "popular struggle" movements. Carried out—sometimes with foreign help—by radicals born and raised in refugee camps in Jordan and Lebanon, many of the so-called actions by "martyrs of the Palestinian revolution" were butchery in political camouflage.

The methods varied from airline hijacking to suicide attacks by boat and even by motorized kites flown across Israel's border from Lebanon, but the victims were almost invariably unarmed civilians and frequently included children. Except for terrifying the Israelis, providing an excuse for their callous control system in the territories, and appalling the civilized world, the bloodshed accomplished absolutely nothing.

Inside the occupied territories, however, the 1970s saw the rise of a spontaneous resistance to the Israeli rule that took a dramatically different form. It was a revolt in the streets of Palestinian towns and villages that was carried out entirely by kids less than sixteen years old—boys and girls too young to receive adult sentences if caught.

Left alone, as Moshe Dayan recommended, their loud protest demos could have been a brief and futile footnote to the West Bank history. Instead, the IDF's dogged attempts to quell the rallies lent them the irresistible appeal of a David challenging a Goliath: kids throwing stones at soldiers who responded with tear gas and bullets. The harder the IDF fought back, the more the sound, smoke, and fury of the children's uprising spread throughout the West Bank towns and villages.

Inevitably, Ramallah, the "Athens" of the occupied territories, produced more of these demos than any other Palestinian town. With its two dozen schools, it had the most children; a hospital that took care of the wounded; several lawyers who defended the arrested protesters; and a good number of well-to-do merchants and professionals who could help pay the fines meted out to the culprits' parents. Although every occupied town and village held many protest rallies, in Ramallah, street fighting became a part of growing up under the occupation.

Whether the occasion was an anniversary of the Balfour declaration that promised a Jewish "national homeland" in Palestine, or the killing of a demonstrator in a nearby village, the response of the Ramallah's hillside schools was so predictable that I—and, usually, a convoy of IDF troops—used to get there in time for the kids' eager action. They poured out of their classrooms at the start of the school day, marched to the Tel-al-Zaatar Circle, and engaged the waiting IDF soldiers in a battle as stylized as an eighteenth-century duel.

With the girls striding up front and the youngest boys prancing along the flanks, the procession would advance within a stone's throw of the troops. The kids would chant defiance to the occupation while the merchants would pull down the shutters to cover the store windows. Finally, the smallest demonstrators—kids no more than six years old—would dart forward and fling the first stones at the soldiers. The troops, by now tense and angry, would leap out of their vehicles and charge the protesters with sticks, tear gas, and live ammunition. Most of the kids would run for cover, but the bravest teenagers would rub their faces with sliced onions to ease the sting of the fumes and keep throwing stones until they, too, would scatter.

Invariably, the showdown would be over by noon. The shopkeepers would run up the shutters and the pushcart vendors would reclaim the sidewalks. The breeze from the desert would replace the stinking smoke, and the streets would fill with traffic. The one o'clock afternoon news roundup on Kol Israel would include a standard IDF announcement that the soldiers had dispersed demonstrators by "firing in the air," a mantra that gave rise to an Israeli joke that the wounded kids were "low-flying Arabs."

But Arafat's faux "revolution," the kids' rebellion, was far from a wasted effort. Their protests were a staple for the foreign news media, whose coverage kept the Palestinian resistance before the eyes of the world. The persistence of the street duels was a morale booster for the youngsters' parents, a generation that was disheartened by decades of Arab defeats. But most important was the impact of the protest culture on the young Palestinians. As Subha Taweel, my then-twelve-year-old best source on the kids' revolt in Ramallah (and, years later, the wife of Arafat) told me, the youngsters had learned they could successfully harass the mighty IDF. The enemy that had routed their parents was defied by their chutzpah and wits. In later years, this lesson fueled the flames of the intifadas.

And it was this highly nationalistic and self-confident Palestinian generation that in the late 1970s and early 1980s became the beneficiary of what may well have been one of the worst blunders of the occupation. It was to give thousands of young West Bankers a cheap and easy access to higher education, most of it in Western-style universities and colleges.

An intelligence colonel in Beit El once tried to explain the Israeli mistake by telling me with a straight face that, when the Palestinians asked for a permission to open new colleges, the Jews as "the People of the Book could not say 'no.'" This was ridiculous. No Israeli government had allowed the establishment of any institute of higher learning for the Israeli Arabs who were taxpaying citizens of the Jewish state and by the end of the 1980s made up more than 16 percent of its population. Moreover, it was widely known in Israel that petitions for the opening of an Israeli-Arab university had been repeatedly vetoed by Shinbet on the grounds that it would likely train leaders for an Arab "fifth column" in the Galilee.

Yet when it came to higher education in the territories, the military government was not just accommodating: it was generous. In 1972 it allowed the opening of a shari'a, an Islamic university, in Hebron. The following year, the Vatican received permission to found a Catholic university in Bethlehem. In 1975, the small, fifty-year-old college in Bir Zeit was given the go-ahead to carry out a major expansion that included the construction of a spacious modern campus and raised its status to a full-fledged university.

Two years later, the military administration approved similar enlargement of the college of Al-Najah in Nablus. And in 1978, the Israelis authorized the al-Azhar Islamic University in Cairo to open a branch in Gaza. By the mid 1980s, one-half of the Palestinian women and one-third of Palestinian men over the age of forty were still illiterate, but about 1 percent of the 1.3 million occupied Palestinians was getting a college education.

In the case of the two shari'as, the motive behind the Israeli benevolence was fairly obvious: by favoring Islam, the military administration hoped to undercut the clout of the secular, arch-nationalistic PLO. The scheme monumentally backfired when the shari'as became the breeding ground for Hamas, the feverishly militant Islamic movement dedicated to the destruction of Israel.

The permission for the Bethlehem university was more difficult to interpret, and there was no visible reason at all for allowing the expansion of Bir Zeit and al-Najah, the two large universities whose payrolls and tuitions were heavily subsidized by the Persian Gulf sheikhdoms.

For me, what explained this puzzle was that this sudden tolerance for an unprecedented upgrading of Palestinian skills was accompanied by Israeli refusal to allow any economic development in the West Bank and Gaza. During my thirteen years in Israel, I repeatedly heard complaints from the occupied Arabs about Israeli denials of their requests to start a cement factory or set up a simple manufacturing plant. Private American aid organizations were tied up in endless Israeli red tape whenever they tried to improve the West Bank's decrepit infrastructure. There was no question that the Israeli policy was to prevent economic growth that might enable the young educated Palestinians to find suitable jobs in the occupied territories.

With only about 100–150 white-collar jobs in the West Bank and Gaza opening each year, the vast majority of the Palestinian graduates who left the new universities each year had only two options for making a living. They could either do unskilled labor in Israel or accept lucrative positions in the oil-rich sheikhdoms. Seen against the background of Yisrael Koenig's doctrine in the Galilee, this dilemma explained the Israeli acquiescence in Palestinian schooling. The universities were meant to be way stations for the exodus of the territories' best and brightest, the young elites who presumably would not be allowed to come back.

That scheme backfired even worse than the rest of Israeli attempts to manipulate the Palestinians. First of all, the job-hunting emigration did not take place. By the time I left Israel, an estimated twelve thousand Palestinian college students and graduates worked as waiters or day laborers in Israel rather than repeating the mistake of the generation of their parents who had fled, only to be denied the right to return. The lessons of 1948 and 1949 had finally sunk in, and among the youngsters the appeal of sumud was stronger than the lure of big paychecks.

Even more important, the new access to higher education produced a profound societal change, especially in the West Bank. A key element was the generosity of Saudi Arabia, Kuwait, and other oil-rich emirates that financed the school construction and paid the tuition for virtually every West Bank or Gaza youngster who was bright enough to enroll.

As thousands of children—one-third of them girls—of the dirt-poor fellahin (peasants) seized the opportunity, the schools became the breeding ground for new Palestinian elites—and this happened while their teachers increasingly included Israeli Arab and Palestinians who were US-educated and, frequently, American citizens. They were as apt to preach democracy as to teach science and calculus.

As could be expected, the ripple effect of this ferment reached every corner of the territories. The college students took their ideas home, where they enjoyed great prestige among their frequently illiterate parents and neighbors. One result was that, even in the hustings, the "apolitical" peasants received a highly nationalistic leadership with which the Village Leagues and the old notables could not compete.

The impact was even greater in the towns, where the university graduates took control of the dozens of charitable societies, social clubs, professional organizations, and labor unions that in the absence of political parties flourished all over the occupied territories. This created a new Palestinian power structure that later played a major role in the first intifada.

The third important change unleashed by the West Bank academia was a sudden flowering of Palestinian journalism. After the Six Day War, the Israeli military administration put up a barrier against precisely such a development by banning Palestinian publications and blacklisting scores of books. The Eshkol government, however, inadvertently put a big hole in the fire wall by annexing Arab East Jerusalem.

As part of the Jewish state, the Arab half of Jerusalem became subject to Israeli press laws that, though not freewheeling, were far less draconian than the rules in the occupied territories. Using this loophole, the new Palestinian college grads established in East Jerusalem more than a dozen dailies, weeklies, and small news agencies that, however heavily censored by the Israeli military censor, provided a platform for a relatively wide variety of political views.

By the mid-1980s many of these young West Bankers acknowledged that thanks to this legal gap in the occupation regime they had more internal democracy and freedom of discussion than the Arab regimes tolerated in Jordan, let alone Syria or Iraq. In this new and intensely nationalistic environment, the old-time sheikhs and Hashemite loyalists were swept off the political map, and the stage was set for the appearance of a new breed of Palestinian leaders. Some of them were among the most promising young people that I as a journalist ever got to know.

Bright, self-confident, and nationalistic to the core, they not only broke with the taboos of their fathers but they unabashedly set out to learn democratic ways from a people who had won their own independence only two generations earlier: the Israelis. To the great credit of the Israeli society, a not insignificant number of individuals not only sympathized with the transformation in the territories, but helped to advance it.

CHAPTER 22

From the mid-1980s onward, more than a score of Israeli lawyers, journalists, politicians, and human rights advocates, mostly the sterling characters I called "righteous"—maintained a dialogue with the new breed of Palestinians and, in effect, tutored their political struggle against the occupation.

An important outcome of this alliance was the emergence of another Palestinian "sumud" strategy—resistance that challenged the Israelis on their own turf. The new Palestinian spokesmen did it by demanding for the occupied Arabs the same sort of civil rights and humane treatment that Israel vociferously demanded for Jews in the Soviet Union, Syria, Argentina, and other countries where they faced discrimination or worse. This approach was pioneered by Raja, Aziz Shehadeh's son, and Jonathan Kuttab, a lawyer and a naturalized American, who founded the West Bank branch of a Swiss human rights organization called Law in the Service of Man.

Raja's group investigated the excesses of the occupation—abuses such as torture, collective punishment, home destructions, and land seizures—and made a valiant effort to come up with facts free of the bombast and inventions that characterized much of Arab reporting. In short order, Raja's office became a respected source of information for both foreign and Israeli newsmen covering the territories.

The most original spokesman of this new type of resistance, however, was Sari Nuseibeh, a young college professor who symbolized the change that until then had taken place on the occupied West Bank. His father, Anwar, and his uncle Hazim—both of whom I had known since my days in Beirut—belonged to the elite group of wealthy, British-educated Palestinians who served King Hussein both ably and loyally and were rewarded by important positions in his court and government. Anwar was a former Jordanian defense minister and Hazim a veteran diplomat and UN ambassador.

Sari, who was born in 1950 and educated in Britain, had the ability and polish of his elders, and yet he was different. An intellectual, a Muslim, and a Palestinian patriot with an English wife, Sari was a truly modern, secular, and independent-minded ideas man. Breaking with the family tradition of royal service, he opted for the much less exalted position of a philosophy professor at the Bir Zeit University, and from this obscure post he fought the Israelis by proposing to play by their own rules. In a way, Sari reminded me of the Czech Good Soldier Schweik who sabotaged the Austro-Hungarian army while professing to be an obedient private.

Tousle-haired, dressed in rumpled tweeds, and consistently cerebral and cheerful, Sari looked and acted like a typical academic egghead whose schedule was just a bit heavier than he could manage. But however late for our breakfast appointments, Sari was leagues ahead of the PLO when it came to psych warfare against the Israeli rule. His basic premise was that the PLO's simplistic order to boycott everything Israeli played directly into Israeli hands. The policy, he argued, not only deprived the Arabs of advantages that could ease the burden of the foreign rule; it foreclosed a resistance strategy that could raise Israeli doubts about the wisdom of the occupation.

Sari could cite a list of benefits won by the Palestinians whenever they departed from the PLO-ordained boycott of Israel. His best example was the belated use of the Israeli press laws in East Jerusalem. In 1967, when Mohammed Abu Zuluf applied for an Israeli publishing license for his East Jerusalem daily *Al-Quds*, the PLO denounced his move as "treason," Arafat's hacks set fire to Zuluf's car, and threatened to kill him.

Fifteen years later, all occupied Palestinians recognized the great value of having their own newspapers. The East Jerusalem publications, though banned in the West Bank and in Gaza, were prodigiously smuggled to the occupied territories by Palestinians returning from their day jobs in Israel, and were avidly read. For the first time ever, the geographically disparate Palestinian community acquired voices that gave the readers a sense of unity and nationhood.

Another PLO taboo that in Sari's eyes did not make sense was the Palestinian use of Israel's institutions. As Sari pointed out, it was not until 1981 that a West Banker—Nablus's mayor, Bassam Shakaa—mustered the courage to defy Arafat and appealed to Israel's Supreme Court against a military order for his expulsion. The Court, Israel's most admirable and fair-minded authority, overruled the IDF. It was the first time the West Bank military administration was prevented from deporting an occupied Arab.

On a more mundane level, Nuseibeh liked to remind his fellow Palestinians of their folly, in which they persisted for more than a decade, of driving only cars with the special license plates issued for the occupied territories. Those who switched to the yellow tags issued in Israel discovered they had a much easier time getting through the omnipresent IDF roadblocks.

With his mind full of ideas and a courage that echoed Aziz Shehadeh's, Nuseibeh advanced proposals that startled both the Israeli and the Palestinian publics.

In January 1986, Sari outlined some of them when I interviewed him for a page-long Q&A that ran in the international editions of *Newsweek*.

Sari's main point was that, if Israel insisted on keeping the territories, "it would be in the best interest of the [then] 1.1 million of us to demand full rights as Israeli citizens," including the minimum wage and social security insurance that was denied to tens of thousands of Palestinians working in Israel. "Annexation (of the occupied territories) would make the Israelis pay for what they are now getting for free," Sari argued, referring to the no-benefits, coolie wages paid to Arab workers by Israeli employers.

Moreover, Sari continued, by converting the entire mandated Palestine into Greater Israel, the Israeli rulers would create an Arab electorate that would cast around 40 percent of the votes in general elections. The result, Sari argued, would be "the first stage of the secular, democratic, binational state of Arabs and Jews in Palestine" that at one time was sought by the PLO. Short of an even more massive expulsion of Arabs than what had taken place in the late 1940s, the hardliners' dream of Greater Israel contained the seeds of a political suicide.

Predictably, the interview caused an uproar in the Knesset. Tehiya cited Nuseibeh's plan as grounds for renewing its demand for the expulsion of all occupied Arabs. Rabbi Kahane quoted the interview as another proof of his contention that democracy was incompatible with a Jewish state. Israeli liberals pressed Likud to explain exactly how it would go about annexing the territories without enfranchising the Palestinians. For a while at least, Sari's message was stirring second thoughts in Israel, as he had intended.

Sari did less well in his own community, where Arafat's followers denounced his proposal as an intolerable defiance of PLO's status as the "sole representative" of the occupied Palestinians. When he caused another stir by accepting an invitation to discuss his ideas with Peres, who was then the foreign minister in Shamir's government, the PLO hardliners expelled Nuseibeh from the Bir Zeit employee union whose chairman he had been until three years earlier.

There was more trouble the next summer when an Israeli newspaper reported that Sari and a veteran Likud functionary had also secretly discussed a peace plan based on a self-determination for the Palestinians and Israel's recognition of the PLO. The encounters embarrassed the Likud, but Nuseibeh paid a price in a coin that was increasingly extracted by PLO enforcers in the Palestinian underground. Shortly after the story surfaced, Nuseibeh was cornered by four masked bullies on the stairs of a Bir Zeit school building and severely beaten.

The attack was unanimously denounced by all fifteen Palestinian publications in East Jerusalem, and it failed to silence Nuseibeh's call for a Palestinian march through the Israeli institutions. A year after the *Newsweek* interview, Sari unleashed another bomb by arguing in the Israeli daily *Ma'ariv* that the 150,000 Arabs in East Jerusalem should stop boycotting the municipal elections.

Once again, Nuseibeh made perfectly good sense. Under the Jerusalem bylaws, all residents—regardless of their citizenship—were entitled to vote for the municipal council. There were enough Palestinians in their part of the city to elect at least one-third of the municipal council and thereby counter the rapidly growing influence of the ultra-religious Jewish right-wingers who were flocking to the city in large numbers.

But once again, Western logic did not carry the day in a world dominated by emotions. An East Jerusalem editor who tested Nuseibeh's scheme by announcing his candidacy for the city council was attacked so violently that he withdrew his bid and publicly apologized for his "mistake." The final blow to Nuseibeh's cerebral approach came a few months later, in December 1987, when a freak traffic accident in Gaza unleashed the first Palestinian intifada.

Within a few days, the entire population in the territories staged a total strike, barricaded all roads, ran up the prohibited Palestinian flags, and stoned Israeli patrols that ventured into the fast-sprouting "liberated zones." It was the start of an unbridled onslaught so sudden and spontaneous it startled both the Shinbet and the PLO.

Especially in the early weeks of the uprising, Arafat and his top bureaucrats in Tunis spent hours making long-distance phone calls to the occupied towns and villages, frantically trying to find out what was going on and how to control the strife. Neither the phone calls nor Arafat's directives telexed to his West Bank supporters were any more effective in influencing events than was Shinbet or the IDF intelligence, both of which eagerly monitored—and occasionally plagiarized—the PLO messages and calls.

The intifada had a life of its own, with several self-styled "command posts" of the uprising publishing "communiqués" that frequently contradicted orders from the PLO. Each town and village had its own militants who procured food supplies, organized defenses against the IDF, and enforced conformity with rules mostly of their own making. Barely out of their teens, most of these minutemen were not taking dictates from anyone.

The violent outburst changed the dynamic of the Middle East conflict. For some Israelis, it brought home the limits on their ability to rule over an unwilling people. As Rabin acknowledged in 1994 by his celebrated handshake with Arafat, at least some key Labor Party figures at long last realized that, for Israel's own good, the era of territorial expansionism should end. But for Israel's hardliners, and for the settlers whom the Labor and the Likud had coddled for two decades, the lesson of the uprising was just the opposite. Their determination to hold on to, and exploit more fully, the Six Day War's conquests only hardened.

On the Palestinian community, the effect of the fighting—which continued until 1993, and resumed more violently in 2000—was similar. As Sari

Nuseibeh wrote me long after I left the Middle East, "right up to the first intifada, many options [for resolving the conflict] seemed open.... However, by 2000 all hopes for this were dashed, and the region became swept by a radicalization current, partly chauvinistic and partly religious. Hopeful ideas became hard to come by. It is as though people on both sides just decided to yield to where they felt history was taking them."

I left the Middle East well before the uprising ended, but I felt certain it was fraught with danger for the Jewish state. Put simply, the Palestinians had decided how to carry on their existential struggle against Israel. Unfortunately, their formula was not Shehadeh's or Nuseibeh's: it was violence.

Epilogue

I came to grips with the latest change in my journey in November 1988, when Leesa, our son, Benjie, and I were going through the security check in the departure hall of the Ben Gurion airport in Israel. To speed up the luggage inspection I showed the serious-looking young security woman my credentials from Israel's Government Press Office. Accredited American newsmen in Israel, especially if they had gray hair, a wife with an Israeli passport and a five-months-old baby born in Jerusalem were not likely to hijack airplanes.

As I expected, the security woman allowed her face to relax a notch and asked where we lived. I almost said, without thinking, "Rehov Hatayassim in Jerusalem." But I checked myself and answered, "United States."

There it was. I finally had a permanent address, and this trip was different from the many times I flew to America during my twenty-six years overseas. I was not on leave, headed for my summer home in Vermont. I was not going to meetings with *Newsweek* editors, and I was not going to have briefing sessions in the State Department and embassies in Washington. Instead, I thought, "I'll get a job that doesn't require travel, and Benjie will grow up in America."

It was an agenda, but later, as we flew over the haze-covered Mediterranean, I realized that's not what I wanted to think about. I needed to draw up a balance sheet of my final transfer. *Newsweek* was offering an early retirement to its senior staff, and I was glad to accept it.

After seventeen years in the Middle East—the crux and climax of my reporting from abroad—I was leaving it for good. I was at peace with that. Professionally, I felt no loss. The Israel-Palestinian conflict was on a trajectory that, I felt sure, would not change for a long time: Israel would continue seizing Palestinian land, and the Palestinians would continue to refuse to accept it. That was the whole story, and the hapless peacemaking and the Sturm und Drang that accompanied it, to paraphrase Rabbi Hillel, were mere "commentary." And I had done enough of that.

But I was also leaving journalism, and that was much more complicated and difficult. On one level, after decades of stressful deadlines, I was ready for life in a quiet suburb and mowing the lawn on weekends. And yet, the decision to give up reporting made me uncomfortable. It was not only that I was giving up a job I had loved since I was in my teens. I knew that just like four decades earlier, when I left Prague for good, I was once again fleeing—running away from something I could not accept and could not change.

By giving up reporting, I was leaving the world that journalists must prowl and scrutinize to meet their obligation to the society, and to have relevance. I was abandoning that mission, and this did not feel good at all. But there was something else that bothered me even more.

I realized that in the haunts I had probed longest and most thoroughly, I never found the cart that, as a youngster, in my dreams I was hoping to push. In the Middle East, raw power struggle, zealotry, and deceit carried the day, and decency was a loser. The "Shining City on a Hill" either was not there or I was not a good enough reporter to see it.

It was a grim obituary of a career that started so hopefully with two hundred mimeographed copies of *Žihadlo*.

I cogitated on that harsh conclusion for a while, but then I let it go. There must be a better way of summing up a big chunk of one's life, I decided. There must be something more cheerful to think about before once again heading into the unknown. And there was something very special about this flight to the States, something that was worth celebrating.

Then I suddenly knew the answer, and I embraced it with a great sense of gratitude and relief even while I was kicking myself. How could I be so blind?

I was about to embark on the best part of the trip. Leesa and I, together. Watching Benjie growing up. Graduating from high school. Going to college. If I am outrageously lucky (and at my age, I would have to be), I may even see him get married.

The journey hadn't been all I wished for, but in one sublime sense, it had a very happy ending: The three of us, going home.

www.ingramcontent.com/pod-product-compliance
Lightning Source LLC
Chambersburg PA
CBHW021648230426
43668CB00008B/547